Y0-CAO-964

The Threat of Soviet Imperialism

The THREAT of SOVIET IMPERIALISM

Edited by

C. GROVE HAINES

KENNIKAT PRESS
Port Washington, N. Y./London

0638994

THE THREAT OF SOVIET IMPERIALISM

Copyright 1954, the Johns Hopkins Press
Reissued in 1971 by Kennikat Press by arrangement
Library of Congress Catalog Card No: 70-122866
ISBN 0-8046-1409-1

Manufactured by Taylor Publishing Company Dallas, Texas

ESSAY AND GENERAL LITERATURE INDEX REPRINT SERIES

Foreword

In August, 1953, the School of Advanced International Studies sponsored a conference in Washington on "The Problem of Soviet Imperialism." This was closely integrated with the School's special graduate Summer Session on the same general topic and, like the conference on "Southeast Asia in the Coming World," which was similarly arranged the preceding summer, was designed to bring together eminent members of the scholarly professions as well as government and business personnel most deeply concerned with the question. The roster of speakers and discussion leaders, to be found in the table of contents, provides a general indication of the broad representation which was achieved, both functionally and geographically. Because of limitations of space, registration at the conference was restricted to 450, most of whom were in regular attendance throughout the five days of its duration. The present volume is the product of that conference.

Although the threat of Soviet imperialism has become increasingly serious over the years, those of us who laid plans for the conference could not have guessed initially how very timely the topic would be. Our preliminary announcements coincided with Stalin's death and the beginnings of what seemed to many to be a genuine relaxation of Soviet aggressiveness abroad and of the stern dictatorship at home. The succeeding months were filled with rumors of internal discords and speculation as to the role and intentions of the new Malenkov regime. By the time the conference assembled, that regime had already been put to some rigorous tests and it was possible to begin reviewing its role objectively and in historical perspective. It was not our purpose to concentrate upon the present dictatorship as such, yet I think it may be said that this volume does provide the kind of authoritative analysis which is required if a reasonable assessment of its place in the contemporary international scene is to be made.

The plan of the book follows in nearly every detail the plan of the conference. There are twenty chapters corresponding to the twenty papers read at the conference and, except for the last of these, there are appended summaries of the general discussions which followed. These proceed in logical order from an examination of the historical background of the problem through an inquiry into its meaning for the present and future policy of the United States. They are organized under five topical headings, each one of which constituted at the conference the subject of one day's deliberations.

The first section deals with the broad aspects of the relationship between the Soviet Union and the non-Soviet world and undertakes to assess the historical and doctrinal factors involved in determining the motivations and estimating the objectives of Soviet policy. This is followed in the second section by an analysis of some of the principal weapons of subversion and attack employed by the Soviets to attain their objectives, particularly trade, propaganda, diplomacy, and the use of force. The third section is concerned with the capabilities of the Soviet Union to deliver the attack: the economic resources and potentialities of the Soviet Bloc; the present status and future possibilities of Soviet science; the number and extent of reliability of devotees represented in the world Communist movement; and the military power which the Soviets can throw into the balance now and in the foreseeable future. The fourth and fifth sections present selected case studies of Soviet expansionist activities, giving particular attention to local circumstances in western and eastern Europe, Africa, Latin America, the Middle East, India, Southeast Asia and China which encourage or retard these activities. The concluding paper focuses its attention upon the response of United States foreign policy to the world-wide challenge of Soviet imperialism.

The most careful planning of a conference which brings together busy and responsible men cannot avoid the hazards of unexpected illness or sudden call to duty. We confronted two major difficulties as the result of illness: Professor William Deakin of Oxford University, who was scheduled to present the paper on "The Role of Force," and Mr. Miron Burgin, who was to serve as discussion leader for the session on "Communism in Latin America," were compelled to withdraw at the last moment. Fortunately, Mr. Jules Menken, who was completing a tour in this country under the Smith-Mundt Act, generously consented to fill in for Professor Deakin. On the day of the scheduled session on "Communism in Latin America," we found that our problem in this case had been turned into a crisis, for Professor Daniel Cosio Villegas of the University of Mexico who was to deliver the main address had had to return unexpectedly to Mexico. Mr. Hobart Spalding of the Department of State, who had agreed to replace Mr. Burgin, stepped into the breach as well for Professor Villegas, and performed the remarkable feat of presenting the address and of conducting the discussion session which followed. The pressure of duty at the last moment prevented two other discussion leaders from appearing at the conference—Col. Robert E. Lee and Anthony Leviero—but their places were most competently filled by Mr. John H. Ferguson, formerly of the Policy Planning Staff of the Department of State, and Mr. Antonio Micocci of the International Information Agency.

In the editing of this volume as well as in the planning and organization of the conference upon which it is based, I had the great good fortune of being able to take frequent counsel with my colleagues at the School and to rely upon them to carry the heaviest burdens for me. The debt of gratitude I owe to all of them is very great indeed.

No one could have had more expert assistance than that which was so generously given by the members of the School's summer teaching staff—Mr. George F. Kennan, Mr. Robert N. Carew Hunt, Dr. Mose Harvey, Dr. Richard Scammon, Mr. Willis Armstrong, and Professor T. Cuyler Young. In particular, I wish to take this opportunity to express my indebtedness to Dr. Mose Harvey whose contributions from the first were indispensable to the development of our plans.

But the largest share of the burden both of administering the conference and of following manuscript through the various stages of its progress to the final printed page was borne by Miss Phoebe Everett, my administrative assistant. To say here that it was her untiring devotion to duty and her extraordinary administrative competence which made the conference a success and this book possible is to state an incontestable fact and yet not to convey adequately the extent of my gratitude to her.

C. Grove Haines

December 19, 1953

Table of Contents

Introduction

CHRISTIAN A. HERTER,
Governor of Massachusetts

The systematic and searching examination of the problem of Soviet imperialism which this volume provides contributes materially to sound appraisal of the Communist challenge. It would be difficult indeed to find an equally imposing array of talented and knowledgeable men such as those assembled by the School of Advanced International Studies for its conference on this topic. The papers which they presented, and which are reprinted here, offer an authoritative and objective review of the issues and problems of Communist imperialism. It is in many ways a sombre book, but if this is the case it is because both the facts of the present and the prospects for the future bear that hue.

Since the end of World War II, there has been much speculation about the real nature of the threat posed by the Soviet Union as the center of the world Communist movement. Was it perhaps more apparent than real, the product of imaginings inspired by unjustified fear or misunderstanding of the driving forces operating in the Soviet Union? We need to remind ourselves that these queries at one time may have seemed more reasonable than they do now. In the atmosphere of hopeful expectation which prevailed after the cessation of hostilities, there was a disposition to look wishfully for the best and to make accommodations to transgressions of the code of international conduct.

Whether it has meant confirmation or disillusionment, the passage of the years has brought a steady intensification of all aspects of the problem. At San Francisco in 1945 there was a flurry of irritation at the arbitrary fashion in which Moscow handled the Polish question; but there were also professions of good intentions and, in any case, the Soviet Union pledged itself to the Charter of the United Nations. Since then, however, Poland has been converted into a satrapy of the USSR and the Kremlin has made a mockery of United Nations principles. In Iran Soviet troops stayed beyond their alloted time but withdrew in the spring of 1946, and for a time there was a readiness to let bygones be bygones. But since then Soviet agents, working through and with the Tudeh party, have continued to exploit every element of unrest. In 1946 and 1947 Moscow converted former independent states of eastern and southeastern Europe into satellites; while this created apprehensions there were those who could construe this as a means, if a heavy-handed one, of ensuring the presence of friendly states on the Soviet Union's western frontiers. Then Czechoslovakia, once before the tragic victim of totalitarian aggression, was forced into the fold of the satellites and Moscow's professions of guilelessness and innocence ceased to ring true. The Berlin blockade which followed soon thereafter added dramatically to the sense of danger, but the success of the air lift and the eventual abandonment of the blockade revived the hope of an orderly accommodation. This too was shaken by the Korean war. Then came Stalin's death and in the weeks that followed rumors of internal discords among his successors no less than the evidence of relaxation at home and abroad, however modest and superficial they may have been, encouraged the hope in some individuals that the problem of Soviet imperialism might still be solved by itself. Yet these hopes too have been dashed. The pattern of Soviet advance and retreat, always followed by a fresh advance, has made it increasingly apparent that the problem of Soviet imperialism is a serious and enduring one which can neither be wished out of existence nor resolved by simple expedients.

What is the real nature of this threat? On the answer to this question will depend in substantial degree the course of policy which the United States and the other powers of the free-world coalition will need to pursue. There has been and continues to be considerable disagreement of view among those who have addressed themselves to the problem. At one extreme may be found those who tell us that inexorable forces of social change and development are bound eventually to moderate the Soviet regime—and they believe that they can see the processes of moderation now at work under Malenkov—so that patience and a readiness to exploit every opportunity to encourage these trends should be the touchstone of policy toward the Soviet Union. For these the threat of Soviet imperialism is considered far less dangerous than it is made to appear. At the other extreme, there are those who maintain that the scourge of communism can never be allayed by anything less than its extinction at its heart and core. Whatever may be the merits and shortcomings of these white and black approaches, they do at least illustrate the need for exhaustive and objective analysis of the problem. Too much is at stake to ask for anything less.

If we are to explain the real nature of the problem we must address ourselves earnestly to a few basic questions such as are examined in this book. What is the best judgment we can make, after review of the evidence, on the matter of Soviet motivations? Is the Soviet Union, after all, mostly a continuation in modified form of traditional Russia, pursuing traditional national policies in an international environment which by accident and circumstance has afforded peculiar opportunities for their realization? How much is there of the old and how much of the new, and to what extent and in what way are they blended? Where does Bolshevist doctrine stand in this regard? Does it really offer a key to the question, or have the basic drives of Bolshevism, insofar as they can be ascertained, been altered, modified, or transformed with the passage of time? And then what paths of inquiry may we follow to answer such questions? How does one ascertain motivations? Does he seek these in contemporary words, which often contradict, or in contemporary deeds which sometimes seem to belie a stated purpose, or can he discover in the historical time-span a clearly definable line of purpose and action which indicates that momentary contradictions and retreats are merely tactical deviations? What does the evidence produce?

The conclusions which emerge in this volume from the examination of these questions indicate that the hard core of Bolshevism remains, that its basic objectives have not been changed, and that it still provides the best, though not the only, clues to Soviet long-range intentions. What this means simply is that the Soviet Union proceeds unswervingly toward the goal of world communism, with all that that may imply for the free world.

It is possible to accept this view and even to agree that the techniques of subversion and attack which the Soviet Union employs bear it out, and still have some doubt as to the seriousness of the danger which is posed. What barriers are strewn in the path of the Soviet advance? May it not be true that it has already consumed more than it can digest? Has it not perhaps exposed itself as untrustworthy and cynical so that it can no longer captivate imaginations where poverty, discontent, and nationalistic strivings prevail? Does it have the means and the power, now or in the foreseeable future, to surmount these barriers, such as they may be? Or can we safely rest at ease in the assurance that we are the stronger of the giants now and for the future as well? These are fundamental questions, too, for which we need to seek the more reasonable answers. It will be found that there is honest disagreement in judgment and diversity of expectation among the authors of this book, and yet it will also be found that there is remarkable uniformity of conviction that the problem is deadly serious and that the dangers to the free world are of great magnitude. Grim as this may be, it is a conclusion which seems unassailable.

The responsibilities of the United States in meeting these dangers are heavy and exacting. We cannot shrink from them, except to our own peril; and we cannot meet them properly, as the leader of the free world, except as we act with sound knowledge and understanding of our adversaries, our friends and ourselves. Though the path we pursue will still be strewn with hazards and pitfalls, we shall be better prepared to avoid them.

PART I

The Soviet Posture Toward the Non-Soviet World

The Soviet Union and the Noncommunist World in Historical Perspective

GEORGE KENNAN,
Former U. S. Ambassador to the USSR.

The problem of Soviet imperialism has been much talked about in these recent years—so much talked about, in fact, that one is sometimes brought to wonder whether profit is really to be derived from its further discussion. The answer is, of course, that it is, provided discussion is honest and conscientious. For in the world of political realities, at least, expression is the indispensable discipline of thought. Without it, thought is certainly not useful, and it is a question to what extent it can be said to exist at all.

Yet one is still conscious of another danger involved in the sort of thing we are doing here: a danger flowing from the artificial forms into which we have to try to compress our reflections, and above all the inadequate and inexact titles by which we have no choice but to permit them to be tagged. Our subject here is an example of this danger. It suggests a well-defined phenomenon of external reality which we here are at liberty to examine with objectivity and detachment, from the further end—so to speak—of our learned microscope. But is it that?

"Soviet imperialism" means a thousand things: it means history; it means language and tradition and the folk-lore of thought; it means the combination, in unknown proportions, of natural law and chance; it means the mystery that stands between free will and predestination; it means, God knows, not only the motivation of people in Moscow but also the way the West has appeared to Moscow and influenced Moscow over the course of the ages; it means not only the elements of strength in Soviet society, but also the elements of weakness in our own; it means, among other things, ourselves, with all our inadequacies, with the limitations of our own vision, with the dangerous gap that exists between the unreality of our comfortable lives and the reality of the physical misery prevailing throughout so much of this world, with the abstruseness and practical sterility that so often mark the process of political thought in any sheltered and peaceful society.

No one can compress a rounded view of these things into a brief dissertation. No one can do more than to flick the surface of this vast, multidimensional substance, the origins of which reach back hundreds of years into the past, and the ramifications of which permeate the entire life of our time. It is in just such a flicking of the surface that I am about to engage.

If we find it useful at the outset to discuss the subject of the Soviet Union and the noncommunist world in historical perspective, surely this is because we see the relationship between these two entities (if such they can be called) as one of tension and conflict, something darkening the life of our times, and because we are trying to understand this conflict in the light of history.

Perhaps this way of looking at things is itself somewhat inexact and misleading. There is probably no such thing as a " noncommunist world " in the sense of a group of national units endowed with sufficient generic characteristics to warrant treating them as a group. And large parts of the noncommunist world would not be subjectively aware of any community with other parts of it in relationship to the Soviet problem. But there is at least a conflict between the will of the men in the Kremlin and the wills of Western governments and peoples generally as to the shape that political realities should take. And as for the peoples outside of the Western community: for most of them, impulses transmitted from Moscow have become important elements in what we might call the topography of their political world. These facts, at least, can be examined in historical perspective.

External conflict, certainly, is nothing new in Russian history. Beginning national life as they did on an exposed plain with few natural barriers or defenses, with no older tradition of political legitimacy, faced with fierce and implacable nomadic enemies, the Russian people have had a national experience punctuated at every point with rivalry, conflict, and violence. The wars of Tsarist Russia, like those of most other continental powers, were primarily with her immediate neighbors. The issue was normally the control of land area and of the human beings resident on it. In this long, painful process certain personal qualities of the Great Russians (not all of them attractive ones) combined with geographical circumstances and with the impact of external historical developments to enable the Great Russians to make themselves the center of a national state, to take into that state a number of other peoples of different national character, and to extend the power of this political entity to a point where it came to embrace the entire great plain running from the Baltic Sea, the slopes of the Carpathians and the mouths of the Danube, in the West, to the Altai Mountains, and, further north, to the shores of the Pacific, in the East.

Naturally, in a process as vast as this, conflict was always present. But this conflict was usually of a nature normal to the habits of the locale and the life of the times. Russia's wars were at no time dissimilar, in early centuries, to wars occurring simultaneously among other rulers and political entities. For her neighbors, Russia was a problem, as indeed the neighbors often were for her. For the remaining world, she was hardly more than a fabulous remote principality, from which travellers returned with lurid tales of the barbaric splendor of the court, the squalor and degradation of the people, the monotony of the landscape, and the rigors of the climate.

It is true that in these earlier times, particularly in the days of the Grand Duchy of Muscovy, many things were noted by foreign observers that seem now, in retrospect, to have had a certain prophetic tinge and to have presaged the conflict of our time. The importance and significance of these observations cannot be denied. Traits were indeed becoming visible in old Muscovy that were destined later to play an important part in the psychological composition of Soviet power. There was a tendency to a messianic concept of Russia's role in history; an intolerance of foreign outlooks and values; a pronounced xenophobia of Russian officialdom; an insistence on isolating the Russian people from foreign contact; a secretiveness and deviousness of diplomatic practice; a seeming inability to understand anything in the nature of a permanently peaceful and equal relationship between states: a tendency to view every treaty of peace as being in the nature of a provisional armistice, a tendency to think of conflict as the normal, peace as the provisional and abnormal. All these things are of course striking, when measured against the habits of thought prevalent today in Moscow. Yet we must remember that many of these features of the early Russian outlook were more common in their own context of time and place than they are today. The tendency to universality of political aspiration, for example, was less startling in a time when the Byzantine Empire was only just disappearing and when the religious wars of the West had not yet reached their climax. What is really strange is not so much that the Grand Duchy of Muscovy should have shown the traits it did in the fifteenth to seventeenth centuries, but rather that a political regime of the twentieth century should have manifested so powerful an atavistic urge and groped so far back into a largely irrelevant past for its political habits and outlook.

In the intervening Petersburg era—the period of the eighteenth and nineteenth centuries when Russia began for the first time to emerge into the affairs of Europe in the capacity of a great power—there was less of this sort of thing. During this period it was primarily in the physical growth of the Russian state rather than in any peculiarities of the official Russian outlook that observant people began to sense the pattern of the future. True: certain of these peculiarities, reminiscent of old-Muscovite patterns and prophetic of Soviet ones, were not wholly absent during those centuries. Custine, visiting Russia under the reign of Nicolas I at a time when these features were shining through with particular clarity, experienced a chill of terror at his prophetic vision of the eventual impact of Russia's massive despotism on the fragile decadence of western Europe. "The eternal oriental tyranny," he wrote, "menaces us incessantly, and we shall be subjected to it if our extravagances and our iniquities render us deserving of such chastisement." It is further true that as the new Russian intelligentsia reacted with increasing sharpness and skepticism to the powerful Western influence under which much of Russian cultural life had developed in the eighteenth and nineteenth centuries, there was a return, particularly among the Slavophil philosophers and historians, to a sort of romantic repudiation of Western values, combined with a messianic belief in Russia's own destiny. What seemed to many Russian thinkers to be the decadence of the West—its dreary bourgeois narrowness of thought and behavior—stimulated this sense of repudiation. Is it our fault, asked the poet Blok rhetorically of his Western friends in a poem written at the time of the revolution, if some day " your skeleton will crunch in our heavy, tender paws? " [1]

But all these things, while faintly prophetic, were not yet really expressive of the East-West relationship as we know it today. This relationship is mainly the product of certain developments of the present century, some of which were, to be sure, of a coincidental nature, but most of which represented the final coming together of great historical movements, bound sooner or later to meet, to impinge on one another and to require mutual accommodation. Let us see what some of these things might be.

The first of these developments was certainly the rounding out of the expansion of the Russian state to a point where further expansion was practically impossible except at the price of conflict with some other great power. Hand in hand with this went the development of Russia into one of the world's major military and industrial powers. It is sometimes forgotten that this was a process well on the way to completion before the Revolution. In the forty years prior to World War I, Russia had been the scene of a fairly stormy industrial development. It seems to me there is reason to suppose that had this process not been interrupted by wars and revolution, the normal workings of the free enterprise system would have produced by this time a level of industrial strength in the traditional Russian territory roughly comparable to what we have before us today.

The second of these great historical developments was World War I and its effects both in Russia and the West. So far as Russia is concerned, the outstanding effect was of course the capture of power throughout most of traditional Russia by a

[1] Aleksandr Blok, *Polnoe Sochineniya* (Publishing House Sovetski Pisatel: 1946). Poem: " *Skify* " (" The Scythisms ").

group of men led by Lenin and inspired by the Marxist ideology as Lenin had developed it.

This meant that Russia had come under the control of men committed to a belief in the unsoundness and iniquity of the social system which, to one degree or another, all the other Western countries maintained and were destined to continue to maintain for a long time into the future. How this curiously twisted and fanatical belief came to find its political home precisely in Russia—a country that fitted very poorly into the Marxist pattern—is another story, and one that I shall not attempt to recount here. It is important to note that this belief on the part of the early Bolshevik leaders was not merely one of detached historical and social interpretation: it was something that involved intimately their own responsibility and actions. The deplorable state of the peoples languishing—as they saw it—under the yoke of capitalism was for them not just something to be noted and regretted: it was something they, as good international Marxists, as Leninist-Marxists in particular, had an obligation to do something about. The cause of the proletariat everywhere was their cause. They were the revolutionaries of *every* country, not just of their own. They challenged the legitimacy and usefulness of *every* capitalistic government, not just the one under which they happened to have been born.

And thus, when these men appropriated to themselves the powers of government in most of the territory known to the world traditionally as "Russia," a new situation was created. With that act, the exercise of internal power in Russia had become associated with a program aiming in effect at the overthrow by force of every Western government and the establishment in power in every Western capital of a violent, embittered, defiant minority group, contemptuous of all real national tradition, challenging most of the accepted national values, hating almost everything their countrymen loved, amenable only to the discipline of the rulers of a foreign state. This was a condition without precedent in modern Western history. It belied the principle of "live and let live" on which the entire structure of international relationships in the Western world had come to rest in the eighteenth and nineteenth centuries. It represented, from the standpoint of international custom, a retrogressive step: a throw-back to the religious wars of past ages—to the quest for universal secular power in the name of an exclusive and intolerant ideology.

At a happier time, at a time when Western society was in possession of its full strength and health, this sort of program and outlook on the part of the Soviet leaders might merely have been ignored and ridiculed and left to expose itself for the childish impertinence that, in essence, it was. Theoretically, this would have been all the easier in the early days of Soviet power for the reason that Russia was then undergoing a moment of great physical weakness. The fact that the Marxist-Leninist outlook was associated with the resources of the Russian state added little in those early days to its physical power. The Bolshevik leaders could rant and denounce; they could attempt to sow doubt and dissension in the Western world. But they had little to draw on in the way of physical resources from the territory under their control. And when, in December of 1918, the new Soviet Government appropriated two million rubles for the promotion of world revolution, this naïve gesture was actually a revelation of its physical helplessness in the face of the vast world-revolutionary task its leaders had marked out for themselves.

Initially, the real difficulty lay not in the control by these men of the resources of an established state, but in the fact that they had come into power, armed with this amazing theoretical challenge to the soundness of Western institutions, precisely at a time when the West, generally, was abnormally sick and weak, exhausted and shattered by the terrible effects of World War I, showing on every hand the signs of strain and shock, its confidence shaken in its own traditions and institutions. The war had not only created new dislocations which were poorly understood and affected people with feelings of restlessness and frustration, but it had also exacerbated changes of a long term nature already in progress in Western society and themselves calling for painful and drastic adjustments.

In the years following the prodigious bloodletting of the first World War, weaknesses and deficiencies stood out all over on the body of Western civilization. It was an easy thing for the

Bolsheviks, with their glib and "*simpliste*" philosophy, to portray as basic weaknesses of the capitalist system things that were actually direct consequences of the great physical and spiritual debauch that modern war invariably represents, or part of the normal tensions of growth and change, made more crucial and painful by the effects of the war. The sparks thrown out by the Moscow leaders, supported by the emotional vitality of a primitive society, struck fire in many places in the tired, shaken Western world: wherever it was weak or divided or lacking in confidence in itself. In this way a curious bond was struck between the Russian revolution and the tensions and discontents of Western civilization everywhere.

Previously, the great countries of the West had been left to work out their internal trials largely in their own way, through the free play of indigenous forces, failure and weakness rendering them more vulnerable only against the limited aspirations of Western neighbors. Now, just at a time when the internal tensions were greatest, an external enemy arose—an enemy not created but self-inspired and self-declared—and so constituted as to take advantage of every centrifugal tendency, every element of self-doubt, every element of sickness or of weakness, in Western civilization. From that time onward, the germ of Communist oversimplification rode like a malignant bacillus, ever present, in the veins of Western society, powerless to disrupt the functioning of the organism so long as health and vigor were present, but ready to seize on the slightest ulterior weakness in order to poison, to disintegrate, and to kill. From the day of the Russian Revolution, the society of the West came to be haunted by a species of foreign demon, geared to take advantage of every gap between Western ideals and Western performance, implacably determined to make the West be all that it purported to be and live up to its highest pretensions, or to accept the horror of totalitarian rule by its own criminal elements in the interests of a foreign state.

Miraculously enough, considering the conditions of the Western world in 1918, nowhere except in Russia herself did society succumb to this demon in those ensuing years. Everywhere in the Western world, even in the new and untried states of eastern Europe, health and strength proved sufficient to resist the virus.

Communist parties remained; but they ceased to constitute in most countries any immediate revolutionary threat; they came more and more to be a sort of traditional fixture of the Western state: a curious receptacle into which there could be poured, decade after decade, all that fringe of the human species that tended by nature to turn against its human environment and to seek fulfillment of its own ego in the defiance of all that others believed and cherished.

Such people always exist; they are a mutation of the species. The presence of real grievances and hardships has only a remote relation to their state of mind. Their trouble is subjective; and if it arises originally in environmental factors, as I suppose it often does, these factors are never—but really never—the ones of which they are conscious, of which they complain and against which they inveigh. There has to be a place for such people in any society; and so far as the Western countries are concerned, perhaps the Communist parties provide as favorable a place as any other, since here you have them all together, identified in a public association, their aims widely known and understood.

But as the ideological threat of Soviet power declined, the physical strength of the territory and peoples under Soviet rule began to increase. The ravages of the war were gradually overcome. Russia began to resume the march of economic and military development which had been in progress before World War I. In this way, with the passage of the decades, the Soviet leaders moved steadily away from their role as intellectual and political gadflies for the Western countries, and closer to the traditional role of Russian rulers competing for position amid the territorial and military rivalries of the eastern European and Asiatic areas.

This situation might have existed for many years, and with no greater detriment to world stability than it had involved in the years of the nineteenth century, had World War I really settled the problems over which it was fought. But this was precisely what it failed to do. What people believed to be a settlement was actually only a state of mutual exhaustion. The war had arisen from a serious element of disunity in Western society: this was the profound disagreement as to the place which the German people, having suddenly emerged on the

European scene as a powerful and vigorous national entity, were to have in the European scheme of things.

But since the war had *failed* to lead to any real political settlement on this point (and by that I mean a settlement roughly acceptable to both parties) and had only produced conditions bound to exacerbate the issue, the entire disagreement emerged again in the thirties in a new and more virulent and more horrible form, in the form of Adolf Hitler and the movement he headed. And in Hitler's aims and methods, marking as they did the most grievous disunity among the Western nations, attended by a readiness on his part to use force against the others, and coupled with the military weakness of the Western democracies, there lay the historic opportunity of which Moscow could hardly fail to take advantage.

For once the battle was on between Hitler and the Western democracies, neither party in the Western quarrel was strong enough to carry out its purpose completely without Soviet help. The Nazis needed help in the form of the nonaggression pact in the early period; the Western allies needed help in the form of 180 Soviet divisions in the later phase. Western disunity was Moscow's chance. For their inability to fight each other without invoking Soviet assistance, and their inability to refrain from fighting each other in the light of this tragic fact, both sides paid a price. That price was in large part the installation of Soviet military and political power over half of Europe in 1945: and there is perhaps a deep historical justice in the fact that that price is being paid today in almost equal measure by the Germans and their Western adversaries in the recent war.

In saying this, I am not seeking to exculpate Hitler and his associates from their heavy responsibility. There could have been no greater betrayal of Western civilization than the mad path on which they embarked in 1938 and 1939. The Nazis confronted the Western powers with the most impossible and tragic of choices. All the hysterical cries and warnings of Goebbels about the Bolshevik menace in the final days of the war could not wipe out this dark responsibility. But the Nazi era was only the last act in a tragic drama that had run through several decades. And for the earlier course of that drama all of us who were prominently involved, and that includes ourselves in the United States, had a share of the blame.

The establishment of the Soviet leaders as the masters over half of Europe was, then, a part of the price that the Western powers paid for their inability to solve their differences without resort to war. I think it important to note that it was precisely this geographic extension of Soviet power that was the principal factor in making Moscow so much more of a problem to the rest of the world today than she was before this last world war. It placed her in command of the resources of eastern and central Europe. It gave her access to the advanced technology of that area. It served to overcome much of her congenital industrial backwardness. At the same time it lamed the productive and recuperative capacities of Europe generally, and rendered impossible the restoration of any real, political stability to the western and central European areas.

And I think it important to note that all of this had little to do with Soviet propaganda or with the political appeal of Moscow's ideas. Moscow's aid was invoked or accepted by both of the Western parties in World War II on a basis of straight military power, in the most old-fashioned sense. And the gains that Moscow made by virtue of this advantage were primarily military, not ideological, gains. Such ideological inroads as the Soviet propagandists were able to make on the European peoples in the final phases of the war were in direct proportion to the degree in which Moscow was able to conceal its real aspirations and to masquerade as a liberal democratic power instead of the center of a ruthless conspiracy. When this mask fell off, the power of Moscow's ideas largely disintegrated. Only the inordinately large French and Italian Communist parties remain in Europe today as living witnesses of the bewilderment and confusion the Communists succeeded in introducing into Europe in the wake of the war.

But I find it difficult to believe that even the members of these parties really want what they appear to want: namely, the enslavement of their own people to a brutal and cynical foreign dictatorship. I am sure that in the great majority of cases their association with this movement is a gesture of despair and impatience, flowing from domestic political frustrations within their respective countries, and that they would reject with horror and indignation if they could see it in the flesh, the real embodiment of the ideas in which they profess to believe. Surely for the Western world in general the Soviet threat today is almost exclusively a physical one, a military-territorial one along traditional patterns, not one of the power of ideas. Starting from what was once a very favorable position, the Soviet leaders have succeeded over the years in divesting themselves of all claim to moral and intellectual leadership in the Western world.

The same, unfortunately, cannot be said of Asia. Here the pattern is reversed. Scarcely anywhere beyond the northern borders of China and Korea does the Soviet Union itself today appear as a military threat to the independence of other people in the Asiatic area. But here the scene is marked by one of the most curious and important phenomena of our time: the appeal of Marxist thought and of the Soviet example, in particular, to people who have not yet come into the enjoyment of sovereign power or who are new to its exercise—above all, to people whose national consciousness and identity were formed under varying degrees of Western tutelage and control and who are now seeking to free themselves from the moral burden of this heritage.

I think we in the West must face the fact that for a great many of these people the repulsion that Soviet realities hold for us is not operable in anywhere near the same degree. Their accumulated resentment of Western patterns is so great that anything that departs completely from those patterns is apt to appear commendable in their eyes by that very fact. The wastage of human life does not impress them. They are prepared to accept physical squalor and cruelty if they can believe that it serves a social purpose. Soviet power is something that is more, rather than less, attractive to them by virtue of the fact that it has been accompanied by physical hardship and deprivation, by sacrifice of the interests of the individual, by a renunciation of precisely that conspicuous luxury, that physical self-pampering, that pretension to a pompous individual self-importance through which the Westerner has made himself hated and despised in so many areas of the world.

The Western world, and our country in particular, must be extremely careful how it deals with this phenomenon of the Soviet appeal to the peoples of the underdeveloped areas of Asia and elsewhere. We must take account of the fact that the past has left an emotional legacy that will not soon be overcome. We must realize that our concepts and example are not always necessarily relevant to the needs of peoples elsewhere. We must contrive to understand, as a normal human phenomenon, the fact that Asian peoples sometimes wish to do things one way precisely because it is *not* the way we do them—because they wish to demonstrate to themselves, and to reassure themselves of, an independence which is new and wonderful to them and in which they cannot yet fully believe. Finally, we must understand the impatience that causes many of them to reject the concept of free enterprise as the best means of achieving rapid industrialization and to look elsewhere for means to this end.

But with all this, they must not expect us to agree with them, or to encourage them, when they look precisely to Moscow for things they will certainly not find there and, in so doing, place themselves and the security of entire geographic areas in jeopardy. It is one thing to ask of us in the West humility and understanding, a recollection of the mistakes of the past, and a tolerance for what is only human and unavoidable. It is another thing to ask us to affirm the reality of things we know to be illusions, and to acquiesce in changes we know to be disruptive of the long-term prospects for peace and stability. Americans can and should have understanding for a desire of other peoples to go their own way, even if it not be our way; but they can have no understanding of a desire to go Moscow's way, when they know too well what that has meant in practice to others who have entered on that path. No American can be expected to view with anything other than abhorrence the proposition that men are best ruled by lying and deceit, by appeals to hatred and suspicion and fear, by the destruction of religious belief, by the denial of moral obligation on an individual ethical basis.

To the extent that Asia manifests a revulsion to the West as a negative reaction to the experience of colonialism, and Western paternalism in the past, and wishes for this reason to strike out on paths of its own, we Americans must find within ourselves the dignity and maturity to accept this, in the confidence that time will eventually develop a better appreciation of all values and a more balanced understanding of American civilization. Even in the field of economic theory, we must learn to be tolerant of approaches we firmly believe to be fallacious. But to the extent that peoples in Asia and Africa indulge themselves in the belief that Soviet-Communist political leadership can bring them anything else than the misery it has brought to all others who have experienced it—to that extent, Americans must view these peoples as victims of a tragic and terrible naïveté, and must take this aberration into account when dealing with them.

People in Asia should be careful about rejecting these American feelings as the expression of some sort of selfish or imperialist interest on the part of the United States—as an effort to entice others into the quarrels of the great powers. If people in Asia were to abandon themselves to Communist deceits, American interests, it is true, would suffer. But the first to suffer would be these Asiatic peoples themselves, and the damage to their interests would be greater and more immediate than any damage to the interests of the United States.

Actually, as of the year 1953, there seems to be reason to hope that the peak of this danger has passed. The real and decisive struggle in Asia has been taking place in the minds of men; and it seems to me that one can discern there a certain turn of the tide of battle to the favor of the forces of realism and common sense. This is not, and should not be, a movement in the direction of any increased pro-Americanism, or any slavish admiration for Western institutions. No sensible person seeks anything of this sort. It is a turn in the direction of a better understanding of the nature of both Soviet power and Western democracy. It marks a more sober appreciation both of the dangers that lie for the Asian peoples themselves in a subordination to the influence of Soviet communism, and of the possibilities that lie in a more mature approach, taking from every source, Communist or Western, that which is relevant to Asia's problems and helpful to their solution but rejecting on principle every political creed and every political influence based on hatred and the degradation of human nature.

These reflections are sufficient, it seems to me, to indicate that for the West, at least, the Soviet threat is only a function and expression of the West's own weakness. It was Western disunity that brought the Soviets into Europe for the first time as a military power capable of placing a temporary veto on the restoration of hope and stability to the European scene. It was the tragedy of the Western impact on Asia—the long record of superficiality and selfishness and pretentiousness vis-à-vis impressionable and observant peoples—that made possible the neuroses and illusions on which Soviet influence feeds today in that area. A distinguished French scholar once observed in connection with the phenomenon of domestic communism that " error must . . . always be regarded as a crisis in the internal development of truth."[2] It may be said, similarly, that for the Western world the Soviet threat is primarily an internal crisis in the West's own development. In this appreciation there lies, in my conviction, the key to the understanding of the correct method of approach to the Soviet problem.

Now up to this point, I have referred only to the noncommunist world. I have said nothing about the peoples of the Soviet Union, or about the regime under which they are languishing. These are of course two different things. They must be mentioned separately.

The Soviet regime, while embodying many traditional Russian features and now showing significant signs of evolution, is still the unique outstanding example of that nightmare of the twentieth century: the totalitarian state. This is in certain respects a new phenomenon in the inventory of political institutions. We do not yet fully know the laws of its development. Plainly, the edifice of Soviet power is faced today with severe strains and crises. These can be observed in its internal structure, which has come to depend on the institution of a supreme and glorified leader but contains no formal provision for the method of his selection. They can also be observed in the satellite empire, where the nature of Soviet power has been thoroughly exposed, where its devices have worn thin, where it is harvesting the crop of hatred and rejection it sowed with such reckless arrogance some years ago, in defiance of the pleas and warning of the Western world. It is our business neither to save it from its follies nor to confuse the issue by attempting to assert ourselves into its difficulties. If our own beliefs are sound, Soviet power will continue to suffer, as it is suffering today, by the

[2] A. Rossi, *A Communist Party in Action* (New Haven: Yale University Press, 1949), 256.

effects of its own unsoundness—its incompatibility with the deepest human needs, and it will eventually earn the retribution it so justly deserves. It is important that this process be permitted to reveal itself with such vividness and clarity that for generations to come, and let us hope forever, men will not again be tempted to seek their political fortunes through the degradation of fellowmen, forgetting that it is themselves who are thereby most deeply degraded.

And as for the Soviet peoples, we can only stand aside, respectful of the ordeal they are undergoing, mindful of the real human sacrifices this has involved, careful not to bestow either praise or blame too quickly where we understand very little of what is going on, maintaining our readiness to be helpful to the extent that we can, when and if the opportunity ever develops. We must not underrate the human damage that has been done by thirty-five years of Bolshevism: the partial brutalization of the youth, the neglect of religious truth, the primitivization of political and social concept, the atrophying of the qualities of individual self-reliance and responsibility. If and when the Soviet peoples ever emerge from this long ordeal, we must not expect them to react like people who had never gone through it. In many ways, they will be in great need of forbearance and understanding.

On the other hand, we must be careful not to approach them with an attitude of superiority and moral instruction. In their long and excruciating subjection to the power of human evil, they have unquestionably sounded depths of human experience beyond the ken or imagination of people in our world. Who knows but what, in the course of this ordeal, spiritual values have not been discovered—or rediscovered—of immense profundity, perhaps even essential to the healthy development of our own civilization? After all we, too, face a crisis at this time in the inadequacy of our own spiritual concepts to the strains of our industrial and urban civilization. Perhaps those who have passed through the purgatory of totalitarianism will have something to tell us that we could not have learned in any other way.

Looking at all these things together, I cannot resist the conviction that there is some great historical logic in the existence at this time of the phenomenon we call Soviet power and in the problem it poses for the world beyond its own borders. To the West it stands as an admonition of the necessity for internal unity and mutual tolerance and a reminder of the immense moral responsibility that rests upon us by virtue of our rise to political and economic ascendency in advance of other portions of the modern world. To the East it stands as an enticement and a test of maturity: as the bearer of something the Eastern peoples must have the strength to reject if their long-coveted independence is to be more than a new disillusionment and failure. As for the Russian people themselves and the other peoples of the Soviet Union, I fear the measure of their tragedy is now beyond our imagination or comprehension. On the great plains of Russia and Siberia, a moral struggle is in progress so immense that it must, it seems to me, be either the final demonstration of civilization's failure or the breeding ground of new spiritual forces of wide historic significance.

All of these developments stress, to my mind, the central feature of our age: the universal interdependence of mankind, which means that nowhere can men be entirely happy while human nature is still being mocked and tortured on other parts of the globe, but also that nowhere need men be completely desperate so long as somewhere else other men are trying to build a decent life based on the principles of charity and mutual responsibility. This does not mean we need lose ourselves in lavish schemes for world betterment by external action. There are many important things to be done; but example is still, after all, the greatest agency by which men help each other. To me, the prime moral dictate that flows for us from these realities is still the cultivation of the cleanliness and simplicity of our own national life, coupled with humility, respect, reservation of judgment, and readiness to be helpful within the modest possibilities of helpfulness, in our approach to others. The deepest duty of American civilization in the face of Soviet power lies still in the being, not the doing.

FRANK ALTSCHUL: *Discussion*

Chairman of the Board, American Investors Co., Inc.

In 1947 there appeared in the July number of *Foreign Affairs* an article entitled "The Sources of Soviet Conduct," by an anonymous individual designated simply as "X." It soon became an open secret that the author was George Kennan, highly influential in the Policy Planning Staff of the Department of State, and shortly to become its Director. Accordingly the thesis advanced at once assumed great significance, and especially the formulation of policy made implicit in the following words: "In these circumstances it is clear that the main element of any United States policy toward the Soviet Union must be that of a long term, patient but firm and vigilant containment of Russian expansive tendencies."

But Mr. Kennan made it plain that in advocating this policy he in no sense accepted as permanent the extension of Soviet power westward on the continent of Europe, evidenced by the enslavement of ninety million men and women held behind the iron curtain against their will. He shared fully the deep desire we all feel to see the prisoner states freed from their present masters. He looked forward to the time when Russian power would retreat to approximately its prewar frontiers. But he knew that before the turn of the tide, Russian power first of all had to be contained. To contain it seemed, in 1947, no trifling objective. While certainly not an ultimate objective of policy, this seems no trifling objective even today.

With remarkable prescience he noted that "the future of Soviet power may not be by any means as secure as Russian capacity for self-delusion would make it appear to the men in the Kremlin. That they can keep power themselves, they have demonstrated. That they can quietly and easily turn it over to others remains to be proved." And a little later he added, "Who can say with assurance that the strong light still cast by the Kremlin on the dissatisfied peoples of the Western world is not the powerful after-glow of a constellation which is in actuality on the wane? This cannot be proved. And it cannot be disproved. But the possibility remains (and in the opinion of this writer it is a strong one) that Soviet power, like that capitalist world of its conception, bears within it the seeds of its own decay, and that the sprouting of these seeds is well advanced."

There are indications that the possibility which he so vividly foresaw is on the way to gradual realization. It is a curious fact that just when there is some reason to believe that the policy he advocated is beginning to bear the anticipated fruit, there should be a continuing effort to distort and discredit it. "Containment" is a static, defeatist policy, the story runs. There must be substituted for it a dynamic "policy of liberation." Yet I believe that any dispassionate observer will be forced to the conclusion that however useful "liberation" may have been as a campaign slogan, unless we are prepared to back the notion with armed intervention, it is not a policy at all. And as we have not the slightest disposition to precipitate a world war in the atomic age, "liberation," I submit, becomes little more than a translation into new and misleading terms of the hopes originally voiced by Mr. Kennan.

In his paper Mr. Kennan has contrived, in brief compass, to place the present global conflict in historical perspective. He has exposed many of the roots of Soviet character and conduct, and has led us step by step to understand how the Soviet leaders, starting, in his words, "from what was once a very favorable position, have succeeded over the years in divesting themselves of all claim to moral leadership in the Western world."

Mr. Kennan holds the conviction that the threat to the West is no longer in the realm of ideas—a conviction unshaken by the spectacle of very large Communist parties in both France and Italy. These, in his view, may be considered to a great extent as expressions of protest against local inequities, involving only the most limited, if indeed any, sympathy with the long-range objectives of Kremlin policy. Peoples of the free societies of the Western world have on the whole learned by bitter experience that whatever there may have been of idealism in the early stages of the Russian revolutionary movement, this has long since been transmuted into a naked and despotic craving for power. For us, accordingly, the menace today, to use Mr. Kennan's words, is "almost exclusively a physical one, a military-territorial one, along traditional patterns."

But turning to Asia, Mr. Kennan points out that there the situation is far different. In this vast area, Soviet imperialism, for a variety of reasons, is still able to masquerade as a liberating force. The ideological weapon is employed with skill and efficacy. The growth of nationalism throughout the Asiatic continent has been accompanied by increasing resentment directed at the colonial powers. This provides precisely the climate in which the Soviet propagandists can draw the maximum advantage from the campaign against colonialism which they have been conducting unceasingly since the days of Lenin. There is an all-pervasive tendency to reject not only European domination but many of the forms of political and economic organization identified with it. Capitalism, like colonialism, has become a word of opprobrium. There is a search for something new and different which expresses itself in a willingness to flirt with Marxism, a disposition to adventure down new paths of social experimentation. Largely unaware both of the evolution of capitalism in this century and of the evil manifestations of Soviet imperialism with which we in the West have, to our sorrow, become so familiar, these distant lands, as Mr. Kennan has said, "look to Moscow for things they will certainly not find there, and in so doing place themselves and the security of entire geographic areas in jeopardy."

This, then, in broad outline, is the challenge we face—primarily military in Europe, and ideological in Asia. To meet it successfully on either front, we must first of all draw the necessary conclusions from a frank examination of some of our own shortcomings. Western disunity, according to Mr. Kennan, furnished Moscow—and one might add continues to furnish Moscow—its chance. And there is a certain contemporary relevance about the sentence which surely by no accident he selected for quotation from Custine: "The eternal oriental tyranny menaces us incessantly, and we shall be subject to it if our extravagances and our iniquities render us deserving of such chastisement." The notion that we might do well to consider the beam in our own eye runs like a theme in music through much that Mr. Kennan has written.

In 1947, in the article previously quoted, he underscored the necessity for us to "create among the peoples of the world generally the impression of a country which knows what it wants, which is coping successfully with the problems of its internal life and with the responsibilities of a world power, and has a spiritual vitality capable of holding its own among the major political currents of the times." He sounded the same note in different words today when he said in closing: "The prime moral dictate that flows for us from these realities is still the cultivation of the cleanliness and simplicity of our national life, coupled with humility, respect, reservation of judgment and

readiness to be helpful, within the modest possibilities of helpfulness, in our approach to others."

And to quote once again from *Foreign Affairs,* "The issue of Soviet-American relations is in essence a test of the over-all worth of the United States as a nation among nations. To avoid destruction it need only measure up to its own best tradition and prove itself worthy of preservation as a great nation."

In the discussion several questions were raised about the intent of certain Soviet policies. One queried whether Malenkov was not more interested in a horizontal division amongst Western peoples rather than a vertical division of nations. The opinion was expressed that every division in the West has been fostered by Russia; although class stratification was initially the first love of the Communist, Malenkov as well as Stalin have held class stratification is not as important as the vertical division of Western national states.

As to whether or not diplomacy should respond to external conditions and exploit weaknesses, such as the East German riots and the recent power struggle in the Politburo, the speaker indicated we should not conceal the nature of our sympathies with the oppressed Germans but we should not overtly interfere and thus offend the ethics of diplomatic decency. For this would mean a disruption of communications between governments, which after all is the first requirement of diplomatic relations.

A third question concerning the lure of Soviet trade, especially in Asia, as a springboard for ideological encroachment, brought forth the response that the Soviet Union has never been a great trading nation. The example of false United States expectations of Soviet trade in exchange for recognition by this country of the Soviet Union was cited. This trade of course never materialized. Russia does not now and has never possessed great surpluses with which to trade, although before 1928 she did have certain exportable surpluses of such raw materials as manganese and timber. But trade is a two-way street. It must be reviewed from both sides. We must think of the net rather than the gross effect.

A last question asked whether Stalinist domestic repressions was a requisite for expansion. The opinion was expressed that the changes that have taken place recently in Russia since Stalin's death have not altered Soviet policy. There has been no modification of the basic ideological outlook of Russian leadership. The evolution of leadership from Lenin to the present is not likely to change, although there may be evolution within their individual capabilities.

The Motivation of Soviet Policy Toward the Non-Soviet World

GEORGE A. MORGAN,
Foreign Service Officer, Washington, D. C.

Knowledge of any kind of human motivation is notoriously spotty and precarious. Even self-knowledge is fraught with passionate illusion. Yet the attribution of motives to one's fellows is among the dearest of human propensities, and apparently a necessity of social life. Even though often fallacious, it is our chief mode of "understanding" men's actions to the modest extent that we do.

When we broaden the inquiry from individuals to groups, the difficulties grow. What does it mean to speak of motivation which, even in a dictatorship, is not fully identical with that of one individual? Whatever we do or should mean, any alleged "knowledge" of it must be more intuitive than demonstrative, and is perhaps possible at all only because we are not exclusively individual ourselves but become social as we learn to speak.

The motivation of policy is esoteric to a further degree. By learning the language and participating in daily life, anthropologists and even quite ordinary people obtain worthwhile results in better understanding an alien culture. But policy, though its roots reach out indefinitely into a social system, takes shape near the top and therefore under highly special conditions. Until the Iron Curtain lifts to the extent of permitting anthropologists to hobnob with the Presidium, such grasp of Soviet culture as may be obtained will at most afford genus, not differentia, of Soviet policy motivation.

A thoughtful study of this topic should therefore begin with a sense of its complexity and elusiveness, and aim not to espouse one or another of the clichés which compete in popular discourse but to develop methods of assessing the evidence, as it grows day by day, in ways which will render the inevitable ascription of motives to Soviet policy as enlightened and useful as our limitations permit.

The present paper is too brief to carry out fully even this modest approach. It will only develop some relevant lines of thought.

Available evidence on the motivation of Soviet policy toward the non-Soviet world, as in the case of other social phenomena, reduces to two primary types: speech and conduct. Neither affords certainty. Any statement may be deceptive. Any act is ambiguous in isolation. Yet by the shrewd and imaginative sifting and cross-checking of words and deeds, including the context within which they are uttered or done, relatively stable probabilities do emerge.

Major statements by Soviet policy-makers offer by far the most explicit evidence, since they contain professed policy already articulated. For this reason they are a convenient starting point for the study of motivation, but it would be unwise to assign them unquestioned primacy. Where there is a clear contrast between speech and conduct, the latter is surely more conclusive. Also the very abundance of textual evidence can warp judgment, much as the unevenness of archaeological remains tends to give the richer sources undue weight in our reconstruction of the past. So in working from policy statements one must try to correct for their inevitable bias in favor of rational as against irrational, planned as against accidental factors.

Yet it is possible to be equally one-sided in emphasizing conduct as evidence of motivation. Words without deeds are empty, but deeds without words are blind, to paraphrase Kant. Conduct bereft of speech loses most of its meaning and approaches the level of the dumb brutes. People who ignore the expressions of Soviet policy in the writings of Lenin and Stalin, for example, and insist on judging merely by "what they do" are not the hard-boiled realists they would like to appear. If they clothe conduct with meaning at all, they tend merely to substitute for an expression of Soviet mentality an uncritical projection of their own unconscious assumptions.

Since a fashionable "realist" thesis is that the Soviet rulers are utterly cynical, opportunistic seekers of power, let us inquire, as a next step, not whether that thesis or its extreme opposite is true, but how power and ideology are probably related in Soviet motivation. Far from being antithetical, they are to a large extent complementary or even identical.

Several things may be said of opportunism in general. Leninist ideology itself is radically opportunistic in one sense: right is what serves the cause of communism, wrong what hinders it. Thus, like utilitarianism, it judges acts in terms of consequences and makes correct choice a matter of assessing the opportunities offered by any given situation. Hence the most Leninist ruling group imaginable would, in a given situation, set a "general line" which judged by our standards would be quite cynical and unprincipled. Yet it would, by hypothesis, be completely faithful to its creed because it would interpret the situation in Leninist categories and make its choice in relation to Leninist ends.

Much talk about the role of ideology in action implies a naïve conception of the way any general ideas affect conduct. No doctrine is self-applying. However intensely and purely a dogma is held, unless it is wholly other-worldly it still has to be related to a concrete case before it can lead to a particular act. This can be done arbitrarily and subjectively, as doctrinaires do, or with practical judgment. The men who have run the Kremlin seem on the whole to have followed the latter model. The regime would hardly have survived had they not. But to admit this, while useful as a step in defining Soviet motivation, is far from denying ideology a very significant part in it. In many ages there have been men of action who were also men of conviction. The great medieval popes, for example, did not exactly spend their lives striking stained glass attitudes, but to conclude from this that their principles counted for nought is a patent *non sequitur.*

Ideas affect action not only in the guise of ends pursued, but also as patterns of thought with which situations are interpreted and means chosen. This is particularly true in the Marxist tradition, which generally professes to be a purely "scientific" cognition of the laws of social change. Leninism is no exception, for all its voluntaristic modulation of Marx—important as that is. It still devotes most attention to principles for the interpretation of fact and the implications thereof for action, while its value categories, covertly smuggled into the system, are comparatively rudimentary. Many of the features of Leninism which seem specially influential in shaping Soviet foreign policy are mainly ideas of fact rather than value: for example, the tragic necessity for conflict in the change of social systems, the dynamics of "imperialism" in decay, the division of the world into two "camps" and the radical hostility between them. Also there is an important reciprocal relationship between ideas and conduct: according to Leninism, the correctness of the interpretation of any given historical situation—the "calculation of the correlation of forces"—is finally known only through successful action. Hence action is a constituent of concrete ideological "truth." Thus in considering the influence of ideology on Soviet foreign policy one should picture it as habits of thought shaping interpretations of the world situation and being tested in the power struggle, as well as decisions consciously related to remote objectives. That the coloring of reality by Leninist categories is particularly evident in Soviet discussions of the non-Soviet world is only natural on the part of men who know it so little by direct acquaintance.

It is sometimes argued that the Kremlin's devotion to power-seeking rather than communism is proved by the regular predominance of short-run over long-run considerations in its decisions. Here again, a fallacy arises from one-sided emphasis on a truism. There is a sense in which any practical man gives priority to the short-run: relying on concrete effort, interacting with the context of men and events, he sees that in order to accomplish next year's purpose he must deal first with what today and tomorrow bring. To that extent the short-run must take priority, because it is temporally and causally prior. So much is obvious: Lenin and his successors have been not so much romantic as pragmatic fanatics. But to prove them unfaithful to their long-range ends one would have to establish more than this commonplace. One would have to show that they never accepted immediate risks and sacrifices in order to move nearer to their alleged goals later on. Yet in fact the history of Bolshevism abounds with illustrations of just the opposite. The cornerstone on which it was founded was the sacrifice of numbers in order to build a party of disciplined revolutionaries, thus losing some short-run support for the sake of ultimate victory. Forced collectivization was a short-run economic loss and a serious strain on the stability of the regime. It is difficult to see what "short-run considerations" could have so perennially required warfare against Social Democrats abroad, notably in Germany where it helped the Nazis to power.

Another misunderstanding about "opportunist power-seeking" in Soviet motivation arises from the habit of lumping Marx, Engels, and others indiscriminately together as authors of "the" communist ideology, and then reproaching later leaders with inconsistency on matters which in some cases were only the doctrine of their predecessors. Lenin and Stalin, indeed, not only departed occasionally from previous theory but altered their own views in important respects, and in fact made it a point of doctrine that doctrine should change with experience. If such change took place with every veering wind of circumstance, the label of opportunism would deservedly stick. But the record shows instead a tough resistance to change, a massive ideological stability, even rigidity, in the face of stubborn fact, which yields only with a slowness like that of religious dogma. Not for nothing has the party line through the years tried to cut a straight and narrow path between "sectarianism" and "opportunism": it manifests a purpose held taut between pertinacity and practicality. The whole story of the Communist movement, from the struggle for power against heavy odds under Lenin to the Korean truce negotiations, shows a "length of will," in Nietzsche's phrase, not easily matched. To belittle this factor would be one of the most serious mistakes one could make in the light of experience.

Perhaps the key relationship of power and ideology in Soviet policy lies in the fact that they are not mutually exclusive but can be merely different aspects of the same thing. Power is an abstraction. It is realized concretely only in particular kinds and patterns. Suppose all Soviet motivation were will to power, the question would remain: what sort of power, in what forms and relationships? To the extent that the writings

of Lenin and Stalin are indicative of how the regime has interpreted history and intended to influence it, their ideology is simply the form of Soviet will to power. To ask crudely whether Soviet aims are ideological *or* power-political is thus as unintelligent as asking, in Aristotelian language, whether a substance has a formal or an efficient cause.

" Will to power " itself embraces a number of meanings. For example, it can mean will to keep the power one has, to get more, or to use it.[1] In each case, the direction may be inward or outward, or both. If one could trace how and to what extent these relationships are particularized in the fabric of Soviet history, it might yield an informative profile of Soviet motivation. The present inquiry must content itself with a few strokes of the brush.

Soviet ideology from its Leninist beginnings has focussed upon power—first its seizure, then its consolidation and increase —with an intensity seldom equaled. In this respect, Soviet preaching and practice have corresponded to a remarkable degree. During the early revolutionary period both speech and action turned hopefully toward revolution abroad, particularly in Germany, while fighting desperately to retain power at home. When foreign hopes failed, doctrine and effort adapted themselves to a longer view, centered on building " socialism in one country " as the main base of world revolution, pending further foreign opportunities in connection with the next world war.[2] War and opportunity duly came, and with them a renewed outward reach for power.

Thus there have been broad swings in the direction of Soviet will to power—now inward, now outward—and on either front the accent has been at times on consolidation, at times on advance. But these have only been differences of emphasis. Both components have always been present on both fronts, and both

[1] Cf. the author's *What Nietzsche Means* (Harvard University Press: 1941), 60 ff. Nietzsche had an early vogue in Russia. Whether the Bolsheviks read him or not, he was in some ways more prophetic of them than was Marx, notably in his conceptions of the " lawgiver " tyrant and " the barbarians of the twentieth century."

[2] Historicus, " Stalin on Revolution," *Foreign Affairs*, January, 1949, 190 f.

fronts have always been active in some degree. So the Kremlin did what little it could abroad through the Comintern during the "socialism in one country" period, and postwar expansion has been accompanied by renewed construction and discipline at home.

It is important to stress this pervasive duality in Soviet motivation and behavior, not as a defect or inconsistency but as a positive and deeply-rooted trait. To some extent it may be characteristic of all living processes, but the Kremlin shows it so much more strikingly than other contemporary sociopolitical systems that it awakens a sense of paradox at every point. For example, sealing off and Sovietizing East Germany impede bids for influence in West Germany and vice versa, yet both lines of action continue, in varying proportions. Thus closure and expansion, digesting what is gained and reaching out for more, are equally essential aspects of Soviet will to power.

Some argue that maintenance of domestic power is the basic motive of the regime, and its expansive hostility toward the non-Soviet world merely a reflex of this, partly necessary for maintaining the tensions by which it governs at home, partly resulting from the insecurity felt by a dictatorship in relation to any power it does not control. This theory seems to be a one-sided reading of what is in fact an organic pattern of interrelationships. There is a truistic sense, of course, in which any regime must give priority to internal stability, no matter how expansionist its foreign policy. Just as no general in his senses will deliberately launch an offensive at the price of losing his main supporting areas, so the protection of the Soviet base naturally takes precedence over furtherance of revolution abroad. This must be a particularly acute consideration for a regime which governs without consent. In addition it is obvious that international tensions are a convenient excuse for the apparatus of the police state. That such tension is stimulated solely or even chiefly for this purpose, however, requires additional evidence, not yet produced, since the converse relationship is equally apparent: controls at home also support adventures abroad. Moreover, the theory in question would lead one to expect a maintenance if not increase of foreign tensions during the early post-Stalin period, but the opposite occurred. It is thus arbitrary and unconvincing to argue that the Kremlin's will to power is primarily introverted. It would seem better to say that this will strikes both inward and outward, creating tensions in each direction which mutually enhance one another.

A related, but less extreme, view tries to distinguish the interests of the Soviet state from those of world revolution, and maintains that the interests of the state now prevail. But if the Soviet state is built as the main base of world revolution, these interests are identical and the alleged difference is purely verbal. The same crowd are running both. To prove more would require a different conception of the Soviet state. But where is the evidence for it? The subordination of foreign Communist parties to Moscow is not decisive here, any more than the sacrifice of a division by General Head Quarters proves that GHQ is merely looking out for itself and not fighting a war. The presumption is that it is doing both, though the perspective of GHQ on relative values may not be as infallible as good discipline must pretend.

A second line of argument for the state versus revolution view is apparently another case of one-sided reading of the facts. It notes that the Kremlin plays the game of "conventional" diplomacy with other states, but ignores the unconventional games that go on at the same time. One could more accurately say that the Kremlin manipulates both as parts of its highly unconventional world struggle.

"Russianism" or Great Russian nationalism, in the eyes of some observers,[3] is replacing Leninism in the motivation of the Soviet state, retaining Leninism chiefly as bait for foreign adherents and for other ancillary purposes. Were this true, it would indeed mean that Soviet motivation is swerving away from world revolution and perhaps toward a revival of something like Tsarist imperialism. That deep inheritances from the Russian past have survived the October revolution and continue to influence Soviet life is only natural, and is readily verified by the similarities in the testimony of foreign observers in past centuries and our own. The question is how far these influences

[3] Edward Crankshaw, *Cracks in the Kremlin Wall* (New York: 1951), Part 2, Chap. 4.

are controlling. Has the Soviet state become essentially national in content as well as multi-national in form?

It seems unlikely. The arguments for the affirmative point to Stalin's toast to the Great Russians, the rewriting of history in their honor, the invidious cultural boasting in recent years, and similar data indicating a special role for the Great Russian culture in the Soviet empire. But this leaves untouched the question: who is using whom? Napoleon used French patriotism, and spread the French Revolution. A discriminating look at what has and has not been revived or invented from the Russian past suggests that Stalin, veteran manipulator of nationality affairs, was using "Russianism" rather than vice versa.[4]

From 1930 until 1945, the appeal to Russian national sentiments had an obvious relation to preparing for and surviving World War II. Since then, while Leninist discipline was firmly restored, there has at the same time been a many-sided process of Russification which includes eastern Europe as well as the USSR. But there is a more practical explanation of all this than the supposition that the Kremlin has surreptitiously been going native. A common language, and its cultural concomitants, are an obvious convenience for unified administrative and psychological control—both directly and as means of making Russian "advisers" more acceptable to other nationalities.

This interpretation also reaches into quite distant perspectives. In a letter on "The National Question and Leninism," first published in 1949, Stalin added a new feature to his conception of the future of nationalities and languages under world socialism. Between the initial stage marked by the proliferation of emancipated languages and the final stage in which all national differences fade away and there is a single world language, he suggested an intermediate stage consisting of "several zonal economic centers for separate groups of nations, with a separate common language for each group of nations." Only later would "these centers combine into a common world center of Socialist

[4] See F. Barghoorn, "Stalinism and the Russian Cultural Heritage," *Review of Politics*, April, 1952, 178 ff.; Leslie C. Stevens, "The Russian Doctrine," *The Atlantic Monthly*, June, 1952, 55 ff. This is not to imply that the relationship may not be reversed eventually: in the long run, means often become ends.

economy with one language common to all nations." He added that national languages would continue to exist along side the common language for some time.[5] The conception of zonal languages was again stated in Stalin's publications on language in 1950.[6] In addition, this discussion made plain that his rebuke to the theories of Marr meant that Russian was not condemned by revolution to die with the past but would have a major role in the future of socialism. Stalin also remarked rather patronizingly that the empires of Cyrus, Caesar, Charlemagne, and Alexander the Great had been temporary " military-administrative unions " lacking an economic base and a common language.[7] The implication for his own empire is evident. While Stalin was formulating these views on language, the Soviet press, particularly in 1949–50, carried general articles on Russian as a new " world language," comparable to English and French.

These bits of evidence suggest the hypothesis that Stalin's postwar emphasis on the Great Russians was at least in part connected with an intention to make Russian the " zonal language " for the orbit of which Moscow had already become the " center." What other centers and zonal languages did he have in mind? It may not have been entirely coincidental that the Communist conquest of China was completed about the time the zonal theory was published, and also that Stalin in his October 1949 telegram beckoned Germany to partnership in " great actions of world significance," including the permanent pacification of Europe. In any case the idea of a plurality of " centers " as a phase in the future of socialism is an interesting variation on the simple monistic formula of " world domination by Moscow," and has political as well as linguistic significance that may not have died with its author. It seems to echo an earlier passage describing the subsequent history of world revolution as a struggle between a system of capitalist and a system of socialist centers. Another passage indicates that each system is to have a main center.[8] Moscow would presumably expect to

[5] *Sochineniya,* Vol. 11, 348 f. The contemporary Russian word " *tsentr* " has an ominous force which the English " center " does not convey.

[6] *Pravda,* Aug. 2, 1950, 2.

[7] *Pravda,* June 20, 1950, 3.

[8] Historicus, " Stalin on Revolution," *Foreign Affairs,* January, 1949,

be such a main center, and finally to become the common world center of the single economy and language in which history comes to an end.

Though Russian nationalism has by no means supplanted Leninism in Soviet motivation, the role of Russian traditions in this field is nevertheless an extremely rich and complex theme to which the present paper can scarcely do justice.[9] That theme touches on a number of nonrational factors which evidently play an important part in Soviet action—its style, its paradoxical contrasts, its scale of sensitivity and insensitivity so different from our own. But, as in the relations between ideology and power, the Russian heritage and Leninism are in the main complementary rather than mutually exclusive factors. Leninism itself profoundly Russified the Marxism on which it fed, and Marxism flourished in Russia partly because even before it was Russified it fitted salient traits in Russian revolutionary feeling and national experience.

The distinctive feature of Soviet as compared with traditional Russian motivation, however, is its dynamism. Part of Russia plus part of Marx formed a mixture far more explosive than either ingredient, and helped make a revolution that is still at work in the ferment of our century. Its driving force is enshrined in Lenin's doctrine of the vanguard of revolution: the party must never wait passively for the "inexorable laws of history" to destroy capitalism. Rather it must tirelessly push forward to exploit every weakness, every advantage. History has to be shoved. Some of the questions most worth asking concern the direction, intensity, and duration of this dynamism.

The interval since the death of Stalin has been too brief to offer the student much except new problems. To a probably considerable degree, the personality of Stalin dominated Soviet motivation for nearly thirty years. Only gradually, and at best incompletely, may we expect to learn how much of both Soviet

203 f. The two passages on "zonal" languages, cited above, expressly refer to a period after the worldwide victory of "socialism," but there is no obvious reason why zones might not begin to form earlier within the "socialist camp."

[9] See George F. Kennan, "The Sources of Soviet Conduct," in his *American Diplomacy 1900–1950* (Chicago: 1951), 107 ff.

excesses and successes were due to his will of steel, cold judgment, skill at intrigue, or trust in cruelty. In the early years some features of Soviet policy abroad were clearly connected with Stalin's struggle against rivals at home, and at all times the need to protect personal power from the enemies it has made must be an obsession pervading the purposes of any dictator or oligarch. What one or more persons contribute to Soviet motivation in similar ways in the future, and indeed whether Soviet power achieves stable personality at all comparable to its past, are still questions in the realm of speculation. Apart from these unpredictable linkages of individual and collective destiny, however, a review of the largely Stalinist Soviet past suggests at least some broad features that may be projected tentatively into the future.

One feature is the impressive fact of a "going concern," to use Sir Halford MacKinder's famous characterization of social momentum.[10] Soviet motivation is harnessed to a vast machinery of interlocking habits and vested interests, including those of the apparatus of repression by which a quasimonolithic shell is sealed about the people. Thus it cannot easily change its basic drives. Many of them are rooted in the fact that oppressive power once seized constitutes a predicament which, like Macbeth's, advances by a relentless inner logic of its own.

The element of social momentum may have increasing importance. Barring the intrusion of new dynamic factors—always possible—one may discern a certain ageing of the Soviet revolution from faith, through will, to habit. The idealistic faith that sustained its preparation and exploded in the fervor of initial success withered away under the cruel will of Stalin, which in turn was embodied in the habits of the succeeding generation, marshalled by cadres whose whole training is postrevolutionary and whose mentality is mainly bureaucratic-administrative. To the extent, however, that Soviet institutions are Stalinism "objectified," as Hegel might say, that ideology will continue to express the general pattern of Soviet motivation even if it fades from conscious conviction into ritual that is mostly taken for granted. Whatever individuals think, the system will "believe"

[10] See his *Democratic Ideals and Reality* (New York: 1919), Chap. 2.

as long as to question openly is tantamount to treason. But though the pattern is apt to persist, the intensity of its dynamism may tend very gradually to run down, over decades, except as refreshed by new stimuli such as internal or external conflict.[11]

This may seem a safe generalization in an age so full of conflict that it can hardly be put to the test. In any case it should not be taken for wishful thinking, since it still allows Soviet dynamism a term of life long enough to be replete with tragedy for all concerned.

One new stimulus for the USSR has been the conquest of mainland China by Chinese Communists. In addition to the obvious problems of collaboration which this entails, it marks the first major reversal of a trend that has dominated Soviet experience with foreign Communist parties since 1917: repeated expectation and repeated disappointment. If one result of that trend was increasing reliance on the Soviet " base," a result of its reversal should be a new seriousness about international communism, and perhaps with it a partial antidote for bureaucratic hardening of the arteries.

One of the most important statements made by Stalin at the time of the nineteenth Congress went almost unnoticed in public comment: it was that " capitalism " has reached a stage of permanent crisis in which growth no longer exceeds decay, and for which the thesis of " relative stability " (acknowledged in 1925) is no longer valid.[12] Since there is reason to believe that the race against stabilization imparted a special urgency to Soviet expansionism since 1945,[13] this announcement seemed to imply that the race was considered won, " capitalist " disintegration having so far advanced that it would never be able to rally enough to stop the general Communist offensive. Such thinking may have contributed to changes in tone and direction of Soviet policy recently observed.

[11] See A. N. Whitehead, *Process and Reality* (New York: 1929), 514 f.; *The Function of Reason* (Princeton: 1929), 18 f. If habit is able increasingly to replace fear as the means of keeping the people in line, that also should favor the slow slackening of Soviet dynamism. But what is lost in speed might be gained in mass.

[12] J. Stalin, " Economic Problems of Socialism in the USSR," Sec. 5.

[13] Historicus, " Stalin on Revolution," *Foreign Affairs*, January, 1949, 212 ff.

But the fundamental sources of the Soviet dynamic remain untouched thereby. Among them the chief so far identified are: the Leninist conception of our age as a tragic, often devious, but always total struggle between systems in which the party must press relentlessly for victory, nourished on the mystique of some older Russian aspirations and obsessions, and embodied in a "going concern" with vast momentum under would-be monolithic controls, haunted by the furies of illegitimate power.

J. H. ADAM WATSON: *Discussion*

First Secretary of the Embassy of Great Britain

We have in Mr. Morgan's paper an extremely illuminating discussion of the whole Communist dynamic in the world today. Mr. Morgan divided his analysis into several main sections, so we may have something to say on each. His points were in essence as follows:

I. Power and ideology are complementary: even in a sense identical. It is an ideology of power; Lenin implemented this. It is an ideology about facts, about how power works in the modern world. Values are rudimentary. What has contributed to the success of the Soviet system is the fact that they have concentrated on certain facts about power, and they saw these facts more clearly than did others.

II. The long-term nature of Soviet purpose—"length of will," as Nietzsche said. Within this there is a duality which makes Soviet policy believe in both internal and external tensions, each supplementing the other. The question I would like to raise is the puzzling one: How far do the very objectives change? Does the ultimate goal alter? No doubt Lenin believed in "tacking" to the wind despite criticism; but the question remains of how far the ultimate objectives are altered.

III. Soviet dynamism—The "going concern." The Soviet system and apparatus run forward of their own momentum.

IV. Then came the difficult question of the conflict between the state interests of Russia and the interests of the world revolution. Mr. Morgan thinks, as I do, that the concept of such a conflict is a fallacy. I believe that among practical statesmen this question has led to the greatest confusion. He made three points here: a. One is a base for the other. It is the same crowd that runs both. This is hard to deny. b. Just because there is conventional diplomacy, just because Malenkov says that all issues *between states* can be settled by negotiations, this does not mean that the world revolution has been given up. c. There are two aspects to Russianism. One is the Russian language and civilization versus the language and civilization of other peoples, within the Soviet Union and the satellites. The second aspect is whether the Kremlin is "going native." I wouldn't put it that way. Mr. Morgan said that part of Marx and part of Russia joined to form an explosive mixture. I would say that it is the whole of Russia, that the Russian element is becoming the more prominent and more dynamic of the two.

Mr. Morgan said "Leninism russified Marxism"; certainly, but Lenin began as an internationalist. He regarded the Russian revolution as almost a historical accident, of one among many European revolutions and argued with Kautsky in these terms. It was not until the invasion of Poland that Russian patriotism was enlisted for the Bolsheviks. They closed the "window on Europe," moved away from Petersburg and all that was implied by that. The iron curtain came down. Socialism in one country was implemented. The "New Soviet Man" as described by Professor Ray Bauer began to be created. Is he not something different from the rest of the world, different from members of the Communist parties in the outside world? A whole generation has grown up cut off from the rest of the world, in ignorance of the West. I felt this in talking to Russians, particularly outside of Moscow. The non-Soviet world is steadily getting more alien and remote to *all* Russians. The new Soviet man sees the world through Lenin's eyes: he reads about the outside world in terms formulated by Lenin and this picture is (1) out of date; (2) constant; and (3) losing out to the living and moving Soviet reality, to the insulated Russian context. The new rulers of Russia, not just the Kremlin but all those who make the system work in many fields of endeavor, are becoming increasingly differentiated from the West, no longer share the value concepts. Lenin was familiar with the West, but today the West is less and less known at first hand by these new Soviet leaders.

A discussion of certain aspects of Mr. Morgan's paper followed.

The first question dealt with the kinds of motivation arising from the domestic scene that could influence foreign relations. It was pointed out that the whole fabric of individual or group aspirations meshed together to influence whoever made the policy decisions that governed Soviet policy. The process of stratification which is going on and which is departing from the earlier utopianism expresses itself in what seem to be strong groups, e. g., armed forces, bureaucracy, economic executives, secret police, etc. As less fresh blood comes up from below, as these groups gain in stability, they are able to filter the information, advice, and suggestions that are brought to the attention of the people making the decisions. The vested interests and tensions of these groups affect modifications in the internal conduct of affairs, which in turn find their outlet in foreign policy as well as domestic decisions.

Another point alluded to was the compulsion arising from the use of arbitrary power without consent of the ruled, by the use of fear and other pressures. Such a predicament has compulsions for the people wielding the power in their relations to the persons kept under that power. This influences decisions about foreign matters. Such a person would not be able to count on the loyalty and support of those people under him during conditions of crisis.

Another question dealt with whether the United States can reverse the Marxist-Leninist propagation that history " must be shoved " by attempting to settle outstanding differences at this time of difficulties for the Soviets. The opinion was expressed that according to the Leninist ideology the mission of the party to push ahead with world revolution goes back to the bedrock convictions about the forces which they believe to be at work in modern times. Current Soviet difficulties hardly went so deep. It was thought most unlikly that a general settlement with Russia was possible. The only way of containing Russia was to be strong enough permanently to prevent her taking a momentary advantage.

The view was also expressed that the United States should not act alone in this matter, but in concert with her Western allies.

The third question concerned the changing emphasis on the importance of economic ideology in Marxist thought and the reliance on the political power in Lenin and especially Stalin. The opinion was expressed that the great bias of the nineteenth century was the notion that economics determine politics. This is found not only in Marx but in Beard, Madison, Parrington, etc. The twentieth century rejected that and adopted an opposite bias. We believe that political power can move the world. If you have control of political power you can shake the economic life of society. This superstition prevailed in the United States also, where we emphasize planning executive power, etc.

Marx, Lenin, and Stalin differed with each other on the relationship between economics and power as a factor. Marx's writings proposed that the working class should seize political power because economic conditions justified it and that no group attempt to seize power until the time was ripe. Mensheviks were able to base their position on Marx when arguing with Leninism.

Stalin's conduct was based on the assumption that the use of force can solve any problem. This constitutes a belief that all can be done by economic planning. Stalin makes (in his last testament) some concession to the need for concern about objective economic conditions, like Marx. But the rest of his writing was based on the reliance on power.

The fourth question concerned the basic contradiction between the fundamental aim of the original Marxist-Leninist doctrine of assuring the welfare of the working people, on the one hand, and the recent Soviet policy of social stratification which favors educated people at the expense of workers and peasants, on the other. The view was expressed that this was a contradiction in the Soviet system and therefore a vulnerability. But its importance would not be exaggerated; and Soviet apologists had a rationalization—namely, that evils like preferential treatment for the educated class were necessary in order to reach the Communist heaven.

The Basic Tactical and Strategical Concepts of Soviet Expansionism

MOSE L. HARVEY,
Chief, Division of Research for USSR and Eastern Europe, Department of State

The danger of knowing something that isn't so with regard to "The Basic Tactical and Strategical Concepts of Soviet Expansionism" is very great. The heart of the problem lies in whether or not the Soviet rulers are Marxist-Leninists, or, perhaps better, Bolsheviks. If they are in fact Bolsheviks, one set of generalizations about their objectives and methods can be made. If, however, they are not Bolsheviks, an entirely different set is required. To say that they both are and are not Bolsheviks is to dodge the issue. For if the term Bolshevik means anything, it is not something a person can partly be. It is like the "little bit pregnant" business. As Stalin put it back in the early days of Soviet Power:

> One thing or the other.
> *Either* we will continue to carry on a revolutionary policy, uniting the proletarians and the oppressed people of all countries around the working class of the USSR with the result that international capital will hamper our advancement in every possible way;
> *Or* we will renounce our revolutionary policy and make a number of concessions in principle to international capital, and then international capital perhaps will not mind "helping" us regenerate our socialist country into a "good" bourgeois republic.[1]

The issue is key to every aspect of the subject here considered. Is there a peculiar sort of Soviet expansionism? Are there cer-

[1] J. V. Stalin, *Sochineniye,* Vol. 11, 54-55.

tain immutable preconceptions that the Soviet rulers have as to what will happen in the outside world? Are there more or less rigid formulas that bind the Soviet rulers in making decisions as to courses of action? The answer to these and a host of related questions lies in the answer to the question of whether or not the Soviet rulers are Bolsheviks.

Nature, it is said, abhors a vacuum, and will exert constant force to fill it. Equally, it might be said, the rational abhors the irrational and attempts constantly to explain it away.

Bolshevism, as elucidated by Lenin and Stalin, and their echoes, is, from our point of view, irrational. Its fundamental tenets are demonstrably contradicted by reality.

Sane men, the mind cries out, cannot be serious in mouthing such claptrap; much less can they base policies of a great power on the assumption that it is valid. The Soviet rulers, reason continues, have proved that they can govern a vast empire, that they can cope with practical problems. They, therefore, are necessarily sane men; they can only be indulging in window dressing when they give vent to such utterances. All of which is obviously neat and logical. It sweeps away with a grand gesture that which is loathsome to the orderly mind.

But can the matter be so simply dismissed? Is not what is involved in reasoning of this sort simply a recreation of the Soviet mind in the image of our own?

Common prudence warns against taking a categoric position on a problem of this nature; it strongly suggests a " yes, but " answer, one that would make possible, with a little mental dexterity, demonstrating at some later date that one had, at the least, not been wrong regardless of what might happen.

Yet if one is to tackle in any meaningful way the problem of the true nature of Soviet expansionism, he must face squarely up to the issue of whether or not those who run the Soviet Union are first, last, and always Bolsheviks.

With trepidation, I take the plunge. It seems to me that the evidence leaves little room for doubt that the Soviet rulers are in fact Bolsheviks. From the Revolution in 1917 down to the present, those rulers have given every indication of a strict adherence to the basic tenets of Marxism-Leninism.

For one thing, they have always talked in terms of Marxism-

Leninism. They have cited Marxist-Leninist doctrine—and this doctrine alone—as the guide and justification for all their actions, policies, views, and evaluations. Every individual—at every level—responsible for the gathering, analysis, or dissemination of information gives every evidence that he views situations and developments in a strict Marxist-Leninist context. Doctrinal dicta appear therefore not only to permeate, but actually to shape, all forces, factors, and media that influence thought processes and judgments of all groups.

Far more impressive, however, is the testimony of Soviet conduct. How many times since 1917 have outsiders jumped on a Soviet action or statement and viewed it as proof of the abandonment of Bolshevism? And how many times have subsequent events torn away the illusion of change?

You will recall the line of argument that came into vogue in 1921, when Lenin announced the New Economic Policy: The reality of power had sobered the visionaries. Bolsheviks were quietly becoming capitalists. The pendulum had, as inevitably it must, swung hard over, and one more revolution had run its course.

It is hardly necessary to dwell upon the disabusement process that followed, to review the quickly inaugurated retreat from NEP, culminating in the resumption of full-scale socialization in 1928-29.

Pass over the rosy-glow interpretation of such developments as the campaign to establish trade relations with Western countries, the studied efforts of Soviet authorities to establish the fiction that the USSR "always meets its commitments" financial and otherwise, and the launching of the United Front in the nineteen-thirty's. Just recall the arguments of the second World War period. World communism was abandoned. The Soviet Union was at last joining the democratic community of nations. Ideological rigidity was being abandoned. Out of the trials and terrors of the war a new sort of Soviet state was arising, one that had as little true connection with Marxism-Leninism as the Russia of Alexander I.

So the views of many went.

But what happened, and how else explain it than that the Soviet rulers were, willy-nilly, still Bolsheviks? How explain the deliberate resumption of a posture of implacable hostility toward the wartime allies, the seemingly calculated step-by-step alienation of public opinion favorable to the USSR, the insistent "division of the world into two camps," the willful creation of international tensions—and all this at a time when the Soviet Union apparently most needed a breathing spell to lick its terrible wounds, needed friendship and help, not enmity and struggle. How else can you explain the ferocity with which the authorities re-tightened the wartime-loosed ideological strait-jacket on the minds of the Russian people, the brutal denial of wartime-generated popular hopes for a better life, the resumption of forced draft efforts to build the economic and military might said to be necessary for completion of the "transition to Communism?"

But, one might object at this point, this was the product of another epoch. With the death of Stalin, a new era has been inaugurated. Whatever Stalin may or may not have been, his successors are hard-headed realists; men of engineering and practical government experience; men on whom the hocus pocus of Marxism-Leninism has as little influence as the incantation of a witch doctor on a bulldozer operator. These men are reasonable, the argument might be continued. Their course is the course that other reasonable men would take if they found themselves masters of the Soviet Union. Granted the first steps are little ones; but they are firm and their direction is clear.

Certainly a great many observers are currently taking just such a position. More or less typical is Sebastian Haffner, writing in the May issue of *Twentieth Century*. While admitting the need for caution Haffner reasoned along these lines:

> After all, a number of facts in the present world situation, and in the profit-and-loss account of revolutionary Communism since 1917, do very strongly suggest the advisability from the Soviet viewpoint of changing over from a dynamic policy to a static one, from permanent revolution to consolidation at home, and from continued cold war to settled peace abroad . . . . A realistic and responsible Soviet statesman must therefore feel driven even more forcefully than his opposite numbers in the West to the idea of dissolving the "camps" and restoring some-

thing like a settled system of world peace, world economy and world trade.

It would obviously be ridiculous to argue that changes have not taken place in the Soviet Union since the death of Stalin. The elimination of Stalin itself necessarily constituted a momentous change. Even if his successors had wanted to follow exactly in his footsteps, varying not a whit in any direction, they clearly would have found it impossible to do so. Stalin was a unique historical phenomenon. To try to operate as if he were still present would have been as vain as attempting to sound an echo without a voice.

But the changes that have been effected recently have been something more than the ones that would automatically derive from the elimination of Stalin. The new rulers have shown no inclination to follow exactly in Stalin's footsteps. They have substituted an all-wise Central Committee for an all-wise individual as the great white father of the cause. They have adopted a somewhat different pattern of behavior in the conduct of diplomatic relations. They have talked more of the responsibility of the government to the people. They have even done a few things—a very few things I might add—to back up this talk. They have indicated that in several important respects operational methods followed in running the economy of the country will be changed. They have dramatically reversed several particular decisions arrived at during Stalin's last months. They have modified existing programs in at least two of the European satellites. They have supported, if not fostered, moves making possible conclusion of an armistice in Korea. Changes then there have been.

But does it follow that there has been a departure from Bolshevism, or if you wish in this instance, Stalinism?

Edward Crankshaw, for example, saw in a passing *Pravda* complaint regarding the lining up of states in accordance with "old and unjustified" ideological principles and social-political systems, evidence of a possible complete break with the past. Writing in the *London Observer* on June 5, Crankshaw said: "If the sentence in the *Pravda* article is to be taken at its face value it means that Malenkov, or at least a powerful group in the Kremlin, no longer believes in the inevitability of final conflict. And this must mean, in effect, that they have abandoned the idea of world revolution as the supreme and overriding aim of Soviet policy. If, in fact, the new men in the Kremlin have abandoned the idea of the division of the world into two camps, they are ceasing to be Bolsheviks."

Happy thought, but is it justified?

What tomorrow may bring, I don't know. But this I think I do know. What has happened so far in the Soviet Union since Stalin's death can no more be added up to equal a departure from Stalinism, or even a modification of the essence of Stalinism, than can Stalin's own Bolshevik article of September, 1952.[2] Analyze the activities of the new regime as thoroughly as you will, give all the legitimate weight possible to the changes that have been made, and as of now—I still am not attempting to speak of tomorrow—you have a Soviet system alike in every essential detail to the system that existed before Stalin's death.

What, for example, could be more Stalinist than the budget announced on August 5 with its continued concentration on the expansion of the industrial base and the military might of the Soviet Union? Even the ingenious little arrangement whereby peasant ownership of cows is to be promoted by cutting in half the taxes levied on peasants who don't now have cows is worthy of a Stalin at his best. Witness also the reaction to the conclusion of a truce in Korea and its emphasis on the great victory of the "mighty movement of the peoples for peace." How does the Soviet reply to the Western proposal for a conference on Germany differ from what you would have expected if Stalin had lived? Could Stalin have improved on the technique displayed in the "unmasking" of "the hired agent of imperialism," the "bourgeois degenerate" Beriya? Whose but Stalin's "basic law of socialism" furnishes the phrases used in the current prattling in regard to the concern of the State and Party for the welfare of the people? How much real difference is there between god-head Central Committee and god-head Stalin?

Something of a "new look" has been effected, yes. But to get a new sort of being from this "new look" requires a remarkable pair of spectacles. Take off the spectacles, and, new look or no new look, you have the same old hag. She may no longer

[2] J. V. Stalin, "Ekonomicheskie Problemy Sotsializma v SSR," *Bolshevik*, No. 18, September, 1952.

pick her teeth in public, but basically she is today what she was yesterday.

But enough of what I consider belaboring the obvious, and what many of you may consider an ardent presentation of one side of the question. There remains the subject with which this paper is primarily concerned, the basic strategical and tactical concepts of Soviet expansionism.

Grant that Stalin was a Bolshevik, that he was a faithful adherent to the Marxist-Leninist cause. Grant also that Stalin's successors are keeping faith, that they consider the tenets of the theology passed down to them as binding as did Stalin, or Lenin before Stalin. What good does it do us? What light does it throw on the problem of what the Soviet Union is up to?

After all, is not Marxism-Leninism—or Bolshevism if you will —so broadly constructed that it permits of almost any line of action that the human mind can devise? Is it not so elastic, so flexible, that it offers no real guide to the attitudes, intentions, and actions of even those who accept it in all sincerity, and without reservation?

It goes without saying that Marxism-Leninism is in no sense of the word a blue-print for a rigid line of action that must be followed under any and all circumstances. The doctrine itself makes a virtue of flexibility. In the words of *Izvestiya* of July 7 of this year: "The Party regards Marxism-Leninism not as a frozen dogma, but as an eternally alive teaching which is constantly developing and enriching itself with the experience of socialist construction in one country and with the entire world's experience of the revolutionary and working-class movement."

Is this by way of saying that Marxism-Leninism amounts to nothing more than a general frame of reference under which the particular leader of the moment has complete freedom of action? Can the ideology be described as calling essentially for only a "correct attitude," it being left to the responsible individual or individuals to work out how this "correct" attitude is to be translated into "correct" action?

If either dissertations on theory, or actions of successive Soviet leaders are taken as a guide, it appears that Marxism-Leninism cannot be so characterized. Despite all the talk about flexibility, and a number of instances of a radical shift in policy, the doctrine holds that certain principles, even rules if you will, are immutable. And these principles or rules are not limited to broad "objectives." They affect operations and they are of a nature that more or less narrowly circumscribes the area of maneuverability open to the particular leader of the moment. Aside from this, there has been an increasingly strong tendency for less absolute principles to become fixed. The operation of the system has been such as to assign a large degree of sanctity to that which was done or said in the past. The burden of proof for a break with past practices is on the initiator of the change. The new must be explained and justified; the old is taken for granted. Thus in practice the flexibility enjoyed by the powers that be is not like that of a fancy Dan boxer. It is more like that of a speeding locomotive. Within certain limits, there can be reversals and changes of course, but these are effected not by flipping a switch, but by a screeching of brakes and a great deal of huffing and puffing, and there are endless pressures to proceed slowly and cautiously.

Marxism-Leninism is not, then, merely a state of mind. It is rather a guide to action and a relatively detailed guide to action at that. It requires that certain things be done, and it rules out certain others.

With regard to Soviet expansionism, or if you will the further extension of the "Revolution," the doctrine is explicit in the case of a wide variety of key details. One can with a reasonable degree of assurance make a number of generalizations about where the Soviet rulers stand on the whole matter.

First, the problem of whether Soviet expansionism is in reality called for. Under Marxism-Leninism, under Bolshevism, must the frontiers of Soviet Russia be constantly extended? The answer is clearly: "not necessarily." The Soviet rulers are obligated to take such measures as may be necessary to maintain their power base in the Soviet Union, that is to preserve "the first land of socialism." Under certain circumstances this might be interpreted as requiring an extension of Soviet frontiers. But a constant territorial aggrandizement by the Soviet State is not demanded.

But what of the Soviet system? Does Marxism-Leninism call for the necessary extension of the Soviet system, which would involve by definition control by the Soviet rulers, to other areas? The answer again appears clear: It most assuredly does.

The essence of Marxism-Leninism is that there must necessarily be a life and death struggle between the proletariat of the world and the rulers of capitalist countries. All preceding historical development has relentlessly led to the unfolding of such a struggle. The USSR is inextricably tied up in this class struggle, the spear head of which, from its standpoint, is now said to have been transferred to the international arena. According to an article in *Kommunist,* the leading Communist theoretical journal, of January of this year:

> The Communist Party of the Soviet Union has always proceeded from the fact that the "national" and international problems of the proletariat of the USSR amalgamate into one general problem of liberating the proletarians of all countries from capitalism, and that the interests of building socialism in our country wholly and fully amalgamate with the interests of the revolutionary movement of all countries into one general interest of the victory of socialist revolution in all countries.[3]

To this should be added Stalin's statement at the nineteenth Party Congress in October of last year. In this he concentrated a major portion of his attention on the problem of the tie-up between the Soviet party and the world revolutionary movement.

> Naturally our party cannot remain indebted to the fraternal parties and must in its turn afford support to them and likewise to their peoples in their struggle for liberation, in their struggle for the preservation of peace. . . . After our party assumed power in 1917 . . . representatives of the fraternal parties . . . gave it the title of "shock brigade" of the world revolutionary and workers' movement. . . . Of course, it was very hard to fill this honored role while the "shock brigade" was the one and only one and as long as it had to fill this vanguard role almost single-handed. But that was in the past. Now things are quite different. Now, when new "shock brigades" have appeared in the form of countries of peoples' democ-

[3] *Kommunist,* No. 2, January, 1953, 15.

racy from China and Korea to Czechoslovakia and Hungary —now it has become easier for our party to fight, yes, and the work goes more joyfully. . . .[4]

The fact of this recent renewal of frank acknowledgment of the tie-up between the USSR and the world revolutionary movement serves to revive the authoritativeness of such earlier statements as Stalin's characterizing the USSR as the " lever " as well as the " base " of the world revolution,[5] and Lenin's emphasizing that the victorious Soviet proletariat, " having expropriated the capitalists and organized its own socialist production, would stand up against the rest of the world, attracting to its cause the oppressed classes of other countries, raising revolts in those countries against the capitalists, and in event of necessity coming out even with armed force against the exploiting classes and their states." [6]

Even if, in contradiction to statements like the above, the Soviet rulers should be inclined to take lightly their ties with revolutionary movements on the outside and to dedicate themselves solely to the task of maintaining themselves in power and preserving the Soviet state, under Marxism-Leninism they would still be compelled to strive for the constant expansion of the Soviet system, for the spread of the Soviet controlled " Revolution."

Soviet theoreticians are currently proclaiming daily that " capitalist encirclement still exists and will continue to exist so long as capitalism itself exists." This, they assert, poses a mortal danger to the very existence of the USSR. For " the objective law of the class struggle," it is said, inevitably drives the capitalists to increasingly desperate attempts to destroy Soviet power. As Lenin is cited as explaining, " a furious resistance of the bourgeoisie in all countries against the socialist revolution is inevitable . . . and will *grow* in proportion as this revolution grows." [7]

[4] *Pravda,* 15 October, 1952, 1.

[5] Stalin, J., *Problems of Leninism,* revised official English translation of 11th Russian edition (Moscow, 1947), 122.

[6] V. J. Lenin, *Selected Works,* Vol. 5, 141.

[7] See, for example, *Pravda* and *Izvestiya* editorials of July 10, 1953, and July 14, 1953, respectively.

Under Marxism-Leninism, therefore, safety for the Soviet Union requires the total destruction of capitalism as a force in the world. Any other course would be to gamble everything. Hence the defensive goals of preserving the Soviet state and maintaining the Kremlin in power merge with, and become indistinguishable from, the offensive goal of expanding the area of Communist domination.

But how does this gibe with the "socialism in one land" line? Soviet theoreticians, as well as propagandists, have dealt at length with this one. The Soviet Union, it is said, has everything necessary for the achievement of socialism and even the transition to communism. Why, then, should there be anything more than sympathetic interest in what happens on the outside? Wherein is there any compulsion to spread the Revolution?

Aside from the fact that one might question, in light of economic realities, whether the Soviet rulers could really believe that they have everything necessary for building socialism, an answer lies in this: irrespective of what it has, the Soviet Union is necessarily stopped from proceeding all the way down the road to the happy valley by threats and problems posed by capitalist encirclement. For the final victory of socialism in one land, revolution throughout the greater part of the world is necessary.[8] "The Soviet Union," *Kommunist* repeated as late as a few months ago, "cannot with its own forces alone destroy the hostile encirclement which raises the danger of capitalist intervention. The destruction of capitalist encirclement and the destruction of the danger of a capitalist intervention are possible only as a result of the victory of the proletarian revolution, at least in several large countries."[9]

There is still another problem. What of the "peaceful coexistence" formula?

Forget for the moment that the formula has invariably been put forward only in a propaganda context, or that in recent years it has been amended to a point where it calls for the virtual surrender of the capitalist "enemy." Take it as it was originally put forward and allow that it meant what it said. What actually

[8] See Stalin's discussion of the point in his *Problems of Leninism*, 156-66.

[9] *Kommunist*, No. 2, January, 1953, 15.

did it say? "Peaceful coexistence is possible, *provided* there is a *will* for it." In the proviso lies the catch. By definition neither a capitalist nor a Bolshevik could, under the immutable social laws that control him, "will" peaceful coexistence with the other without automatically ceasing to be a capitalist, on the one hand, or a Bolshevik on the other.

If anything is axiomatic in Marxist-Leninist doctrine it is that imperialism and socialism, capitalist rule and Bolshevik rule, cannot live side by side. Irrespective of the inclinations of any individual, or group of individuals on either side, mortal struggle is made inevitable by the operations of unchangeable social forces. This is the heart of the dialectic. This in brief is what it is all about. Marxism-Leninism—Bolshevism—is by definition world revolution, is a drive for the constant extension of Soviet power. Take this aspect away and nothing meaningful is left.

This raises immediately a second major question. Grant that the object of the Soviet rulers is the extension of their system to other lands, in what way is this to be brought about? Is it to be an automatic process, with reliance being placed upon the workings of the forces of history? Or does it require causative activity on the part of those who desire the change?

Marx's analysis of the course of social development held that certain things will be because they have to be. Fixed laws determine human activity as surely as they determine physical phenomena. Man is as powerless to change social laws as he is to change physical laws, or to escape the results that they automatically produce.

Marx held that social laws were inevitably bringing about the destruction of capitalism and were inevitably preparing the way for the transfer of power from the bourgeoisie to the proletariat.

If something is inevitable it would seem that one should act as if it were inevitable. In all logic, therefore, there was no reason for Marx's activist call for the workers of the world to unite. History would do their job for them, would present them with the fruits of victory, regardless of what they did or did not do themselves. There was no reason why the workers shouldn't bask idly in the sun, fully assured—now that Marx had penetrated the secrets of history for them—that harvest time was coming as certainly as day would dawn.

In effect, the first followers of Marx accepted this point of view. Not in an extreme sense, of course, but essentially. Activity was deemed desirable and was undertaken, but fundamentally this was directed toward preparing for what was coming, not toward causing it to happen.

Lenin, however, was different. Either because he was a revolutionary first and a Marxist second, or because he wanted to develop a rationale for an early revolution in Russia, where, according to Marx's thesis, it could occur only after capitalism had evolved infinitely beyond the level it had thus far attained —or both—he rejected out of hand the passive "wait and it will happen" point of view. Moreover, using Marxism only as a general base he developed theoretical concepts to justify his position.

These concepts, it goes without saying, profoundly altered Marxism. Marx saw the "proletarian revolution" developing as a result of the great majority of the population being first proletarized and then inevitably driven to a state of desperation and revolution by a relentless and unending increase in capitalist exploitation. Thus under Marx revolution would come spontaneously and inevitably. For it to come, however, capitalism would have to develop to a point where the greater part of the population had become proletarized and where the contradictions besetting capitalism had become so intense as to force an increase in the exploitation of the workers to a point where it was no longer endurable to them. Obviously, then, revolutions could occur only in very advanced capitalist countries.

Lenin, in effect, substituted another revolutionary force for the class-conscious, now-at-the-breaking-point proletariat of Marx. He had to if he was to have revolution in the "weakest link in the capitalist chain." Lenin's substitute force was to be an artifically created one, whereas Marx's was to be a natural one. Lenin's force was to be brought into being by a revolutionary party, professional and not mass in nature, bringing together at the proper moment a number of different forces that allegedly inevitably exist in capitalist society. The proletariat was only one of these forces, although an important one. None of the forces alone, not even the proletariat, would be capable of producing a revolution. A revolutionary situation could arise only through the combination of all of them. While the existence of the several forces was automatic, their necessary combination into a single revolutionary movement was not. It would require skillful planning and constant activity, struggle if you will, on the part of the professional revolutionary party. It would be greatly helped through some cataclysmic event, notably war.

Lenin's description of the forces that he looked to to furnish the raw materials for building a revolutionary movement, or achieving at a given moment a revolutionary situation, varied from time to time. In general, it might be said that he considered the forces to include any group, any condition, and any activity that could be exploited, directly or indirectly, in the drive to undermine and destroy the hated enemy. Thus the peasantry, national liberation movements in colonial countries, warfare between capitalist countries, quarrels within the ruling class of a country, petit bourgeois elements that happened to be discontented, as well as activities of the proletariat, were all grist for his revolutionary mill. He generalized to the effect that the "revolutionary movement" was a "proletarian" movement, but his specific admonitions called for something entirely different.

Stalin summed it up in terms of three groups of forces: first, a main force consisting of the Communist party, which is the vanguard of the whole movement, and the proletariat proper; second, direct reserves consisting of the peasantry and other intermediate strata of the population of a given country and the proletariat of neighboring countries; and third, indirect reserves, consisting of conflicts between nonproletarian classes in a given country and conflicts among different capitalist countries.

Stalin in his original discussion of these forces seemed to be talking only about the Communist movement within a particular country. When he discussed the movement in a world sense, however, he used, although somewhat ambiguously, the same analysis. In the world movement context, the main force consisted of the Soviet Union and foreign Communist parties, with the other forces forming direct and indirect reserves of the Soviet Union.

To Stalin as well as Lenin, the problem of extending the area of the revolution was the problem of mobilizing and maneuvering these various particular forces so as to weld them into a single unified force capable of being used, as Stalin put it, "for achievement of the main object of the revolution at the given stage of its development."

For this an activist approach is necessarily an absolute essential. There can be no waiting for the fruit to fall from the tree. In the words of Stalin, which for once appear to be crystal clear:

> Some comrades think that, once there is a revolutionary crisis, the bourgeoisie must be in a hopeless position; that its end is therefore predetermined; that the victory of the revolution is thus assured, and that all they have to do is to wait for the fall of the bourgeoisie and to draw up victorious resolutions. This is a profound mistake. The victory of the revolution never comes by itself. It must be prepared for and won." [10]

Which again brings us to another major question, our third. How is victory for the revolution to be "prepared for and won?" What measures and activities are called for? What concepts govern their selection and the tempo of their application?

First, are distinctions made between different types of methods in terms of generalized principles regarding admissability or even preferability? In particular, can it be said that the aim is to employ only, or even principally, such indirect methods as political pressure, psychological warfare, and subversion, with direct methods such as insurrection, armed attack, and formal warfare excluded, or at least relegated to an only-at-a-last-resort status?

Here, I believe, little discussion is required. Clearly no type of activity is ruled out, or put in a less preferred category, on the basis of principle. Anything and everything is permissible, is even required, if it promises to be successful. Thus, depending upon circumstances, the fight may be carried on through organizing propaganda campaigns, executing political maneuvers in parliaments, agitating for this or that "cause," organizing mass activities for one purpose or another, denying markets necessary

[10] Stalin, *Problems of Leninism*, 464-65.

for the disposal of capitalist surpluses, creating war scares, exposing the enemy through formal negotiations, exerting economic pressures, precipitating and supporting armed uprisings, launching or inducing local wars, precipitating general war. Such activities may be utilized singly or in combination. Several, even if they are contradictory, may be carried on in the same area at the same time.

Theoretically, there can be nothing static about the choice and use of these various forms of attack. Instead, it is obligatory that shifts in emphasis and even in types of measures be affected as often and as rapidly as the situation may seem to demand. In the words of Stalin, the object must always be " to put in the forefront precisely those forms of struggle and organization which are best suited to the conditions prevailing during the flow or ebb of the movement at a given moment, and which therefore can facilitate and ensure the bringing of the masses to revolutionary positions, the bringing of the millions to the revolutionary front, *and* their disposition *on* the revolutionary front." [11]

A change from one particular " form of struggle " to another does not involve in any sense a change in the nature of the struggle itself. The struggle is a life and death affair. It is no less a life and death affair when primary emphasis is placed on " sweetness and light " forms of struggle than it is when the emphasis is on direct attack with no holds barred. The only thing involved is a judgment that the life and death struggle can be more effectively prosecuted by substituting for the time being the indirect method for the direct.

This should put in proper perspective the problem of what is implied by the concept of an ebb and flow of the revolutionary movement. As an ebb sets in, as prospects for immediate revolutionary gains decline, revolutionary activity does not decline. There is simply a change in the forms of struggle. The fight continues, according to Stalin's paraphrase of Lenin, " by means of replacing old forms of struggle and organization by new ones, old slogans by new ones, by recombining these forms [of struggle], etc. . . ." [12]

Similarly, a general retreat from a course adopted does not

[11] *Ibid.,* 75. [12] *Ibid.,* 70.

represent any lessening of the intensity of the struggle. Under certain circumstances, in particular when disaster otherwise threatens, operational concepts call for backtracking to whatever extent necessary to save the situation. But the backtracking does not stop the war; instead it is a move in the war. "The object of this strategy," said Stalin, "is to gain time, to demoralize the enemy, and to accumulate forces in order later to assume the offensive." [13]

It is important to note that except for situations where necessity appears to dictate, retreats from lines of attack are not called for, are not even admissible. It has sometimes been said that Lenin advocated a "stop and go" technique—a sort of "two steps forward, one step backwards" approach.

Nothing could be more alien to Leninism. Under Leninism, forward movement, once begun, must be continued unless objective conditions make a halt or a retreat necessary. A basic principle of strategy, according to Stalin, is the "undeviating pursuit of the course adopted, no matter what difficulties and complications are encountered on the road towards the goal." [14]

Stalin explained that such firm adherence to an established course is necessary in order that the vanguard may not lose sight of the main goal of the struggle and that the masses "may not stray from the road while marching towards that goal and striving to rally around the vanguard." [15]

This explanation relates to a key point, the very nature of the revolutionary movement under Leninism. Lenin's revolutionary movement, you will recall, derives its force from the artificially effected combination of a number of particular forces existing in society. The forces are, in effect, brought together and held together by motion. Given a cessation of motion, and the combination becomes unstable, tends to break apart, with the result that the whole revolutionary movement of the moment is threatened with disintegration. The vanguard "loses sight of the goal" and the masses "stray from the road" and abandon their intention "to rally around the vanguard."

In other words, the Communist leaders are not as free as we sometimes think to execute sudden twists and turns. Useful as a really clever "new look" might be in confusing and befuddling

[13] *Ibid.*, 74. [14] *Ibid.*, 173. [15] *Ibid.*

the enemy camp, it would produce similar results in the Communist camp, and perhaps with far more sweeping results.

Also because of the artificial and essentially transitory nature of the Leninist type revolutionary movement, the Communist leaders are under considerable compulsion to capitalize immediately on any opportunity that may arise to achieve a solid success. It is often said that the Soviet leaders must automatically view any situation of the moment against a "history is on our side" backdrop; that no matter how favorable a particular situation appears, they must necessarily believe that it will become more favorable at a later date; and that the weight at any given time is consequently against a decision for action.

Actually the reverse is the case. The favorableness of a given situation derives from the success achieved in combining the various potentially revolutionary forces, that is, from the fact that at the given moment the vanguard is aroused and ready for action, the peasants and other potential allies are arraying themselves behind the vanguard, rivals for the leadership of the masses are for the moment indifferent or helpless, and confusion and disorder reign in the ranks of the enemy. Because this combination of happy circumstances exists at a particular moment, it does not follow that it will also exist tomorrow. The peasants might fall away from the vanguard, the capitalists might recover their bearings. Thus to delay is dangerous. It may mean a delay of years, even decades in the attainment of an important objective in the eternal struggle.

Once an opportunity arises, action, immediate action is, therefore, the only permissible course.

"History," Lenin said, "will not forgive revolutionaries for procrastinating when they can be victorious today . . . , while they risk losing much, in fact, everything, tomorrow." [16]

So much for particular concepts. There remains, however, a general point that must be emphasized, one that lies at the base of all else: There is no place in the Marxist-Leninist outlook for genuine compromise, for any reconciliation of differences. Struggle against the capitalist enemy is the law of life. To end it, even to interrupt it, would be to die.

[16] V. J. Lenin, *Selected Works,* English Edition, Vol. 6, 335.

Kommunist, the authoritarian Soviet theoretical journal, made this point as clearly and frankly as possible in an article contained in its January 1953 issue. Here it was stated:

> The Soviet Union is conducting and will also conduct in the future a policy of building communism in our country, although the gentlemen capitalists do not like it. The Soviet Union is conducting and will also conduct in the future a just, liberating and peace-loving foreign policy, in spite of the shoutings, blackmail, and threats of the warmongers.
>
> J. V. Stalin unmasked and branded the capitulants who insisted on pacifying the imperialists at the price of continuous concessions on questions of principle and at the price of satisfying their imperialist appetites. The imperialists of Great Britain, the USA, and other countries demand that the Soviet people give up its sympathy for and support of the liberation movement of the working class of other countries, that the USSR sanction the imperialist policy of the international bourgeoisie in the Far and Near East, in Southeastern Asia, in Latin America, on the African continent, etc., that it give up the monopoly of foreign trade or at least 'soften' it, etc. J. V. Stalin showed that the Communist Party and the Soviet Government cannot agree to these and similar concessions unless they renounce themselves; . . .
>
> Leninism teaches us that the imperialists cannot be pacified' with small concessions as was suggested by all kinds of liberals who broke with the theory of class struggle and who slid down to the position of rightist opportunism. Concessions, big or small, to the imperialists on radical problems and problems of principle weaken the positions of the socialist country and encourage the imperialists to intensify their pressure on the socialist and democratic countries and raise new and still more insolent demands. It is clear that only people who have broken with Marxism can follow this road. As Comrade Stalin teaches us, the laws of class struggle demand the intensification of the attack on the positions of reaction, and not concessions to reaction and reactionary classes. The successes on the class struggle front are being won in the course of a bitter struggle against the enemy. This also fully relates to the struggle for peace and democracy and against imperialistic reaction

and war. Comrade Stalin teaches us not to yield to the sudden attacks of the warmongers and enemies of democratic freedoms and not to give in to any provocations and intimidations on the part of reaction, and more persistently to unmask their mean actions in the eyes of the masses of the people and strengthen the collaboration of the toilers of all countries. This is the key to victory.

The agents provocateurs, the mongers of a new war and their rightist and socialist tuft hunters strive to present in a false light the consistency of the Soviet Union and its observations of its principles, its firmness in putting across its domestic and foreign policy, which expresses the socialistic essence of the Soviet regime and the Soviet State, as an alleged deviation from Lenin's thesis concerning the possibility of a peaceful existence of two systems, a socialist and a capitalist system. As a matter of fact, the liberating and anti-imperialistic nature and consistency of Soviet foreign policy and the implacable struggle with the warmongers have not only failed to shake the thesis of Lenin and Stalin concerning the possibility of a peaceful coexistence of the two systems, but are also a necessary condition for the possibility of such a coexistence.

The conditions which have determined the possibility of peaceful coexistence of the two systems in the past continue to operate also at the present time. The Soviet people are persistently struggling for the conversion of this possibility into reality. Marxism-Leninism teaches us that a possibility is not converted by itself into reality; an active struggle must be conducted for its realization. In order to convert the possibility of a peaceful coexistence of the two systems into reality, it is necessary to strengthen the country of socialism and the whole democratic camp with all possible means, to unmask the warmongers systematically, also to defend henceforth the policy of international collaboration based on the adoption of coordinated decisions to counter-balance the policy of dictation conducted by the American and British imperialists, to strengthen the ranks of the adherents of peace in the whole world, and to utilize ably the differences in the camp of the warmongers in order to frustrate their nefarious plans.

However, that means that not the way of gifts to the aggressors and warmongers is to lead to success, but the way of decisive resistance to their aggressive intentions, the way

> of decisive unmasking of their base plans, and the way of mobilizing the masses for a struggle against these plans.
>
> While supporting any revolutionary movement, the working class always preserves the independence of its movement and considers the struggle for democratic reforms as a necessary step which secures the development of class struggle for socialism.
>
> The struggle for democratic demands under conditions of imperialism does not distract the working class from the solution of its future socialist problems, but brings their solution nearer in every possible way. Such is the dialectic of historical development. On one occasion Lenin wrote: 'The socialist revolution is not one act and not one battle on one front, but a whole period of aggravated class conflicts and a great number of battles on all fronts, i. e., on all questions of economics and politics, battles which can be ended only with the expropriation of the bourgeoisie. It would be a radical mistake to think that the struggle for democracy is capable of distracting the proletariat from the socialist revolution or block it or overshadow it, etc. On the contrary, just as a victorious socialism which does not realize full democracy is impossible, a proletariat which does not lead an all-sided, consistent, and revolutionary struggle for democracy cannot prepare itself for a victory over the bourgeoisie.[17]

Is this by way of saying that so long as the Soviet rulers remain Bolsheviks they can not seek a genuine East-West settlement, can not accept in good faith established norms of international conduct, can not abandon—or even " put on ice "—their drive to effect the destruction of rival powers?

It can hardly be read as saying anything else.

Struggle thus remains the key to Soviet tactical and strategical thinking. Relaxation, " normalcy " in the conduct of relations with others, peace as we understand the term, are by definition incompatible with what the Soviet leaders avow to be their solemn obligation to history. To ask quarter is, in their own words, to invite destruction; to give quarter is to betray themselves. The contest, they themselves insist, must be to the death.

[17] D. Chesnokov, " Rech I. V. Stalina na XIX S'ezde Kommunistichesksi Partii Sovetskogo Coinza-Programma Borby za Mir, Demokratiin, Sotsializi " in *Kommunist*, No. 2, January, 1953, 21-34.

JOHN HIGHTOWER: *Discussion*

Chief Diplomatic Correspondent,
Associated Press, Washington, D. C.

In the folklore of experts on the Soviet Union one of the sayings is that there are no experts: there are only varying degrees of ignorance. This vacuum, this lack of comprehensive information, is responsible for one of the phenomena chiefly characteristic of our attitude toward the Soviet world—I refer to our great reliance on experts instead of observers. In this peculiar situation, created by Soviet secretiveness, we necessarily esteem the second guess, whereas with other nations we insist upon the firsthand look.

However, the logic of Mr. Harvey's analysis seems to me to proceed upon a straight line. His major assumption is that Bolshevism is the key to all understanding of Russia. His second assumption is that the people who count in Russia in this month of August, 1953, must either be non-Bolsheviks or else hard-shell, straight-down-the-middle Marxist-Lenists.

Mr. Harvey then offers evidence to demonstrate that the rulers of the contemporary Soviet empire are faithful disciples and absolutely orthodox interpreters of Marxism and Leninism. This opens to him the whole field of classical Communist literature from which he then draws his facts and conclusions about the intentions and behavior of the men who are pushing the buttons—or fighting for control of them—in the Kremlin right now.

I would like, however, to raise at this point a question: Are people like that? Specifically, are the Soviet leaders like that? What of their Russian historical inheritance? Also are the revolutionary ideas which have come down to these modern kremlinites still truly revolutionary or have they become simply adjuncts of Soviet power?

It sometimes seems that to try to understand Soviet conduct—to foretell Soviet strategy—largely in terms of what Marx wrote a century ago, what Stalin wrote a few years ago, and what Malenkov wrote yesterday is like trying to prophesy the life pattern of a modern Lutheran layman from the writings of Martin Luther and yesterday's Sunday School lesson.

The Soviet tyranny has recently undergone, in Stalin's death and Malenkov's succession, a tremendous change of personalities.

Beria's purge proves the presence of violence. Other forces of which we see violent evidence are at work in the satellites.

The question I am now seeking to pinpoint is whether we have adequate resources of information and adequate techniques for meeting the challenge of this opportunity? How accurately can we gauge, and how far can we go in exploiting, this apparent weakness in the Kremlin's empire? Fundamental to this, of course, is the question: What are the real purposes and strategy of Russia's rulers right now—today?

Let me point out some other and different considerations. In the period from the Russian revolution to the Roosevelt administration here, the dominant American attitude was one of stern excommunication of the land of communism. We didn't like the Reds; since we disapproved of them and couldn't trust them, we wouldn't speak to them at all. In the second phase of our relations with the Soviets we tried under considerable difficulty to get along with them, understand them, and make them our friends. That was true for a long period which, with time out for the Stalin-Hitler treaty interlude, lasted from 1933 through most of 1945.

Since the fall of 1945 we have been engaged in another phase of relations with Russia, based on bitterness, deep suspicion and fear, and marked by a terrible armaments race. This time there is a speaking relationship, but the language is pretty tough.

During the war years the United States government held that Russia was not intent upon world expansion; all it really wanted was a defense in depth in eastern Europe and a friendly reassurance now and then from countries like the United States. In the Hitler-Stalin pact period, the Soviets were a bunch of cynical power politicians. Just now we regard them as consecrated to the Communist doctrine of world conquest. There have been other interesting variations in American attitudes. There have been times, for example, when Soviet military power was represented as overwhelmingly great and other times when it was represented as something less than devastating. These representations have shown a tendency to vary with Washington's budget problems.

These bits and pieces suggest that United States attitudes toward Russia may not be determined exclusively by objectively definable realities of Soviet character. Internal American needs and events seem to exercise a certain influence. At times we appear to judge the Soviets in terms of our own national experiences and in accordance with what we would like them to be. At other times we react to some spectacular behavior on their part, in evident surprise, as if it could not possibly have been expected. On still other occasions we seem to judge them primarily by what they say about things rather than what they are doing about them.

It is true that over most of its history the Soviet Union does not appear to us to have changed in any such degree as we have with our periodic succession of new governments. Yet it seems to me desirable to remember that changes in Soviet personalities and Soviet power have occurred. There have been the expansions in eastern Europe and Asia; there have been the recessions involving Iran and the island of Bornholm. New strains and tests have been imposed on the Soviet system. It is questionable whether Marx, Lenin, and Stalin knew ahead of time all the answers to all the questions which contemporary Russia, Soviet Russia, has faced and must face in the years ahead.

PART II

Techniques of Soviet Subversion and Attack

*Soviet Use of Trade as a Weapon**

WILLIS C. ARMSTRONG,
Deputy Director, Office of International Materials Policy, Department of State

Soviet trade and trading methods have from time to time been depicted as a tremendous threat to free economic and political institutions, and a sense of alarm has been evident in many quarters. Consequently, it is in order to review objectively the place of Soviet foreign trade in the general contest between the Soviet Union and the free world. One should not expect to find anything very startling or new; the factual record is reasonably clear; and there is the normal latitude for conjecture which characterizes any discussion of the Soviet Union.

One or two qualifications should be made quite clear, however. The definition here of Soviet foreign trade does not include trade between the Soviet Union and its satellites. Such commerce is said to be treated as foreign trade by the Soviet Union, but the available evidence shows it increasingly an extension of Soviet domestic economic activity. Furthermore, by Soviet foreign trade is meant only the trade relations of the Soviet Union itself with the countries of the free world, and not the external trade relations of Soviet satellites, although this should perhaps be regarded as an extension of Soviet foreign trade activity. If we were to deal here with the foreign trade of what is described as the Soviet bloc, some of the observations made below would require modification.

The first consideration should be the economics of the problem. Russia is not an important trading nation. It never has been, and it has been even less important since the 1917 revolution than it was before. The reasons for this are clear. The country possesses an abundance of resources of great variety, and

* This is an unofficial and entirely personal statement. It does not necessarily correspond to the official opinion of the Department of State or of the United States Government.

can potentially satisfy its food and raw material needs by domestic development. Some of these items occasionally show an export surplus. Before the Soviet regime, these surpluses resulted from normal economic processes, but since 1928, at least, an export surplus in the Soviet Union has been what the government says shall be available. The goods could in most cases be absorbed by a voracious internal market, but Soviet planners realize they must import, and therefore must export, to pay their way. Of course, they could export gold, but they ordinarily do not, as they seem to hold orthodox capitalist views about this desirable and comparatively useless metal.

Thus the Soviet Union exports in order to pay for imports. Most of its exports are useful—such as grain, timber, manganese ores, and other raw products. A small amount of manufactured goods is exported, primarily to obtain certain goods or favors from particular countries. Some of its exports are luxury items, such as furs and caviar. In general, the foreign sales of Russian goods do not bulk large in the import patterns of many countries, and in many instances they could disappear from world markets with only a ripple. The rest of the world could find some other sources of supply, and after a brief period of adjustment Russian goods would not be missed. It might be tough on those who habitually wear mink and eat caviar, but they could doubtless be conspicuously luxurious in some other way without much shock. In a few countries there would be a real problem of adjustment to the loss of Soviet goods, but it could be solved by genuine cooperation among the countries of the free world.

Soviet purchases in other countries are again a marginal factor in world trade. From time to time selected industries in certain countries have profited by sales in the Soviet market, but no long-term dependence has really developed, and the rate of growth of the economies of the rest of the world far outstrips any program of Soviet buying. The countries of the free world could presumably find ways and means of absorbing the shock which would come if the Russian market were not there. Furthermore, the Russians have shown an unpleasant tendency to concentrate on buying goods of high military and strategic significance, and a reduction or elimination of such sales has recommended itself to other countries as the course of prudence. This may entail some economic loss, but the security gain is clear. The USSR is compelled to import only a very few items in order to maintain its civilian economy at current levels. The more it seeks to expand and improve this economy, however, the more it needs imports to overcome its relative backwardness in applied technology. The Russians do not appear to be retarded in pure science, but they do seem to have their troubles when they try mass production of the more complex items of machinery and equipment, except perhaps in the direct military field.

The chief point which strikes the observer is that Soviet policies have been directed at self-sufficiency. This is probably out of reach as an objective in technology, but it is not remote in the case of individual products. The emphasis on self-sufficiency means one very important thing to foreign buyers and sellers. The Soviet Union may be a good customer for some years and then may suddenly disappear without warning, because it has learned to make the article itself in adequate quantities. The Russians may also offer particular commodities to certain buyers in the free world over a given period of time and then may vanish as a supplier, again without warning. This may happen because the Soviet goods are needed at home, or because the Soviet government has decided it can sell them to better advantage elsewhere. Doing business with the Russians does have its risks.

These characteristics of Soviet foreign trade have been present from the time the Bolsheviks seized power in Russia. No previous Russian government followed a more autarchic or more protectionist course in foreign trade than has the Soviet regime. The very institution of a state monopoly of foreign trade was designed to make this effective. This system was not substantially modified during the New Economic Policy period, when there was private enterprise in Russia. There was of course no alternative after the elimination of domestic private enterprise in the nineteen-thirties. The monopoly seeks a position of minimum liability and maximum flexibility, and has no compunction about voiding contracts or changing its mind if the Soviet rulers decide that such action serves their interests. Under the circumstances, it is potentially and theoretically available for use as an instrument of foreign policy, and perhaps could be far more useful for this purpose than the foreign trading institutions and practices of private enterprise countries.

The course of Soviet trade has been profoundly affected by domestic and foreign economic factors. In the nineteen-twenties the Soviet economy was weak, and the Soviet government needed good economic relations with other countries. The total foreign trade of the USSR was fairly impressive up to about 1932 because of relatively heavy requirements for goods to compensate for the economic destruction of World War I, the Civil War, and the Intervention, and to get a start on the basic industrialization of the first five-year plan. To buy these goods the Soviet Union had to export, and at the end of this period it found itself selling primary products of forest, mine, and farm on a declining world market. At considerable domestic sacrifice it had to increase its exports to be able to meet its external financial obligations. It was then subjected to foreign trade restrictions because it was said to be engaged in dumping. The severe adverse effect of the world depression on Soviet foreign trade was perhaps one factor in a renewed Soviet drive toward relative economic isolation in the nineteen-thirties.

International political and military events have likewise profoundly disturbed the Soviet economy and consequently its international trade policy. The Soviet Union acquired a huge volume of imports during World War II, furnished on credit by its allies, while its exports dwindled close to zero. In the period 1941–45 the USSR could not make use of foreign trade as a weapon, because it was a suppliant for aid.

From this recital it may readily be concluded that the Soviet government was in no position to take real political advantage of other countries by use of trade as a weapon, either during the first fifteen or more years of its existence, or at a later time when it was under heavy military pressure. In both cases its economy was weak by comparison with those of other countries, and this experience has doubtless reinforced Soviet leaders in their drive toward relative self-sufficiency. At other times the Soviet economy probably suffered from domestic political disturbances, as in the mid-thirties, and from a need to repair war damages, in the years immediately after 1945.

Thus far we have touched on the economic aspect of Soviet foreign trade, and a conclusion that it is of marginal importance for the rest of the world appears inescapable. We must concede that this margin is far more significant in some countries than in others. A few countries, because of their resources and needs, have a sound economic basis for a healthy and profitable trading relationship with the Soviet Union. Foreign trade is of limited importance in Soviet economic plans, except for a very few commodities where the Soviet Union does not have domestic production. It is quite important in technology, where the USSR must import know-how and machinery if it is to catch up with its capitalist rivals. We have further observed that the economic leverage the Soviet Union is able to exert has for a good part of its history been rather poor—perhaps one reason for its great drive toward autarchy.

We have also noted the institutional aspect. The Soviet foreign trade monopoly is an instrument potentially capable of being used for the attainment of noneconomic ends, to the extent the Soviet economy has the strength to support such use. The most fertile ground for such use is to be found either in countries where manufacturing industries are particularly susceptible to cyclical unemployment, or in countries heavily dependent upon the sale of individual raw materials which are normally affected by wide swings in price. Governments in modern times are highly sensitive to unemployment or low levels of income, and may respond eagerly to Soviet purchases when markets and employment are uncertain. A marginal economic factor may well make the difference between prosperity and collapse in a certain area or a specific business, and clever operation by Soviet traders can take advantage of such situations. Careful use of these possibilities can be of real political advantage to Soviet diplomacy, especially where public opinion is aroused over the threat of unemployment or general economic instability.

It may thus be admitted that under certain conditions, in certain areas, and to a limited extent, the Soviet Union perhaps advances its foreign policy by the use of trade negotiations and actual transactions. Trade has, however, not been a primary weapon, but rather an auxiliary. Where it has worked, the other side has frequently been beset by severe economic problems, has overestimated the prospects of Soviet trade, or has underestimated its capacity to adjust itself to changing economic circumstances in the rest of the world. There have been certain major limiting factors: the first is that the Soviet economy has at times been weak; the second is that it has been governed by a policy of autarchy; the third is that the trading nations of the free world are not unskilled in driving a bargain. There is no reason to assume that the Soviet Union always out-trades them, in either economic or political matters. In fact, the net advantage may well remain on the side of the free world country.

The Soviet Union has, however, sought to make use of the device of talking about trade, of implying that large orders will develop, of persuading unknowing peoples that their economic problems would be solved if their governments and businessmen would only see the light and enter into close trading relations with the Socialist fatherland. Since, in many countries, the general public is aware that economic conditions could be better —and nearly everywhere they always could—and since this same public is usually only too unconscious of the real facts concerning foreign trade, a climate of opinion has been built up which clamors, now and then, for closer trade relations with the Soviet Union. This is not an example of the direct use of actual trade in diplomatic and commercial relations with other governments and business firms in their countries, but rather an element of the general propaganda line of the Soviet government. This line naturally seeks to influence public opinion in a given country to put pressure on its government to yield to some Soviet demand. It finds its base in Communist organizations in other countries, but this base acquires additional support from business and labor groups as a result of the use of talk about trade in the general propaganda presentation. The talk is directed at groups not immediately concerned with foreign trade, or not informed about it. It helps build a backlog of good will for the Soviet Union, and it costs the Soviet government practically nothing.

An outstanding example occurred in 1946. France was short of grain and was importing great quantities from the Western Hemisphere with some financial assistance. The Soviet Union sold a much smaller quantity, for cash dollars, to the French, most of it carried from Odessa in American ships. The Soviet propaganda line, well publicized by French Communist agencies, implied that the grain was a gift, that the quantity was significant in solving the French grain problem, and that no other country was doing anything so specific to help. Probably a great many Frenchmen glanced at headlines, concluded the USSR was really being very friendly and helpful in a practical way, and went on munching breakfast rolls made from American wheat.

Of course, this sort of thing can be counteracted, and is being met, by effective publicity in the free world. But it is not uncommon to find people in many countries of the free world who discount the efforts of their own governments and business firms, who do not know the facts of foreign trade, and who assume that the Soviet Union is prepared to be of real assistance. This is the most receptive ground for the Soviet talk about trade. It represents a challenge to the free world to tell the facts, and fortunately a good deal of progress has been made in this direction.

A recent Soviet propaganda move in The Economic Commission for Asia and the Far East (of the United Nations), for example, was to allude to the possibility of large availabilities of Soviet capital goods and industrial equipment for sale to Southeast Asian countries. There was at the time a shortage of such goods, and the capacity of the manufacturing countries to make prompt deliveries was limited by defense requirements. The Singapore Chamber of Commerce called the Soviet bluff by staging a session in which explicit questions were asked of Soviet representatives concerning spare parts, servicing, delivery terms, prices, guarantees, and credit. The Soviet group was apparently not well briefed on these points, and the offer evaporated into the air from which it had come.

It might be in order to speculate at this point as to what the Soviet Union could do in the trade field if it chose to give wide scope to its trading institutions and policies. It could dangle many enticing prospects before foreign sellers, many more than it does. It could offer essential goods at cut prices, to enable hard-pressed countries to save their precious foreign exchange. It could cause havoc in certain commodity markets by dumping its goods and blaming the effects on competitive sellers. It could enter and leave markets at will. It could create speculative enterprises in sensitive markets, designed to spread suspicion, distrust, and ill-will as by-products of manipulation. The Soviet economy could stand it, up to a point, and any sacrifices in the Soviet standard of living which it entailed could be imposed on the people by the will of the government. In other words, the Soviet Union could become a disturbing factor in some fields of foreign trade, but it would have to be willing to buy and sell more than it customarily has. It would run the risk of being out-traded, and the process would be expensive.

Such a course would be contrary to the usual Soviet practices of frugality. Furthermore, it would require operators with a sound working knowledge of foreign markets, and with wide latitude and discretion in their instructions. Soviet officials are seldom granted this privilege, and furthermore are usually so isolated from the outside world that they lack the personal contacts and background to make such a program effective.

This brings up a rather interesting point. The world is accustomed to Soviet political diplomacy, with its quick changes of pace and tone, its rigid instructions that are occasionally changed over night, and its blatant disregard of fact and reason. But in foreign trade the real test is the actual transaction, and here the Soviet diplomat cannot function without the support of Soviet economic institutions. Now these institutions are embedded in a highly complex structure of manufacturing and agricultural enterprises, trading and banking corporations, ministries, scientific institutes, and administrations, presumably supervised by a planning board. This intricate and cumbersome machinery has been hard at work for many years trying to devise an acceptable and practical substitute for the capitalist market, which, in a perhaps rather imperfect way, makes the economic decisions in the free world, with varying degrees of regulation and intervention by governments. There is some question as to how successful the Soviet planners have been. Certainly they have built an economy capable of producing far more goods than it could before, but the position of the average consumer appears not to improve very fast. The USSR remains a shortage economy and a seller's market, which can be administered without great institutional strain. On the other hand, the outside observer may properly ask whether the system is well-designed to develop the kind of economy where flexibility and ready adjustment to changes in consumer demand are important assets.

The question is a proper one because the Soviet Union has developed a great deal of institutional rigidity. It must have, because there are so many people in the administrative complex, and the Soviet political climate tends to develop the cautious administrator. Also, the Soviet government is by no means immune from interdepartmental bickering and contests of strength, similar to those which appear in governments with which we are more familiar. Of course the penalties for the loser are somewhat greater in the USSR, and at the same time a decision in a complex economic matter cannot be made without a lot of clearances, unless complete chaos is to overtake the system. It may be asked, parenthetically, whether the economic system of the Soviet Union can develop to a point of responsiveness and flexibility comparable, for example, with that of the United States. Since there is no market in the proper sense of the term and since all actions must be determined by rules and administrative decisions, masses of bureaucrats are required. The more complex the economy, under the Soviet system, the more officials will be needed. It may well be asked whether such a system can ever catch up with its own overhead, let alone with the economic systems of the free world.

In this context, foreign trade as conducted by the Soviet Union's businessmen in the Ministry of Foreign Trade is a highly regulated thing, sometimes so regulated and controlled that it cannot take advantage of real economic opportunities as they develop. Even in wartime, as our experience in handling Russian lend-lease showed, Soviet representatives are encumbered by extensive rules and regulations and have little or no power of decision. Every question waits for instructions from Moscow, and sometimes these are very slow in coming.

This excursion into Soviet domestic affairs has been for two purposes. The first is to suggest that the Soviet system of planned economy has a large self-limiting factor in its expansion and development, which would circumscribe the extent to which the Soviet Union would have resources to use freely in a general economic offensive in the rest of the world. The second is to indicate that although we may readily concede that the foreign trade monopoly is theoretically adaptable for use as a political instrument, we must also recognize that it is inherently a part of the total Soviet economic machine, and as such is susceptible to the same institutional inertia as the multifarious ministries at home, which may well render it incapable of really effective action on a wide front. Of course these two limitations could be removed, but a basic shift in Soviet administrative methods would be required, and there is little current evidence that this is taking place. It would appear, therefore, that under present conditions there does not seem to be much danger of a successful general offensive by the Soviet Union in international trade, given Soviet autarchy policies, institutional rigidity, limited production, and high overhead.

Since the free world, with a few exceptions, has relatively little need of Russian products or markets at present levels of economic activity, and since the Soviet economic and political system makes it difficult for the government freely to operate as an effective market force in international trade, perhaps we may conclude that trade is not in fact an important weapon in the Bolshevik arsenal. Talk about trade is admittedly important, and can be more so, depending on the measure of economic health in the free world. If the free world is sound, however, and if its economy is expanding, it should be easy to combat the additional political capital which the Soviet Union creates by talking big about small trade. There are so many people in different parts of the free world who do not possess the essential facts, however, that the educational job is a large one. Furthermore, many people seem to be imbued with the idea that there is something morally wrong about private enterprise, and something inherently better about anything which describes itself as socialism. This perhaps proves that the Bolsheviks got there first with the ideas, at least with some people. The important point to make, and to demonstrate by action, is that free economies get there first with the goods and the real income.

Some of the inherent weaknesses of the Soviet system may help the free world, but it is unwise to count on them. We must assume that the Soviet rulers will try to use trade to foster their political objectives, but we must not allow ourselves to be frightened by Soviet trade and trade methods. The countries of the free world are striving to build a healthy economy, reduce trade barriers, protect security, encourage economic development, and expand output and employment. If the free world puts primary attention on its own economic strength and at the same time continues to expose the facts of Soviet economics, trade, and politics, the Soviet trade weapon can do it little harm.

JOHN H. FERGUSON: *Discussion*

Deputy Director of the Policy Planning Staff, Department of State

The subject of trade between the free world and the Soviet Union has engendered a great deal of heated political discussion during the past few years. During this period of tension, it is clearly not in our interest to permit international trading relationships which result in a net gain of strategic importance to the Kremlin, and the major trading nations of the West have now imposed restrictions on exports to the USSR to prevent it from achieving such an advantage.

Mr. Armstrong has said that Soviet foreign trade is of marginal importance to the rest of the world, although the margin is far more significant in some countries than in others. We would all agree, I think, that the Soviet Union uses its trade for strategic military purposes as well as for general economic and political ends, so it may seem surprising that the Russians have not further stepped up their efforts to attract trade with the West, particularly in those items of military value.

Mr. Armstrong explains the marginal importance of Soviet foreign trade by describing the economic weakness of the USSR, the skill of Western traders in driving a bargain, and the institutional rigidity and inertia of the Soviet system. These have certainly played their part in reducing Soviet trade as a factor in total world trade. And another reason may be the obverse of Mr. Armstrong's point that the Russian market is an unpredictable and undependable market, since it can be manipulated at will by the Soviet government. All internation-markets have a degree of unpredictability, both with respect to price and availability. Part of the Soviet push for total self-sufficiency surely derives from an unwillingness to depend on any supplies not under the direct control of the Kremlin.

In describing Soviet capabilities, Mr. Armstrong seems to place the primary emphasis on the economic weakness of the Soviet Union compared to other countries. He has said that at few points during the past thirty years has the Kremlin been in a position to use trade as a major weapon. It is true that up to the present time Soviet trade has been more a potential threat than a real one. But it may be useful to look at some of the aspects of this potential threat.

One aspect is the possible use of gold. As Mr. Armstrong has remarked, the Soviet leaders seem to hold orthodox views about the desirability of accumulating stocks of gold, but it is still odd that they have not made use of their gold stocks in international trade. I believe the estimate of annual gold production in the USSR is around $400 million, and their gold stocks have been estimated at several billion dollars. Whatever economic weaknesses there may be in the Soviet Union, it would not be much of an economic strain for them to utilize gold already accumulated as a temptation for countries that have severe foreign exchange problems.

But apart from gold, the rate of growth of general Soviet economic strength has to be considered when we are examining Soviet foreign trade as a potential threat. During the first years after the last war the central economic problem in Europe was to get the European economies functioning at a rate that would provide for the increases of population and overtake the deficiencies and obsolescence that characterized the late prewar years. With vigorous efforts on the part of the European governments and with U. S. assistance under the Marshall Plan, rates of production were achieved which were relatively satisfactory. The future rate of increase in national production in Europe, moreover, barring unforeseen contingencies, may be from 3 to 5 per cent annually over the next few years. The annual rate of increase in national production in the United States is of about the same order of magnitude.

But let us look at the Soviet Union. There the rate of increase has been estimated to approach 10 per cent annually, and there are estimates that a somewhat lesser annual rate could be maintained over the next ten to twenty years. If such annual increases were to be maintained, then, at a point in time not too distant, the Soviet Union could match or surpass the production of the United States and Europe in absolute, and not merely relative, terms.

I have mentioned these figures on production, for the purpose of discussion, as a possible measure of the potential threat—a potential threat that could drastically alter the present international trade patterns.

Mr. Armstrong is quite correct in saying that one important element in avoiding economic and political harm from Soviet trade and increased Soviet production is to build healthy economies in the Free World—to encourage economic development and expand output and employment. These are good general goals and I doubt whether anyone here would quarrel with them.

The difficulty, it seems to me, is that even with present levels of Soviet orbit trade many countries experience serious political trouble in attempting to adjust their trading patterns to noncommunist markets. Japan comes to mind as a very urgent case. If Soviet goods available for foreign trade are greatly increased, the specific economic problems will certainly be magnified even if the general economic problem seems logically soluble. And the psychological effects will be much sharper if the USSR is in fact prepared to engage in trade transactions and not merely to talk about them.

The Ideological Weapon in Soviet Strategy

FREDERICK C. BARGHOORN,
Yale University

The subject of this paper is vast but its aim is modest: to attempt to summarize and interpret Soviet ideological and propaganda material as I have read it over a period of years. Naturally, I have been assisted in this reading by the study of various books and articles on totalitarianism and on Soviet totalitarianism in particular. A few of these works will be referred to subsequently. At the outset I should like to call attention to the deep insights contained in the profoundly pessimistic but brilliant article by Hannah Arendt entitled "Ideology and Terror; A Novel Form of Government," published in *The Review of Politics* for July, 1953. Dr. Arendt's thought, like that of Paul Kecskemeti and Waldemar Gurian, emphasizes the dangers which result from regarding mankind as material to be "fabricated" in accordance with certain axioms which are to be carried out regardless of any moral, traditional, or even logical considerations. Bolshevism grew out of the adoption of Marxism by some members of the Russian radical intelligentsia, a social group which, as Berdyaev pointed out, lived "by ideas alone." In fact, as Gurian put it in his most recent book, Lenin was the "apotheosis and nemesis" of the Russian radical intelligentsia.

I am emphasizing the importance of a central core of ideas in the Soviet Communist pattern of thought and communication because I believe there is a danger in our current preoccupation with Soviet military and political strategy and tactics to overlook the fact that at the basis of this whole movement and process lies the ideology.

At the same time, however, students of ideology and doctrine must constantly remind themselves that Bolshevism is a complex of ideological, economic, political, and military factors, none of which can be understood in separation from all the others. It derives from two main factors. These factors dominate Lenin's writings. They are ideology and organization. One might, in fact, say that Lenin's system was an ideology of organization and an organization of ideology.

After the Bolshevik revolution in Russia in 1917, a third major factor entered the situation. This was the territorial-human base seized by Bolshevism. The imposition of Bolshevism upon the peoples it captured produced a totally new type of state which has played an increasing role as the major factor in Soviet politics. This new state is the instrument of an ideology which is antinational, antitraditional, anticapitalist, but certainly not socialist. This state and the ideology which brought it into being but which has increasingly served as its instrument and justification pursue an unlimited and unrestrained drive for power. Whatever contributes to the power of the rulers of this state is viewed as both useful and good. Everything else is useless and evil, and must be denounced and vilified until such time as it can be destroyed and remodelled in the image of Moscow. In other words, as Lenin said, it is a question of " we " versus " them."

It is a paradox of our time that this political and moral monstrosity has been able to employ for its own purposes and with great success the ideals, principles, and symbols of men and movements which were, are, and should be in bitter opposition to it. Again and again Soviet communism has used nationalism against nationalists and internationalism against internationalists. It also makes use of a specious legality and correctness against the law-abiding. Perhaps its greatest triumph is that it employs democracy against democrats and capitalism against capitalists. How have these results been achieved? Whatever answer this paper can give is furnished mostly in the discussion of the content of Soviet ideology which follows. Here, however, certain preliminary considerations must be set forth.

The Protean nature of communism is certainly one factor contributing to its success. Moscow has never hesitated to develop whatever propaganda line it thought would be useful in a given situation. The ignorance of the opponents of communism has been another major factor. In a sense, the victories of communism have been the revenge of the despised. Lenin and Stalin, like Hitler, were too often brushed aside as ignorant fanatics not worthy of the attention of serious students or the concern of responsible statesmen.

Even today, the student of this subject is hampered by a serious lack of monographic literature. There are numerous excellent studies of propaganda in general and a few valuable studies of Soviet propaganda from a theoretical point of view, such as those of Professor H. D. Lasswell. There are also good works on individual Communist parties, among which Langer and Swearingen's *Red Flag in Japan* is outstanding. Another recent valuable work is Franz Borkenau's *European Communism*.[1] For the most part, however, such works help us to understand the strategy and tactics, but not the origin and growth, of Communist movements.

Let us now turn to an outline of the content, appeal, and dissemination of Soviet Communist ideology. Protean as it is, the ideological weapon can be treated under two main rubrics. Central to both aspects is the inner core, a combination of ersatz faith and ersatz science. Marxism-Leninism, in its Soviet version, orients a man to the world and makes him believe that he can control it. It gives him a feeling of being "in the know." Once this doctrine gets possession of a man, he feels that he alone is in possession of the truth and of righteousness, and that he has a right to do or say anything which serves this truth and the movement in which it is embodied. It is for this reason that Communist propaganda permits itself such a wide range of means. Once the correctness of the end is assumed, and is guarded against any doubt, all means are permitted. This utilitarian and instrumental attitude toward truth has been set forth with great brilliance by Arthur Koestler in his *Darkness at Noon*.

Once one grasps the nature of this attitude it is not difficult to analyze Soviet propaganda. The propaganda is the ever-changing instrument of ideology. Soviet doctrine calls this approach to truth "partyness" ("*partiinost*"). Because of its dominance, social science, philosophy, and intellectual life in

[1] Paul Langer and Rodger Swearingen, *Red Flag in Japan* (New York: 1952); Franz Borkenau, *European Communism* (London: 1953).

general as we understand it—and as it has always been understood in civilized society—is impossible under communism. To convince oneself that this is so it is only necessary to read the documents of the postwar " cultural purge " in the Soviet Union.[2]

The ersatz faith offered by communism is a substitute not only for religion, but also for morality and philosophy. The writings of Toynbee and others have emphasized the religious aspect. One point which needs to be made in this connection is that the mere existence of a well-organized religion is no automatic guarantee against Communist penetration. An aspect of Russian Communism which has been little studied is the fact that so many of the precursors of communism in Russia, and also converts to communism itself, came from the families of priests or had been students in theological seminaries. One thinks of Chernyshevski or of Stalin, the student in an orthodox theological seminary.

In western Europe, communism is strongest in Italy. Some of the top leaders of the Indian Communist party come of Moslem background. Without attempting to explain this almost unexplored phenomenon, I should like to suggest that perhaps communism represents the inversion of faith by the disillusioned. This is a phenomenon wider than the field of what is ordinarily known as religion. Communism permits the believing type of person to reject his faith and keep it too. He rejects the faith which he considers has failed him, usually because its leaders fail to practise it, at least in his eyes, and replaces it by a new set of ideas and symbols into which he infuses the content of his old sentiments. Those who have studied Russian Nihilism will be familiar with some aspects of this phenomenon. Some of Dostoevski's and Turgenev's characters well represent the image of the pre-Bolshevik.

If Communist ideology furnishes an ersatz faith, it also furnishes an ersatz community. It is partly because of this that " proletarian internationalism " has such an appeal. But this is not merely a matter of treason to the nation: it also includes all the phenomena of alienation or rejection with respect to the smaller social groups in which men live. The Communists

[2] Excellent collections of this material are available in George S. Counts, *The Country of the Blind* (New York: 1949).

have been skilled in furnishing substitutes for all kinds of social groups. Communist parties and their fronts to some degree achieve this purpose. We must not, of course, consider that this phenomenon results from mere cunning. People would not adopt such desperate solutions if they did not feel maladjusted or frustrated. Two points should be stressed in this connection. The first is that ours is an age of unprecedented cultural interpenetration, conflict, and, to a certain extent, disintegration. The other is that Soviet communism is a system of sociological analysis which has universal application. Both its "logical" aspects and its Messianic characteristics impel it to interest itself in literally all cultures, civilizations, and social groups. Even experienced students of communism are occasionally surprised by the attention paid by Moscow to the most varied and sometimes insignificant groups. Recently I was amazed to read in a Soviet publication that "in Equatorial Africa the natives walked through the forests for twenty or thirty kilometers to meetings, called to discuss the Stockholm petition."[3] Such reports from all over the world are perhaps intended to demonstrate the irresistible force of Soviet ideology.

A more recent and familiar indication of the extent and thoroughness of Moscow's sociological interests is of course furnished by the Mau-Mau disturbances. The synthetic character of the identities fashioned by Moscow for those who are tempted by its ideology is apparent to any student of Communist history. Perhaps Beria after his arrest pondered some of these same questions. The history of purges of Communists and fellow travelers, in particular of foreign Communists, who either fell victim to the purges in 1936–38 or were turned over by the Soviet secret police to their Nazi counterparts during the Nazi-Soviet pact, is only one of the more dramatic revelations of the true character of the ersatz community promised by Leninism-Stalinism.

The most powerful weapon of Soviet communism in the area of its pseudo-religious appeal is, however, a kind of synthetic nationalism. From the beginning, the Soviet leaders have employed this weapon with deadly effect in both domestic and foreign affairs. They appealed to Russian nationalism against

[3] A. L. Orlov, *Borba narodov mira za mir* (Moscow: 1951), 74.

their opponents in the Soviet civil war. Appeals to love of the "fatherland" were of course a major feature of Soviet propaganda during World War II. In foreign policy, Soviet-encouraged "national Bolshevism" in Germany was a weapon against the Western allies in the early nineteen-twenties, when crocodile tears were shed over the plight of a "colonial" Germany being exploited by the West. This theme was set forth with surprising frankness in the debates at the Twelfth Party Congress of April, 1923. Western-oriented Bolsheviks such as Rakovski argued that the Soviet constitution should be drafted in such a way as to appeal to the Germans and other "oppressed" victims of Western capital. Stalin and his victorious cohorts retorted that it was more important to appear to satisfy the constitutional aspirations of Soviet populations related to great Eastern countries such as India and China.[4] Among other things, one is struck by the opportunistic character of a political doctrine in which constitution-making becomes a branch of propaganda. Similar observations could of course be made about the "Stalin Constitution" of 1936 and the various amendments thereto, including that of February, 1944, which ostensibly created "Ministries of Foreign Affairs" of the constituent Soviet republics.

Soviet propaganda made its most effective use of nationalism in the period of the "United Front" in preparation for World War II. The cynicism of this policy becomes apparent to anyone who reads Dimitrov's speech at the Seventh Congress of the Communist International. Here Dimitrov said in effect, "The Fascists are making excellent use of nationalism, so why should not we?"[5] Soviet exploitation of the wartime resistance movements against both Germany and Japan was a logical continuation of the policy adopted at the Seventh Comintern Congress. False nationalism was employed simultaneously against the Axis

[4] *Dvenadtsaty sezd rossiiskoi kommunisticheskoi partii* (Moscow: 1923); see especially 596-607; the nationality question was the main subject discussed at this Congress, and it is the best source for an understanding of the intricacies and sophistries contained in the Soviet "nationality policy" even to this day.

[5] Available in various sources. I read it in *Abridged Proceedings, Seventh World Congress, The Communist International,* No. 17–18 (Vol. XII, Sept. 20, 1935); 1218–21 deal with the nationality question.

and against the Allies. On the one hand, there were such organizations as the "Union of Polish Patriots" and of course the various resistance organizations in East and West. On the other hand, there was the appeal to desperate and disillusioned German patriots contained in the "National Committee for Free Germany" and the "Union of German Officers." The tactics of provocation and slaughter employed in connection with these movements of course betray their true character.

Since the war, this policy has been employed primarily against the United States. Probably the most potent weapon of Soviet propaganda in both Europe and Asia and perhaps also in Latin-America is an exploitation of national sentiment in which the Communists attempt to inflame all factors of national idealism on the one hand, and envy and jealousy on the other hand, against the United States. The rationale of this policy was again set forth in Stalin's article, "Economic Problems of Socialism in the U.S.S.R." published just before the Nineteenth Party Congress in October, 1952, as well as in the major speeches delivered at that congress. At present, Soviet propaganda is wooing the peoples of the Far East. On July 10, 1953, the front page of *Pravda* contained not only the news of Beria's disgrace and doom, but also a photograph and the text of a speech by a Japanese scholar who was awarded the Stalin Peace Prize. One wonders whether this probably sincere victim of Soviet ideology knows anything about the history of Moscow's nationality policy. Concurrently, the only people besides the Russians to whom the adjective "great" is constantly applied in the Soviet press are the Chinese. Such recognition is intended, no doubt, as an easy way of flattering the Chinese.

Thus we see that nationalism, which Professor Carleton J. H. Hayes in his studies published some twenty years ago, characterized as the "secular religion of our age," is invaded by Soviet communism, the doctrine which of all historical doctrines has proved itself most capable of mimicry and camouflage. One could discuss at length the numerous doctrines in which this form of totalitarianism has succeeded in masquerading. It is hardly necessary to point out how much more successful it has been in this respect than was its only major competitor, National Socialism in Germany. This treatment of Bolshevism as a kind of ersatz faith might be concluded by a brief reference to the ersatz peace offered by communism. Anyone who has studied Lenin and Stalin understands that Communists regard war as both inevitable and desirable. The only qualification is that the war must not be so destructive as to endanger the existence of the Communist movement. By concealing the above fact and projecting their own aggression to their opponents, the Communists have succeeded in winning the sympathy of pacifists. It matters not that they despise pacifists and punish pacifism by death in countries under their control. But in addition to performing this remarkable feat, the Communists also turn their peace agitation into a combination of threats and blackmail, directed against those who fear the power both of the Soviet army and of its agents, the Secret Police and local Communists. Despite all this, there are certainly many sincere people, including scientists and even clergymen, who, for religious and moral reasons, have become fellow travelers or perhaps even Communist party members because they have identified the cause of communism with that of peace. War has been the greatest agent for extending communism and undermining civilization in our time. Most of the extension of communism can be traced to the first and second World Wars. It is only when we keep in mind these facts and the problems caused by what G. Lowes Dickinson called the "international anarchy" that we can understand the complex relationship between communism, war, and peace.

Thus far some of the aspects of Communist ideology have been discussed which appeal to idealism and in some cases to an irrational despair with the state of the world. One thread that runs through this type of response to the appeal of Communist ideology is a desire to punish those whom the Communists brand as criminals responsible for the suffering of mankind. The punitive note was very strong in Lenin himself, as is apparent to any student of his writings.

But in addition to this pseudomorality of communism, tinged with hatred as it is, there is also what might be called the "positive" and "rational" aspect of communism. If many idealists turn to the materialism of communism, it is also true that many materialists cloak their ambitions in the idealism of communism. The gamut of appeals to desires for material, power, and status advancement is enormous. Communists seek to gain allies by pointing to their—and their potential allies' own victims'—common enemies. One can start with the simplest grievances induced by poverty or bad working conditions. These are convenient weapons in the hands of Communist agitators and manipulators who hope to climb to power on the backs of the workers.

Above this elementary and individual level are the dissatisfied members of the middle and upper classes. Students of revolutions have for a long time been in agreement that counter-elites composed of able and discontented members of the middle or upper classes are the major factors in revolutionary leadership. To such people, whether they be primarily idealistic or primarily selfish, membership in the Communist conspiracy offers a vast aggrandizement of their ego. This is the more tangible and material aspect of the synthetic community offered by communism. It must be rather tempting to citizens of weak or backward countries to join a movement of such grandiose scope, even if it means subordinating patriotism to the interests of a mighty foreign state. One wonders also whether or not the more sordid appeals of membership in the *apparat,* of trips to the movement's world capital, and the various other Communist fleshpots do not have a considerable force. The appeal can be particularly great to intellectuals in countries which do not provide them with satisfactory scope and adequate compensation for their activities.

A kind of synthesis of the selfish and idealistic appeals is furnished when the Communists hold out hope of national regeneration to backward countries. This is the appeal of "ersatz capitalism," which has been dealt with in an interesting fashion by the Soviet refugee Hermann Achminow, in his book *Die Macht im Hintergrund.*[6] At present world communism seeks to use North Korea and China as show windows of industrial and cultural progress to influence the peoples of Asia. At the same time, and perhaps even more important, there is a stream of propaganda regarding the success of Soviet policy in the non-Russian republics of the Soviet Union. Several speakers at the Nineteenth Party Congress, particularly Beria, presented what were obviously intended to be seductive statistics about the in-

[6] (Ulm: 1950).

dustrial, educational and cultural progress of the Soviet peoples of the Caucasus and Central Asia.[7] The recent work by Walter Kolarz, *Russia and Her Colonies*,[8] is part of a growing body of literature which exposes the ruthlessness of the exploitation and colonization which lurks behind Soviet claims promising national and cultural fulfillment.

We have dealt briefly with the ideology of organization, which promises place and purpose to the spiritually displaced and the frustrated careerists of all lands and cultures. Let us now examine briefly some of the methods by which these "victims and executioners," as Hannah Arendt calls them, are recruited. To be effective, an ideology must be disseminated. This simple truth has too often been forgotten by the opponents of communism, but by its advocates, never.

Far more than other political leaders, the Bolsheviks have realized the importance of direct personal agitation and propaganda. To bear their message to each political, cultural, and social group, they have trained native personnel to carry the ideology to the target. It is startling to realize how many men who are now heading powerful Communist movements or even governments began to receive their training in Moscow and other Soviet centers from the earliest days of Soviet power. The careful screening and indoctrination of prisoners of war was begun in 1917–18. Some of these prisoners furnished delegates and even cadres for the Comintern, organized in 1919. Among these early guests and students were such men as Ho Chi Min. Equally well-known but eventually less satisfactory was Tito, who started his career as a soldier and officer in the Red Army. Some idea of the scope of this operation can be gained from Stalin's speech on the "Political Tasks of the University of the Peoples of the East," which he delivered on May 18, 1925. This was the fourth anniversary of the institution. Stalin pointed out with pride that the University comprised representatives of not less than fifty nations and national groups of the east.[9] This

[7] For an interesting analysis of this theme, see the article by Klaus Mehnert, "Worte an Asien," in *Ost-Europa*, Heft VI, 2. Jahrgang, Dec., 1952, 463–64.

[8] New York: F. A. Praeger, 1952.

[9] I. Stalin, *Sochineniya*, VII (Moscow: 1947), 133.

process of recruiting and training national cadres to serve in the Kremlin's political army has never ceased. It has been very successful in spite of the frightful casualties suffered by these foreign cadres, especially in the great purges of 1936–38. As of 1945, 57 per cent of the Chinese Communist Central Committee were Moscow-trained.[10]

For the most part, only selected personnel are brought to the Soviet Union. The process of recruitment normally begins in the country of origin. These bearers of the ideology reach high place in the Soviet apparatus only as the culmination of a long process of removing them from their spiritual environment. As the report of the Royal Commission in Canada brought out, the process begins in apparently harmless "Marxist study groups," which serve not only as channels of indoctrination but also as surveillance and screening devices. The personnel thus trained are employed not only for espionage, and, if they are highly successful, as policy advisers in the international Communist conspiracy, but also as agitators in various activities in their native countries.

There are other devices for the dissemination of Communist ideology which, taken together with the foregoing, aim at control of the field of perception. This control is designed to create and protect the system of ideas and its accompanying imagery, supplied by the Kremlin. As Gurian and others have pointed out, this process requires the creation of an artificial reality. Often it involves extensive operations in managing even the physical environment. Among other things, architecture is pressed into the service of politics and Moscow dazzles its subjects and its foreign "guests" by the new and probably quite impressive skyscrapers which they are shown. Some of these activities belong in the area of what George Kennan has referred to as the "manufacture of illusion." Those familiar with Russian history know that this aspect of Bolshevism has deep roots in the Russian past. Not only were there the Potemkin villages, but as the historian Klyuchevski pointed out in a fascinating but little-known book, there was a whole series of other similar devices, extending back many centuries. For example, it was the

[10] Robert C. North, *Kuomintang and Chinese Communist Elites* (Stanford: 1952), 72.

habit of the Muscovite rulers to cause large crowds of people to gather along the path travelled by foreign ambassadors in order to create the impression of a dense and vigorous population.[11]

The iron curtain is only one, although perhaps the most important, of the devices which enable the Soviet rulers to project the desired images into the minds of their subjects and to the audience beyond Soviet borders. It is, however, of vast and almost incalculable importance. Because of the iron curtain and its backstopping devices of censorship, only persons of great knowledge and imagination can get the "feel" of life under Communist control. This is perhaps one reason why refugees from iron curtain countries seem to people in the West to be so excited. The reality which the refugees have experienced differs so much from that to which we are accustomed that our minds tend to reject it. At the same time, realization of this fact drives the refugees to frustration and despair. Considerable progress has been made in bridging the gap between the knowledge and experience of these refugees and the pattern of experience of the free peoples, but much remains to be done in this field.[12]

Closely related to the iron curtain is the Soviet management of cultural relations. Basically a protective device against the unmasking of Soviet reality, the iron curtain also serves the purpose of whetting the curiosity of foreign intellectuals. By making it hard to get at, the Soviets in some cases succeed in enhancing the enticing quality of their system for the susceptible. Cultural relations, like almost everything else, can thus become a weapon of Soviet policy. Since memories are short, it is not generally known that the United States government, for example, worked very hard to facilitate cultural relations in the years immediately following World War II. Nothing came of these efforts, which foundered on the rock of Soviet obstruction and confusion tactics.

In the weeks following Stalin's death, it appeared that

[11] See V. O. Klyuchevski, *Skazaniya inostrantsev o Moskovskom gosudarstve* (Petrograd: 1918).

[12] An important contribution in this field is the work of publication being done by the research program on the USSR, sponsored by the Ford Foundation.

the Kremlin was again flirting with the idea of a limited restoration of cultural relations with non-Soviet areas. Several articles appeared in *Pravda,* the theme of which was that the USSR was ready to go at least half way in this direction. However, in view of the past record, the non-Communist world had a right to be skeptical about the value of these feelers. For one thing, they were accompanied by warnings to Soviet citizens that they must heighten their vigilance against foreign enemies. At the same time, it was made perfectly clear that only carefully selected guests would be welcome. For example, *Pravda* for June 15 in its lead editorial entitled " The Word of Truth " stated that the Soviet Union would welcome guests who came with " honorable intentions." Perhaps we should not leave this subject without pointing out that, strange as the Kremlin's attitude is toward cultural relations, and prepared as Moscow is to turn all such matters to its propaganda advantage, one of the pitfalls against which the West should guard is to avoid creating the impression that it, and not Moscow, sets up barriers to the free contact and exchange of people and ideas. A sophisticated application of a *quid pro quo* policy would seem to be in order here.

Much has been published in the last year or two regarding the organization, coordination, and vastness of the Soviet ideological effort. I recently talked to a student from India who pointed out how successful the Soviets are in making available their ideological and propaganda literature in his country. Besides spending vast sums of money and assigning well trained cadres to this task, the Kremlin sees to it that adequate research, training and information facilities are placed at the disposal of its ideological warriors. It is this aspect of the effort that is least known in the West. Area research institutes and training programs have been highly developed in the Soviet Union from the earliest days of the regime. Soviet embassies are staffed by large press departments, which prepare comprehensive analyses of the local press and publications. Counterpart groups in Moscow subject this and other material to further analysis and codification. Special academies, such as the military-diplomatic Academy of Foreign Languages, and huge foreign language institutes furnish a corps of translators and interpreters. All this machinery helps to provide the Soviet propaganda and ideological media with up-to-date facts and a knowledge of the areas to which they direct their output.

Finally, a word should be said about Soviet ideological and propaganda tactics. In the broad sense, ideology is strategic and propaganda is tactical. The " party line," based on ideology and the requirements of the Soviet state, gives firmness and body to Soviet propaganda. Inconsistent though the propaganda may be in time, it is usually consistent in space. This creates the impression of confidence and firmness. Borkenau in his recent study points out that although the Communists in France had shamelessly denounced their previous principles, they were able to inherit the support given by French radicals to the Socialist and other parties before the war in the postwar French elections. Among the factors responsible for this success, he points out, was the fact that the Communists had " always acted in unison." [13] Anyone who has studied Soviet propaganda is aware not only of its dullness, but of the cheap sophistries and rhetorical tricks constantly employed by it. However, its massive organization and above all its doctrinal base confer upon it a kind of power which can overcome the susceptible and deceive the ignorant or gullible.

How successful is Soviet propaganda, and the ideology on which it is based? Despite the seriousness of the subject, we have very little information on which to base an answer. However, the continued strength of the Communists in Italy and France, and such recent dramatic events as the anti-American demonstration in Teheran engineered by the Iranian Communists indicate that this propaganda is disconcertingly successful. How is it possible to induce thousands of Iranians to shout " Death to the American imperialists! "? Somehow, the Communists have succeeded in identifying America with the conditions, institutions, and persons these misinformed and perhaps desperate people regard as evil and hostile. Similarly, the Communists are able to bring about riots in southern India of persons who feel that the Indian government has violated their right to speak and use their own native language in public institutions. The systematic way in which the Communists ex-

[13] Borkenau, *European Communism*, 455.

ploit such national and cultural grievances is indicated by a book published by the Soviet Academy of Sciences in 1949 entitled *The Crisis of the Colonial System.*[14]

What has been stated here should be considered as diagnosis rather than prescription. But I should like to conclude with some suggestions as to how to deal with the problems posed by Soviet Communist ideology. In the long run, an ideology is only as strong as its power to interpret reality meaningfully. Therefore ideologies and counter-ideologies operate within the framework of the basic trends of history. The Communists will not be able to claim that they are riding the wave of the future, if, despite their efforts, facts and realities expose the falsity of their claims. There are good reasons for believing that the process of decay of Communist ideology is already well under way. To argue this thesis would require much space, but we can suggest a few features and indications of the process.

Defections and revolts in iron curtain countries are among the symptoms. Perhaps more fundamental is the process of "petrifaction" of culture, to use Professor Timasheff's term. The root causes of this ideological decay are complex; among them may be distinguished the conflict between Soviet reality and professions, and the ever-increasing tension between the interests of the Soviet state and those of international revolution. And, as Achminow and many ex-Marxists such as Isaac Deutscher have argued, there is a conflict of generations and of social types within Soviet communism which must some day lead to profound changes.

The above considerations should not make us overly hopeful. The short-run trends are threatening. To stem them, we must not only rededicate ourselves to our basic values of freedom, free critical discussion, and respect for individual rights and welfare; we must also demonstrate to the desperate and the impatient that the Communist short-cut is a path of self-destruction. Above all we have a duty to bring to these people,

[14] In Russian (Moscow and Leningrad: 1949); see 123 ff. on the 1948 resolution of the Indian Communist Party demanding that India be made a "federation" of nations. Communist policy in India cloaks its disruptive aims in nationality and other emotionally appealing disguises.

potential converts to communism, a positive message and program. The basic question is, can we help them to realize their own as well as general human values? It is here that ideological and propaganda strategy have a vital task to perform.

There is one other point to make. We must beware of the pessimism so fashionable today. Horrible as totalitarianism is, it does not turn men into robots. In an age of atomic and hydrogen bombs, we cannot afford to despair of influencing the elements capable of reason and valuing survival, even in countries under totalitarian rule. All this will of course require favorable conditions of work for those who must perform the exacting and delicate tasks involved. It is to be hoped that they will not have to fight a two-front struggle against the experienced Soviet opponent abroad and unreasonable criticism at home.

ANTHONY H. LEVIERO: *Discussion* *

The New York Times

Professor Barghoorn has shown us how relentlessly Soviet ideology and propaganda are used together to achieve Communist aims. Propaganda is the ever-changing yet consistent instrument of ideology. Even in the drafting of the Russian constitution there was the propaganda design of making it "appear to satisfy the constitutional aspirations of Soviet populations related to great eastern countries such as India and China."

He points out how peoples of the West have been duped by the cunning and fraudulent use against themselves of their own ideals, principles, and symbols. General awareness that the Kremlin uses democracy against democrats and capitalism against capitalists has come tragically late.

The ignorance of the opponents of communism has been a major factor contributing to Soviet success. Professor Barghoorn reminds us that the victories of Communists have been the

* Mr. Leviero traveled with President Eisenhower to Denver and could not be present at the conference. Mr. Antonio Micocci of the United States Information Agency served as moderator for the discussion period.

revenge of the despised. Lenin and Stalin, like Hitler, were ignored as fanatics. Complacent in the potential, rather than the actuality, of our strength, we in the United States were far too contemptuous of Soviet leaders while they were building up vast power, and were secretly planting their ideology in the breast of virtually every country in the world. It comes as a shock now that Moscow-trained agitators are behind the trouble in British Guiana as they are among the Mau-Mau natives of Africa.

It may well be, as Professor Barghoorn believes, that the process of decay of the Communist ideology is well under way. But the important question here is which will proceed faster: the deterioration of the ideology or the accretion of Soviet strength in atomic and hydrogen weapons? Dr. Barghoorn states that Communists regard war as inevitable and desirable so long as it does not jeopardize the existence of the Communist movement. Will Russia resort to atomic war before her political structure cracks up? That is the dilemma of the West. Meanwhile, will the West be resolute and continue to build its strength —unified strength?

Dr. Barghoorn stresses the importance of the pseudo-Communist faith and the pseudo nationalism that have been propagated so relentlessly by the Kremlin and that are still winning many adherents. The world revolution, set back somewhat in Germany, moves on elsewhere. The hour is late, and another question is how the free world can offset the influence of Moscow-trained leaders who have emerged all over the world. The messiahs from Moscow are thoroughly trained to breed discontent. Is it enough for us to show natives how much better it is to use a steel instead of a wooden plow? Or are our missionaries equipped to bring hopeful answers to cultural, economic, and political questions?

Unity, a lesson that the United States and the free world can learn from the Communists, is the need now. Suspicions and nationalism still afflict western Europe. In our own country there still is some confusion over national objectives. The promise of a strong new foreign policy has not been fully realized yet. More recently, however, there has been a salutary recognition that power and deeds alone must speak for the United States. Will our voice be firm and clear?

Dr. Barghoorn warns that we cannot afford to despair of influencing the elements capable of reason and valuing survival in the age of the atomic and hydrogen bombs. He realizes that we have a duty to bring a positive message and program to desperate and impatient people who are still being tempted by communism. He asks whether we can help them to realize their own as well as other human values. It is an extremely difficult task because we ignored the march of communism for too many complacent years. Now in the era of the showdown Dr. Barghoorn rightly suggests that those who must lead and fight for us should not have to do so on two fronts, with demagogues clawing at them from the rear on the home front.

The Role of Diplomacy in Soviet Imperialism

C. E. BLACK,
Princeton University

The role of diplomatic negotiations and intercourse in the conduct of Soviet foreign policy must be examined with reference to the Soviet theory of international relations. This theory assumes that the dialectic of history, in its inexorable march towards world-wide communism, must necessarily result in conflicts between the Communist and noncommunist worlds, or in Soviet terminology between "socialism" and "capitalism." At the same time this theory maintains that these conflicts will extend over many years. The spasmodic periods of war and revolution are separated by long periods of international and domestic peace. The first round of revolutions followed World War I, and resulted in the victory of Bolshevism in Russia and eventually in Outer Mongolia. The second followed World War II and resulted in the territorial expansion of the USSR and the establishment of Communist governments in eastern Europe, in northern Korea, and in China. Between these rounds of revolution are the long periods of watchful waiting, preparation, and correct relations between the Communist and noncommunist worlds, known in Soviet terminology as "co-existence." [1]

[1] The Soviet theory of international relations is discussed in greater detail above; T. A. Taracouzio, *The Soviet Union and International Law* (New York, 1935), and L. B. Schapiro, "The Soviet Concept of International Law," *Year Book of World Affairs, 1948* (London, 1948), 272–310, provide useful introductions to the legal aspects of the Soviet approach to international relations.

The necessity of making provision for both struggle and cooperation in the field of international relations is always kept clearly in mind by Soviet leaders. As Vyshinsky asserted in unmistakable terms in 1938: [2]

> In working out the Soviet theory of international law, it is necessary to start from the fact of capitalist encirclement in which the USSR is placed . . . as well as the fact of the struggle and rivalry between the socialist and capitalist systems, and also the ever-increasing cooperation of the USSR with certain capitalist countries both in the economic sphere and in the sphere of preserving peace.

It follows from this approach that Soviet foreign policy must be geared to situations of stability and instability occurring simultaneously. Hence also the ability of Stalin to state, without contradicting himself, both that peaceful "co-existence" between "socialism" and "capitalism" is possible and that the inevitability of wars will continue until "capitalism" is abolished.

It should also be noted that the Soviet leaders envisage their country as the primary base from which world revolution will be spread. They regard Moscow as the center of a system of states which must wage a relentless struggle against other countries, with due consideration for the ebb and flow of revolutionary opportunities, employing all the methods known to statecraft including if necessary armed force. It is this motivation of the Soviet regime, frequently and explicitly stated, that gives its foreign policy and hence its diplomacy a special significance.[3]

[2] A. Ya. Vyshinsky, *Osnovnye zadachi nauki sovetskogo sotsialisticheškogo prava* [*Basic problems of the science of Soviet socialist law*] (Moscow, 1938), 52, restated on page 186 as one of fifty-four theses presented to the First Conference of Legal Scholars that met on July 16-19, 1938, under the auspices of the Institute of Law of the Academy of Sciences of the USSR; the implications of this position are discussed in Schapiro, *op. cit.*, 283-87.

[3] For an interesting development of this theme, see Part IV of "The Programme of the Communist International. Adopted by the VI World Congress on 1st September 1928, in Moscow," *International Press Correspondence*, Vol. VIII, No. 92 (Dec. 31, 1928), 1756 ff.; a valuable review of this phase of Soviet doctrine is available in Historicus,

In order to implement a foreign policy tailored to this theory of international relations, great flexibility is required. To achieve this flexibility Soviet policy employs military, economic, and ideological means, and particularly two instruments that deserve special attention: the Communist party, and the procedures of diplomacy. The former is the more important instrument during the revolutionary periods. It is closely controlled by the Politburo or Presidium, and has at its disposal all over the world a wide variety of public and secret organizations integrated by a strict discipline. Diplomacy, although in the long run a secondary instrument, is nevertheless essential to the implementation of policy. The periods of "co-existence" are, after all, of much longer duration than the periods of revolution. Moreover the revolutions would not come off at all without long and careful preparation. Hence diplomacy is held in high regard in the Soviet Union, and the prestige acquired by it during the periods of "co-existence" is essential to success in the periods of revolution. Soviet diplomats are carefully trained, and, thorough treatises on international law and diplomatic practice are published for their guidance.[4] Although the Soviet Union recognizes

"Stalin on Revolution," *Foreign Affairs,* Vol. XXVII, No. 2 (Jan., 1949), 175-214.

[4] Leading Soviet treatises in this field include: E. A. Korovin, *Mezhdunarodnoe pravo perekhodnogo vremeni* [*International law of the transition period*] (Moscow, 1924), and *Istoriia mezhdunarodnogo prava* [*History of international law*] (Moscow, 1946); A. V. Sabanin, *Posol'skoe i konsul'skoe pravo* [*Diplomatic and consular law*] (Moscow, 1930); E. B. Pashukanis, *Ocherki po mezhdunarodnomu pravu* [*Outlines of international law*] (Moscow, 1935); A. D. Keilin and P. P. Vinogradov, *Morskoe pravo* [*Naval law*] (Moscow, 1939); V. P. Potemkin, ed., *Istoriia diplomatii* [*History of diplomacy*] (3 vols., Moscow, 1941–45); V. N. Durdenevsky and S. B. Krylov, *Mezhdunarodnoe pravo* [*International law*] (Moscow, 1947); V. M. Koretsky, *Ocherki anglo-amerikanskoi doktriny i praktiki mezhdunarodnogo chastnogo prava* [*Essays on Anglo-American doctrines and practice of private international law*] (Moscow, 1948); B. E. Shtein, *Sistema mezhdunarodnoi opeki* [*The international trusteeship system*] (Moscow, 1948); *Diplomaticheskii Slovar* [*Diplomatic dictionary*] (2 vols.; Moscow, 1948-50); D. B. Levin, *Diplomaticheskii immunitet* [*Diplomatic immunity*] (Moscow, 1949); V. M. Shurshalov, *Rezhim mezhdunarodnoi opeki* [*The international trusteeship regime*] (Moscow, 1951); E. A. Korovin, gen. ed., *Mezhdunarodnoe pravo* [*International law*] (Moscow, 1951); and

only those aspects of international law that it has explicitly accepted, these recognized portions are extensive. Thus the Soviet Union was able to play an active role as a member of the League of Nations, accepting the international system on which the League was based and participating actively in the formulation of new rules and codes.

In the first period of " co-existence," between the two world wars, the Communist party organizations around the world played a secondary role in Soviet foreign policy. Between 1924 and 1936 they were probably more of a nuisance than a help, and even after the adoption of the " people's front " tactics their role was not important. During this period of relative eclipse the Communist parties underwent several purges, and from these they emerged fully subservient to Soviet policy and hence more serviceable than ever. The Communist International and the Commissariat of Foreign Affairs did not cooperate closely at this stage, and the former was apparently not highly regarded by Stalin as an instrument of policy.

With the advent of World War II, however, everything was changed. The Soviet leaders recognized that the war presented an opportunity, if properly handled, for a new round of revolutions, and the Communist parties were put to work to exploit the situation. To facilitate this task the Communist International was disbanded, and the Communist organizations abroad were brought under the direct supervision of the Politburo, and under the administrative control of the secret police. The larger framework of Soviet foreign policy remained the preserve of diplomacy, but in the areas set aside for Soviet imperialism it was the Communist parties that carried the ball for Soviet policy and the role of diplomacy was to run interference.[5]

It is in this role of running interference for Communist aggression during and after World War II that diplomatic intercourse and negotiations as conducted by the Soviet Union must

translations by A. A. Troianovsky of Harold Nicolson's *Diplomacy* (Moscow, 1941), Jules Cambon's *Le Diplomate* (Moscow, 1946), and Sir Ernest Satow's *Guide to Diplomatic Practice* (Moscow, 1947).

[5] See Bruce C. Hopper, " Narkomindel and Comintern: Instruments of World Revolution," *Foreign Affairs,* Vol. XIX, No. 4 (July, 1941), 737-50, and Franz Borkenau, *The Communist International* (London, 1938) and *European Communism* (London, 1953).

now be examined. The considerable prestige achieved by Soviet diplomacy in the interwar period of "co-existence" made it an invaluable instrument for the purpose which it was now to serve. It is true that the Western world could not ignore the Soviet doctrine of the strategy and tactics of revolution that had been widely discussed and disseminated in this period. It is also true that in an unguarded moment before the revolution Stalin had stated—in connection with a discussion of "bourgeois" diplomacy—that "Words are one thing, actions another. Good words are a mask for the concealment of bad deeds. Sincere diplomacy is no more possible than dry water or iron wood." [6] Yet in the long run the reputation achieved by Soviet diplomacy in the League of Nations, for instance, counted for more than the logic of Marxian dialectics or isolated statements of the Soviet leaders, and so the prestige of Soviet diplomacy in Western eyes remained in general unimpaired.

The need for the USSR to provide a diplomatic screen for its aggressive moves will become clear if one recalls the situation at the end of World War II. In eastern Europe, for instance, the Soviet armies overran a region inhabited by well over one hundred million persons in large measure hostile to communism. The task of the Communist Party of the Soviet Union and its local agents was to seize control of the government of each country, and under the circumstances this involved several essential tactical measures: the neutralization of local military forces; the temporary cooperation of the Communist parties in "people's fronts" with the peasant, socialist, and liberal political parties; and the delay in elections until these could be conducted in such a way as to assure Communist victories. All these tasks were assigned to the Communist organizations.

The role of diplomacy was to assure the Western allies of the USSR that none of these measures were intended, and at the same time to gain the consent of the West to the establishment of conditions that would facilitate their implementation. A comprehensive review of all the negotiations conducted in connection with the postwar Soviet imperialism is beyond the scope of this essay, but an analysis of three characteristic situa-

[6] I. V. Stalin, *Sochineniia* [*Works*] (Moscow, 1946), Vol. II, 277, from an article published in the *Sotsial-Demokrat* (Jan. 12/25, 1913).

tions will serve to illustrate the role of diplomacy. The use of diplomacy in winning control of a friendly state is well illustrated by the relatively simple case of Czechoslovakia. More complex were the diplomatic negotiations relative to the former Axis satellite states of Rumania, Bulgaria, and Hungary. Finally, in order to redress somewhat the balance, an example should be given of the failure of Soviet diplomacy to provide adequate cover for Communist activities. Soviet diplomacy in the United Nations concerning the Greek case illustrates such a failure. While these represent only three of the many examples that could be cited, they illustrate essential features of the role of diplomacy in Soviet imperialism.

The Soviet conquest of Czechoslovakia illustrates the role of diplomacy in its most uncomplicated form, because of a number of unique circumstances. Many Czechoslovakian statesmen were disillusioned with the West as a result of the events of 1938-39, and this disillusionment fed the romantic Panslavism that has been an important strain in Czechoslovakian thought. Of more immediate significance was the conviction on the part of Beneš that he could undertake a policy of "coexistence" with the Soviet Union without endangering Czechoslovakia. This conviction was based on the view that Soviet aggressive tendencies would be modified under pressure from the other great powers, and that at home the Communists could be appeased by the rapid development of a welfare economy after the war.[7]

However these views may be judged by posterity, they certainly facilitated the first step of Soviet diplomacy which was to convince the Czechoslovakian government-in-exile that the USSR had no intention of sponsoring a Communist seizure of power. Beneš informed Eden that he "accepted as a reality what the Soviet Union promised" and from his "previous experience . . . had no reason to doubt its word." [8] Molotov was thus not faced with a difficult proposition so far as the government-in-exile

[7] Curt F. Beck, "Can Communism and Democracy Co-exist? Beneš's Answer," *American Slavic and East European Review*, Vol. XI (Oct., 1952), 189-206.

[8] "Memoirs of Eduard Beneš," *Nation*, Vol. 167, No. 4 (July 24, 1948), 101.

was concerned, and his vigorous defense of the proposed treaty with Czechoslovakia at the Moscow conference of Foreign Ministers in October, 1943, wore down the objections of the Western allies.

The Soviet-Czechoslovakian Treaty of Friendship, Mutual Assistance, and Postwar Cooperation, concluded in Moscow on December 12, 1943, contained in Article 4 an explicit pledge on the part of the two signatories of noninterference in each other's internal affairs, and this provision served as the justification for many further concessions by the Czechoslovakian government-in-exile.[9] Of these, the most important was the composition of the provisional government of Czechoslovakia, negotiated by Beneš in Moscow and proclaimed on April 5, 1945, in the Slovakian town of Kosice. In this government the Communists insisted upon and obtained the key ministries of interior and information, as well as effective control over the army and the conduct of foreign affairs. This Communist position was further strengthened when American troops, implementing an earlier Soviet-American military agreement, halted their advance and permitted the Soviet army to liberate Prague.

The subsequent development of events in Czechoslovakia is well known.[10] The Communists built up their domestic organization rapidly under the cover of the Soviet-Czechoslovakian treaty, but there was no overt Soviet interference until July 9, 1947, when Stalin demanded that Czechoslovakia reject the invitation to attend the Marshall Plan Conference. By this time the

[9] For the text of this treaty, see *United Nations Review,* Vol. IV, No. 1 (Jan. 15, 1944), 14; and *Soviet Foreign Policy During the Patriotic War* (2 vols.; London, 1946), Vol. I, 250-52.

[10] The principal accounts are: Ivo Duchacek, "The Strategy of Communist Infiltration: Czechoslovakia, 1944-1948," *World Politics,* Vol. II, No. 3 (April, 1950), 345-72; and "The February Coup in Czechoslovakia," *World Politics,* Vol. II, No. 4 (July, 1950), 511-32; Otto Friedman, *The Break-Up of Czech Democracy* (London, 1950); Sir Robert Bruce Lockhart, *Jan Masaryk: A Personal Memoir* (New York, 1951); Hubert Ripka, *Czechoslovakia Enslaved: The Story of the Communist Coup d'État* (London, 1950); Jan Stransky, *East Wind Over Prague* (New York, 1950); Edward Taborsky, "Beneš and the Soviets," *Foreign Affairs,* Vol. XXVII, No. 2 (Jan., 1949), 302-14; and Paul Zinner, "Marxism in Action: The Seizure of Power in Czechoslovakia," *Foreign Affairs,* Vol. XXVIII, No. 4 (July, 1950), 644-58.

democratic forces had lost their independence of action, however, and when the Communists decided to carry out a *coup d'etat* seven months later they met with no organized opposition.

In evaluating the role of diplomacy in this incident of Soviet imperialism, it appears that its chief contribution was in winning the initial pre-liberation concessions from the government-in-exile. The prestige of Soviet diplomacy, nurtured during the interwar period, was sufficiently great to facilitate the seizure by the Communist organizations of key positions from which they were not to be dislodged. At the same time the role of Beneš was perhaps not as guileless as may appear from the events. His judgment of his ability to deal with Communists at home was not entirely mistaken, for it is known that they were rapidly losing popular support and had to resort to the desperate measure of a *coup* for fear of a decisive setback in the free elections scheduled for the spring of 1948. It was rather in his estimate of the restraints that the Western democracies would choose to exercise on Soviet imperialism that the judgment of Beneš was wrong, and for this temporary negligence of the West he was only in part responsible.

The role of Soviet diplomacy in the Communist seizure of the three Axis satellite states of Rumania, Bulgaria, and Hungary was much more complex than in the case of Czechoslovakia, since it involved simultaneous negotiations over a period of several years with both the Western allies and the victims themselves.[11] First Soviet diplomacy had to convince the Western allies that it had no aggressive designs on these countries. It then had to gain recognition by the Western allies of a sphere of influence over them. Later it had to obtain their consent to the armistice terms desired by the USSR. Soviet diplomacy also had to gain acceptance of the peace treaties at a time when Communist control of these countries was rapidly becoming a reality. Finally

[11] Brief discussions of these negotiations from the viewpoint of the Western democracies are available in Redvers Opie, and others, *The Search for Peace Settlements* (Washington, D. C., 1951); and Mark Ethridge and C. E. Black, "Negotiating on the Balkans, 1945-47," in *Negotiating with the Russians* (Boston, 1951), 171-206.

it attempted, and this time failed, to gain admission to the United Nations for what were now three Communist satellites. An examination of these five separate steps will illustrate the role of diplomacy as one of the instruments of Soviet foreign policy.

The first step was the familiar one of disclaiming imperialist intentions. Although this was accomplished in part by propaganda, it was the formal statement of the Soviet case by diplomatic representations that give it its strength. These disclaimers took several forms. The Soviet accession to the Atlantic Charter in September, 1941, and its signature of the United Nations Declaration four months later, represented a general Soviet pledge to "respect the right of all peoples to choose the form of government under which they will live." The fact that shortly thereafter in negotiating the Anglo-Soviet Treaty of Alliance a modest attitude was revealed, served to strengthen further the Soviet case. It is true that on this occasion a demand was made for recognition of the territorial gains made under the Nazi-Soviet pact, but since this demand was withdrawn under Anglo-American pressure the impression was conveyed of a moderate policy in this region.

To these rather vague indications were soon added more specific disclaimers. Thus in April, 1944, while negotiations for armistice terms with Rumania were in progress, Foreign Minister Molotov issued a formal statement that the USSR had no intention of interfering in the internal political and social affairs of Rumania if it turned against Germany—an event that occurred four months later. The most specific and comprehensive pledge of non-intervention on the part of the Soviet Union, however, was that given at Yalta in February, 1945. In the Declaration on Liberated Europe, Russia and its two Western allies agreed to assist the liberated peoples, including those of the three satellites under discussion, "to form interim governmental authorities broadly representative of all democratic elements in the population and pledged to the earliest possible establishment through free elections of governments responsive to the will of the people." These series of pledges, with which Stalin or Molotov was in each case associated, had a powerful cumulative effect on the Western allies and were an important factor in their recognition of a Soviet sphere of influence over the three satellite states and their neighbors in eastern Europe.

This second task of gaining recognition of a Soviet orbit was a more difficult one, for it involved not merely formal Soviet pledges but winning specific concessions from the West by diplomatic negotiations. The initial obstacle that Soviet diplomacy had to overcome was that presented by British plans for a campaign from Italy into Yugoslavia, which borders on all three satellites. Since this proposal first came up at a time when the Soviet army was still worrying about Stalingrad, its execution would have frustrated Soviet plans in the Balkans. The full force of Soviet diplomacy was therefore brought to bear on blocking the execution of this plan. This was done by stressing the predominant need for a Second Front, and by supporting American objections to the British proposal that were based on military considerations. The abandonment of the Balkan campaign was not solely the result of Soviet diplomacy, but it played a skillful role in bringing about this decision.

Once the menace of a Balkan campaign by the West had been blocked, Soviet diplomacy turned to the positive side of the task. Recognition of a Soviet sphere of influence had to be won by negotiations, and negotiations involved concessions. The concessions made by the USSR were equivalent to those made by the West only in form, however, but not in substance. Two specific cases are involved. One was the establishment of Allied Control Commissions and the other, negotiated at the same time, was the Anglo-Soviet agreement for a division of the Balkans into spheres of influence. In the first case the Western allies gained a free hand in the Allied Control Commission in Italy, while conceding Soviet predominance in the military occupation of Rumania, Bulgaria, and Hungary. In the second case the British interest in Greece was conceded, in return for a recognition of the predominant Soviet influence in the three satellites. The influence of the two powers was to be shared in Yugoslavia under this agreement. The formal equity of the concessions in these two agreements is clear enough. What was not apparent, was that in the three satellite states the Western allies were surrendering in large measure the possibility of influencing the future course of events, while in Italy and Greece the USSR maintained overt and covert organizations that continued to exert a powerful influence. These agreements, reached by diplomatic negotiation, thus served to give the Communist organizations in the three satellite countries the full protection of the Soviet High Command, while offering them at least a fifty-fifty chance of success in the two countries left in the Western sphere of influence.

The recognition by the West of a Soviet sphere of influence over the three satellites took place at the same time that the armistice terms were being drafted, and formed an integral part of these negotiations. The Soviet leaders realized that their bargaining position was strong in the post-Stalingrad phase of the war, and they therefore sought inclusion in the armistice terms of the demands that they wished to see in the final peace treaties. Thus the principal boundary and reparations features of the armistice terms, negotiated rather casually by the Western allies, were little changed in the final peace treaties.

The predominant position achieved by the USSR at this stage was now used with great effect in the negotiations regarding the formation of provisional governments for the three satellites. The Soviet government was able at first to present itself in the satellite states as the official agent of the Western democracies, and unsuspecting democratic leaders in these countries were faced with the choice of accepting Soviet proposals or appearing to flaunt the entire United Nations coalition. Under these circumstances the Soviet government had no difficulty in the winter of 1944–45 in installing "people's front" governments in which the Communists held the key positions. Throughout this transitional period from armistice to peace, the effective representatives of the USSR in the satellite countries were Russian agents of the Communist party of the Soviet Union. In dealing with the Western democracies diplomacy remained an essential instrument, but within the areas where Soviet imperialism was successful the diplomats and even the military commanders played a secondary role.

If Soviet diplomacy achieved its essential aims in the armistice negotiations, one may well question why so much value was placed in obtaining the consent of the Western democracies to the peace treaties. One reason certainly was that the relatively gradual process of the "people's front" tactics in these three countries required the continued deception of many leaders who still had considerable political influence. An open break with the Western allies would have created a political crisis before the domestic instruments of force were firmly in Communist hands. Moreover the three satellites represented only one sector of Soviet imperialism, and the pursuit of Communist objectives elsewhere in eastern Europe as well as in other parts of the world depended on a continuation of the appearance that the policies of the USSR had the support of the Western democracies.

The Soviet desire for the conclusion of the satellite peace treaties was sufficiently strong to give the Western democracies some leverage for bargaining, and certain Soviet concessions therefore had to be made. In the long discussion of the peace treaties at Potsdam, at four meetings of the Council of Foreign Ministers, and at the Paris Peace Conference, the principal issue was the democratic character of the provisional governments of Rumania, Bulgaria, and Hungary. The Western allies took the stand that the terms of the Yalta Declaration had not been honored, and that peace treaties could not be signed by governments not established through free elections. The Soviet diplomats, after prolonged argument, recognized that these objections would have to be met in some manner. They therefore made a number of concessions in form that did not affect the "commanding heights" of political power already held by the Communists.

These concessions included the holding of free elections in Hungary in 1945, which set back for some two years the formal establishment of a Communist regime, as well as the postponement of elections in Rumania and Bulgaria and an agreement to admit two leaders of the democratic opposition to the governments in each of these countries. The modest concessions evoked a handsome response. The government of Hungary was recognized by the United States even before the elections were held, and recognition was granted to Rumania in 1946 and to Bulgaria in 1947. American willingness to sign the peace treaties after these nominal Soviet gestures was due in large measure to the hope that the withdrawal of Soviet occupation troops would facilitate a return to political freedom. This hope was illusory, however, for by this time the firmness of Communist control lay in hands other than those of the Soviet army. The purely tactical character of the Soviet concessions is illustrated by the fact that on the day after the U. S. Senate ratified the Bulgarian peace treaty, Petkov, the leader of the democratic opposition, was placed under arrest.

The Soviet effort to gain admission of the three satellite states as members of the United Nations illustrates the limits of their diplomatic methods. After recognition and peace treaties had been won, the Communist regimes cast aside all pretense. They moved rapidly to transform these countries into "dictatorships of the proletariat" patterned on the Soviet model, and this necessitated frequent violation of the provisions for the protection of human rights that had been included in the peace treaties. This finally aroused the Western democracies, and they rejected the package deal under which these and other Communist states would have been admitted at the same time as Italy and six other states supported by the West. By maintaining that each country should be admitted on its merits, the Western democracies succeeded in blocking the admission of the Communist states at the price of a Soviet veto on the admission of the other seven states. This was a rather peculiar issue for the West to insist on so strongly, but this position was perhaps taken less on its merits than as an indication of a belated change in Western policy. In the meantime Soviet diplomacy had succeeded in protecting the Communist regimes while they consolidated their domestic position, and with this achievement it turned its attention to other problems.

The Soviet effort to provide a cover for the Communist seizure of Greece was undoubtedly not a diplomatic action of the first importance.[12] It is nevertheless interesting because it involved the complex machinery of the United Nations, and in certain important respects represented the obverse of the situation in Rumania, Bulgaria, and Hungary. In Greece it was the

[12] See Harry N. Howard, *The United Nations and the Problem of Greece*, Department of State Publication 2909 (Washington, D. C., 1947); and C. E. Black, "Greece and the United Nations," *Political Science Quarterly*, Vol. LXIII, No. 4 (Dec., 1948), 551-68.

British army that was in occupation, and it was the Western democracies that were trying to implement the Yalta Declaration. To this extent Soviet diplomacy faced many of the problems in Greece that confronted Western diplomacy in the three states to the north.

In view of this situation, the assignments of Soviet diplomacy were to prevent the holding of free elections in Greece, to obtain the withdrawal of the British army, and to discredit the existing Greek government. If this could be accomplished, the strong Communist organization in Greece that had been well supplied during the war with British and American gold and arms for its guerrilla operations would have a much better than even chance of seizing power.

In Greece an early Communist *coup* in 1944 had been defeated by prompt British military action, and the Communist guerrillas had agreed to surrender the bulk of their arms and to disband. This agreement was not honored, however, and the guerrillas cached large supplies of arms and withdrew their forces to the northern mountains and to the adjacent territory of Albania, Yugoslavia, and Bulgaria. In the meantime the restoration of peacetime political and economic conditions had been proceeding apace in Greece, and the government laid plans for holding elections under British, American, French, and Soviet supervision as a guarantee of their freedom. The refusal of the Soviet government to participate in the supervision of these elections, which were held on March 31, 1946, left it free to repudiate the new Greek government. It now stepped up the propaganda campaign denouncing this government as having "monarcho-fascist" leanings.

At the same time Soviet diplomacy undertook a campaign in the United Nations to obtain the withdrawal of British military forces from Greece. Two formal complaints were lodged in the Security Council in January and August, 1946, one by the USSR and the other by the Ukrainian S.S.R. The first charged that the presence of British troops in Greece represented a threat to the peace, and the second claimed that the reactionary policies of the Greek government were responsible for the growing civil strife. The Security Council did not take action on either of these charges, but when the United States proposed that a commission of investigation be sent to look into the second charge, the proposal was vetoed by the USSR.

Up to this point, Soviet diplomacy had not succeeded either in preventing the establishment of a freely elected Greek government or in obtaining the withdrawal of the British forces, but the situation was now changed when a renewed Communist guerrilla offensive began to make important gains in the summer and autumn of 1946. Retained and equipped by the three northern neighbors of Greece, the Communist guerrillas launched vigorous attacks on villages and towns and on occasion retreated north of the border when the Greek army came too close. Under these circumstances the Greek government itself took the case to the Security Council, maintaining under Article 34 of the Charter that this aid to the guerrillas had created a situation endangering the peace. The proposal that a Commission of Investigation be sent was again made by the United States, and this time the USSR accepted it. This acceptance nevertheless did not take place until a significant change had been made in the proposed terms of reference of the Commission. Whereas the American resolution had instructed the Commission "to ascertain the facts relating to the alleged border violations," the revised version broadened this assignment to include both "the facts" and "the causes and nature" of these border violations.

With this change in the terms of reference, the Commission of Investigation could be turned into a useful instrument for undermining the already somewhat precarious position of the Greek government. Under the procedures negotiated in the Commission, two investigations were in fact conducted: one of the border violations and the other of the Greek government. Although some of the Soviet efforts to swamp the Commission with Communist propaganda were blocked, Soviet initiative was responsible for 16 of its 33 field investigations and 126 of the 238 witnesses heard. These investigations and witnesses supported the Soviet view that the Greek charges were unfounded and that "the causes and nature" of the trouble lay in the character of the Greek government. Two reports were also submitted by the eleven-member Commission in June, 1947. The majority report documented the original Greek charges and a minority report supported the Soviet case. The latter was signed by only two of the members, the USSR and Poland. At the same time Communist pressure exerted in the right places was such as to compel France to abstain from signing the majority report, and to win from Belgium and Colombia a conditional signature.

Certainly in this case Soviet diplomacy won only a partial success, for it was unable to cast serious doubts on the Greek case. Although a Soviet veto blocked the acceptance by the Security Council of the recommendations of the Commission, when the case was taken to the General Assembly the Soviet proposals were defeated. Nevertheless, the real victory in Greece was accomplished only in part by Western diplomacy, for it was Western economic and military aid to the Greek army that finally brought Communist aggression to a halt. Had it not been for the Truman Doctrine, announced on March 12, 1947, while the Commission of Investigation was in Greece, the interference run by Soviet diplomacy might have become an important factor by confusing the issues and delaying international action.

The central theme of this essay has been the manner in which diplomacy was used in close integration with other instruments, principally the Communist organizations and the Soviet army, in support of Soviet imperialism. It seems clear that in none of the cases discussed was Soviet diplomacy alone responsible for Communist success. The cover provided by the Soviet army was doubtless more important for, with certain notable exceptions, the limits of Soviet imperialism in Europe correspond closely to the line reached by Soviet troops at the end of the war. It should not be concluded from this, however, that the role of Soviet diplomacy was not significant or that the full extent of Communist expansion could have been achieved without its assistance. The small cost at which the Western democracies were induced to accept Soviet disclaimers of imperialist intentions, to recognize a Soviet sphere of influence in exchange for unequal concessions, and to give their approval to the armistice terms and peace treaties, was the vital contribution of diplomacy to Soviet imperialism.

At the same time one cannot but question whether the prestige gained by Soviet diplomacy was not merely utilized, but in fact squandered, in this second round of revolutions and whether this prestige can be sufficiently revived during the present period of "co-existence" to be serviceable once again should a third round of revolutions occur. Certainly the Western democracies demonstrated after 1947 that they had learned their lesson in Europe, and have mobilized their political and military resources so that in the future they will be able to undertake diplomatic negotiations from positions of greater strength.

It is only because these lessons were learned by the West that one can contemplate without great apprehension the negotiations that are being conducted today, with Soviet diplomacy or its first cousin, in other parts of the world. The truce talks in Korea, for instance, have exhibited many familiar characteristics. In the two years that these talks have lasted, the Communist position has changed from one of great relative military weakness to one of almost unbeatable strength. The West has accepted a five-member supervisory commission in which two of the states are disciplined mouthpieces of the USSR while the other three are neutral in the effort of the United Nations to stem Soviet imperialism. In the partitioned Korea that will result, the Communists will doubtless have a powerful organization in the south with full Chinese and Soviet support while it is not difficult to imagine that the United Nations may discourage corresponding activities on the part of free Koreans. In appearance, these terms seem to be another victory of diplomacy in support of Soviet imperialism. The assumption that this is not in fact the case, rests on the hope that the Western democracies have now learned that in dealing with the USSR and its associates it is not the diplomatic forms that count but the reality of Communist power that these forms are intended to conceal.

RAY L. THURSTON: *Discussion*

Deputy Director, Office of European Affairs,
Department of State

At the close of his talk Mr. Black referred to the Korean problem as an example of the difference between Soviet diplomacy and Western diplomacy. I should like to amplify his point. In the opening period of the Korean hostilities, in June, 1950,

American diplomacy was able to achieve solidarity with the rest of the world by an idealistic appeal which emphasized unsullied objectives. The galvanized American people enabled United States diplomacy to reach a high level of performance. In the long hard pull following this dramatic beginning, however, some of the weaknesses of our diplomacy were revealed, particularly in the realm of staying power. As against this tendency of ours to proceed in fits and starts, we found revealed in the Korean episode the stubborn and persistent character of Soviet diplomacy.

I should also like to refer to Dr. Black's thesis regarding alternating periods of "cooperation" and "revolution" as applied to Soviet diplomacy. Cooperation hardly seems the word to use with respect to Soviet diplomacy at any time, and certainly not with regard to the situation between the United States and the Soviet Union. I must also object to the use of the word "revolution" in the European context. The post World War II changes in eastern Europe were manipulated from above.

How do we define diplomacy? The classic Western definition assumes a common field of interest between sovereign governments. It is the job of the diplomat to find this common ground and to build on it. But there is a fundamental difference between Soviet diplomacy and that of the free world. Soviet diplomacy is predicated upon an assumption that there are no enduring common interests between the Soviet Union and the so-called capitalist countries. The Soviet goal is to destroy the capitalist world. The Soviet diplomat is, therefore, part of a world-wide conspiratorial and ideological scheme. Within his embassy he is the instrument of such nondiplomatic agencies as the secret police and the Communist party.

I should like to express one last general thought about the differences between our diplomacy and that of the Soviet Union. When our diplomats are engaged in important negotiations, the spotlight of domestic and public opinion is focussed directly on them and exercises a day-to-day pressure on their deliberations and decisions. The Soviet diplomat and the government issuing instructions to him are not concerned with public opinion in this sense.

The discussion centered about three principal issues. The first question was whether Soviet diplomacy should be viewed as fundamentally a stalling device to prevent agreement either as a prelude to military action or, in the case of post-Stalinist diplomacy, to hold the line while insecurities within the Soviet bloc are being reduced. It was pointed out that while the one stable factor in Soviet diplomacy is the pursuit of the goal of the Soviet Union to exploit any given situation to its fullest possibilities, Soviet diplomacy does often assume a negative form. There are many examples in this field. Both the Austrian treaty and the Korean war are excellent examples. Another one that was cited was the action of the Soviet Union to block the efforts of the Bulgarian government in 1944 to get out of the war. The Bulgarian government wanted to negotiate directly with the Soviet Union but this attempt was met with a unilateral Soviet declaration of war on Bulgaria. The Bulgarian government at that time was one that the Soviet Union did not wish to see in power after the war.

It is well known that the Soviet Union often uses diplomatic forums to foster disagreement and then utilizes the disagreement as propaganda for the Soviet case. On the other hand, the Soviet Union has been known to keep treaties when it is in its interests to do so. It is very difficult in any given case to decide when the Soviets are serious about reaching diplomatic agreements and when they are interested only in propaganda or other objectives. In Korea there was a period when we assumed that they were not serious about reaching agreement. After Stalin's death we decided they were serious because of the internal problems which existed in the Soviet Union. Reference was made to the Soviet note of August 4 responding to an allied invitation for a meeting to discuss the German question and to a Herblock cartoon on that subject in the Washington *Post* captioned "Nyes or Nyet?".

Considerable interest was expressed regarding the relationship between Stalin's death and subsequent Soviet diplomatic moves. The thought was expressed that we should expect less unity and boldness in Soviet policy during this period of uncertainty. The implication is therefore that through negotiation, tensions can be lessened for the time being and conditions can be made more favorable for a period of "co-existence." There may be an analogy here to apparent Soviet moves aimed at putting greater emphasis on the production of consumer goods rather than capital goods. A genuine move by the Soviet Union in this direction would support the "co-existence" thesis. There is an obvious relationship between any such domestic steps and Soviet foreign policy.

Even before Stalin's death, vitriolic criticism of American racial policies had been toned down in Soviet discussions in the

United Nations. It has been noted that a change of Soviet personnel has occurred; there is more geniality. The Soviet representatives have been especially friendly to Latin Americans and to representatives from underdeveloped countries. Tactical changes in Soviet diplomacy do not alter its purposes, which are (1) to divide the non-Soviet world by playing off countries against each other by propaganda and other means, and (2) to keep together the Soviet world. Diplomacy plays only a minor role, it must be admitted, in the second objective.

Although it was agreed that it will be very difficult to reach concrete conclusions regarding current Soviet diplomatic tactics "until the documents are published," it was also pointed out that American diplomacy must take decisions on the best possible guesses at this time.

The last problem discussed was the place which such concepts as "co-existence" and diplomatic negotiations have in the face of the Bolshevik theory of irreconcilable camps and the admittedly implacable objective of the Soviets to destroy the West. It was pointed out in this connection that what really counts is the reality of power which diplomacy conceals. This is what we mean by negotiation from strength. The change in the real power of the two camps can be reflected in diplomatic negotiations. We pursue negotiations with the Soviets for positive ends of our own, not accepting history for what the Marxists say it is. Insofar as the Soviet point of view is concerned, it is not easy to define exactly what they think is meant when they use the word "co-existence." Perhaps if we can view history as the prison which Marxist dialectics make it, capitalism is like a prisoner condemned to death but with the date of execution not yet set. In the meantime, the Soviet masters of the prison house have to deal with the prisoner in day-to-day affairs. This is the Bolshevik perspective and need not concern us unduly since in fact we are not the prisoners of history they imagine us to be.

The Role of Force in Soviet Policy

JULES MENKEN,
International Affairs Analyst

The use of force is central to Communist theory and Communist practice. Whereas the American Declaration of Independence takes for granted "a decent respect to the opinions of mankind" and affirms that governments derive "their just powers from the consent of the governed," whereas the preamble to every British Act of Parliament states that it is "enacted by the King's [or Queen's] most Excellent Majesty, by and with the advice and consent of the Lords Spiritual and Temporal, and Commons, in this present Parliament assembled, and by the authority of the same," Lenin defines the "dictatorship of the proletariat" as follows: "The scientific concept of dictatorship means nothing more than unlimited power, absolutely unconfined by any kinds of laws or regulations but resting directly upon force. . . ."—"unlimited power, based on force and not on law."

Stalin worked Lenin's idea out in detail. According to Stalin, "the dictatorship of the proletariat is the weapon of the proletarian revolution, its organ, its most important base, summoned into life in order, first, to crush the resistance of the overthrown exploiters and consolidate its achievements, and secondly to carry out the proletarian revolution to the end, to carry out the revolution to the complete victory of socialism." Hence, Stalin concludes, "the dictatorship of the proletariat cannot arise as the result of the peaceful development of bourgeois society and of bourgeois democracy; it can arise only as the result of the smashing of the bourgeois state machine, of the bourgeois army, of the bourgeois civil service, of the bourgeois police. . . . In other words, the law of the smashing of the bourgeois state machine is a preliminary condition for such a revolution, is the inevitable law of the revolutionary movement in the imperialist countries of the world."

These and similar passages are of course well known to students of Marxist thought. But familiarity should not cause their true significance to be overlooked. In Plato's *Republic*, the unlovable Thrasymachus is also an advocate of the social and political use of force. But Plato permits Thrasymachus to put forward his theories only in order that Socrates may destroy them. What is significant about the Marxist formulation is that, as Stalin put it, " Marxist-Leninist theory is not a dogma but a guide to action."

The internal application of Lenin's and Stalin's ideas within Soviet society is only too familiar. No rulers of any state have ever used force more ruthlessly. The peoples of the Soviet Union have been the first victims of the fury of Soviet policy. Agricultural collectivization, the Great Purge of 1936–39, and forced labor on a gigantic scale have brought violent or premature death to untold millions. Entire peoples—among them the Chechens, the Crimean Tartars, and the Volga Germans—have been uprooted from their ancestral habitations and transported to strange lands at incalculable cost in life and suffering. Among lesser examples of the ruthless internal use of force is the Soviet suppression in the early nineteen-twenties of a Turkomen rising, which was unknown until the fact was reported by General Anders. The ruins which still remained twenty years later, states the Polish leader, bore silent but terrible witness to the scale of violence used against this small people.

Just as no political inhibitions or moral scruples restrain the rulers of the Kremlin from using force internally to extend or maintain their power, so also Communist theory and practice place no limits (except the probability of ultimate success) on resort to war as an instrument of policy. On this topic Lenin, Stalin, and Mao Tse-tung all speak with one voice. In *Left-Wing Communism: An Infantile Disorder*, which was published in 1920, Lenin wrote: " Everyone will agree that an army which does not train itself to wield all arms, all the means and methods of warfare that the enemy possesses or may possess, behaves in an unwise or even in a criminal manner. But this applies to politics even more than it does to war. In politics it is even harder to forecast what methods of warfare will be applicable and useful under certain future conditions. Unless we master all means of warfare, we may suffer grave and even decisive defeat. . . . If, however, we master all means of warfare, we shall certanly be victorious." Another (and better known) passage gives classic expression to Lenin's views. "We live," he wrote, "not only in a state, but in a system of states, and the existence of the Soviet Republic side by side with the imperialist states for a long time is unthinkable. In the end either one or the other will conquer. And until that end comes, a series of the most terrible collisions between the Soviet Republic and the bourgeois states is inevitable."

After quoting this forecast of inevitable wars, Stalin commented: "Clear, one would think." Stalin also stated his views on war in a letter written to Maxim Gorky on January 17, 1930. "We are in fact not against *all* war," Stalin told Gorky. "We are *against* imperialist war, which is counter-revolutionary war. But we are *for* liberating, anti-imperialist revolutionary war, regardless of the fact that this kind of war, as is well known, is not only not free from the 'horrors of bloodshed,' but actually teems with them." In other words, Stalin opposed wars which might threaten the Soviet Union, but favored wars which, because they are (in his language) "liberating, anti-imperialist, revolutionary," would extend communism and Soviet power.

Mao Tse-tung's views on war have found expression not only in his decade-long and most successful development of so-called "Soviet areas" as bases from which armed attack could destroy the regime whose overthrow the Chinese Communists were seeking—a technique which is being used again today in Indo-China, and which in appropriate circumstances can be repeated indefinitely—but also in his important lectures, *Strategic Problems of China's Revolutionary War*. "In China," Mao says, "the main form of struggle is war, and the main form of organization is the army. . . . Without armed struggle . . . there will be no victory." Mao has also written: "A revolution or revolutionary war is on the offensive. . . . A Soviet war lasting ten years may be surprising to other countries, but to us this is only the preface."

Whether the Communist war against the free world will last

for ten years depends in part on Communist strategy. Any strategy assumes certain purposes and certain forces—which may exist already or may have to be created—and seeks to achieve its purposes by appropriate use of the forces available to it in relation to the obstacles to be overcome. Stalin fully recognized this truth, and applied it with a master's hand. "Strategy," he wrote in his lectures on *The Foundations of Leninism,* "is the determination of the direction of the main blow at a given stage . . . , the elaboration of a corresponding plan for the disposition of . . . forces . . . , the fight to carry out this plan throughout the given stage . . . ." Words and phrases omitted here show that Stalin was then thinking in terms of revolution from below; but this fact does not qualify the truth or lessen the relevance of his main thought, which his action on countless occasions illustrated and emphasized, and which we may be certain that his successors will adopt and apply within the measure of their very considerable abilities.

From the standpoint of Moscow and Peking, what should be the direction of the main blow at the present stage? The answer depends on the reply to another question, viz., what is the main Communist purpose? To this question, at least, the answer is clear: the main Communist purpose is a world Communist revolution, or the establishment of world communism, which expresses the same essential idea in different language. But this is not quite the whole story. It is inconceivable that either Moscow or Peking would be satisfied if the United States, Britain, Germany, and Japan—the main noncommunist centers of industry and of actual or potential military power—were to have a Communist revolution on their own, and if the rest of the world followed suit. Such a situation, which would merely carry forward present world tensions within a nominally Communist frame, would not satisfy Moscow or Peking at all. The Soviet and Chinese Communist leaders, whatever words their ideology and policy may require them to use, seek the substance of world power, and not its shadow. What the Russian Communists, who are the dominant members of the Communist third of the globe, really want to establish is a world communism which centers on the Soviet Union, on Russia, and on Moscow. The race-proud and culture-proud Chinese Communists may think differently; but whatever seeds of future conflict their views may hold, China's industrially weak and technologically backward condition makes such differences unimportant in practice today.

Given the purpose of establishing world communism, the direction which the main Communist blow must take is clear. If Moscow and Peking are to attain their common goal, they *must* destroy the power of the United States. No alternative can suffice. While the United States exists and is strong, an impassable road-block bars the way to world communism, the rest of the free world is heartened and sustained, the hope of liberation will burn unquenchably among the peoples under Communist rule, and the ultimate downfall of the entire Communist structure is implicitly threatened. If the great despots in Peking and the Kremlin, and the myriads of their lieutenants and henchmen, are to sleep quietly at night, the United States and all the strength, aspiration, and promise that it stands for must be utterly and finally destroyed.

How is this to be done? In the first instance, the problem is not necessarily one of direct attack. Ordinary prudence and common sense require that the Kremlin, before embarking on major military action, should try to weaken the United States by nonmilitary means and by policies involving the use of force on a small or secondary scale, if at all. Along these lines there are many possibilities. The global political and strategic situation today obviously comprises two areas of major power. On the one hand, there is a central Communist land-mass, which is in physical contact with about a dozen states whose political, industrial, and military strength varies, but is in no case sufficient to withstand major Communist aggression unaided. On the other hand, there is the United States, which vast oceans separate both from the noncommunist states whose independence is a major or a vital American interest, and also from the Communist world which is its mortal enemy. In terms of conventional weapons, the logistic situation is greatly to the Communist advantage. In political terms, the Communists oppose a closely knit and centrally directed bloc to a loose constellation of independent states whose respective hopes, ambitions, jealousies, and fears create deep divisions between them, and make it most difficult to achieve an effective common policy. In addition, the

Communists still wield an ideology of illusion which even today seduces the loyalty and focuses the dreams of millions.

In this situation the most important immediate aims of Communist policy are fairly clear. Moscow must seek by every means to break the North Atlantic alliance, and in particular to divide Britain and France from one another and from the United States. Moscow must also do its utmost to bring under Communist control four areas—Germany, the Middle East, Southeast Asia, and Japan—whose industrial capacity, raw material resources, and man-power potential make them key pieces in the world strategic pattern. The Kremlin has long been working to achieve all these things; and for the time being its policy need involve no use of armed force more extensive than the combat groups which the Tudeh Party must be presumed to be training and equipping in Iran, or the handful of tactical and strategic advisers and the comparatively small supplies of weapons with which the Chinese Communists have for many months been aiding the Viet Minh rebels.

At this point one of the great paradoxes of history emerges. Even if Moscow were to attain all the major strategic goals within immediate reach of Communist forces on the mainland of Europe and Asia, this immense achievement would still not yield the supreme prize of Soviet domination over a completely communized earth. The main task would still be unaccomplished. The United States would still have to be destroyed. The terrible loss of its friends and allies, the transfer from the free to the Communist world of all the peoples and industrial resources of Europe and Asia, and the loss of many strategic materials would strike a heavy blow at the ability of the United States to defend itself. Whether such a defense would succeed in the long run no one can foresee. What is certain is that the United States would still be a formidable military power, the more dangerous to an aggressor since its people would then have their energies heightened and their unity reinforced by the manifest perils of a life-and-death struggle. At this stage, moreover, if conventional weapons alone were used, the scales of advantage might tilt somewhat towards the United States; for in this situation an enlarged but by no means unified Soviet Empire, its subjected peoples baleful with sullenness and hatred, would have to face all the hazards and logistic disadvantages of fighting beyond the seas.

When atomic weapons are considered, the picture alters fundamentally. Western Europe for the past five or six years has lived under the shield of American atomic power. The risk of American atomic retaliation is still a major check on direct Soviet action against Germany and Japan. But this situation is not permanent. It rests on one-sided American possession of atomic bombs in numbers. Once the boot is also on the other foot, once the Soviet atomic stock-pile becomes large enough and the Soviet Air Force strong enough, Moscow will possess the technical means both to prevent American interference with Communist advances elsewhere in the world, and also to attack and perhaps destroy American power at its source in the United States.

This possibility needs to be looked at more closely. It is often said that fear of American atomic retaliation on a scale which would devastate the entire Soviet economy and bring the Soviet state down in ruin will prevent Moscow from striking first. But this answer is altogether too easy. What the risk of American atomic retaliation will really do is to make Moscow try to eliminate it by a prior blow. Soviet espionage is efficient, as we all know to our cost. The Kremlin must therefore know very well the location of most American radar stations and atomic air bases. It certainly knows the names and locations of the main centers of American industrial and political power. Among other places, the essential information is published in the *World Almanac*. According to census data printed in this source, there were in 1950 fourteen American cities with metropolitan areas whose population numbered a million or over, another nineteen with populations between half a million and a million, and forty-four more with populations between 250,000 and half a million. The combined population of these seventy-seven cities and their metropolitan areas numbered 71½ million, or 47.4 per cent of the census population of the continental United States. In those cities is also concentrated a high proportion of American industry.

Atomic bombs now have about ten times the explosive power of the bombs which devastated Nagasaki and Hiroshima in 1945, or perhaps three times the destructive power of those bombs after allowing for atmospheric and other losses. How many modern atomic bombs would be required, if not to wipe out those cities, at the very least to inflict terrible casualties and disorder, and to paralyse their industries for a time? If we assume three modern atomic bombs per million of population, we will perhaps not go far wrong. The general pattern which a treacherous Soviet surprise attack could very well follow thus becomes clear. The first blow would probably be delivered by ordinary bombers against the radar stations which give warning of invaders in the American skies. A second wave of perhaps two-hundred attacking planes would try to destroy the airfields in the United States and other countries from which atomic retaliation against the Soviet Union could be launched. A third wave, perhaps also numbering about two-hundred planes, would attack some seventy-five metropolitan areas and other key centers. The only questions are whether Moscow has only Hiroshima-type bombs, or also possesses more modern kinds; and how many bombers would get through and place their bombs effectively. If only the older type of atomic bombs are available, more must be used to inflict the same hurt. In order to lessen the risk of failure, the Kremlin might in any case use a larger number of planes and bombs.

Whether Moscow will in fact start a third world war is one of the most obscure and highly debated subjects in the world today. Important sections of Western opinion hold that the main danger of war springs from Soviet fear of the United States, and that the same fear is the chief cause of Soviet armaments. A vicious and lying domestic propaganda extending over many years may indeed have misled the ignorant Soviet masses, and a wholly unwarranted but genuine fear of American intentions and of unprovoked American attack may therefore exist among them. That the rulers of the Kremlin should really have similar fears is inconceivable, for men who could harbor them would be fitter for the lunatic asylum than for the responsibilities of ruling the Soviet Empire and pursuing the hazardous policy aimed at world domination on which Moscow has embarked.

On the entire question of whether the United States or Moscow-centered world communism is the true aggressor, the salient facts are too often forgotten. The American will to peace and efforts to promote and establish peace—like the British efforts and will in the same direction—stand unequivocally in the record for the whole world to see. The Soviet story is very different. It is true that Moscow has continuously talked the language of peace. But Moscow's words and Moscow's deeds tell utterly different stories. Soviet efforts to foment world revolution go back to the earliest years of the regime. Those efforts have not been confined merely to propaganda and subversion both in the West and among the Eastern peoples. As long ago as May, 1925, the Third All-Union Congress of Soviets passed a resolution instructing the Soviet Government to strengthen what was called—in the double-talk which even then characterized Communist pronouncements—the "defensive might" of the Soviet Union by measures which would "(a) secure a corresponding expansion of the armaments industry and run all the rest of the State industry of the Union in such a way as will in peacetime take into account the needs of war-time; (b) improve armaments and saturate the Red Army with them; . . . [and] (f) pay profound attention to the military training of the entire population."

In order to judge the relevance of this resolution to a genuinely peaceful policy, the situation at the time need only be recalled. In 1925 Stalin was already fairly firmly in the saddle; he must therefore have approved the resolution, if he did not actually draft it. The first Five-Year Plan still lay three years ahead. In May, 1925, the negotiations which led to the Locarno Agreements of the following October were well under way, the armed forces of Britain and the United States had been cut almost to their very low peacetime minimum, a relatively liberal regime ruled Japan, and the only army of any size in Europe outside the Soviet Union was the French army, which was maintained against Germany.

Men who do not want their countries to be overrun by world communism must therefore hold that the truth is very different from the fair picture of Soviet motives presented by those who argue that Soviet policy is based on fear. Neither the immense existing Soviet strength and prodigious program in conventional armaments. nor the vast resources which the Kremlin is certainly devoting to atomic weapons, make sense unless the

Politbureau are preparing to use them should occasion and opportunity arise. A policy of bluff calls for no such extravagance; a policy of true peace does not need to be supported by the largest armed forces the world has ever known except during the two world wars of this century.

Alike in families and in states internal freedom is normally a precondition of external action. If a man and his wife are quarrelling bitterly, they are unlikely to agree on plans for a new house. It is therefore often argued that the internal tensions which exist throughout the satellites—and which are certainly parallelled by great stresses inside the Soviet Union itself—will compel Moscow to hold its hand. It is believed further that the struggle for power now going on in the Kremlin will also make foreign war impossible.

Both of these assumptions may be challenged. Riddled by hatred for Russia as the satellites undoubtedly are, the Moscow-controlled secret police, the country-wide network of spies and informers, and Communist knowledge of conspiratorial methods and of the dangers which must therefore be guarded against have apparently prevented effective, organized undergrounds from developing anywhere in eastern Europe. Moreover, though the satellite armed forces may be unreliable and unuseable for combat purposes, no published evidence suggests that they could not be employed on line-of-communications and similar duties so as to save Soviet manpower. Again, though the output of satellite factories may be low in quality and unsatisfactory in quantity, Soviet methods are well adapted to extracting a maximum from unwilling workers; while sabotage is too dangerous to the individual and his family for it apparently to be practised on any significant scale. The situation in the satellites, therefore, though it would certainly prove troublesome and perhaps dangerous in the event of a long war, would not necessarily cause Moscow to refrain from launching a war which it believed would be short and successful—the only kind of war, that is, which the men of the Kremlin are likely to contemplate.

The struggle for mastery inside the Politbureau is no more reliable as a preventive of war. While it is going on, a lull may perhaps prevail—though even this is not certain. Sooner or later, however, the pattern of dictatorship which is the rule alike in

Russian and in Soviet history must be expected to emerge again. Whether the new master of the Kremlin will then steer towards war or will set a different course must depend on whether his purposes and the purposes of his associates remain in the consistent Communist tradition, or whether the Leninist-Stalinist heritage—and also the *mystique* of Russian expansionism—are at long last and finally abandoned.

Will the men of the Kremlin—and in particular the man who becomes master of his fellows—abandon the aim of Soviet- and Kremlin-centered Communist world domination? Any answer involves a political, a psychological, and a moral judgment—and also a judgment of character which combines these and other factors as well.

Politically, there can be few reasons why a thoroughly indoctrinated Communist should become an apostate. In one of its most important aspects Marxism is a criticism—to a considerable extent justified on Christian and other religious grounds—of the evils of nineteenth century capitalism, and of evils in the present social structure of the West which our own generation has either inherited, or failed to reform, or made for itself. In another no less important aspect communism is a form of social wish-fulfilment of unsurpassed seductiveness, a doctrine which seems to promise—though the promise is false—the material abundance and the opportunities for a better and richer life which are the age-old dream of discontented and impoverished men. The power of this promise is especially great among colored and Eastern peoples whose judgment has been clouded and warped by a century of what is felt as humiliation at white men's hands. In political terms these and related forces are crystallized in a congeries of small states, most of them weak as well, which appear unable to unite even in the face of an immense common threat from without. In a somewhat similar situation, the great Jenghiz Khan and his successors cut an entire world of small states to pieces and devoured them one by one. Why, then, should the strong Communist world ruled from the Kremlin—a world whose masters are united at least for the time being by common ambitions—not hope to have a similar success?

Politically, a subtle change has entered the Kremlin since

Stalin's death. Nearly thirty years is a long time for a single individual to dominate the thought of a large segment of mankind as Stalin dominated the thought of the Communist world both inside and outside the Soviet frontiers. One important element of Marxist dogma—the belief that time and history are inevitably on the Communist side—may indeed be implicit in Marx; but in the domination it has established over the present generation of Communists it owes more than is realized to Stalin's own character. Two of Stalin's outstanding traits were his almost superhuman patience, which enabled him to wait until situations which he thought were developing favorably in fact matured, and his unsleeping (if also unavowed) memory of the distance he himself had travelled from the misery and impotence of his early years—a journey he never intended to retrace.

Stalin's successors—Malenkov not least among them—have grown up in very different circumstances. They did not have to create a revolutionary party out of nothing, suffer exile while they waited for circumstances in which they could snatch an insecure power, and then consolidate the power they had won so precariously with the sword in one hand and organization charts of the secret police and of Five-Year Plans in the other. The atmosphere of their early manhood was quite different. They may, it is true, have fought in the Russian Civil War. But they fought from inside the ranks of a Party which already had power —and they fought to make that Party prevail, and to advance their own careers along with it. Their temper is therefore different from the temper of Stalin and his generation. They are less patient, more assured, less alert to risks. They not merely want to see the triumph of Communism; they want it to come in their time; and they also want the glory of achieving and establishing it. For Malenkov's generation the inevitabilities of history a century hence are not enough. World communism must be achieved while they are living—and they must be the men who establish it.

Similar forces operate in the moral sphere. "The fundamental problem of Leninism," Stalin once wrote, "is the problem of power." In one of its deepest manifestations in human personality, power is self-assertiveness. In all generations one of the supreme problems of morals has been to curb such self-assertiveness with the standards and sanctions which ethics and religion impose. Marxism sweeps all such standards and sanctions away. For the Communist no criterion is significant except success in furthering communism. In the case of the topmost Communists who determine the content of Party doctrine for the time being, this means that all restraints to self-assertiveness are swept away except those that calculation of probable success or failure imposes. By its wholly pragmatic self-assertiveness, communism thus eliminates all normal restraints. In doing so it opens another of the sluice-gates which can sweep mankind into war.

One of the most difficult problems of politics arises from the fact that students of politics are usually men of mind and intellect, whereas successful politicians and statesmen are men of will and action. Each of these two very different human types can enter the other's field only by a strong effort of imagination. The normal sensitiveness of men of mind and intellect, their feeling for the feelings of others and their ordinarily high ethical gifts, make it exceptionally hard for them to understand a very different type of men whose highest good is the effective imposition of their own will. Where men of mind and intellect see problems but not solutions unless attainable without the use of force, men of action and will see situations which they will drive a way through if they cannot go round them. In extreme cases, men of action and will are not only prepared to cut the Gordian knots which restrain them; like Samson, they will also risk bringing down the temple in which they stand rather than continue to accept the servitude and humiliation of a world which they are unable to mould to the self-assertive will of their hearts' desire.

All these are reasons why the role of force in Communist thought and practice is central. But force in its international application means war. If and in so far as this reasoning is correct, Communist policy will move in the direction of war. This does not mean that major war is inevitable; no analysis, however subtle, no human logic, however powerful, can establish inevitability in such a matter as a proposition in geometry can be rigorously and finally proved. What this argument does establish is that war is highly probable. Force occupies a central place in Communist thought and practice; and Communists will avoid recourse to it only if they fear that its use will fail.

The meaning of this for the Western world is clear. Since the Communists will all but certainly resort to force—that is, since they will go to war if and when they think the chances favorable—it is the duty of the West to create an armed strength and establish a political unity that cannot be overcome. The West must do more than this. At present the atom and hydrogen bomb and the long-range bomber offer almost irresistible temptations to the men with the mentality of international gangsters who call their tyranny world communism and seek to spread it over the entire earth. What the leaders and peoples of the West must ensure is that the concentrated evil which communism in its falsity and callousness embodies shall not only fail in its efforts to bring mankind under its slavery, but shall also destroy itself by the evil of its nature and the violence of its endeavours.

MARIO EINAUDI: *Discussion*

Cornell University

Mr. Menken's views on the Soviet use of the military weapon provide a dramatic climax to our analyses of the variety of ideological, political, and economic instruments available to the Soviet Union in its relentless warfare against the West. In view of these, we must attempt to find an answer to this question: what are the priorities that the Soviet leaders themselves are going to establish when they review the armory of weapons, ideological, political, economic and military, available to them?

One is struck, in reading Malenkov's address of August 8, 1953, by the emphasis given to the economic and the political factors, and by the de-emphasizing of the ideological and the military ones. The Soviet Union has perhaps reached a stage in which she has secured a moderate measure of freedom of movement in economic affairs. The Kremlin might direct the use of certain plants either to increase politically significant exports, or to shift home production from capital to consumer's goods. Undoubtedly this is an important issue for the West.

No less significant, however, has been the political coloration of Mr. Malenkov's speech. One of its characteristic and relatively novel features has been a sweeping diplomatic *tour d'horizon* of the type which by tradition I had always thought was reserved to British prime ministers.

In this connection it is worth noting that we are today confronted by this curious paradox. Malenkov is addressing France in the most soft-spoken and enticing language that country has heard in recent times, while he is reserving his sternest and severest language for Germany. This is not due to chance, for Malenkov knows that the United States government is reserving its sweetest language for the Bonn government of Chancellor Adenauer, while France is addressed with increasing frequency in the language used for naughty and rebellious and ungrateful children. At a time when the European Defense Community and the entire policy of European federalism hangs in the balance, it is obvious that these developments must call for the most careful consideration on the part of the American government.

In the discussion that followed the question was asked why, if the atom bomb is a deterrent in western Europe, it had not been in eastern Europe and in China.

The opinion was expressed that the Soviet Union was clearly convinced that the United States would not use atom bombs in areas over which the United States was not prepared to go to war. This is in contrast to the Soviet Union's realization that the United States will use all available means to oppose an attack on western Europe. Mr. Menken stressed the military importance of EDC uniting what is at present a divided continent. He thought the effort important in order to restore to Europe some of its lost faith. He added that moral and political problems were at least equally important and had to be solved before military instrumentalities could be fully effected.

In reply to further questions the speaker stated that even if it were proved that the new Soviet 1953 budget did indeed provide for a shift to consumer goods production, the probabilities were that the Soviet leaders could afford a slight change in emphasis without in any way weakening their military potential, so that a greater production of consumer goods should not be taken as signifying the renunciation of the use of force.

It was further added that the Soviet government was taking into account possible domestic strains caused by war. Its tendency would be to discount them in case of a short war.

Given Mr. Menken's views of the high probability of war, the question was raised of the value of any attempt at negotiation that would seek to arrive at a partial settlement of outstanding disputes. The speaker clearly favored a policy of negotiation if this was feasible. He went on to point out that as against the great legend of Stalin as the man of peace the intentions of the West were unquestionably profoundly peaceful; it was still necessary, however, to make the Western position unmistakably clear before the entire world, including the propaganda-corrupted Soviet home public, and by so doing clearly to shift the burden of failure of negotiations to the Communist side.

PART III

An Assessment of Soviet Strength

Economic Realities and Prospects of the Soviet Bloc

HARRY SCHWARTZ,
The New York Times

Economics, we are sometimes told, is the dismal science. In no area does this description apply more appropriately than in that of Soviet studies. The problem of Soviet imperialism would not engage our attention nearly so much if it were not for the fact that among the other components in the arsenal of the Soviet bloc, there is a large and very effective base of military economic potential. It is this economic strength which we shall examine here.

The simple facts about the size and population of the Soviet bloc are enormously impressive. It occupies more than one-quarter of the habitable land surface of the earth, with a population of approximately 800 million people, or nearly one-third of all humanity. Within this vast region there is to be found virtually every important natural resource, be it mineral or nonmineral; and among its numerous inhabitants there are great human resources as well. From the people now living in the Soviet bloc there have come many individuals who in the past have been outstanding in the fields of science and technology. It is not out of place to point out here that among those who came to the United States are men such as Leo Szilard, one of the basic workers on the atomic bomb, Mr. Sikorsky of helicopter fame, Major Seversky of airplane fame, and Dr. Ipatieff, one of the world's greatest petroleum chemists. Obviously, we do have in the Soviet bloc a rich reservoir of resources, both human and nonhuman, which can be exploited for man's economic goals, whether they be for war or for peace.

Yet in spite of these riches, the single fact that strikes one most clearly is the general poverty of this area—China, the Soviet Union, and eastern Europe. As a generalization it can be said perhaps that there is no other area of comparable size on earth which is as poor. The United Nations in 1949 made a study of incomes in different countries of the world which illustrates this condition. The Soviet bloc with roughly one-third of the world's population accounted for only about 18 per cent of the total income and production of goods. Average per capita income within the Soviet bloc was about $110.00, whereas in the rest of the world it was over $250.00.[1] In other words, speaking very roughly the people of the noncommunist world were on the average two and one-half times as well off in 1949 as the people in the Soviet bloc.

Although this comparison is useful, we should not let the fact of the poverty of this vast area obscure our vision of a second related fact, namely, that even within the Communist area there are very important and sharp income variations. According to the same United Nations study, the per capita income of Czechoslovakia in 1949 was $371.00. The per capita income of the Soviet Union was $300.00. But the per capita income of China was only $27.00. I wonder if our psychological warfare specialists have thought of the political dynamite there is in the notion of sharing the wealth in the Communist world. Why should the Chinese not be upgraded to something closer to the Russian level? But I leave that to others to consider.

Of course there are many reasons for this poverty in the Soviet bloc. Much of the land, particularly in the Soviet Union, is rather unsuited if not unuseable for agriculture because of climatic and soil conditions. Moreover, in most of this area industrialization began only comparatively recently or has barely begun, as in the case of China. The Soviet Union is, of course, the basic area of industrial strength. China, on the other hand, is still a nation in which perhaps 80 per cent or 90 per cent of the population are still engaged in agriculture, and industrialization is merely a very superficial phenomenon.

In the face of this poverty, which some may be tempted to

[1] *New York Times,* December 9, 1950, p. 1.

identify with weakness, the question arises as to why we need be concerned with the Soviet threat? The view is sometimes advanced, and even supported by allusion to production statistics for heavy industry in the Communist world and the noncommunist world, that we need not worry about the " Soviet threat."

The argument is usually presented about as follows: The Soviet bloc as a whole produced last year roughly these quantities of major commodities—approximately 47 million metric tons of steel, 460 million metric tons of coal, 56 million metric tons of oil, 33 million metric tons of pig iron, and 190 billion kilowatt hours of electric power. The noncommunist world, on the other hand, last year out-produced the Communist world by about the following ratios: three times as much steel, pig iron, and coal; five or six times as much electric power; and ten times as much natural petroleum.

On the basis of such comparisons some have been tempted to say that the noncommunist world had nothing to fear, that there is no possibility of the Soviet bloc challenging us either economically or militarily. But the implicit assumption in this reasoning is that the distribution and utilization of resources is the same within the Communist and noncommunist world. This is most decidely not true. We must understand that a basic facet of Communist economic policy is the overwhelming concentration of resources for direct or indirect military strength—in other words, either for the production of arms or for the production of those machines and raw materials which will ultimately help in the production of arms. Mr. Malenkov gave us a key statistic recently on just how great that concentration is. He told the Supreme Soviet that in the year 1953 approximately 70 per cent of the total industrial production of the Soviet Union will consist of means of production. To the best of my knowledge there is no simple, comparable figure available for the United States economy but a very rough guess would be that at most 25 per cent of the American industrial production went for what the Soviets put in their Category A, that is, means of production. For comparative purposes, then, we can think of the two economies as consisting of a relatively weak Soviet bloc which puts three-fourths of its industrial output into direct and indirect military production, and of our own relatively strong economy which puts only one-fourth of its output into that area.

If we bear in mind this concentration, we can understand that the Soviet Union uses each ton of steel, each gallon of gasoline much more effectively than we do or are likely to do, short of anything but all-out war.

Given the absolute resources of the Communist world today, then, in terms of output, capital, and technology, there is no reason whatsoever to suppose from an economic point of view that they cannot have produced the hydrogen bomb, just as there is no reason to believe that they have not produced atomic bombs and are continuing to produce them. From all we know of the Soviet economy and of the way in which resources are utilized, we should expect that they have the capability and are producing every weapon of war within the range of man's inventive genius. We should not be misled by comparisons merely of over-all figures because in over-all American production is included tens of millions of tons of steel which we use turning out Buicks and Cadillacs and Lincolns and refrigerators and washing machines and dishwashers and which the Soviet Union certainly does not "waste" in any such fashion.

It may be argued, of course—and I think with more justice—that the relative weakness shown by the over-all figures for Soviet production, as compared with non-Soviet production, would be telling in the case of a protracted war. It may be argued that in the event of a war, after the United States and western Europe have had a chance to convert fully to all-out military production, then the ratios between noncommunist and Communist military production would be more or less similar to the ratios between basic raw material production, and the Communists wouldn't have a chance. That kind of reasoning had some validity in the past; but I would submit that it probably has little validity for the future. In any future war it is very unlikely that the Western world would be able to convert to military production simply because much of the vast plant and many of the workers who work in that vast plant would have been destroyed within the first few hours or days of that war.

Capacity in being at the start of a future world war may be

thought of largely as capacity which will have been destroyed shortly after that war breaks out.

It may be useful at this point to make a few observations about one or two other facets of the Soviet economic system. One is the transportation system. For the Soviet bloc as a whole, that is clearly very weak. In mechanized transportation, it depends primarily upon railroads, which are very inadequately developed except for the area roughly between the Elbe River and west of Moscow. Nor is the automobile transportation system satisfactory, because of the general absence of paved roads and the relatively small number of motor vehicles. In any future war Soviet transport would probably be one of its primary weaknesses, although again one can be misled by historical notions of protracted war.

Petroleum also is probably insufficient for a long war, but the deficiency is not nearly as great as it was a few years ago, and petroleum output is one of the most rapidly rising facets of the whole Soviet bloc productive setup today. They certainly have enough petroleum for the kind of atomic war which depends on an initial devastation of the enemy.

Thus far we have been concerned with existing Soviet potentials and their present utilization. But we need also to project our thinking forward and make a reasonable estimate of Soviet bloc capabilities in the future. A thesis which has been developed by a number of writers—Mr. Peter Wyles, writing in "Foreign Affairs," Mr. Theodore White, writing in "The Reporter," and others—is that judging by past trends, Communist production is growing about 10 per cent a year. Our own production, on the other hand, is growing only about 3 to 5 per cent. Now, it is argued, if we take these percentages and extrapolate them and then look ahead ten or twenty or thirty years, there will be a point in the not too distant ftutre at which the Communist world will out-produce us and therefore exceed us in military economic strength. The Communist hare will have outstripped the Capitalist tortoise. This is a new school of economic defeatism, not unlike the secular stagnation school of the nineteen-thirties.

I want to challenge that school of thought although I also want to give it its due. The basic difficulty with this kind of mechanical extrapolation is that it leaves too much out of account. It is entirely reasonable, on the basis of the kind of argument I have sketched above, to suppose that by 1960 the Soviet economic bloc would probably have production of some key materials amounting roughly to the following amounts: 70 million metric tons of steel, 55 or 60 million metric tons of pig iron, 650 million metric tons of coal, 70 million metric tons of petroleum, and 300 billion or more kilowatt hours of electric power. This is 25 per cent more than their present production. Certainly if by 1960 the Communist were to have any such production of these basic commodities, together with related production of machinery and other raw materials, there would be no question but that the Communist world could out-produce us militarily, unless we stepped up military production greatly. However, these production figures are unlikely of attainment because the projections from which they have been derived ignore the basic tensions and difficulties which accompany vast changes and which have been particularly manifest in economic growth in the past.

These difficulties and tensions are easy to discern. First is the fact that within the Soviet Union a great many of the richest sources of raw material, particularly coal and iron ore, have been seriously depleted by the frantic concentration within the past quarter of a century upon the resources of a few highly localized areas. In coal, for instance, the Donetz Basin is today a far leaner, far less satisfactory source than it was ten or twenty years ago. In iron ore, the Magnitogorsk and Krivoi Rog are today giving far poorer iron ore than they gave even ten years ago. The Magnitogorsk material which was thrown away ten or fifteen years ago is today close to the average level of richness. What this means is that the Communist world is more and more having to go to new resources which are either geographically distant or which are technologically unsatisfactory, such as the ores in the Kursk Magnetic Anomaly. Thus, simply from the exhaustion of some of their richest natural resources, difficult problems are already arising.

More fundamentally, the Communist world is facing today the fact that its past extraordinary concentration upon heavy industry has been possible only because of the great neglect of the standard of living of the people and the production of consumer goods, agricultural products, and housing.

Even Mr. Malenkov has admitted the truth of this observation. He said recently that the Soviet people do not have enough consumer goods and that the quality of Soviet consumer goods is often poor. Ostensibly for this reason he announced certain concessions. The Soviet economy is going to produce more consumer goods. The regime is going to tax the individual peasant less heavily, and so on. This might lead to the conclusion that the Communists intend to divert a large part of their industrial potential and resources from heavy to light industry and to agriculture; and that they must, therefore, in the future, have a much slower rate of economic progress than they have had in the past. I doubt that this is the case although, of course, it is not outside the realm of possibility.

If we analyze Mr. Malenkov's statements and figures, we find, I believe, that what he is really trying to do is to make certain peripheral, not fundamental, concessions. A small increase in the amount of consumer goods and relatively minor concessions to the collective farm peasants have been promised. None of these small concessions announced so far are basic, nor are they as important as some of the things that have not been done. The forty-eight hour week is still the basic work week of the Soviet economy as it was under Stalin. The entire corpus of legislation setting down stringent rules regarding work discipline for both industrial workers and collective farmers is retained intact despite the promise made at the end of March, at the time of the Amnesty Decree, that this legislation would be significantly eased. The basic nature of the collective farming system has been reaffirmed and the farmers have been told that if they do not put in their obligatory minimum number of works days, they are going to have their taxes raised 50 per cent. Mr. Malenkov has also announced that heavy industry is the "basis of the foundation" of the Soviet economic system, and you certainly do not destroy the basis of the foundation of anything if you can help it.

Thus the strategy of the new rulers appears to be, for the moment, both at home and in the satellite areas, to make relatively small concessions in the Soviet Union and relatively greater concessions in the satellite countries like East Germany and Hungary. These concessions will help consolidate their power for the time being. Later when they feel that their power is more secure, they can return to the Stalinist path.

Here, then, is really the key problem of our time from the economist's point of view. Can Mr. Malenkov and his associates carry out this policy of limited retreat? In spirit, this is simply the new economic policy of the early nineteen-twenties with the difference that the commanding heights of the Malenkov regime are far more powerful and extensive than those of Lenin while Lenin's concessions were more far-reaching than Malenkov's. We don't know whether Malenkov will win or lose his gamble, but I think that for the short run ahead there may be some slowing down of the Soviet heavy industrial program. For the long run, however, they are going to try to push ahead as rapidly as before and they will come up against the basic technology and raw material factors I mentioned earlier. All these considerations suggest the need for caution in forecasting Soviet bloc economic progress.

Two special problems may be anticipated in the future. One is Malthusian. The Soviet population, according to Mr. Beria before he was "unmasked" as an "imperialist agent," is now growing by more than three million people a year. If you multiply this by ten or twenty years, you can see that the Soviet Union is going to have a difficult time just keeping up with the growth of the population. China is going to have an even more difficult time because one of the first results in China of the Communist rule should be a much more rapid increase of population than they have had in the past.

Finally, one other possibility of discord arises from the economic factors involved here. The magic word among the Communist leaders is still "industrialization." This is the new god of communism, replacing Marx. In particular, the Chinese want to industrialize. They want to be able to build their own tanks, their own planes, and their own atomic bombs. Much as they may claim to love the big Russian brother, they would rather produce their own armaments. They have said so time and again.

If the Chinese are to meet the kind of industrialization

schedule they have in mind, they have got to get help from abroad. They must get machinery. They must get raw material. They also need technical know-how. This is one of the most difficult problems in the Moscow-Peking relationship, because the Soviet Union can have no great excess of capital goods if it is to continue its own rapid industrial expansion. What the Chinese want could swamp any surplus Moscow has had.

Where, then, is China going to get the capital goods for its future industrialization? On the answer to that question may well depend much, not only in the economic sphere but also in the political and military sphere.

In planning our national policy in the weeks and months ahead, we will be wise to base ourselves on a balanced view of the Soviet bloc's economic strength. The attempt to present such a view has been my purpose. The Soviet economy is capable of great technical and production feats. We have no alternative but to prepare our own defenses against the flood of weapons that has been and is being turned out in the Soviet Union. But the very concentration upon military-economic potential may very well be the Achilles heel, politically, of the Soviet system. For the moment the Soviet leaders are seeking to correct that weakness and to give their people some of the benefits of economic progress which have been denied them for so long. But we shall need far more convincing evidence than we now have to shake our conviction that fundamentally the Soviet economy is a war economy and is likely to remain one for the foreseeable future.

Only when the Soviet people have far more influence upon their government and their economy than they have under today's oligarchial rule is this situation likely to change. But when that happy time will arrive, no man can tell.

RAYMOND H. FISHER: ***Discussion***
University of California

Mr Schwartz referred in his talk to the thesis of Peter Wiles [1] and Theodore H. White [2] relative to the higher rate of expansion of the economy of the Soviet Union and its satellites, and indicated that it is a thesis with which he disagrees. Although I reserve judgment as to whether this thesis is well founded or rests on a shaky interpretation of the statistical data, I believe it is a point of view worth considering—particularly in some of its implications.

According to the reading of the data by Mr. Wiles and Mr. White the Soviet Union and its European satellites are increasing their productive capacity at a more rapid rate than are the noncommunist countries, including the United States. The rate of increase in Soviet industrial output is calculated to be between 12 and 15 per cent per annum compounded annually, which means that it doubles every five or six years. Moreover, the increase is part of a long-range plan and is executed with determination. In contrast, the rate of increase in western Europe is placed at about 5 per cent per annum compounded annually, as is that of the United States. Extrapolating the present rates of growth of the Soviet Union and of western Europe, we can expect that Soviet industrial capacity should become equal to that of western Europe by 1960.

Meanwhile, the rate of industrial growth in the satellite countries is also greater than that of western Europe. If the present difference continues, eastern Europe should overtake western Europe by the middle 1970's, though the law of diminishing returns will probably postpone it for some ten years.

Combined with this high rate of growth is the fact that up to the present the emphasis in the expansion of industrial capacity of the Soviet bloc has been on heavy industry, upon capital or producers' goods, with deliberate neglect of consumers' goods. This Mr. Schwartz has made clear. Such emphasis on producers' goods is possible in these countries because of the centralized

[1] "The Soviet Economy Outpaces the West," *Foreign Affairs*, XXXI, No. 4 (July, 1953), 566–80.

[2] "The Challenge of Soviet Economic Growth," *The Reporter*, VIII, No. 11 (May 26, 1953), 9–14.

and comprehensive planning and control which the state exercises over the economy and the people. The governments of these states have been able to ignore consumer demands and interests—and make the people accept it until recently, at least—and to force a rate of savings and investment in capital goods which have not been possible in the noncommunist countries except in time of war, and then only by the imposition of extensive controls. However, recent developments in the satellite countries indicate that their governments may have gone too far in neglecting consumers' interests, though, on the other hand, the Soviet regime has managed to do so with considerable impunity for twenty-five years. One can point to the great poverty which has resulted for the peoples of the Soviet bloc and minimize the threat which they hold for us, but that ignores the point stressed by Mr. Schwartz that productive capacity and ability to direct it to the ends of power are more significant than the standard of living.

This higher rate of industrial expansion and emphasis on heavy industry might remain matters of academic interest were it not for the revolutionary objectives pursued by the Soviet Union. Western Europe's superiority in industrial production, along with our own industrial might, has given the West a sense of security which is due for reconsideration. Sober thought requires that we look seriously at the threat—and challenge—which the growing economic strength of the Soviet bloc poses for us.

The one threat which comes to mind first is the military power which Soviet industrialization makes possible and is intended to make possible. Since Mr. Schwartz has already elaborated upon the military potential of the Soviet Union, it is superfluous to repeat the argument here. Rather, I would point to a second threat—perhaps challenge is the better term—which this industrialization holds for the West. It is a challenge which I feel merits more attention than it has received.

This threat, or challenge, is the appeal which the technique of rapid industrialization promises to make in certain parts of the world. One may well ask whether Asiatic peoples are going to be content with the slower, even though more humane, technique and methods of industrialization associated with liberal democracy in face of the demonstration by the Soviet Union and its satellite states that centralized planning, party and police control, and forced savings provide a more rapid way to the industrialization which promises freedom from foreign domination. To peoples mired in poverty and sensitive to Western imperialism, the effectiveness of Soviet methods of industrialization and the promise of a higher standard of living may well lead them to overlook or minimize the costs of such methods. For many Asiatics, human beings are not the precious entities that they are in the West, and to such Asiatics the results of forced industrialization may appear well worth the cost. As a student of history I sometimes wonder if the historian of 2053 will look back upon this age and conclude that the significant contribution of the Soviet Union was not its efforts to put into operation the teachings of Karl Marx, but that it made the first, perhaps crude, attempt to develop a technique of rapid industrialization of backward peoples.

Be that as it may, it seems to me that liberal democracy must show that rapid industrialization is possible under its system if Soviet influence, which means Soviet imperialism, is to be checked. *The Economist* (London) for December 20, 1952, puts the issue forcefully in these words:

> A democratic government is a poor saver. . . . An authoritarian government on the Eastern model, willing to exact large forced savings and itself taking responsibility for most of the objects of investment, can save what it chooses. But in a liberal society, saving depends on self-help. It is the . . . people as individuals and as shareholders in enterprises who must save. . . .
>
> China's transformation will take place under the star of Communism and total rule. If the Soviet analogy holds good, the people will be battered into economic growth. India, in choosing the way of liberal democracy, has renounced the weapons by which spectacular progress can be achieved. Left to its own poverty, it cannot win the race to economic strength in which, in the eyes of all Asia, it is now engaged against China.

This challenge may well go farther. Malenkov's recent speech points to an increase in the production of consumer goods in the Soviet Union. Whether this increase be one resulting from more emphasis on consumers' goods at the expense of producers' goods or from an over-all increase in all production makes little difference in the propaganda appeal which such an increase can effect among the poor peoples of the world. But supposing that the Soviet leaders decide at last to make the raising of the standard of living of their people their primary goal, shifting the emphasis of their plans to light industry. To be sure, in terms of our own principles, improving the well-being of the Soviet peoples is, by itself, highly desirable. Yet would not this have an explosive effect on the peoples of the backward and undeveloped countries of the world, with the likelihood that the explosion would be turned to the advantage of the Soviet Union and to the detriment of the noncommunist world?

It is not the possibility that the depressed peoples of the world may have their standard of living uplifted that disturbs me. Far from it. It is the possibility that it may be Soviet power which brings about the uplifting that gives cause for concern. I would much prefer that Western power did it and that the resulting explosion would work to our benefit, not to the furthering of Soviet imperialism. It is with this idea in mind that I think we should concern ourselves with such a Soviet prospect to the end that we forestall it as a reality.

An Evaluation of Soviet Scientific Capabilities

CONWAY ZIRKLE,
University of Pennsylvania

In spite of the fact that secrecy has become a Soviet fetish, the present status of science in Russia is known with fair accuracy. A nation may be able to conceal certain specific discoveries or certain technical applications, but the general state of its scientific research and development cannot be hidden or camouflaged. The scientists of the world know just how their own specialties are faring everywhere, and this is fortunate for us because we should know what the Russians are accomplishing in science. Only last December the American Association for the Advancement of Science published a symposium, *Soviet Science*, in which the major developments in Russia were described. I refer you to this work for an account of what the Russians are doing and what their physical capacities are. In this paper I shall confine myself to the imponderable factors for these furnish us with clues as to the future of science in the Communist world. Science is now growing at an unprecedented rate, and the future of any nation, its ability to work good or ill, will depend in great part upon whether or not its technology will enable it to keep up with its rivals.

We know the present status of Soviet science and we understand a great deal about the social forces which have conditioned its development—about the alarms and excursions which have reduced it to its present level.[1] If conditions in Russia continue

[1] Conway Kirkle, *Death of a Science in Russia,* (Philadelphia: 1949); "The involuntary destruction of science in the U.S.S.R," *Scientific Monthly,* 1953, Vol. 76, 277-83.

as they are, we can say definitely that her science will have no real future of its own. It will deteriorate, although it may be kept functional by what it is able to smuggle in from other countries. Conditions in Russia, however, are not static; they are changing constantly, and these changes will determine the fate of her science. When we try to predict these changes, however, we are faced with a great uncertainty, for here we enter a realm where our basic information is too incomplete to allow us to draw definite conclusions. The best we can do is to list the most reasonable alternatives; we are on much firmer ground when we evaluate the effects of the specific actions which the Russians may, or may not, take. A reversal of the present policies might well restore all the Russian sciences to health, but, as things now stand, we can write off a number of Russian sciences as nonexistent.

To evaluate Russian science adequately, to bring to bear all of the pertinent data, would enable us to place Soviet science in its proper setting in the general picture of world science. However, we would have to trace the history of science, to explain its vicissitudes, its growths, stagnations, and decays; and, if our exposition were to have meaning, we would have to identify the basic conditions which help or hinder science. Here we can state only that the growth of science has been extraordinarily spotty—both as to place and time. At no one time, however, has science ever been healthy over more than a tiny portion of the earth's surface, nor have the scientists themselves formed more than a minute fraction of the population of even the leading scientific nations. The real growth of modern science, from the Renaissance until late in the nineteenth century, was in fact limited to a minor portion of Europe, to the central and northwestern regions. Science in the rest of the world was both derivative and backward. In spite of the fact that some good science and a few outstanding scientists were found in both the United States and Russia, it was not until the last seventy-five years that these nations made their bid to become leaders in scientific research, and it was not until after the first world war that their bids could be taken seriously.

First-rate science, of course, depends upon the existence of first-rate scientists, and there are no techniques for developing just anyone into a scientist. Those who can be so developed are always rare. They are extreme Mendelian segregants—scarce even under optimum conditions. Nothing is easier than to increase the number of men we label scientists, but nowhere is it more dangerous to substitute quantity for quality than in the development of a scientific personnel. The failure to recognize this led perhaps to the first major error of the Communists. Their continuing failure to recognize that all men are not equal is still a major hazard to the recovery of their science. But granting the possibilities of a recovery, what are the Russian potentialities?

This question is easy to answer—they are good. We know definitely that Russia can produce scientists who are really "tops"—she has already done so. Some Russian scientists have been as good as any which have been produced anywhere. They have not been as numerous as those of England, France, and Germany, and the per capita production in Russia may never begin to approach that of Switzerland, Sweden, or Holland, but Russia has the potential of producing great scientists. In the early days of communism, when Lenin gave Russian science the full support of the state but before the dead hand of bureaucratic stupidity descended upon it, it made truly great progress. If Russia had been able to solve the problem of giving her scientists all of the state support they could use profitably, yet at the same time keeping them free, her science would have maintained its eminence and the whole world would have been the richer. Her failure to solve this problem was complete and tragic and, in time, disastrous. Perhaps this problem cannot be solved by a totalitarian state.

We should consider, however, what might happen if Russian science should develop under ideal conditions and with no limitations on it except those set by nature. Our conclusions, of course, cannot be precise, for allowances must be made for a large margin of error in our speculations. However, if we consider the history of Russian science, the unfavorable conditions which have inhibited it in the past, the size and quality of her present population, and her interest in and support of science, we can arrive at some provisional conclusions. It is safe to assume that the number of her first-rate scientific contributions would be less than those of either the United States, Germany, or Britain, but more than those of France, Italy, or the smaller European nations. At times she should rank first or second in a science—third, fourth, or fifth in others—in some even less but, over the years, she should be very good indeed. However, all of this presupposes that she discovers some method by which she can get out of her present difficulties and recover from the blight of her totalitarianism.

For Marxian authoritarianism has interposed a number of major hazards to the development of an honest and objective science. We can consider here but three of the more striking of these hazards. They are, first, the forced production of great numbers of really stupid and opportunistic "scientists," who, for self-protection have had to destroy both the integrity of their science and the able men who might expose them. Second, the final control and planning of science in Communist lands remain in the hands of nonscientists—of career bureaucrats whose personal fortunes often conflict with the demands of intellectual integrity. And third, the prevalence of Marxian dogmas which are in direct conflict with present scientific knowledge and thus limit the advancement of science. We can be certain that Russian science will not prosper unless these hazards are removed. Moreover, there is one other basic condition which will have to be altered before her science can recover, i. e., the Communists will have to correct their widespread and almost universal disregard of the truth. Where the truth is not valued for its own sake, science will lead a precarious existence.

The attempt to make good scientists out of essentially stupid men is so obviously futile that it is difficult for us to understand why any nation would attempt it. Yet this is what the Russians have tried to do, and they seem to have been led into the attempt through a blind application of a doctrinaire equalitarianism. Apparently they believed that anyone could be developed into a scientist. Now it is quite true that no nation has ever developed all of its potentially good scientists. Many studies made on the origins and numbers of American scientists, for example, demonstrate this clearly. But the number which can be produced at any one time is never unlimited. In terms of the whole population, it is always small, and when attempts are made to develop a great many scientists very quickly, it does not take long before the available talent is exhausted. There is no real limit, of course, to the number of men we can label as scientists if we lower our standards sufficiently, but when the number of prospects is increased beyond certain definite limits, a catastrophic decrease in their ability occurs. Some figures from our own population are illustrative. There are 50,000 names in the last edition of our directory of scientists, the *American Men of Science.* This represents only one citizen in every 3,000. From 1903 to 1943, some 2,600 scientists have been "starred" by their colleagues. If 1,500 of these are still living, they would represent one citizen in 100,000. The most eminent of our scientists, members of the National Academy of Science, number less than 500, or one citizen in over 300,000—less than one scientist in 100.

Now obviously the leading scientists do not have a monopoly of our national brains. For instance, many engineers and physicians have the potentialities of becoming first-rate research workers in pure science. But we need good engineers and good doctors of medicine. Brains are also not out of place in the legal profession, in management, in higher army brass, in congress. We desperately need brains also in our political and administrative leadership. However, the question before us is not how many American citizens can become first-rate scientists, but what proportion of our available brains can we afford to dedicate to science. An excellent brain devoted to atomic physics is an excellent brain not devoted to the advancement of legal theory, to the history of art, to international relations, or to military strategy or logistics. These same limitations apply to Russia.

Signs are multiplying that we cannot increase greatly the number of our scientists without lowering their quality to a dangerous extent. And another danger—the sciences are already beginning to deplete the brains of competing occupations. Right now in our undergraduate institutions certain sciences have their pick of students with the result that some disciplines have to be content with second-raters. The National Science Foundation has been granting predoctoral fellowships for two years now. While it is true that some of their screening procedures have been defective and major errors have been made, little can be gained by merely increasing the number of awards. The limiting factor with us seems to be talent, not money. The situation in Russia is similar, but the Russians have not realized it.

In the days of Lenin, they started to create scientists in wholesale lots. They got quantity, but the average quality was so low that a great many could not pass their university examinations. But this inconvenience was overcome by a typically communistic remedy. Cooperation was the answer. The students were divided into small groups who passed their examinations altruistically, with mutual aid and assistance. When a group was successful, all the members became scientists. Some of the horrifying examples of ignorance and stupidity which some Soviet scientists now display can be traced to those who passed their examinations cooperatively.

We must not overlook the fact, however, that Russia still has many good scientists and that, in certain fields, some of them are still doing excellent research. In other fields, however, the good scientists have been swamped by the incompetents and have been forced by the clamor of their colleagues and by political pressure to recant and to foreswear any knowledge which conflicts with Marxian orthodoxy or which the average run of the new "scientists" find puzzling. The best illustration of this is to be found in genetics. Anything in this science which is too complicated for Lysenko to understand is now wrong and reactionary. We in the West see little of these horrible specimens, for only rarely are any of them allowed to leave their homeland. Occasionally, as when some party-line biologists were sent to the International Botanical Congress in Stockholm (1951), and later sent to comfort the faithful in England, we catch a glimpse of them. They turned out to be fascinating, for they do not know how funny they were. If all Russian scientists were as bad as their biologists, Russian science would be a joke —but in certain other fields Russian scientists are really good.

Can the Russians recognize their mistakes and correct them? Perhaps, but there are obstacles in the way. They must first change some of their basic concepts and, in addition, they must have the fortitude to face some inconvenient facts. They must learn to judge between two conflicting hypotheses on the basis of the evidence—and not on eloquent but unsupported claims.

They must learn not to accept automatically the hypotheses which promise the most. One of the reasons why the Central Committee of the Communist party decided in favor of Lysenko and outlawed genetics was that Lysenko promised more than any good scientist would dare promise. In fields where the results cannot be measured simply or directly, the big promise may win until it is too late too correct the choice. The naïve environmentalism of the Communists makes big promises seem reasonable—even promises which cannot be checked without complicated scientific controls, and we have evidence that those in final authority in Russia have no understanding of scientific controls.

Any hypothesis which promises less than the maximum is suspected automatically and is taken as evidence of sabotage; those who support it are attacked as bourgeois reactionaries and enemies of the people. In addition to this, all research which discloses unwelcomed facts is discouraged. The study of identical twins, for example, gives some valuable data on both the hereditary and environmental variables, but the implications of the discoveries made here were obviously resented. It is significant that work at the Maxim Gorky Institute on identical twins was stopped suddenly in 1939 and nothing further was heard of the psychologists in charge of the work.[2] Intelligence tests also give results that the Communists do not like, so intelligence tests must go. C. G. T. Giles, writing this year in the party-line magazine, *Anglo-Soviet Journal* (Vol. 14, 11–15), in an article entitled " Why Soviet teachers oppose intelligence tests," states that:

> . . . The revolt against testing came first from the teachers and from parents. Teachers found that I. Q. tests gave results contradicting those obtained by individual observation in school, with a wide margin of error. Moreover, they found that such tests underrated especially children from unfavorable environments. (Quite true, but are there unfavorable environments in the U.S.S.R.?) *Above all, the generally accepted norms seemed to deny the possibility of educating the children needed to provide sufficient*

[2] H. H. Newman, *Multiple Human Births,* (Chicago: 1940).

> *people qualified up to the necessary standard.* (Author's italics.)

So, down with intelligence tests! There seems to be no immediate prospect of improving the quality of the new crop of Russian scientists.

The second hazard to the development of a sound science is the fact that the final control and planning of science in Communistic countries is in the hands of nonscientists. Professor Michael Polanyi has described the ill effects of this system so accurately and eloquently that there is little that I can add.[3] Polanyi has shown that when the final authority in science is not possessed by the scientists themselves, quacks will flourish and ultimately dominate the field. This occurs because the technically untrained are unable, in the last analysis, to distinguish between scientists and charlatans, and secondly, the plausible oversimplifications of quackery always have an immense popular appeal. Even with the very best intentions, the political authorities cannot decide scientific questions. It is only when science is autonomous and scientists are free to expose quackery as it arises that imposters can be exposed before they reach positions of power.

This is true in all nations and not just in Russia. We have many examples right in Washington. What we call "scientific method," tests which are quantitative, with sufficient controlled experiments, seem to be just beyond the grasp of the generality. A recent incident, for example, is to be found in the method of establishing the claims of a very famous battery additive. In a Congressional Committee hearing, Senator Edward Thye of Minnesota is reported to have said (*Time,* July 6, 1953, 18): "That means more to me than the technical talk of a bunch of chemists. . . . If a good, hard-fisted businessman has used the product . . . and is fool enough to come up and place orders month after month, what is the matter with him? Or otherwise, what is the matter with the Bureau of Standards test?" This "satisfied customer" method, which so impressed Senator Thye, has been, of course, the standard procedure of the patent medi-

[3] I refer you to his paper, "The Autonomy of Science," *Scientific Monthly,* 1945, Vol. 60, 141.

cine manufacturers for several generations. Testimonials have "proved" many times that any nostrum can cure anything. Fortunately, the American Medical Association has other standards. But we can imagine what would happen if our scientists were not free to protest and if they had to hail Secretary Weeks and Senator Thye as the greatest scientists of all time.

In Russia, not only is the party line in science drawn by nonscientists, but in addition certain dogmatic formulas of research are insisted on. Here it is not the hard-fisted businessman who is "our hero," but the working men and women, the shrewd laborers. This research stance is harmless enough in itself, merely a pinch of incense on the altar of Jove, but when it is used by a charlatan, it may undermine a science. Indeed, this was a technique which gave Lysenko his start. I quote from an unpublished manuscript of a distinguished Russian scientist now doing research in the United States:

> But Lysenko did not push his fortunes in the USSR on the basis of these experiments. He started to make experiments and check them, not at the experimental stations or in the Institutes, but in the so-called "House-laboratories" at the collective farms. These laboratories were organized at the collective farms by the Government chiefly for propaganda purposes. They were headed by farmers entirely ignorant in the methods of conducting experiments. Lysenko made his experiments . . . at these collective farms. While the scientific institutions and experimental stations found that these experiments did not show increase in yield of old well-adapted varieties, the "house-laboratories" at the farms which conducted the experiments under wrong methodological conditions showed unprecedented increase in yield. Not educated in the rules of conducting the experiments, the farmers generally planted the vernalized seeds earlier than the control, they gave them better soil and feeding conditions, cultivated the plantings after vernalization earlier to receive better results because each farmer and every collective farm was afraid to show negative results. If the results were not promising or were negative, Lysenko and Present considered such a collective farm a bad farm and the farmers poor workers. Negative results were not published by Lysenko and Present. At the same time they cried in the newspapers about their success

> and about the farms which helped by their good work to embed the new methods of agriculture. Such farms received fine reputations and their administrations could expect to obtain different rewards from the Government. In such a way the new methods were approved. Of course, the people at scientific institutes and at the experimental stations could not agree with such methods of evidence.

This was the beginning of Lysenko's climb to power. Obviously he was not safe as long as honest scientists were free to oppose him. The elimination of these scientists then became a " must," which was achieved at the meeting of the Lenin Academy of Agriculture from July 31 to August 7, 1948. When he reported that the Central Committee of the Communist party had approved his stand, all opposition ceased and five scientists found it expedient to recant. Lysenko then got control of biological research in the Communist world.

The social control of science by the Communists has lasted long enough now to bring to light perhaps its most serious aspect. All scientists must conform. Those on the losing side of a controversy either recant or else—Siberia is always in the background. Those who would avoid disaster know what they have to do, and that is to be on the winning side. They may even enhance their own personal security by denouncing their colleagues, whose published work has committed them to the losing side. The effects of this situation can readily be recognized. In fields where the politicians interfere, all are reduced to the lowest common denominator. Scientists who are either intimidated or merely disgusted act just like the quacks. In consequence, the Soviet career politicians have no way of discovering what their scientists really believe. They have cut themselves off from the truth. Even if Stalin, Malenkov, or Molotov had wanted to know the truth about Mendel, they could not learn it. They could find no reason to believe what anyone would tell them.

The third hazard is the Communist party line in science. Only recently have we learned how far this line extends and how much of modern science it excludes. Enforced literally, it would even forbid the utilization of atomic energy as it is wedded to the nineteenth century definition of matter, but fortunately for the Soviet physicists, they are allowed a number of verbalistic evasions. If their atom bombs explode, their double talk is not analyzed semantically.[4] The Soviet chemists are also allowed to quibble, provided their work remains useful. Both Albert Einstein and Ernst Mach are major villains in Russia and their contributions cannot be acknowledged openly,[5] as Lenin himself set the line which excludes them. Practically every basic concept of modern physics is condemned and the materialistic philosophy of communism extends even so far as to deny the theory of resonance in chemistry. The party line also runs right through astronomy where it approves certain hypotheses concerning the origin of the solar system and forbids others.

These sciences, however, have thus far escaped all purges and heresy hunts. Here lip service to dialectic materialism and to communism is apparently sufficient. If the scientists watch their words, their scientific work is not injured by too much party-line meddling. Much excellent work is still being done in these fields. In mathematics, where the party line does not interfere, Russian work is truly excellent. Any country could be proud of the Russian mathematicians.

Communist orthodoxy has done its major damage in the biological, medical, and agricultural sciences. In these fields intellectual integrity has been destroyed and the scientists liquidated. Marx and Engels in the eighteen-seventies set the party line in evolution theory and in heredity; their archaic notions have now congealed into a holy doctrine. It took this doctrine from 1926 to 1948 to gain complete control of genetical theory but, when it did, the results were spectacular. The utter destruction of Russian genetics rapidly ensued.

In 1950 the Soviet physiologists found that it was their turn to be put through the wringer. Here the line was set by Pavlov, a great physiologist in his time. Russian physiologists, even

[4] The dilemma of the Soviet physicists is explained in a paper, *The diamat and the point of view of modern physics,* by Paul S. Epstein (mimeographed in English), printed in French in *Preuves,* 1951, No. 10, 3.

[5] V. M. Tatevskii and M. I. Shakhparanov in *Voprosi Filosofii,* 1949, No. 3, 176; translated (mimeographed) by Irving S. Bengelsdorf.

Pavlov's own students, who had the temerity to go beyond him, have been rebuked and compelled to confess. They are allowed to work but only under supervision, and the attacks on them continue. As late as April 15 of this year, Biryukov, in *Izvestia,* questioned the sincerity of their confessions of error. Cellular pathology, cytology, psychology, and psychiatry have almost disappeared, and what is left of them exists only on the sufferance of the Commissars. Soil science is still practically limited to the little that Vasilly R. Williams could understand; and Russian statistics now has the function of "proving" that whatever decision the Party makes is the correct one.[6]

One aspect of this impact of Communist orthodoxy on Soviet science we should note most carefully: it affects the different sciences differently. In physics or engineering, where the validity of research can be measured easily and directly, it does little damage. In medicine and agriculture, where many factors enter into the end results and where quackery is often difficult to expose, its effects have been fatal. In certain of these fields, no scientists are left.

Science can be advanced only by those who revere the truth. In the past, science has lived in many lands and has made great progress in regions which now produce nothing. Science can be destroyed and has been—often. Wherever the climate of opinion is hostile to intellectual honesty, the existence of science is precarious. How do the Russian Communists look upon the truth?

The great geneticist, William Bateson, visited Russia in 1886. One of his observations sounds as if it were written yesterday:

> He found that the information given to him by Russians was unreliable. It was not that they meant to lie, but they did not know what the truth is.[7]

The recently published proceedings of the various Russian academies and scientific institutions are now available, and we can tell from these just how the Russians ignore the truth. We know what they said and did when genetics, physiology, and statistics were warped to fit the current orthodoxy. Not once were any real scientific data presented; the facts seemed unim-

[6] S. A. Rice, *Scientific Monthly,* 1952, Vol. 75, 71.

[7] J. G. Crowther, *British Scientists of the Twentieth Century,* 257.

portant. What was important was the proper pose, the proper stance. Quotations were split so that the meanings could be misrepresented. Discredited experiments were presented as fact, e. g., in 1948 the results claimed by Kammerer were quoted as valid although Kammerer himself had confessed in 1926 that they were faked. Many other examples could also be cited. History, of course, in Russia is made to order, but the specifications are constantly changing. As Bertram D. Wolfe expresses it:

> Histories succeed each other as if they were being consumed by a giant chain smoker, who lights the first volume of the new work with the last of the old. Historians appear, disappear and reappear; others vanish without trace.[8]

Specifications are changing also in so many fields that the Great Bolshevik Encyclopedia apparently cannot be completed. The earlier volumes must be burned before the later ones can be finished. It might be well to insert here a quotation from Frank Rounds, Jr., taken from *A Window on Red Square*:

> The thing hardest to take in Russia is not so much the secret police, not even slave labor with all the human cruelty involved, as bad as these things are: to my mind the thing hardest to take, day in and night out, is the lie—the big meaningful lie and the glib little lie. More than anything in the world I hate the cool willingness of the handful in the Kremlin to lie about *anything*, any hour; and not only a willingness, but a rare ability to do so. And this willingness and ability seem to be at the root of the whole system.

Now, what of the future of Russian science? Within limits, it is anybody's guess. We can be certain that, under decent conditions, Russia will produce many great scientists and their contributions will deserve our full respect.

The question which now faces us is: will or can the Communists create an intellectual climate in which science can thrive? In the distant future we may hope for the best, but present conditions are discouraging. Even if the Central Committee has the best possible intentions, their power for good is

[8] *Foreign Affairs*, 1952, Vol. 31, 39.

limited. We know what they must do if Russian science is to recover, but it may be psychologically impossible for them to take the necessary steps. They would have to take most drastic action.

The party line would have to be reversed in statistics, soil science, physiology, psychology, clinical medicine, pathology, evolution theory, and genetics. Can this be done? Perhaps—it is remotely possible. Some reversals have already taken place. Stalin himself changed the line in linguistics by merely writing a paper, and Russian linguistics was given the chance to make up for lost time. Then, too, some of the quacks who rode to power with Lysenko have already been liquidated, and Lysenko himself is now criticized in no uncertain language. Perhaps his days are numbered, but no steps have yet been taken to reverse his biology. The Communists have also started to hedge in soil science, for now Williams' theories (in double talk) "must not be applied too literally and dogmatically." The famous group of Moscow doctors who confessed to malpractice, murder, and treason have, after the death of Stalin, unconfessed themselves. The woman doctor, who was one of the chief accusers of the group—which included, incidentally, her own husband—and who was decorated by the state for her efforts, has been rebuked and has had her prize taken away from her. She may even have had to take her husband back! These instances show that the Russians can reverse a party line in science. Will they do so in the sciences which they have injured most?

In some sciences, the reversal of the party line is easy. In soil science, only Williams need be repudiated. The line in statistics can be changed as easily as it was in linguistics. In physiology all that is needed is to allow the science to grow beyond the point reached by Pavlov. The same is true for psychology. In pathology, however, the Communists will have to repudiate Engels himself, and this will be harder. The real difficulty will arise if attempts are made to revive genetics and evolution theory, for here not only will Michurin and Lysenko have to be repudiated, but also Stalin and the Central Committee of the Communist party. And in addition to all this, the Communists will have to confess that the biology of Marx and Engels is in error, and this may be impossible.

But the Kremlin faces another problem. How will they know what they should do? They cannot trust the advice of their own scientists, for now the Russian scientists will tell their masters what they think their masters want to hear. Can the Kremlin take its view from the scientists of the free world? They know something is wrong with their science, but can they trust the bourgeois scientists? Might not the scientists who are the tools and slaves of the capitalists play some sort of joke on the true believers in Marx?

How can Soviet science recover? There is a long hard road ahead. Mathematics is sound; astronomy, physics, and chemistry can be freed from the verbalistic nuisances without too much trouble. Geology can be relieved of its "practical application" shackles. These sciences will recover if only they are let alone, if they are supported but freed from political meddling. But disciplines which are now controlled by quacks cannot be rescued so easily. Fields in which no scientists remain can recover quickly only if scientists from abroad are imported to teach a native crop or if Russian students are sent abroad to study. Can this happen? What honest geneticist would now care to go to Russia to work, and what dangerous thoughts might not Russian students acquire abroad? Foreign scientific publications can and are being bought by the Russians in great numbers. This helps, but more is needed. At best Russian recovery will be very slow. But we must not forget that the sciences which *directly* affect the Russian military strength are the ones which have been injured least.

We can readily see that the Soviet authorities have gotten themselves into a very serious dilemma. We should watch their actions with the greatest interest and should be alert to discover just what actions they take. No matter what they do, they should be very amusing.

LAZAR VOLIN: ***Discussion***
Department of Agriculture

In appraising the present state and the potentialities of science in Russia, I think that it is instructive to glance at the pre-Soviet stage of Russian history, particularly the half century preceding the revolution of 1917. For this period witnessed a flowering of Russian science, as a phase of a general cultural upsurge. Many branches of science, both natural and social, made remarkable strides and a number of Russian scholars won world-wide recognition.

This took place under political conditions that were much less auspicious for scientific and general intellectual progress than in the West, though more favorable than those prevailing under the Soviet regime, whether under Lenin, Stalin, or his successors. From a mere pupil of the West, Russian science in that half century was increasingly becoming a valuable collaborator, standing on its own feet, but always maintaining close and friendly ties with the older Western science. I dealt with this point in greater detail in the symposium on Soviet science, mentioned by Professor Zirkle. What I want to emphasize here is the development of a genuine scientific tradition in pre-Soviet Russia; a tradition that emphasized quality of scholarship that knew no "iron curtain" or fatuous and vicious anti-Western propaganda, harping on often spurious achievements and claiming priority of practically all scientific and technological discoveries. It was this legacy from pre-Soviet Russia that provided a solid foundation for such further scientific development as took place under the Soviet regime. In fact, most of the illustrious scientists of whom the Soviet propaganda boasts had won their spurs, and some even died, before Lenin and Stalin became dictators.

Now, the significant fact about the prerevolutionary Russian science is that it won a substantial measure of that autonomy on which Professors Zirkle and Polanyi so strongly, and, I think, rightly, insist, as a *conditio sine qua non* of a healthy development of science. That a charlatan like Lysenko or even scholars like the historian Pokrovsky, or the soil scientist, Williams, or the philologist, Marr, could then set up, with the sanction of the government, an official dogma for every scientist to follow in his university teaching and research, was simply unthinkable. And this was true not only in the natural, but also in the social, sciences. Even in prerevolutionary Russian institutions of higher learning, teaching of economic theory from a Marxist standpoint was not uncommon.

But this situation was not achieved in Russia without constant vigilance and without a continuous struggle with the Czarist regime and its bureaucracy on the part of the scholars and students supported by progressive public opinion. Such a struggle on any significant scale is inconceivable today. It is impossible now, for instance, to imagine resignation of a large part of a university faculty protesting government interference with academic self-government, such as occurred at the University of Moscow in 1911. This is what augurs so ill for the prospects of science under Soviet totalitarianism.

For, if the scientific community cannot combat, or even protest against, the arbitrary interference of political authorities and if it cannot obtain the support of an independent public opinion, which simply does not exist in the USSR today, then who can change the climate that is so detrimental to scientific progress? The government itself? It is true, as Professor Zirkle points out, that the Kremlin senses that not all is well with Soviet science. For instance, a typical editorial in a recent issue of a Soviet agronomic journal complains of insufficient criticism of shortcomings in research work in agricultural sciences, contrary to the directive of comrade Stalin that ". . . no science can develop and thrive without a conflict of opinion, without freedom of criticism."[1] And the editorial then proceeds to cite from Malenkov's report at the Nineteenth Communist Party Congress in October, 1952, to the effect that,

> In a number of branches of science there has not been fully liquidated as yet the monopoly of separate groups of scholars pushing aside the growing fresh forces, fencing themselves off from criticism and attempting to solve scientific questions by administrative fiat. No branch of science can successfully develop in a stifling atmosphere of mutual praise and hushing up of errors; efforts to establish monopolies of separate groups of scholars invariably generate stagnation and decay in science.

Well, Professor Zirkle and I could not have done better in condemning the state of science in a totalitarian regime than

[1] *Sovetskaya Agronomiya,* 3, 1953, 6–14.

these authoritative Soviet statements. But, wait, a few paragraphs further on, the same editorial pontificates:

> The development of criticism and the free exchange of opinion among scientists presuppose, first of all, an increasing struggle and exposition of all kinds of reactionary bourgeois and idealistic manifestations in our science, [and] the strengthening of the only correct materialistic Michurinist [that is, Lysenkoist] teaching. Free exchange of opinion among scientists does not mean unhindered propaganda of any doctrines, including those that are antiscientific and erroneous, but calls for an irreconcilable struggle with such views.

And so on and so forth in the same vein, including approving references to the infamous purge of the geneticists "under the direction of the Central Committee of the Party and of Comrade Stalin personally." Now you have here the tragic problems of Soviet science revealed in a nutshell.

But fine words by Soviet rulers about the freedom of criticism and the danger of monopoly do not mean, in practice, free exchange and competition of ideas in the realm of science any more than in the other spheres of intellectual life under Soviet dictatorship. Such double talk cannot conceal the iron fist of a relentless party-state control and surveillance of science as of every other aspect of life under a totalitarian regime.

The dethronement of a gauleiter in this or that science occurred from time to time in the past and will, no doubt, occur in the future. Even so strongly entrenched a gauleiter as Lysenko, in biology, I think, is not immune, and there are, in fact, some indications, as Professor Zirkle noted, that he is slipping. After all, if so powerful a political figure as Beria could be liquidated, and if Karl Marx himself could be revised by Stalin, why not Lysenko, once the Soviet rulers become aware of the damage he is causing to Soviet agriculture. And, even in the Soviet Union, a little boy may be occasionally found who will at least whisper into the proper ears that "the king is naked," even if he does not cry out loud. But experience demonstrates that relief in such cases is likely to be partial and temporary. Another doctrinal monopoly, another dictator, individual or collective, replaces, under Soviet conditions, the one that has fallen. The fact, moreover, that the Kremlin values science exclusively for utilitarian ends—primarily for the enhancement of the power of the Communist state—is likely to lead to the neglect of pure science. This would tend to accentuate the adverse effects on scientific progress of a police state environment.

Therefore, I cannot be more encouraging about the general outlook for Soviet science than Professor Zirkle has been. I also agree with him, and I think it worth emphasizing, first, that not all sciences are equally weakened by Soviet totalitarian control; second, that fine work is still being done in many branches of Soviet science which warrants careful watching; and third, it is still too early to conclude that the deterioration, which undoubtedly has set in in Soviet science, has had an adverse effect on the Soviet military potential. Finally, despite the bleak prospects of Russian science under the Communist regime, its glorious history gives a ray of hope for a brighter future if and when Russia becomes again a free country.

The World Communist Movement

ROBERT N. CAREW HUNT,
Great Britain

The world Communist movement is so vast a subject that to attempt a brief survey of it is an alarming prospect. It is, however, one which is relevant to the subject of our conference —Soviet imperialism. Yet as to the precise degree of relevance there may be differences of opinion. National Communist parties undeniably assist the advance of Soviet imperialism. The difficulty is to determine to what extent Soviet imperialism is concerned with the advance of communism, or simply uses communism to further its ambition to attain world power. For in fact the difficulty is an illusory one, since the Russians would assuredly introduce their own social and economic order into any country over which they obtained control.

As to the motive which leads them to seek such control, we should do well not to be too dogmatic. Certainly the Russian leaders are not animated solely by a crusading zeal. Yet they have inherited a mission, and it is one which they cannot hope to carry out as long as they are opposed by any important group of countries. The desire for world power and the desire to introduce everywhere the Soviet way of life are simply the obverse and reverse of the same medal.

Hence, the constantly repeated statement that the Russians make use of Communist parties to promote their own foreign policy begs the question, as it leaves undetermined what that policy is. Every party member is told that his ultimate loyalty is to the Soviet Union. It is easy to take a cynical view of this. Yet the plain truth is that the strength of world communism over the years has advanced *pari passu* with that of the Soviet

Union. Were the Soviet regime to disappear, world communism would not present the problem that it does today.

The Soviet way of life, which we call communism, is the particular brand of socialism which was introduced into the Soviet Union after the October Revolution. The Russians contend that it possesses a universal validity, so that it provides the model to which every country should conform, and indeed must ultimately do if the dialectic is any guide. As they were responsible for it, they have claimed the right to interpret the principles on which it rests, and to determine the strategy and tactics which national Communist parties must adopt to give effect to these principles; and every party has long recognized the justice of this, even though it has been to its own hindrance. Any consideration of world communism must start therefore with the form which communism assumed in Russia.

What then is Russian communism, and why has it taken the form it has? No two authorities entirely agree in their answer to these questions. What is suggested here is that it is the consistent and ruthless application of Marx's teaching, and that it has led to a police state is only what might have been expected. The core of Marxism was that the "bourgeois state," that is, the whole socio-economic apparatus of bourgeois society, must be utterly destroyed, and that it was impermissible to use any part of it as the basis of a new social order. But in view of the primacy attributed to the economic factor, that part of it which had above all to be abolished was the private ownership of the means of production, the root cause of the class struggle. The productive resources must be transferred to society. Only then would be ended what Engels, following Saint-Simon, describes as "the anarchy of private enterprise," and it would become possible to plan social production intelligently. As to how it is to be planned no word is said. But just as the goal of Hegel's dialectic is the Idea acquiring complete self-consciousness in the Absolute, so that of the Marxist dialectic of history is a society free from conflict and thus self-sufficient. In such a society we are left to infer that social production will somehow plan itself. As Engels declares, "the administration of persons is replaced by the administration of things," though how the one can be administered without the other he does not explain.

In fact, however, no one has yet devised any workable system of the public ownership of the means of production which does not eventually mean that the state takes charge of them, as it (or rather the Communist party which controls the state) does in Russia. It is probable that Lenin's support of the Soviets was always conditional upon the party having the last word. When he wrote *State and Revolution* in 1917, did he genuinely believe in workers' control of industry, or did he only advocate it knowing that it would lead to confusion and thus pave the way for the dictatorship of the party? It is hard to say. What is certain is that it was tried and failed, and that within a few months he was himself demanding the most draconic disciplinary measures against the workers. Yet at one point in *State and Revolution* he showed a remarkable prescience. The transference of the means of production to public ownership and a planned society are of the essence of socialism, though it is only within our generation that planning has assumed its present highly technical form. The problem has always been to reconcile the two, unless the first is to be understood in a purely formal sense, and the only group of Western Socialists squarely to face it were the Fabians whose leaders were state planners to a man and markedly undemocratic. What Lenin saw was that a nation-wide planned economy was incompatible with the parliamentary democracy of the West. If production is to be planned, some body of persons must do the planning, and this becomes impossible if the plan may be reversed at any moment by a vote in a popular assembly. Under capitalism the planning is unconscious. It is not a perfect system, but if its destruction is held, as it was by Marx, to possess an absolute value, the only practicable alternative is for the State to take over production as the *Communist Manifesto* declared that it would do. In this event it will have to adopt a number of measures—such as the direction of labor, the fixing of prices, and the prohibition of strikes—and take the necessary steps to enforce them. No Western democracy, based on universal suffrage, is likely to tolerate this save in the emergency of war.

Lenin has been bitterly criticized for his autocratic conduct. But, apart from the chaotic conditions into which the revolution had plunged the country and which were scarcely favorable to the emergence of a democratic regime, he was simply following his master. The "revolutionary dictatorship of the proletariat" is not a democratic doctrine, and to tack on to it such devices as the "recall" and the acceptance by officials of "workers' wages" does not mean that the government will be democratic, but only that it will be inefficient. Even if the proletariat constituted an immense majority of the population, which it never has done or is likely to do in the foreseeable future, it would have no right to eliminate other sections of society, as Marx clearly intended it to do. Certainly there was nothing democratic about his direction of the First International, nor was there any trick to which he would not resort to rid himself of opponents.

As for Lenin, it is surely asking too much to expect that a man who has spent his life as a revolutionary agitator, and has at last brought about the revolution he desired in the teeth of opposition from many of his closest associates, should pay any regard to parties which he knew to be hostile to his policy—and this in a country in which such democratic procedures were virtually unknown. Thus he suppressed the Mensheviks and the Social Revolutionaries, and then, turning to his own party, forbade the formation of any faction which might become the focus of an opposition movement. The basis of "one-party" government was laid. There could be no justification for any other. If it agreed with his own it was superfluous; if it did not, it was counterrevolutionary.

But equally Lenin was resolved to create an organization which would replace the Second International and direct the proletarian world movement. Such an organization would be a convenient instrument for promoting those revolutions in other countries, and particularly in western Europe, on which survival of the Russian republic was held at that time to depend. This objective was realized by the formation in March, 1919, of the Third International or the Comintern. Yet when it was set up, Russia was so weak and isolated that the Bolshevik leaders made no claim to direct it, and seem genuinely to have contemplated the eventual establishment of its headquarters in some Western capital.

The policy which made it what it was to become, was laid

down at its Second Congress, held in Moscow in July-August, 1920. As E. H. Carr has pointed out, it met at a time when the Red army was sweeping into Poland, and the Bolshevik leaders had persuaded themselves that this " revolutionary war " would kindle that revolution in the West which, despite their presumed dialectical analysis of the situation, had somehow unaccountably tarried. The validity of Soviet principles appeared triumphantly established, and the leaders were only concerned to assert them in their most uncompromising form. Hardly had the congress dispersed than the Red army was defeated outside Warsaw and retired as rapidly as it had advanced. But by this time the famous *Twenty-One Conditions of Admission to the Comintern* had been adopted, and they were never formally amended.

For Lenin had now discovered that none of the parties which had so far affiliated to the Comintern were in the strict sense Communist at all; and faithful as ever to his conception of the " narrow " party, he insisted that all Socialist parties must now decide between revolutionary action and reformism. Thus he split the labor movement in every country, while the formation, at this congress of the Profintern, caused a corresponding split in the trade union movement. The immediate consequence was that the Italian Socialist party left the Comintern at the Livorno Congress of 1921; while the majority of the German workers remained faithful to the Amsterdam International and seceded. Yet, granted his premises, Lenin's policy was the correct one, and it has made the Communist movement what it is. It was better that Communist parties should start as small militant groups which knew what was required of them rather than that they should be absorbed into larger organizations whose members did not share their views.

The Second Congress established the Soviet leadership of the Comintern upon an impregnable basis. Under existing circumstances Moscow alone could provide its headquarters, and this gave the Russians a predominant position as the Comintern Statute laid down that the country which was the seat of its Executive Committee should provide five of its fifteen to eighteen members as against one from each of the larger national sections. Yet this predominance was by no means primarily attributable to the Comintern's organization. It was at least equally due to the emotional attachment of all foreign Communists to the Soviet Union. Thus although considerable freedom of discussion was permitted up to the Seventh Congress of 1935, the views of the Russian delegation, which were those of the Politbureau, were commonly decisive, while any national congress or conference would similarly defer to a Russian emissary.

The fiasco of the " March action " in Germany of 1921 convinced Lenin that his expectation that the proletariat of the West was ripe for revolution had been too sanguine, and that a long period of preparation would be necessary. The Third Congress of that year adopted therefore the slogan of " To the Masses," which was simply an extension of the policy he had advocated in his *Left-Wing Communism* of 1920, and which the Theses of the Second Congress had reaffirmed. The new policy was actualized in what became known as the tactics of the " United Front." Communist parties were to engage in joint action with other labor groups for the realization of concrete and nonrevolutionary aims, such as the shortening of hours and the raising of wages. Such action would either be initiated on the leadership level (" United Front from above ") or on that of the workers (" United Front from below "), but the objective would be the same, to represent the Communist party as the true champion of working-class interests and outbid and otherwise embarrass the Socialist leaders. The Fourth Congress of 1922 devoted a good deal of attention to the tactics to be employed, but was not otherwise of much significance. Its keynote was the need to strengthen the Soviet Union, which had maintained its revolution but had not received from the world proletariat the support to which it was entitled. This foreshadowed the doctrine of " Socialism in one country," announced by Stalin two years later, which aimed deliberately at building up the Soviet Union as the " home base " of the world revolutionary movement.

The application of United Front tactics became an important element in the " party line " which, with the passage of time, the Comintern laid down with an increasing inflexibility. The execution of this line confronted the local party leaders with a dilemma from which few escaped. To obtain control of the masses they must work in with other left-wing leaders, who might not welcome a collaboration of the true nature of which they were well aware. At the same time, they must use this collaboration to bring about revolutionary action when and where Moscow judged advisable. To combine these policies successfully was a virtual impossibility. If the leaders entered upon a collaboration which did not lead to the desired revolutionary consequences, they would be branded as "opportunists"; if they attempted a revolutionary action which proved abortive, they would be accused of "putschism" or "sectarianism," that is, of taking action without having first secured the necessary mass support. What was never to be questioned was the infallibility of Moscow, and for any failure to carry out its directives they must take the blame. The Comintern possessed the inestimable advantage of being able to shift the line as it wished; and in proportion as its national sections fell completely under its control, its directives tended to assume a global character, so that a policy which might assist a revolution in one area was equally imposed upon others where it could only lead to disaster. Further, the local leaders might at any time fall from grace for having faithfully carried out a policy which had been changed overnight. What was orthodoxy at one moment became "right" or "left deviationism" in the next. But of this they would receive no warning until they were informed that they had betrayed the proletarian cause.

How little consistent was the policy of the Comintern is revealed in its congresses. Thus the Fifth Congress of 1924 discovered that capitalism had achieved a "temporary stabilisation," and that this demanded that Communist parties should adopt a more uncompromising policy, which was tantamount to the abandonment of United Front tactics. The congress approved a decision, reached earlier in the year, that the basis of the party should henceforth be the factory cell, thus emphasizing its proletarian character while weakening the genuinely democratic element which had existed when the Communists had foregathered in their districts to discuss political issues and elect their own representatives. Street cells were not indeed abolished, but they were to be regarded as secondary, and any Communist who belonged to a factory, workshop, or office was to make this the center of his party activities. The result was to increase, as was intended, the authority of the party machine, and it is from this time that Politbureaus began to supplant the more representative Central Committees. But in December, 1926, the swing to the left observable at this Congress was checked by the replacement of Zinoviev by Bukharin as head of the Comintern, and in the following year Trotsky was exiled and the movement of which he had been the leader was crushed.

The Fifth Congress was faced with the aftermath of the disastrous German rising of October, 1923, the last attempt for many years to engineer a revolution in western Europe. With its failure, the focus of revolution shifted to China, where the local Communist party had recently concluded an alliance with the Kuomintang. The notion of using national liberation movements to undermine " capitalist imperialism " was not a new one, and the tactics to be adopted had been laid down by Lenin at the Second Congress. The concept of the " dual party " was an extension of these tactics dictated by expediency, and is the embryo of the later concept of the National or People's Front dominated by the Communist party, which would keep its own organization distinct. The original policy of the alliance was not without an element of realism. Its failure was ultimately due to the Comintern's misapprehension of the nature of the Kuomintang and to its continued belief, in the face of all evidence to the contrary, that it was possible to bring about a revolution of the approved " bourgeois democratic " type by uniting with a party which did not desire one. Yet the rival policy advocated by Trotsky would certainly have been no more effective, and the arguments which he used to attack Stalin after the alliance had broken down carry no conviction and were of disservice to the Chinese Communists in so far as they prevented Stalin from dissolving it, because to have done so would have involved a loss of face.

Thus the Sixth Congress of 1928 met once more under the shadow of failure, and the Comintern now adopted a policy of ultraradicalism. The phase of the stabilization of capitalism was declared to have ended, and catastrophic crises in the capitalist world were imminent. There was to be no more talk of the " peaceful coexistence " of the two world camps, since the Soviet

Union was in danger of attack. The Socialists were now labelled "Social Fascists," and no further cooperation with them was permissible. Whether Stalin believed in this new estimate of the situation is impossible to say. But he had now embarked upon his so-called "left course," and it was this that the policy of the Comintern was required to reflect.

How far the adoption of these tactics by the German Communist party contributed to bringing Hitler into power is too controversial a question for discussion here. Certainly whatever services the party may have rendered were ill-requited, as it was virtually crushed out of existence. But the French Communists suffered almost equally. Obedient to instructions, they fought the 1928 elections on the slogan "*classe contre classe,*" and attacked the Socialists with no holds barred. The result was to reduce their parliamentary representation to fourteen deputies. So serious indeed was the decline of the party that in 1930 Thorez was summoned to Moscow for a reprimand; but the same tactics were adopted at the 1932 elections, and the number of Communist deputies fell to ten. Yet it was not until 1934 that Stalin began to cast round for protective alliances, such as those which he concluded with Czechoslovakia and with France. The culmination of this new foreign policy was the adhesion of the Soviet Union to the League of Nations, hitherto apostrophized as a "den of robbers" and the organ of the iniquitous Versailles system.

This reorientation foreshadowed a major change in Comintern policy, which was officially adopted at the Seventh and last Congress of August, 1935. Dimitrov, the hero of the Leipzig trial and the symbol of resistance to fascism, replaced as president Manuilsky, who had been loudest in his denunciation of the Socialists as "Social Fascists." His report consigned to oblivion the entire tactics of the Sixth Congress. The defense of democracy was now to be the primary objective, and Communist parties were not only to return to the United Front tactics of sponsoring "partial demands," but were to form "Popular Fronts" with antifascist parties of any political complexion, despite the "Twenty-One Conditions" which had explicitly forbidden such combinations. The report revealed indeed the old ideological antagonism, and the "Trojan Horse" tactics which it advocated made it appear unlikely that the overtures of the Communists would be welcomed. None the less the concept of the Popular Front made an immediate appeal to the French electorate, and in the 1936 elections the Communists returned seventy-four deputies. World revolution was now abandoned, and as if to show that this was no empty gesture, the more notorious of the "old guard" revolutionaries were summoned to Moscow and liquidated. And with world revolution went internationalism, for it is from this period that dates the deliberate encouragement of Soviet nationalism and the rewriting of Russian history which this rendered necessary.

The line laid down by the Seventh Congress was maintained until the signing of the Stalin-Hitler Pact of August, 1939, when the Comintern abandoned its antifascist crusade, a policy the implications of which the Communist parties of the West failed to appreciate when war was declared, and which was immediately reversed when the Germans attacked the Soviet Union in June, 1941. With the new situation, which brought Russia into alliance with the Western democracies, the Comintern became increasingly an embarassment, and in June, 1943, it was formally abolished. The necessary doctrinal rationalization was provided. The Comintern had fulfilled its essential function by bringing the world proletarian movement into existence. But it had been outgrown by the development of that movement, and had become a hindrance to the strengthening of national working-class parties, which had now come of age as was proved by the upsurge of the masses against Hitlerite tyranny. It will be observed that the decree made no mention of the policy which the Comintern had been formed to promote, and referred only to the organization for carrying it out. But the disappearance of the Comintern marked the end of the era during which Communist parties had periodically assembled to lay down what was, at least in theory, a common policy, while it left the Soviet Union free to prescribe the line which any particular party was to follow. Thus Stalin, who had never taken the Comintern seriously as an instrument of world revolution, was able to make a contribution to the allied cause which cost him nothing.

It was not until the great interruption of fascism and war (from approximately 1931 to 1945) was over that the Soviet

Union, itself much transformed, resumed its earlier line of advance. Its policy towards its former allies has since passed through three main stages. The first dates from 1945 to the middle of 1947, and was marked by a return to the Popular Front tactics of the Seventh Congress. The Soviet Union had obtained in the satellite states large accessions of territory, but the Communist parties of these states were numerically weak, and although they were soon to become swollen, the new members were untrained and unreliable. The strength of the anti-Communist forces in these countries, combined with Russia's pledges to the West, imposed a policy of gradualism, while too drastic a display of police state methods would have hindered the attempts of the French and Italian Communist parties to ingratiate themselves with the Socialists. In this period, therefore, Communist parties participated in left-wing governments with a view to extruding the noncommunists at the appropriate moment, as they did in the satellite states, but proved unable to do elsewhere.

By early 1947 the Western powers had become aware that they were confronted not simply with a hostile state, but with an implacable enemy bent on their destruction and combining great military strength with the control of a world-wide subversive organization. The result was the Marshall Plan of economic aid to Europe, to which Moscow replied by setting up the Cominform in September, 1947. Zhdanov's inaugural address indicated that Soviet policy had moved sharply to the left. All the old arguments against capitalist imperialism re-emerged, and nationalist movements in backward areas were now to be given active encouragement. The Communist parties of the West were to return to revolutionary tactics, and thus during the winter the French party organized a series of militarized strikes which caused havoc in the working class and the trade unions. The defection of Tito was one of the principal causes which contributed to the abandonment of this line, and after a period of uncertainty, the policy of Moscow entered upon its third stage, marked by a return to United Front tactics, and in particular by the " peace campaign " which has been ever since the most favored weapon for confusing Western opinion.

The precise function of the Cominform has aroused much

speculation. Officially designated as "The Information Bureau of the Communist Parties," it is ostensibly a newspaper office responsible for publishing the Cominform organ *For a Lasting Peace,* which issues Moscow's directives in eighteen languages. Its organization bears no resemblance to that of the Comintern, as it has no Congress, Politbureau, or Central Committee. Nor does it profess to be a representative body. Only eight parties—those of the satellite states and of France and Italy—sent delegates to the meeting at which the Yugoslav Communists were expelled, and to that of November, 1949, which defined the tactics to be employed in the "peace campaign," while since this last meeting no others have taken place. Nonetheless, the tactics which its journal announces are at once accepted by the Communist parties of all five continents, and it may well be regarded as more desirable that they should be promulgated by a body whose precise composition is veiled in mystery rather than by a widely publicized international congress.

In the years following the revolution, the Russians had waited anxiously for proletarian risings in the West, and had done their utmost to promote them. They were now to receive almost embarrassing support from the East. Indeed the greatest event in the history of postwar communism has been the triumph of the Chinese Communists. After the failure of the earlier Comintern tactics, Mao Tse-Tung had built up his party along the frontiers of the Chinese Central Provinces until forced to remove to the borderland regions of the north. The development of this party seems to have occasioned an uneasiness in Moscow which was by no means simply due to scholastic pedantry. That the Russian revolution was proletarian and the archetype of all future revolutions was an article of faith, and on it was based Moscow's claim to direct the world-revolutionary movement. It was indeed recognized that in backward areas the revolution would be "bourgeois-democratic" and not proletarian, but this had been provided for by laying down that the bourgeois-democratic phase would be proletariat-controlled. To admit that the Chinese Communist party was based on the peasants, which Marxist-Leninist theory relegated to the role of allies of the proletariat, was to concede to it a character of its own. It would be a peasant revolution and a law unto itself, since the principles which govern the proletarian variety would not necessarily apply to it.

But Mao was careful to preserve appearances and not to challenge the validity of the accepted doctrine. Thus he was at pains to represent his movement as "proletarian" even when it was not of his party and to shift the center of gravity of his party back to the cities as soon as this became feasible. He has indeed claimed the right of interpretation in accordance with Stalin's often-repeated slogan that "Marxism is not a dogma but a guide to action," but he has made no important deviations from the official creed of which his own theoretical writings are an orthodox exposition. Thus the Chinese experience has been cloaked in Marxist phraseology, and is propounded as the line to be followed by all Asiatic Communists.

In what light Mao is regarded by the Russian leaders is a matter of speculation. The probability is that they do not want revolutions anywhere unless they can control them. But at least he has given them no further cause for anxiety than they must expect if they foment in large countries revolutions which are eventually successful. The present Sino-Soviet alliance is based upon a broad community of interests, and it would be unwise to build upon Mao as a potential Tito.

The Russians have been assisted in their task of imposing communism on the satellite states by the presence of the Red army; and it was to its absence that its letter to the Yugoslav Central Committee, the Central Committee of the Russian Communist party incautiously attributed the failure to impose communism upon France and Italy. Apart from this auxiliary, the Communists have only been successful where they have ceased to base the movement on the proletariat whose interests they theoretically represent. Both in Russia and China they have succeeded in seizing power by taking over the leadership of an "anti-feudal" revolution, to use the Marxist phrase. In Russia they exploited the desire of the peasantry for land; in China, the rising tide of nationalism. These forces have proved far more potent than the contradictions of capitalism in which Marx was primarily interested, and modern communism has had to extend its doctrine to cover them. It is in this, and in its development of power politics, that Leninism and Stalinism differ from classical Marxism. The latest evolution of communism in this direction is to be found in the form in which it has been worked out for Asia. Yet it would be an error to conclude that there is any fundamental distinction between the Russian and the Asiatic versions. Communism is much the same wherever we find it. It is the rule of a self-styled élite which has induced the masses to accept its leadership by promises of economic security which can only be fulfiled at the expense of political freedom. It constitutes, in fact, a return to the "social relations" of precapitalism in which the functions of the slave or serf are determined by their masters.

N. S. TIMASHEFF: *Discussion*

Fordham University

Professor Hunt's paper is a scholarly study of the successive phases in the directions and orientations given to the world Communist movement by its leaders, the men in the Kremlin. These phases seem to be firmly established by historians and political scientists. But, first, behind the zigzags of the phases caused by changes in the situation on the international scene, one perceives a gradual change in the long-range orientation. Second, a social movement is not limited to the leadership and the directions it gives. These are also the masses and their responses; therefore, the question arises: what are the forces attracting human masses toward the movement and maintaining their cohesion? It is worthwhile to spend some time on each of these problems.

Professor Hunt is right when saying that it is difficult to separate Soviet imperialism into two components: (1) advance of communism and (2) ambition of the men in the Kremlin to achieve world power. It is, however, equally true that there has been a gradual shift of the objectives of the world Communist movement from the former to the latter component. In the beginning, emphasis was laid on the creation of a world-wide society of victorious proletarians embodying the teaching of the founding fathers of communism and the developments added by later authorities. That world-wide society would be free of political coercion and be based on the collectivization of the means of production; it would embody complete equality, not only formal as is the case in " bourgeois " democracies, but also social, economic, and cultural; it would liberate men from the yoke of the traditional family and religion, as well as of national prejudice; finally, it would renovate the intellectual and esthetic culture.

Thirty-five years later, the objective could be described as Soviet Russian World Empire. In this formula, Soviet stands for a specific blending of the central core of Marxism, the collectivization of the means of production, with despotism. Such an organization of society, it is believed, can and must be achieved under the leadership of the Russians who are now ascribed the role of the senior partners in the fraternity of nations liberated from the yoke of capitalism. Since the nation is represented by the party, and the party by its leadership, the formula is tantamount to saying that the world society of the future must and will be led by the men in the Kremlin.

But the society of the future looks now quite at variance with the original blueprint. The world empire led by the men of the Kremlin will not necessarily embody the principle of total equality; it can come to compromise with religion and be reconciled to the survival of the family; it would recognize a hierarchy of nations and their cultures, and the world culture of the future society could take over a large number of culture elements from Russia's past.

But the main difference concerns itself with the structure of leadership. The difference between the earlier and later conceptions is well reflected in the Kremlin's attitude toward the unexpected success of the Chinese Communists. As correctly stated in the paper, Moscow only reluctantly granted undivided support to Mao, for his victory was merely the victory of Communist principles but not another step toward the formation of the Soviet Russian world empire. Thirty-five years earlier, similar events would have elated Lenin without qualification. In principle, Lenin and his associates pondered the shift of world leadership to the Communists of a more advanced nation provided it were smart enough to overthrow their capitalists.

The second problem which could and should be discussed with great profit is that of the forces of attraction exerted by communism and, of course, of the forces weakening or dissolving that attraction. These forces are manifold; however, no good method is known to single them out. One of the possibilities to replace guesswork by statements based on observation and inference from them would be the study of electoral returns in countries where elections are or were free, provided that there are reliable data as to the percentage distribution of the electorate.

The first test of the inner strength of communism took place in Russia during the elections to the Constituent Assembly (1917). These elections were held in the midst of a revolutionary turmoil generated by a complete disintegration caused by two and a half years of poorly conducted war and eight months of universal abuse of the newly gained freedom. Still, the result was 25 per cent of the votes for the Communists, with the rest against them.

In Europe between the two world wars the victorious and neutral countries were not hard hit by communism, at least up to the emergence of the great depression. In France, England, the Lowlands, and the Scandinavian countries the Communist vote was low. But in 1932 and 1936, the Communists increased their strength in France. The Communist vote was sometimes high in defeated Germany and, somewhat surprisingly, in Czechoslovakia, a country which was rather prosperous and ruled democratically.

The electoral returns for the period after the end of the Second World War can be summarized in this way:

1. Nowhere did communism attract the majority of the population. In one case only, Czechoslovakia in 1945, did communism attract more than one third (38 per cent).

2. Nations with long democratic tradition, like the Lowlands and the Scandinavian countries, insofar as they were not exposed to direct Communist pressure, displayed strong forces of resistance which checked the attraction of communism. The highest percentage of voters gained by the Communists was 12 (Belgium, 1946); in all cases, this percentage declined from earlier to later elections. The spell of the spectacular victories of the Red army and of the contribution of communism to the movements of resistance dissipated, and the policies of the men in the Kremlin obviously antagonized the democratic minded nations.

3. Two countries, Finland throughout the years and Hungary in 1947, gave to the Communists between 19 and 22 per cent and 17 per cent, respectively, despite the fact of being, in general, under Communist dominance. When one realizes that condition, the figures seem to be rather low. In Finland, this can be ex-

plained by the democratic spirit of the country. Relative to Hungary, the main force of resistance was the attraction exerted by the Small-Holders (peasants') party which promised a sweeping agrarian reform without collectivization.

4. Nations exposed to direct contact with the Soviets, like Germany and Austria, displayed strong anti-Communist feelings; in Austria, the Communists gained 5 per cent of the electorate in 1945 and 4 per cent in 1949, and in Western Germany, 6 per cent in 1949.

5. France and Italy have become and remained the stronghold of communism in free Europe. The French have consistently given to communism from 26 to 29 per cent of the votes, the Italians about the same in 1948 and 1953, with an increase in the later elections when compared with the earlier. The constellation of factors behind this phenomenon is probably this: (a) national pride hurt by crushing defeat followed by liberation from the outside; (b) inefficient democracy, in France especially in the thirties and in Italy throughout the twentieth century, until the catastrophe of the Fascist revolution; (c) unsound social structure, namely the large percentage of dwarf farms in France and of the rural proletariat in Italy; and (d) lack of direct exposure to communism. Some of these factors were present also in societies which have resisted communism more valiantly; but their combination in France and Italy is unique.

6. The strength of Communist attraction in Czechoslovakia (more exactly, in the Czech part of the dual nation) is rather puzzling. Of course, national pride was badly hurt by Munich; the attraction of communism could be then explained by repulsion against the West; but there is little evidence confirming this hypothesis. On the other hand, Czechoslovakia had a rather efficient democratic system between the two wars; her social structure is rather sound; and also, after World War II, the Czechs had direct contact with communism so that they could learn from experience what communism really grants the nations succumbing to its temptation.

Communist attraction providing the movement with large human masses is a subtle phenomenon. The tentative conclusions which can be drawn from European electoral returns must be supplemented by studies of the differential attraction of communism in various Asian and Latin American countries as well as by case studies of individual conversions to communism. This seems to be a very important task indeed.

Present and Potential Military Capabilities of the Soviet Bloc

VICE ADMIRAL L. C. STEVENS USN (Ret.),
Former U. S. Naval Attaché to the USSR

The present and potential military capabilities of the Soviet bloc can be summed up in the single word "formidable." They are so impressive that their very existence, under Communist control, provides the key to understanding the actions of most of the world in its international relations since the end of the last World War. Under their shield Soviet Russia has again and again dared to do things which are normally regarded as a justifiable *casus belli*. Because of their location and extent, the free world, which economically and technologically stands far ahead of the Soviet Union, has again and again taken a course of action which was not to its own liking, a course of action not necessarily of timidity, but of prudence in the face of known facts.

Whether or not the Soviet Union would have used its military capabilities if we had been less prudent is beyond the scope of this paper, which is limited to military potentialities. Presumably others have adequately covered the other factors that enter into the general problem of war or peace—factors, many of which are unique in the case of the Soviet Union.

You will all remember that Stalin once asked cynically, "How many divisions has the Pope?" It is a responsibility of our own military men, without necessarily the same cynicism, to look similarly at the hard facts, tangible elements such as the number of divisions, tanks, submarines, and aircraft that are at the disposal of the Soviet Union.

There are some intangibles whose appraisal is also the responsibility of military men. Training, discipline, and organization are intangibles, and in these factors the Soviet armed forces are known to be competent and to have gone far towards impressing their competence on the armed forces of their satellites. Richard Chancellor, the first discoverer by sea of the Kingdom of Muscovy, had this to say of the Russian army in 1553:

> [In] their warres . . . they runne hurling on heapes . . . that which they doe, they doe it all by stelth. But I beleeve they be such men for hard living as are not under the sun.

These intangibles still characterize the Russians of today.

Military men when acting as such must deal in the elements with which they are familiar and which they can evaluate. Some of the great military disasters of history, including Pearl Harbor, have been due in large part to reliance on mistaken estimates of enemy intentions without a full appreciation of capabilities. Now there is no doubt but that the Soviet bloc today possesses a large margin of tangible military power both in Europe and in the Far East. It has the capability of militarily overcoming whatever resistance can be immediately opposed to it, and can also launch direct airborne attacks on the Western hemisphere, both from its own bases and from surfaced submarines. The Soviet Union has an extensive radar network extending from her European frontiers along her Arctic borders to the Pacific, and German-derived guided missiles are in Soviet hands. Not only are the land forces of the Soviet bloc formidable, but they are backed by a formidable air potential. These are known facts and can not be disregarded.

The solid foundation of this strength is manpower—one-third of the world's population—which can be and is organized into military formations, while still affording adequate numbers to provide for industrial and agricultural needs.

Unlike the Western world, the Soviet Union kept a large conscripted army intact at the end of World War II. It has remained at a figure of about 2,500,000 men, relying upon modernization and replacement of equipment, strenuous training, and potential rapidity of expansion. It is organized into some 175 major divisions, 22 of which are in East Germany. One sometimes hears the strength and size of the Red army disparaged, particularly in comparisons of wartime mass effort with the West, because the Soviet divisions are much smaller than those of the West, but it should be remembered that the Western excess is largely composed of supporting rather than combat troops. The Soviet divisions are able to get along without most of the behind-the-line functions that absorb much manpower in our army, and, unlike most of our troops, they can live off the country, except for technical supplies and munitions.

A standard Soviet infantry division of 11,000 men comprises three rifle regiments, a regiment of artillery, and an armored regiment of fifty tanks. Mechanized divisions, and tank, artillery, and anti-aircraft divisions vary from this in size and of course specialized equipment. In the taking of Berlin in 1945, about 20,000 guns were concentrated. Since the war I have seen some of those or similar guns in Russia, stored almost as far as the eye can reach. Mass mobility is stressed by the use of mechanized forces in break-throughs. The total number of tanks, in which the Soviet Union excels, is estimated at well over 40,000.

An important factor in Soviet capabilities is the location of these massive ground forces. In addition to the twenty-two divisions in East Germany, fifty-one divisions, estimated at nearly 700,000 troops, are maintained near the Western frontiers, seventeen divisions with 220,000 troops in the Caucasus, and nearly half a million men in approximately thirty divisions in the Far East. Air forces are similarly deployed, and naval forces are distributed between the Black Sea, the Baltic, the Far North, and the Far East. There are no oceans which separate the Soviet armies from free Europe and free Asia. Her troops and those of her satellites are on the spot.

The Soviet-trained and organized European satellite armies consist of seventy-four line divisions with about a million and a half men, and Chinese forces in being are estimated conservatively at some 2,500,000 men. This comes to a total land force for the bloc of almost 500 divisions and 6,000,000 men organized, trained and ready to go. Compare this with the 100 or so divisions with which what is now the Western world ended the war in Europe, Asia and the Pacific. The total armed forces of the Soviet bloc are now approaching 9,000,000 men. Soviet-trained reserves are estimated at 8,500,000 men, and the Soviet army alone could probably mobilize a total of 13,000,000 men within one year.

Since the war, the Soviet navy has concentrated on building submarines, destroyers, and cruisers. It consists of 3 old battleships, 20 cruisers, about 150 destroyers, and well over 300 submarines. The submarine force includes true ocean-going craft which are capable of cruising and operating throughout the great oceans, including off our own coasts. Less than a third of their submarines are of this sort, but they are increasing in numbers. This is the most significant element of their naval power, for the submerged speed provided by German developments toward the end of the last war, when too late for Germany, has complicated the problem of antisubmarine warfare to an almost fantastic point. I have seen Type XXI fast German submarines on the assembly ways in Leningrad. When one remembers how close the Allies came to disaster in both world wars because of a much simpler submarine threat from enemy forces that were initially much smaller in numbers, the Soviet capabilities here are far from reassuring to us.

The air power of the Soviet bloc is largely in the hands of the Soviet Union itself. Our own Air Force estimates that the USSR has 20,000 first line aircraft in organized units, with large numbers of reserve aircraft. More than 1,000 of these are believed to be heavy bombers derived from our own B-29's, which are capable of carrying the atomic bomb. The European satellites have about 1,500 aircraft, including many jet fighters, and the Chinese Communists have some 2,300 aircraft, including about 1,400 Soviet-made jet fighters. There are more than 70 major fully-developed airfields in eastern European Communist territory, and about 30 major air bases in eastern Siberia and Red China.

We know that the Soviet Union produces fissionable materials in quantity and that it conducted one atomic test in 1949 and two more in 1951. As you know, it requires a vast effort to produce a stockpile of atomic bombs, but there is every reason to believe that the Soviets by now have a respectable stockpile. The necessary technical information on the thermal type bomb as well as the fission-type bomb was obtained by them through espionage, and Malenkov has announced that the West no longer has a monopoly on the hydrogen bomb.

The one restraining force on their eventual use against us is our own immediate retaliatory power with similar weapons. As regards capabilities of the more distant future, a time may come when the Soviet Union will have sufficient atomic strength to fatally cripple the United States in a single blow. This is, of course, the ultimate nightmare situation which puts an urgency on reaching a solution to the problems here being considered. Even in that ultimate situation, it should still be possible for us to strike equivalent retaliatory blows.

It is my own opinion that that apocalyptic day is far enough in the future to permit an orderly approach to those problems, and that, although we dare not drag our feet, so much water flows over the dam with the passage of time that we need not yet despair if we cannot see a clear solution at the moment. It seems desirable to point out that it is this ultimate military capability which, far more than our cold-war tax burdens, gives priority to reaching a solution before it may be too late.

In the Soviet Union, practically all information regarding capabilities is on a top secret, need-to-know basis, and the punishment for security violations is ruthless, swift, and brutal. This, coupled with the extraordinary precautions taken in preserving the Iron Curtain, makes arriving at definite and precise data a difficult business for the outside world. The validity of the exact figures is open to argument, and the more the figures are broken down into such elements as specific types and models of equipment, the more room there is for argument. Such arguments can have a considerable effect on the detailed manner in which we should build up our own strength to cope with the Soviet threat, and can be of importance as well in modifying our over-all expenditures on national defense. However, my subject covers only the military capabilities of the Soviet bloc, and not what the United States should do about them. No matter how they are qualified, the figures I have given are valid for the order of magnitude of Soviet strength, which is indeed formidable.

Now there is nothing new or startling in all this. In one form or another, it has been known for some time. If there were anything new or startling, I would doubtless either end up in the pokey for releasing it publicly, or else be accused of saying something that was not so.

Let us now consider some of the military weaknesses of the Soviet bloc, for it seems to me that capabilities and limitations go hand in hand. The military and other resources of the Soviet bloc are ample to wage the minor armed conflicts of what we call the cold war, particularly since it is essential to this phase that Soviet forces be not directly engaged. But a global war is another thing, where lack of sea power as we know it would chain the Communists to the Eurasian land mass.

I know of no developments in aircraft or guided missiles which will appreciably diminish the role of the great oceans in the next few years as an ultimate factor in global warfare. It takes many years to create sea power, and the Soviets have no aircraft carriers, which are the keystone of world-wide sea power. So, unless a final atomic cataclysm some day becomes a reality, or unless the United States fails to cope with its internal problems and becomes militarily weak, losing its allies, America, its sea power, its air force, its great industry and technology, must eventually be reckoned with.

Although it seems clear that Soviet armed strength in being and its strategic location is such that any resistance that can be opposed to it can initially be overcome, it is not so clear that the Soviet Union can successfully carry out a prolonged aggressive war. The Soviets have their own peculiar problems in using their troops in foreign lands, problems which are vastly more difficult for them than those which they would meet in a defensive war carried out on their own homeland. The Soviets themselves recognize that the Dekabrist revolt of 1825--that first great uprising to attain a constitutional government—was a direct result of what Russian troops saw when they were out of the country in the Napoleonic wars ten years and more before.

Information regarding order of battle and equipment for the Soviet Union is by its nature apt to be more reliable than that regarding stockpiles of munitions, supplies, and such vital war commodities as petroleum and petroleum products. When confronted with unknowns, the responsible military man can only play safe and not underrate the enemy. The economic and scientific status of the Soviet Union has been covered elsewhere.

Let me, however, say that most of our statistics on economic figures regarding the Soviet Union are put out by the Soviets themselves, and it is naïve to expect the Bolshevik regime to put out figures with the normal Western motive of reflecting actual conditions. Although I may seem to wander from my subject, it is pertinent in appraising military capabilities, and I believe that the Soviet bloc is weaker economically than it is generally regarded in the West. Here I have particular reference to qualitative factors, which seldom are reflected in economic analyses.

I doubt very much if the additional conquered resources of western Europe would be readily exploitable by the Soviet Union. The Russians lack the ability of the Germans in this respect as well as in ability to govern in any way by terror and force, and additional sullen populations, controllable only by force, could be a debit rather than a credit, except for what could be expropriated on the spot.

Soviet industry at home is fairly well dispersed, but what seems to me to be more important, it is more primitive and less of a delicate organism than is industry in the West. Although this may be a strength rather than a weakness under bombing attacks, the ability to continue to produce under what might be called normal atomic bombing is still very much of an unknown. We should not underrate the military contributions made by the West to Russia's victory in World War II. Food is a factor that is as essential in war as guns. The Soviet bloc now has tremendous populations to feed, and it is well known how necessary to the Russians was the nearly two-and-a-half-million tons of food shipped there by America, Britain, and Canada in the last war.

The vastness of the land that is controlled by the Soviets and the advantages of shorter internal communications constitute another strength of military importance, which may well be more than offset by the low state of development of the railroads that tie the vast areas together and by the absence of highways and east-west waterways. Although the Soviets have not sincerely sought international agreements, in the absence of such agreements, the enormity of the Soviet areas requires large armed forces in place for protection alone, without reference to the use of those forces in aggressive action beyond the frontiers.

But modern military operations tend to involve more complex factors than the wars of a hundred years or more ago, and it seems to me that in contemplating the Soviet Union, whether in the uneasy peace which is called the cold war or in another global conflict, the military problem is less than ever before a purely military affair of opposing orders of battle. When viewed on a compartmented military basis, the strength and potentialities of the Soviet bloc remain impressive. Of course the military viewpoint is never completely compartmented, but in the case of the Soviet Union we are up against something new, where intangibles have far greater meaning than ever before. And the cold war has shown them to be skilled in the exploitation of intangibles. In my opinion, however, one of the most important intangibles is the reliability of the Communist populations and that of their armed forces themselves. All of the satellites have known comparative freedom in recent years, and Soviet strength is far from being consolidated there, as attested by recent disorders.

It seems easier for the military man to appraise discipline than morale. Everyone knows that the oppression of the Bolshevik regime creates discontent, but it is customary to balance out this factor by the obvious fact that discipline is strong enough to keep under control under present conditions whatever discontent there may be. It is also customary to consider that morale is high in forces that are winning military victories. The most that conventional military thinking would be justified in doing would be to consider the intangible of loyalty to the regime as a plus, much as plus values are counted in appraising a bridge hand. After all, it is the experience of the past which teaches us never to underrate an enemy, and we have had so little experience with populations subjected to pressures like those of the Soviet bloc that the classical approach is very apt to underrate the factor of loyalty. The Soviet regime is a dictatorship, but it is a unique dictatorship, and one with which we are only beginning to acquire experience. Moreover, the peoples of the Soviet Union are unique. Attempts to apply past experience with other dictatorships and other peoples can well be misleading.

Now there is no questioning the simple military virtues of the Russians. They are tough and courageous, and they have a patriotism and love for their native soil that is extraordinarily powerful and moving. But the army, although a conscript army, is genuinely a peoples' army. In peacetime, it is privileged in many ways and even protected from many of the realities of Russia. In Russia the only real believers in the regime are the young. As soon as their schooling is ended and they become responsible cogs in the vast mechanism of the Soviet Union, they see and experience things which are so much at variance from their dream that there are few of them that are not disillusioned within a few years. This process effectively prevents another nightmare from becoming a reality—the rise of new generations of heartless robots. During its compulsory peacetime army service, Soviet youth is still protected from some of the grim realities of Soviet life, but in a great war, older, more questioning men would be called into service. In the rapid expansion of a major war, the army more than ever mirrors the towns and villages, with all their unhappiness and latent, hidden disaffection.

The methods of the regime, which are necessary for its survival, do not breed loyalty, but fear. During the Great Purge of the thirties, tens of thousands of officers were liquidated, not because they were guilty of treasonable acts, but, in characteristic Bolshevik fashion, because they were potentially disloyal. And it was the sailors of Kronstadt who were the first to revolt against the Bolshevik regime which they had helped mightily to bring to power. News of many another revolt continues to trickle through the Iron Curtain, revolts always suppressed, to be sure, but always recurring, a process which is known to have continued into the postwar days.

It is true that the Great Purge followed close on the heels of the period of forced collectivization when literally millions of peasants were done to death in the name of communism. But such things are not yet forgotten in Russia, and purges are a necessary continuing factor in a Communist regime, a factor which is required by its basic philosophy.

It is impossible to believe that important components of military leadership are not vulnerable on the score of loyalty to the regime, and after all, the armed forces constitute the only element that can take decisive action. The support of soldiers is basically necessary for every successful revolution, and, under war conditions, the swollen peoples' army has weapons in its hands. Thousands of its professional leaders remember what happened to their own in the Great Purge—to Tukhachevsky, Kork, Yakir, Putna, Uborevich and the rest. The system of informers and commissars or political deputies is welcomed only by those who are completely loyal to the regime, for it is primarily a mechanism for eliminating even potential disloyalty, and in wartime the Soviets have found it militarily necessary to slacken that system.

The Bulganins and the Vasilevskys come from the ranks of the Chekists and commissars, but the Rokossovskys have had their teeth literally knocked out by Bulganin's sort. There is, moreover, hardly a family in Russia that has not suffered at the hands of the regime, and they do not forget. The fact that the army leaders may be party members is beside the point, for the old revolutionary fire has been so often and so long betrayed that it has died out, and cynicism and force is not an adequate substitute cement for the party. There are countless Russians, including even part of the *apparat,* which is the core of the party, who still have a conscience.

The regime has never given the people reason to trust it, but has depended on propaganda which was worn very thin in many places. The party's *Agrogorod* project had to be dropped even before Stalin's death because it was too hot to handle, and although Stalin's successors have already rejected his latest peasant economy, the party will have to cease being the party before it inspires true loyalty. And in the Soviet Union, the party is the state.

It is a peculiarity of Russia that this party-state is not identical with the native land which the people love so passionately. The regime devotes much of its most skillful propaganda towards furthering this identity in the minds of the people, but it still must overcome the difficulties created by itself, and the people are wary.

When the Germans went into Soviet territory, their reception by the people gave them an extraordinary opportunity to bring the people to their side against the regime. Estimates of troops alone that went over to the Germans run as high as 4,000,000 men, with willing prisoners extending all the way from the Ukrainian front to Leningrad. The Germans were not only unprepared to deal properly with such numbers, they were politically unprepared. There were two schools of thought; one which believed in dividing and conquering, which could well have set the nationalities against the Great Russians, and the other which advocated turning both Great Russians and the non-Russian peoples against the regime. If the latter school of thought had prevailed, the outcome of the war might well have been different, but Hitler treated both Russians and nationalities as *untermenschen* and sought to make the conquered land a feeder province of Germany. This, coupled with the genuine skill of the regime in capitalizing on it, served to unite both Russians and nationalities in support of the state.

The greatest future danger, however, in furthering the illusion of identity between the land and the state would seem to come from our own ineptness and lack of knowledge and skill in handling such problems. Here is the true field of psychological warfare with the Soviet Union. Most of us know by now that it is dangerous to confuse Soviet imperialism with Russian nationalism, and that the nationality problem can be approached only on a basis of noninvolvement for Americans, but the other elements in aligning the peoples with us are subtle and poorly understood. I am not talking of "winning the hearts and minds of men," for that is an over-simplified formula. The Russian heart and mind is alien to us, and the complexity of the problem is indicated by the fact, as one of the most bitterly experienced of todays' emigre scholars has pointed out, that the Soviet peoples accept various aspects of the regime in varying degree.

We do not know precisely how the vulnerabilities of the Rokossovskys and the Zhukovs can be made to flower. We do know that the regime is even more aware than we of the dangers of the situation to itself, and that it will spare none of its skill and experience in meeting that situation. A Russian is so conditioned to propaganda as such that he can smell out any of our efforts to use him for our own interests. It has been my experience that he will cooperate only so far as he himself considers that his own interests are concerned. He will even try to use us for his own ends, but I do not believe that he can be bought.

And if we do not learn how to work with the Russian people and its armed force towards a common end of a decent homeland for them, the great limitation which they place on Soviet capabilities will not even be a possible plus value for us, and we may some day see Gogol's famous words come true with even greater arrogance than now. More than a hundred years ago, in comparing Russia to a swift *troika,* he had this to say:

> The steeds of the troika that is Russia, with the whirlwinds riding in their manes, "almost not touching the earth with their hoofs, have been transformed into a single line flying through the air, and the troika . . . rushes on. Whither are you going, Russia? No answer is given. The sleigh bells ring out with a wonderful sound, the air thunders and, torn to bits, becomes a wind; the troika flies past everything that there is on earth; and all other peoples and governments, looking askance, stand aside and give it the road."

SAMUEL L. A. MARSHALL: *Discussion*

The Detroit News

I come to my task less as a critic and reviewer than as a rifleman reinforcement. From such knowledge as I have, there is little which could be added to Admiral Stevens' appraisal of Russia's military resources. He hewed to the line of his subject: the presentation was realistic and timely. The speaker went to the heart of the matter—the sheer massiveness of Russian military power, coupled with a vastly increased ability in our time to give it sound technical direction and supply it with fighting equipments which are good enough.

But as a military critic I cannot forbear to express my personal unhappiness about the *capability* approach to the analysis of great military problems, for when it becomes unduly emphasized naught but illusion will come of it. I am confident that Admiral Stevens agrees as to its limitations and dangers, else he would not have made those digressions to speculate about the imponderables and to discuss the possibilities of method according to circumstance. War, and the risks of war, are never a matter of counting the chips on both sides of the table, and then coming forth with a plus or minus answer. The wisest man in this nation, having full knowledge of our weapon count, productive capacity, and human resources, still could not forecast the true capability of the United States for a war with limits yet undefined, fought with weapons the effects of which remain unmeasured, engaging peoples whose moral strength in the face of unfathomed danger is unknown and unknowable. But he might, if he puts his brains to it, and called for help from all quarters, begin to envisage the main conditions of the battlefield, superinduced by weapons changes, and from some understanding of the increased pressures, see at least in part the new tactical order.

This is the type of research and reform which military systems through all history have been most reluctant to undertake. It is easy, relatively, for a few men to fashion a new and deadlier weapon or a faster machine. But it is inordinately difficult to get thousands of men to accept wholly new patterns of action deriving therefrom, ridding themselves of the bind of convention and conservatism. The inertia of traditional thought is all against it and of that, in Admiral Mahan's words, comes the great evil. Capabilities?—what meaning have they as an index in the power struggle? I'm afraid not much. We have been wrong too many times—wrong about Hitler's Germany, wrong about the staying power of Russia, wrong about the ability of Japan to accomplish much with little through sheer audacity, and finally wrong about the genius and tenacity which enabled the primitive army of Red China to stand against the most modern engines of war.

To me at least, Admiral Stevens' paper said this: "True we will err one way or another, but let's not again make the mistake of underrating the force moving against us." His ancient quotation from Chancellor should remind us of Frederick the Great's remark: "It isn't enough to kill Russians; one must still knock them over." And they're getting a little harder to knock over all the time.

Still, the most marked phenomenon of the past thirty-five years is the unwillingness of Western peoples to acknowledge fully that capacity for military growth which has already been demonstrated by Russia under the Revolution. We are alternately fearful and contemptuous. One emotion or another is substituted for that greater awareness of fact we so much need. Conceding that their average soldier is brave, admitting that by fluke they may be on their way to possession of the hydrogen bomb, we keep telling ourselves that they are not technically-minded and aggressive enough to withstand *fully armed* whatever magic lightning might be loosed against them tomorrow. *That is the rumor that Americans like best to believe about Russians because it is so very comforting.*

In a way, we are victims of the same judgments which for so long Russians held of themselves. Summing up three centuries of warfare, Kuropatkin wrote in the early nineteen hundreds that his country would always have to lean on strong frontiers and its armies must always prepare for long retreats, such would be the weakness of its weaponing and its generalship. This was the considered view of the ablest student of war that Russia had produced, speaking from the bitterness of his experience as the leader of a defeated side. He had witnessed the Russian fleet foul off against some neutral fishing smacks in the Dogger Bank, shed some of its armor plate when it ran into a stiff breeze off the French coast, and sail nakedly on to the ultimate catastrophe at Tshushima.

Nothing happened in World War I to belie Kuropatkin's estimate. Millions of Russians died in vain endeavor, the victims of stupid generalship and a corrupted supply system. During the Spanish Civil War their tanks reacted like punk; we saw the so-called plate riddled by rifle bullets, and we heard the experts say, " Russians will never be able to pickle armor plate." It was at about this same time that engineers were returning to my home city of Detroit from working in Russia, bringing the word, " Their factories will never be able to fabricate a modern plane."

But their tanks do well enough on the modern battlefield and their fighting planes are efficient enough to be of some concern to us even when fought by the relatively unseasoned Chinese pilot. When the Germans first invaded Russia, they sent back word that the Russians did not know how to mass artillery, and made the mistake of sending forth their aircraft singly. But in less than one year the Russians had learned, and what they learned they did not appear to forget. In the early Finnish invasion, and again at Bialystok, Smolensk, and Kiev, as the Germans hit, they responded as a clumsy mass, seemingly incapable of sharp maneuver under skilled control. But later in the war, the rebound from Stalingrad, the crossing of the Dnieper, the advance up the Danube and the crossbuck operation through the Baltic States were first-class examples of the skilled handling of extraordinarily massive forces in the attack. The Russians had acquired what they hitherto had lacked—light and leading in proportion to the mass brought to the field of battle.

But we seem no less ready to counter them with newer and bigger cliches. Today their vast superiority in armor is acknowledged. Yet it is said that the fact is immaterial, since the tank idea is obsolescent and without decisive relation to the future battlefield. A comforting thought! But no new thought-through theory of the form of future war yet supports it. And I have heard it seriously said by our makers of military doctrine that the Russians will not again use mass, and that in any case, mass has had its final day. We would all like to think so. But where is the sufficient proof?

There is the old story about the bushman who was given a new boomerang and then went crazy trying to throw the old one away. What little I might add to Admiral Stevens' fine paper would be badly put if it raised any such hazard. It is not saying they are supermen invulnerable to our slings and arrows to suggest that it is our national tendency to underrate both their power and their capacity for military growth and that this is not the course of prudent wisdom.

In the period which followed World War II, I had many of Germany's higher commanders serving under me for a prolonged period. We used them to conduct comprehensive staff studies of enemy operations on the western front and against Russia in the east. The generals who had fought in Russia were a group apart. They were shocked men, bowed down by the weight of terrible experience. They had dealt with mass—mass in its full military meaning—and they responded but numbly as they discussed it. It was as if they still could not comprehend its meaning and what to do about it. They said to me: "We learned at last how terrible is war."

Maybe the reflection seems beside the point in this age of super weapons; but considering the plain geography of the problem, I simply do not think so. I am sure if those same commanders were here they would pay warm tribute to Admiral Stevens' paper. And if we could hear Frederick's ghost remind us that Russians have to be knocked over, that might help also. The Admiral says Russia could mobilize 13,000,000 in one year. I do not know the validity of the figure. I do know it is a tremendous number of men. No nation in history has ever come near to such a mark—13,000,000 men in one year. The United

States has just run out on a war wherein it was never able to get more than seven divisions to the battlefield. Those are sharp, and in my judgment, critically decisive contrasts. And when men either in or outside the military establishment treat them as if they were without particular significance, they have not, to quote Admiral Nelson's phrase, "prepared their country against the acts of a mad government." Capabilities as an index cannot be treated in separateness from trends in existing programs, particularly here in the United States where the besetting tendency is ever to make a lesser military demand upon our average individual.

Having described the Soviet military capability as "formidable" in his direct statement, Admiral Stevens added during the discussion period that the USSR is at present too weak to launch a world war. In his judgment, the country can increase consumer-goods production markedly and still promote peripheral wars of the Korean type, but the critical test of its ultimate aggressive design against the free world will come when it is strong enough (in atomic and air power) to launch a "crippling, surprise attack upon the United States."

He indicated this is a somewhat distant peril. The question was asked: "If the Soviet Union carried out a Pearl Harbor type attack on the United States, how could we retaliate, how could we continue a long war?" His answer was that no atomic attack could be fully devastating to the United States and that by the hour Russia has a sufficient stockpile, our military installations will be so protected that full retaliation will still be possible. The second part of the question went unanswered.

In his view, the possession of atomic weapons by Britain and France, *provided they are on our side in future war,* would adversely affect the military position of the USSR, acting as a deterrent. But if they should drift from alliance with the United States, their possession of A-weapons would be a blow to this country.

Is there any fresh sign that Soviet strategists have revised their views which rejected the *blitzkrieg* theory of the overland attack? As the speaker understood Russian theory while he was Naval Attache in Moscow, the Russians do not reject the *blitzkrieg* principle; their strategists simply premise that the lightning stroke unsupported by the total follow-up is unavailing. Were they to undertake total war, he said in answer to another question, what performance could be expected of satellite troops is impossible of analysis. Being closer to the West, they are more subject to defection. But if they were employed mainly as line-of-supply forces, they could still be a major prop to the Soviet fighting system. Whether, in the cold war period, there would be increased hope for the West if the Russian army, rather than the Communist party, held control is another such imponderable, subject to guess but not estimate. The party is the enemy of the West. Its line and teaching have not permeated root and branch of the fighting establishment. But whether the army would incline toward the same policy as the party is beyond prediction.

However, in discussing the respective roles of Marshals Bulganin and Zhukov, Admiral Stevens implied that the Russian army emotionally leans towards its leaders who have succeeded on the battlefield, and has a "lack of confidence" in those who have risen to power through the bureaus. Bulganin is regarded by soldiers "as a politician." Zhukov is "still popular" with the common soldier, and for that reason may have fallen from grace.

There is nothing to be gained, the Admiral said, by retaliating against the USSR for its obstructing of the activities of our military attaches within Russia. He made two points in support of the proposition: it is not practicable to hurt the Russians more than we are being hurt; further, the restrictions put on our official representatives are no worse than what the Russians impose on their own people.

PART IV

The Soviet Union and the Western World

Soviet Policies and Successes in Eastern Europe

JOHN C. CAMPBELL,
National War College

The open revolt of the German workers in East Berlin and the Soviet zone, the rioting of Czechs in Pilsen, the announced "new economic policy" in Hungary, the rumblings and grumblings from one end of Moscow's satellite empire to the other—all these events give timeliness to an already difficult subject, which is also a somewhat dangerous one, since whatever conclusions you reach may go out the window with tomorrow's headlines.

In any case I'm not going to try to answer all the questions that are being asked, such as: What is the relation between these events and the changes in Moscow? Will Stalin's successors be able to hold the empire he put together? What should the United States do? It is difficult enough to guess what has actually happened in eastern Europe in the years that have already gone by, but I shall do what I can to put recent events into the perspective called for by my subject—Soviet policies and successes in eastern Europe—and by the broader topic of the conference—Soviet imperialism.

Put in its simplest form, Soviet policy has been to establish absolute control over the nations of eastern Europe, making them for all practical purposes—military, political, and economic—provinces or rather colonies of the Soviet Union; provinces later perhaps—constituent republics like the ill-starred Baltic states—but colonies now. At a time when the colonial dependencies of the Western powers have been gaining their independence, these formerly independent nations have been subjected to treatment unequalled in the worst period of European exploitation of " backward " peoples.

We shall consider here only the states now in satellite status, rather than of the annexed territories and the zones of occupation, which while a part of the picture of Soviet imperialism in eastern Europe nevertheless present special problems. And only brief mention will be made of two countries where full Soviet control was not established: Finland, where for reasons of their own the Soviet rulers chose not to destroy democratic institutions; and Greece, where Soviet political policies went beyond the perimeter of Soviet military power and were stopped by American and Greek firmness. A third area of failure—Yugoslavia—we shall come to later.

It is not necessary to go into the details of the way in which Soviet imperialism fastened its grip on Poland, Czechoslovakia, Hungary, Rumania, and Bulgaria. It is a familiar story. It has been told by Western diplomats and journalists who witnessed it, by democratic political leaders and by many exiles and refugees who were its victims, and even by Communist leaders and propagandists themselves in surprisingly frank revelations of their strategy and tactics. Developments have varied from country to country but have had many common factors: the pressure of Soviet military forces (even without direct intervention in most cases, their forces were the threat always in the background; they were the anvil, as one observer has said, on which the hammers of Soviet political and economic action beat free peoples into slaves) ; direct political intervention (Rumania) ; the use of picked Soviet agents as local political leaders; the abuse of armistice and peace-treaty provisions and violation of other international agreements; the exclusion of Western influence (the Western powers, much as they disliked it, had to accept the role of spectators rather than actors in this drama) ; the seizure of key governmental posts; the use of front organizations and Communist-controlled splinter parties; the undermining of coalition governments; the denial of free elections; the smashing of democratic parties and organizations; the exploitation of old frontier and nationality disputes; economic spoliation and pressures; treason trials and purges; and above all the unbridled use of terror from which no one, be he ex-bourgeois politician or professional man, average worker or peasant, or Communist party functionary, can escape.

The only way to avoid getting bogged down in this problem is to list the major lines of Soviet policy and action, and to comment briefly on what the results have been in each case.

First is military security. It was clear from Soviet policy before the war—indeed from Tsarist policy before that—that the major Russian preoccupation with these countries is to organize them as a safety belt, to prevent the use of their territories or their armies by any potentially hostile power. So strong is the impulsion, both Russian and Communist, to control of this area that there is no legitimate reason for surprise that the Soviet leaders have ruthlessly asserted it. The only surprise is that people in the West had hopes that they would not.

The Soviet leaders were able to make sure of that primary purpose by the conduct of their military operations, and of their diplomacy, in World War II. The sweep of the Soviet armies through eastern Europe was the decisive factor in giving the USSR the security protection it sought, and it also determined the destiny of the unfortunate inhabitants of that area. The security system has now been consolidated by a network of military pacts, by the keeping of Soviet troops in Poland, Hungary, and Rumania, as well as in Germany and Austria, and by the complete rebuilding of the satellite military establishments under Soviet officers into adjuncts of the Soviet armed forces.

The Soviet leadership has, in fact, gone well beyond any defensive strategic concept by maintaining over twenty divisions in East Germany, a deployment area of great strategic importance, by building up the satellite armies to over one million men, well beyond any defensive needs, and beyond peace treaty restrictions where those exist, to the point where Soviet and satellite forces together cast their shadow over all of Europe and stand as a threat to the security of the free nations beyond their borders. Nothing brings home to free Europeans the reality of the Soviet threat more than to see the Russians encamped on the Elbe and the Danube, and to hear the ancient European capitals of Prague and Budapest speaking with the voice of Moscow.

But no system can give absolute security. So far as it rests on Soviet military power it may seem secure enough. But Soviet forces may not stay forever in Germany, in Austria, or in the satellites. And a system which is based in countries whose populations are fundamentally hostile, and which relies to any degree on satellite armies, on men drawn from the disaffected mass of the subject peoples, carries no guarantee of permanence, no matter how many Rokossovskys or Panchevskis may be placed in posts of command. The satellite forces must be counted in the world balance on the Soviet side now. What they would do in a war against the Western powers, what they would do after a few military defeats even on a local front, what they would do in a moment of crisis when called upon to suppress their own peoples—these are questions which can hardly be answered with assurance, here or in the Kremlin.

Second is the objective of absolute political control. This the Soviet leadership apparently regarded as essential to the security of its ultimate hold on the area. This meant that the willingness of a Beneš or a Mikolajczyk or a Nagy—and of the Western powers for that matter—to recognize Russia's special security interests but to retain a free political life for their countries met with no corresponding desire for compromise but only with a fixed determination to destroy them.

This was actually an unequal contest in that the local Communists were supported, or rather directed, by a neighboring great power whose influence was everywhere evident. Their opponents looked to the Western powers but did not find sufficient support there to save the situation. Without minimizing this factor, however, some of the elements of internal weakness which contributed to the final outcome should be pointed out.

I do not subscribe to the oft-expressed theory that "these countries never had any democracy anyway" and that the Western insistence on representative governments and free elections was merely a quixotic idea of President Roosevelt or of Secretary Byrnes. I do not mean to equate Czechoslovakia's history and Albania's, or to present the rule of the "colonels" in Poland or the royal dictatorships in the Balkans as anything other than what they were, but the nations of eastern Europe had all passed through the fires of a long struggle for independence and free institutions. Their governmental practices were often, in Western eyes, distinctly undemocratic. But they could and can still distinguish between freedom and bondage, for they had experienced both. Never have they had a full-fledged freedom for all the people, but on the other hand never such a total enslavement as has been forced upon them in the last eight years.

But what were some of the weaknesses which made the Soviet task easier and made more difficult the efforts of the Western powers, inadequate as they may have been, to prevent the ultimate tragedy? Most of the noncommunist political organizations were lacking in dynamic leadership and in popular support. Many were already discredited because of prewar inadequacies, or had not recovered from suppression by prewar dictatorships and wartime fascist-type regimes. Some were tainted by their association with or tolerance of those regimes. Except in Czechoslovakia, the so-called bourgeois parties had quite limited support in the population. The peasant parties did not have the well organized, politically effective mass support of that great majority of the population which was peasant. The Socialists were weak because, with few exceptions, they were not solidly founded on strong unions and a significant working class. Their leadership teemed with opportunists and with men who could be seduced by Communist appeals to working-class solidarity against the revival of fascism. The unsolved problems of the prewar era, the chaos induced by the war, and the dissolution of constituted authority that accompanied the collapse of old regimes and the coming of the Soviet armies—all these factors created a state of social flux and revolutionary change in which victory went almost by default to the side which had firmly set its revolutionary goals and had the organization, the ruthless determination, and the necessary outside support to achieve them.

Whether the same techniques would work elsewhere, in western Europe for example, is questionable. The specific conditions which obtained in eastern Europe—including Soviet freedom to act in an area recognized as a Soviet military theater, and insufficient knowledge of Soviet intentions and methods—are not likely to be duplicated elsewhere. And we may hope that the world has learned at least a few lessons from what happened in eastern Europe.

Third on my list of items is what we can conveniently call Sovietization, by which is meant the attempt to remake the whole pattern of life of these peoples. The Soviet leadership has chosen this course in preference to one by which they might increase the element of consent and cut down the requirement for coercion, by leaving intact some aspects of local society while still maintaining full control, thus avoiding the upheavals of rapidly forced and brutally executed large-scale social changes which have complicated the process of exploitation and intensified the resentment and hatred of wide segments of the population. Partly for doctrinaire reasons, partly because in the long run these nations are slated to be an integral part of the Soviet system, the decision was made to drive them to the goal of socialism along the only "correct" road, that already traveled by the Soviet Union. There is no room for any "capitalist remnants" that might become a focus of opposition.

And we need not dwell on the constitutional forms, which in the latest versions are approaching the Stalin Constitution of 1936, or on the theory of "people's democracy," which seems to mean different things at different times in different countries. One thing it is not is a permanent compromise of capitalist and socialist elements, although that was the talk in the early days when it was still necessary to conciliate noncommunists. Since 1948 both Soviet theorists and their satellite pupils have made it clear that "people's democracy" means the dictatorship of the proletariat though "not in the Soviet form." There is no stopping halfway, as Stalin has said, on the road to "socialism." Every year the satellite states, already Soviet in content, come closer to the Soviet form.

In the economic field the Soviet leadership has driven the satellite nations relentlessly toward the Soviet-type economy, following the two main lines of rapid industrialization, at the expense of both worker and consumer, and collectivization of agriculture, at the expense of the independent peasant. Industrial production is now well above prewar and still going up, though the obstacles loom larger as time goes on. Goals have had to be revised in Czechoslovakia, the chosen producer of heavy goods, which has been forced to undergo major changes in its economy. In Hungary the recent change in government coincided with the announcement that the pace of industrialization had been too fast. But this is only a temporary respite.

Meanwhile in agriculture the socialized sector continues to grow, although not at the same rate everywhere, and generally is marked by intensive campaigns and then halts for consolidation. In Bulgaria over 50 per cent of the arable land has been collectivized, but it has stayed at that point for the past two years. In Czechoslovakia it has reached 45 per cent fairly rapidly, amid great unrest. In Poland it has hardly begun. The Soviet leaders, and even more their local puppets, have no desire to invite the travail and bloodshed which marked the farm collectivization drive in the USSR. But the goal is set and the march to socialized agriculture goes on.

All this is not just for the purpose of proving the superiority of the Soviet economic system. The big point, so far as Soviet policy is concerned, is that these are the methods by which the human and material resources of the satellites can be put to work in the Soviet interest. The various five-year plans are meshed into the Soviet plan. The industries and the farms of the satellites produce what the Soviet Union needs for its over-all economic and politico-military strategy. Forced to cut down their trade with the West, they have been tied up in a network of economic relationships and trade treaties, "coordinated" by the Soviet-run Council for Mutual Economic Assistance in Moscow; there are arrangements which catch the satellites in a price squeeze and deprive them of the opportunity of being "exploited" by the Western "imperialists" at world market prices which would be much more advantageous to them; and there is the device of joint companies by which the key industries of Hungary and Rumania have been placed under Soviet direction. All this fraternal cooperation adds up to what is perhaps the only example of the classical Leninist description of imperialism that exists in the world today.

We have learned a good deal about these economic relationships from satellite officials who have fled to the West. The world has learned even more from the Yugoslavs, who have made a special point of documenting the case against Moscow's "unequal relationships" with its lesser Socialist brethren. "It was precisely economic relationships"—this is Milovan Djilas talking to the U. N. General Assembly in 1951—"largely founded in force and political pressure, which the Soviet Government endeavored, even partly succeeded, to impose on Yugoslavia and which it did impose on a large scale upon other East European countries, and which were intended to provide the basis for the subjugation of Yugoslavia."

Yugoslavia's defection, of course, was the most spectacular and damaging Soviet failure in the entire period since the war. Not only was a strategic area lost, but the psychological effects of this heresy of the favored satellite leader, the eldest son of the church, were such as to challenge the whole structure of international communism. It illustrated the fundamental dangers that still existed for the Soviet leadership, even when they had virtually liquidated their pro-Western, bourgeois opponents, in the increasing difficulties with satellite Communist leaders, who had to take some account of conditions in their own countries as well as of the demands made on them by Moscow. Here we get into the murky waters of relationships within the Communist family, where our sources of information are more limited. Much has come to light in the process by which the Soviet and Yugoslav Communists, each in self-justification, have washed so much dirty linen in public. But there are still many matters on which one finds it difficult to speak with any certainty, and one of these is how close the Soviet Union came to even greater losses and defections in its satellite empire in the period surrounding the open break with Tito.

According to one theory, the vigorous American policy begun in 1947—the Truman Doctrine, the Marshall Plan, and the prospect of a strong and united western Europe—not only turned the tide against Soviet imperialism in the West but threatened its still not fully consolidated hold on the East. To the Kremlin the satellite reaction to the Marshall offer showed possibilities of an attraction which, in view of the obvious economic needs and of their own inexperience or ambitions, the local Communist and coalition leaders might be unable or unwilling to resist. At the same time there was much talk about Balkan and east European federation, of which Tito would be the obvious leading spirit; he was then making a triumphal tour of the satellite capitals. All this was climaxed by Dimitrov's public espousal in January, 1948, of the idea of a customs union and eventual federation of the whole satellite area, with the obvious implication that such a grouping, even though Communist, would have some independence of Moscow. The Polish Communist leaders expressed themselves favorably toward the idea. Dimitrov probably thought so too. Stalin himself had proposed at least a South Slav federation.

But the Kremlin had definitely not cleared it. In fact, it reacted with a violence all out of proportion to the offense, largely because of the situation building up with Tito. *Pravda* denounced Dimitrov's proposal, and Stalin, according to the Yugoslav story as told in Vladimir Dedijer's book on Tito, read the riot act to both Yugoslavs and Bulgarians at a meeting held in Moscow in early February. Czechoslovakia, where the non-Communist elements were gaining ground, was seized by *coup d'état* that same month. And steps were taken immediately to reduce Yugoslavia to obedience. When these steps failed, the Cominform was called in to condemn Tito as a heretic. However confident Stalin may have been that he could replace Tito and his colleagues with " loyal " Communists, he was willing to take the risk that they could stand their ground and that Yugoslavia would be lost to the Soviet orbit. This amputation was a grievous loss but, as an acute British observer has written, " it saved the life of the patient," and a well-planned series of purges and bloodlettings restored the appearances of health.

That the Soviet hold on the remaining satellites was in such danger as this interpretation makes out is not certain. In any event, frustrated though they were in their attempts to intimidate or crush Tito within his own country, the Soviet leaders succeeded in containing Titoism within Yugoslavia's borders. But the depth of the Titoist challenge should not be minimized. The ideas behind it cannot be contained by force, for they rest in part on nationalism, which no governing group can ignore. And they have a special potency in the Communist world in that they attack the Soviet leadership in its own Marxist language and with its own weapons. Tito has called down upon himself the fury and invective of the Kremlin to a degree unequalled by any Communist since Trotsky. His is a poison which is particularly virulent and particularly contagious. They have, however, been successful in their measures of quarantine, temporarily at least, and the Gomulkas, Rajks, Kostovs, and Slanskys, whether they were potential Titos or not, have been disposed of.

Before concluding mention should be made of certain factors which underlie both Yugoslavia's successful defiance and the nearly universal nonacceptance of Soviet-Communist rule in the satellites. These factors are the traditions and deeply held convictions of the people, whether they be manifest in devotion to religion, in national patriotism, or in the peasant's stubborn attachment to his parcel of land and his way of life. These are conservative rather than revolutionary forces. They did not bring about Yugoslavia's break with Moscow. But they have made it possible for Tito to maintain it, however much he as a revolutionary Communist may scorn them, and even though they may be in many ways hostile to his regime. They cannot overturn Soviet rule in the satellites. But they can undermine and frustrate it, increase the problems and burdens, and demonstrate its impermanency. They make it possible for these nations to endure the long night of terror and despair, as they have at other times in their history.

No matter how thoroughly they try to educate the young and re-educate the old, the Soviets have not destroyed these forces as they have destroyed the old political institutions, the old parties and the old leaders. Some say they can do it in time when a new generation, knowing only communism, grows up. But even a generation is a short span in the life of a nation, and nationalism should prove resistant to all the devices of totalitarianism except annihilation.

To these elements of resistance is now added the increasing restiveness of the urban working class, which is growing in numbers and importance with the rapid expansion of industry. These proletarians, ceaselessly driven to greater production efforts for less and less in return, are reaching a state of sullen discontent, sometimes flaring into open violence, against the "proletarian" regimes which govern in their name.

This can hardly be a period of security and serene confidence in the future for those who occupy the seats of authority, or even for those who pull the strings behind the scenes. Besides the unsettling and potentially dangerous problems of local control, there are now the great uncertainties of developments at the seat of all power. Whatever the course of shifting policies and struggles for power in Moscow, they are bound to have repercussions in the satellites.

I do not want to give the impression, however, that the Soviet empire is about to collapse from within. On the contrary, so far as I am aware, the system of control is intact and is not about to break down in the near future, barring a general international crisis or some fundamental change in the USSR itself or in Soviet policy. It is true that the puppet East German regime was only saved from oblivion by the intervention of Soviet troops. But East Germany is a different proposition, from several points of view, from the satellites. And even so, the fundamental fact is that Soviet forces did intervene, and they would probably intervene in any satellite state, if necessary. Whatever line the new Soviet leadership may take toward the satellites—and Mr. Malenkov, who had a hand in setting up the Cominform, is not without responsibility for what has already been done in this field—it is not likely to deviate from Stalin's insistence on the crucial importance of this area to Soviet security.

I have avoided saying anything about United States policy, since my topic was Soviet policies and successes. Soviet successes, which are not inconsiderable, have been our failures, or rather our losses, in terms of the world balance. These are losses that were perhaps inevitable, given the postwar situation in which the United States found itself. We may regret instances of our lack of foresight, of misplaced hope and confidence, or of less than realistic negotiation. But the United States is not the arbiter of the world, least of all in areas which the Red army overran in our common war against Hitler.

The United States has in a comparatively brief period grown up to worldwide responsibilities, and to a realization of what Soviet imperialism is and what it means. So long as we keep a clear understanding of what we face, safeguard our own security, and devote our efforts to building a world in which nations can live in peace and in freedom, so also will we serve the cause of the eventual return of those nations now held captive to their rightful place in that free world community.

S. HARRISON THOMSON: **Discussion**
Editor, Journal of Central European Affairs.
University of Colorado

Mr. Campbell has presented a penetrating analysis of what and why the Soviets have accomplished in central and eastern Europe since 1944, as could be done only by one in constant and conscious touch with movements in this sensitive area. I find myself in hearty agreement on almost every point, and I want simply to pinpoint a few of Mr. Campbell's statements, and perhaps here and there to footnote his so adequate generalizations.

On the basic assumption that Soviet Russia has, as a part of a long-term policy, decided to incorporate these border peoples into the Soviet Union—a statement, by the way, which opens large vistas of the how and the when and the immediate repercussions of such an event—we are presented with three "major lines of Soviet policy and action" in this area. The first is *military security*. The "second is the objective of *absolute political control*." The third is Sovietization or "the attempt to remake the whole pattern of life of these peoples."

I should like to comment on each of these objectives and their effectuation. Mr. Campbell remarks that the Russians desire to organize these countries into a "safety belt." The use of this term inevitably suggests the classic concept of the "*cordon sanitaire*" which was neither sanitary, salutary, nor a cordon. I venture to suggest that the image here might be regarded as inept. It seems much more probable that Soviet plans call for a neutral zone to the *west* of these presently captive states—to stretch from Finland and indeed all Scandinavia to include all of Germany, Austria, Italy, and perhaps even Yugoslavia. It is not a pleasant prospect, but few prospects in this complex of issues and tensions are pleasant. I doubt if any serious student of Soviet policy could long harbor the thought that the Kremlin imagined it could keep Germany divided for long. But who dares forget the history of German-Russian relations through the centuries, a story of quick shifts from animosity to bosom friendship, yet and still a story of permanent contiguity. The East Germans have been treated completely differently from the Poles, the Czechs, the Rumanians, and the rest. They have been mercilessly exploited, callously driven, and prodigiously lied to, but no one could deduce from a picture of their treatment since 1945 that the Soviets planned to stay there for good. The same holds for Soviet action in Austria.

I feel it necessary to insist on this distinction precisely because a failure to grasp its significance might easily lead us to misunderstand, to our regret, possible Soviet withdrawal from the German lands. If we should interpret this withdrawal as weakness or the action of an enfeebled dictatorship, we would be grievously mistaken. I shall return to another aspect of this differentiation between Soviet treatment of the German lands—a part of the neutralized area—and what Mr. Campbell and I unhappily agree is now slated for organic inclusion in the greater Soviet Union, the real captive states.

Mr. Campbell treats with some care the matter of Soviet "security" and the training of satellite armies. He uses the figure of "over one million men" for the latter. This figure would appear to me to be low. One could argue very easily for nearly two million in regular armies and another three or four in paramilitary reserves or trained police and auxiliary militia units, to says nothing of women in uniform. These larger figures—and there are reputable estimates that run even higher—are not to be lightly challenged. It would be easy, as well as unfortunate, to emphasize unduly the disaffection of the rank and file of the satellite armies, although perhaps in 1945 to 1948 we might have. But the officer cadres have been purged and purged, re-recruited, drilled, and indoctrinated. A few Jareckis do not tell the whole story by any means. Another five to ten years of training will further strengthen the morale of these armies, and the harsh punishment to disaffected individuals will not encourage more of it.

Under the second rubric, the Soviet demand for "absolute political control," Mr. Campbell quite properly brings up the question of the weaknesses within these countries "which made the Soviet task easier." This sad reality, it seems to me, is not generally recognized at its true value. Things move so fast we are inclined to forget all too quickly the events of the day before yesterday. Those events, in this case, I conceive to be the Nazi occupation of these same countries that are now occupied by another and not less brutal or systematic conqueror.

From 1938 to 1945—over six years—the Germans had, with ruthless and methodical precision, set out to exterminate the intellectual, social, and economic leadership of the smaller peoples they had set their heel upon. The Nürnberg Documents tell the story, but it was much more graphically told on the faces and in the actions of those that survived, and who came face to face—in 1944 and 1945—with a new threat to the freedom of their country in the frightening hordes from the East. Their older leaders were gone or broken. There was no reserve pool of young minds trained in the ways of peace. And six years of deceit, badgering, fear of delation or of capricious murder, denial of the elemental rights of man, six years of gradual starvation, of body not least, but of mind and heart too—this is but a poor preparation for resistance to the insidious political semantics of an organism the whole world now knows planned thirty-five years ago to take advantage of precisely this deep and desperate fatigue. Certainly, as Mr. Campbell says, "most of the noncommunist political organizations were lacking in dynamic leadership and in popular support." That leadership had been shot or hung and that "popular support" had been starved and broken by the Germans. There were no young or middle-aged to take their place.

Mr. Campbell then goes on to emphasize the aims and procedure of sovietization, a process of transformation that would alter every human expression, enter into every human motivation, and revolutionize every facet of human society. There has been made mention of the concept of the "new Soviet man." We could easily pay too little regard to the import of this concept. All up and down the new peoples' democracies one can hear this clarion call to the new creation, the new man cast in the new mold of the Soviet man. There's the "new freedom," the "new democracy," "the new truth," but most of all there is to be the new man, with a new will (obedient to the party), a new energy, beyond that of decrepit capitalistic man, with new Stakhanovite productive capacities that make capitalistic norms of production seem puny, and a new set of joys and satisfactions that make the old bourgeois concepts look pale and tawdry.

They begin to work this transformation early, and keep it up through life. To examine the school curriculum and the guided play for children in these captive states confirms in a very subtle and accurate way if such confirmation were necessary, the assumption Mr. Campbell makes and which I fully endorse, that it is the Soviet intention to incorporate these nations absolutely and completely into the Soviet Union. There are almost no native fairy stories being printed in these lands—they have been consistently replaced by Russian fairy tales. It may not be irrelevant that the Russians have always been masters of the fairy-story. Native art in almost every manifestation is being replaced by Russian art. The motion picture industry of both Poland and Czechoslovakia is spending most of its time and energy turning out Russian films. By now, more than half of the books published in *all* these countries—and the parallel development is tremendously significant—as if by a single order are translations of works by Russian authors. The same holds true in art, music, education, poetry, the novel and the drama.

In economics, law, sociology and what is euphemistically called history, the percentage is much higher. *Most* of the scientific works, from the life sciences to mathematics, are by Russians. Foreign languages may be learned in these countries, but with a unique difference from the jejune method used in bourgeois lands. Because the content of the writing and the intent of the author are the principal criteria of quality, an anthology of the best French, for beginners as well as for advanced students, contains long extracts of the majestic and resonant prose of that master of French style, Josef Vissarionovré Djgashvili of hallowed memory. His German is superior to that of Goethe, his Italian brooks no comparison with either Dante, that stale Florentine failure, or Mazzini, that amateur demagogue.

This new Soviet man of the peoples' democracies will speak many languages, but he will have but one mind, one will, one hope, one fatherland—the Soviet world, with Russia its core and Moscow its head. An enforced isolation so comprehensive as this, so soundly based in human psychology, so well calculated to mold the mind of a whole people from the cradle to the grave, is to us, I can only think, frightening in its total depravity. Yet there it is, in front of us, actively at work among people with a millenium and more of Western openness and reason. Ten more years of this Soviet success—for that is what we are talking about—will take a full century to undo.

Here we can remember, from earlier and more carefree days, the first lines of Virgil's *Aeneid*. "I sing of arms and the man." We have heard recently much talk of *arms*. But the *man* must not be forgotten. Whatever the success of Soviet procurement and manipulation of arms we may decide to recognize, we cannot gainsay their formidable success with the man. Indeed, I know of no such conscious and calculated effort to uproot, as it were by a surgical operation, a whole culture and put another in its place, on this scale and with this easy and early success, in all recorded history.

In the discussion the question was asked if it was not true that Tito had grown too powerful and that therefore the Kremlin had given the order to cut off his head. Mr. Campbell answered that this factor is to be added to the economic explanation contained in his lecture. This is the over-all explanation, he explained—Tito's refusal to submit to such sweeping control as desired by the Russians—especially economic controls. The Russians did not allow Yugoslavian industrialization on the scale desired by Tito and caused a drain of capital goods.

In response to the question, what is your opinion of the theory that Titoism is an *organic* disease of Stalinist communism and not due, primarily, to historic traditions, economic conditions in Yugoslavia, and other factors, it was agreed with that Russian Communist party domination of local leaders naturally frustrates their desire to disagree and to represent local interests in contrast to those of Russia--especially economically. This situation can foster revolt, as in Yugoslavia. Titoism, however, is less likely in places where the Communist party is a revolutionary opposition force, dependent to a great extent on the USSR.

Finally, Mr. Campbell was asked to discuss in more detail the use of Soviet nationals in important posts in the captive states. Mr. Campbell answered by stating that there are many Soviet nationals hidden in key positions. There are M.V.D. agents in the eastern European armies and in key industries in particular. All the top positions in the Polish Army are held by Russians. There are also Soviet citizens who were born in the eastern European states, and who have returned there, but who do not seem to have given up their USSR citizenship. There are many more among the satellite political leadership. There also appears to be an amalgamation of citizenship concepts and citizenship laws going on in eastern Europe, which appears to work especially for Russia's benefit.

Mr. Thomson then mentioned that the process in question has been going on for eight years now. It began with the Polish army in 1944. The extent of the use of Soviet nationals in important posts in the captive states is deep, but unclear. Perhaps there are 15,000 officers of Soviet nationality in the Polish army—perhaps 30,000 noncommissioned officers. The Polish air corps and navy are fully controlled by Soviet nationals. This process goes into all ministries similiarly, and occurs in countries besides Poland.

*Soviet-Communist Pressures on Western Europe**

A. ROSSI,
Author of A Communist Party in Action
Paris, France

At first glance, what we call the " iron curtain " divides Europe into two zones between which there is a deep gap, and the differences all seem to turn into opposition. East of the line of demarcation the Communist parties, while in the minority, came into power between 1944–45 and March, 1948. It is not a majority which gives them the power, it is power which assures them the majority. In the West the Communist parties have neither a majority nor the power.

In the East, Soviet occupation or Soviet pressure has, directly or indirectly, played a decisive role by entering into combination with the political tactics and work of organization of the Communist parties.[1] In the West, while the connection between Communist action and Soviet pressure has not been entirely lacking, it has not been possible to develop it or push it to its logical conclusion. In the first place, in a great many countries of the West the Communist parties were, and still are, very weak. They became parties of the masses only in France and in Italy. Even these large parties were unable to follow the same path as their brothers in eastern Europe for the following reasons: (a) The strength relationships which developed in France and in Italy between Communists and noncommunists after the Liberation did not permit it; (b) the world situation called for a

* The translation of this paper into English from French was made by Theodore H. Leon and John O. Walker.

[1] We have sought to describe the stages of the Soviet Communist march to power in the satellite countries in the study entitled " Theorie des démocraties populaires," *Prévues*, Paris, May, 1953.

certain amount of caution on the part of the USSR, which it could not have discarded without bringing about a serious and premature break with its former allies.

In metropolitan France, in the first two postwar national elections, the Communists obtained 26 per cent of the votes (5 million out of 19.8 million votes cast) in October, 1945, and 28.5 per cent (5.48 million out of 19.2) in November, 1946. In Italy in the first elections to the Constituent Assembly (at the beginning of June, 1946), the Communists obtained only 19.7 per cent of the votes (4.28 million out of 21.76). But their situation was less favorable than these figures indicate. There was no territorial contiguity between France or Italy and the USSR. Furthermore, in so far as there were Allied troops in these countries, they were American and not Soviet. This latter factor was of the greatest importance. When the letters between Tito and Stalin were published, after the break between the Yugoslav Communist party and the Bolshevik party of the USSR, Stalin, in order to disparage the merits to which the followers of Tito laid claim in bringing about their success, insinuated in his letter of May 4, 1948, that the Soviet army had been able to intervene in Yugoslavia, " creating the conditions which were essential for bringing the Communist party to power," while " unfortunately it did not contribute, and could not contribute, the same assistance to the French and Italian Communist parties." [2]

In the autumn of 1952, during the campaign which the French Communist party conducted against two of its leaders, Andre Marty and Charles Tillon, it was a question of the attitude which the party had adopted during the first months following the liberation. Marty and Tillon reproached the party for not having taken advantage of the situation, which, they said, was favorable to it, in order to seize power, as was done in the satellite countries. They condemned the party for having dissolved the " patriotic militia "—that is to say, Communist militia —for having surrendered their arms to the government and having agreed to the integration of the *Francs-tireurs et Partisans* (F. T. P.) into the regular army. They affirmed that these

[2] " Exchange of letters between the Central Committee of the Yugoslav Communist Party and the Central Committee of the Communist Party (Bolshevik) of the USSR," *Le Livre Yougoslave* (*The Yugoslav Book*), (Paris: 1950), 110-11.

measures had constituted a form of barter with General de Gaulle, then president of the provisional government, so that the latter would allow the return to France from Moscow of the secretary general of the party, Maurice Thorez, in spite of his desertion from the French army at the beginning of October, 1939, and the ignominious sentence which had been passed upon him for this reason. This is not the place to analyze all the elements of this policy, but it is interesting to note the reply which the Political Bureau of the party made to these criticisms:

> In August, 1944 the war was not yet ended. It was possible that the alliance which formed the front of the capitalist powers might turn against the Soviet Union. If a pretext had been given them, the Americans, who came to fight in our country at the eleventh hour (sic), in the fear of seeing the Soviet army advance too far toward the West would not have hesitated to ally themselves with Hitler in Europe and with Japan in Asia in order to align all the forces of international capitalism against the socialist countries. Even in France, in spite of the considerable progress in its influence, the Party would rapidly have been isolated and it could only have ended in a " bloody failure " because De Gaulle would have been supplied with a pretext for calling on the aid of Anglo-American arms in order to crush the uprising.[3]

There is no need to emphasize the false and anachronistic nature of this representation of the state of mind of the United States at that time, but it is certain (a) that the French Communist party was not in a position in 1944 and 1945 to seize power in France (or in Italy); (b) that even if the party had been able to do so, Moscow would not have urged it in this direction, because a success of this nature would have unleashed an Anglo-American reaction which the USSR wished to avoid at any cost.

Never has the separation between East and West in Europe been interpreted by the USSR as signifying a definitive or even stable delineation of mutually guaranteed and respected zones of influence. If Winston Churchill had ever seriously thought

[3] Resolution of October 3, 1952, of the Political Bureau of the French Communist party, *Humanité,* October 4.

that, his policy would have suffered a set-back bordering on failure. While modifying its attitude according to the relative importance to it of the different countries and problems, the USSR has practised everywhere, even in the West, a policy of being at hand (*politique de présence*), and of being at hand actively, according to the means at its disposal. It brought about the paradoxical situation that the "iron curtain" was for it never a frontier, whereas it was one for its former allies. The road which leads from the east to the west of Europe is, in Soviet strategy, a one-way street. This strategy corresponds to the deep and permanent characteristics of a policy which has motivated it for over a third of a century, and today it is impelled in that direction by its own weight, as a result of the situation created in Europe and in the world by the outcome of the second World War.

From the point of view of geopolitics, to which the Germans were attached and which the Russian Bolsheviks have rediscovered, a radical transformation has taken place in the respective positions of the USSR and the West, considered in the European framework. Within this framework, the USSR acquired a preponderant role after the defeat of Germany and the weakening of France. This USSR, which scarcely twenty years ago appeared to be condemned to live almost on the fringe of Europe, now enjoys a power tending toward hegemony. The expansion of the USSR has moved so much toward the West that one might say today that western Europe is living on the fringe of the Soviet or Sovietized world.

Soviet Communist pressure on the West is first of all, independently of the other factors, the consequence of this reversal of the strength relationships. A simple glance at the map of Europe suggests the least optimistic conclusions. Public opinion does not consider the few hundred kilometers which separate the Soviet zone from the French border, for example, as a valid margin of safety. We saw this at the time of the first incidents in Berlin between the occupying powers during the latter months of 1948, and to a greater extent at the time of the outbreak of the Korean war; the uneasiness of a portion of the population of the West was great, bordering at times on a sort of resigned despair and panic. The "capital" declaration of Maurice Thorez to the Central Committee of the party in February, 1949, contributed to fix general attention on this aspect of the problem, for it gave a rather clear reply to the question posed by the non-communists: "What would you do if the Red army occupied Paris?"

"If," stated the Secretary General of the party, in case of war, "the Soviet army was led to pursue the aggressors as far as our territory" the workers and the people of France "could not behave toward the Soviet army any differently than the workers and people of Poland, Rumania and Yugoslavia," etc.; that is to say, they would welcome the Soviet army as an army of liberation and would give it their full support.[4]

This declaration was taken up by the leaders of all the other Communist parties of the West. In France it provoked, among Communist circles, not panic, but, on the contrary, a surge of hope, to such an extent that their leaders had to intervene in order to calm them. When the Central Committee of the party met in April, 1949, Leon Mauvais, in his report cautioned the militants who had envisaged the declaration of Thorez "from the angle of the possible arrival of the Red army at Paris and as the means of settling certain accounts" [5] by taking advantage of this arrival in order to liquidate their opponents.

Gradually the apprehension of the populace was stilled. First the propaganda of the Communists and their allies succeeded, as we shall see, in replacing the picture of a Red army hurling itself on the countries of western Europe which were yet free by the other, highly emotional, picture of an American army dragging western Europe into the maelstrom of a war against the USSR. Then other arguments of an oversimplified, and hence all the more effective, nature gained a hold over the mind of the public. Why, they said, if the Russians are so strong and formidable, have they not given the push which could topple the still weak structure of Europe in a state of reconstruction? The Russians, they remarked, tolerate the Berlin enclave; they have not reached

[4] *Humanité,* February 22, 1949. About five months previously the Political Bureau of the French Communist party, in a statement made on September 30, 1948, had contented itself with proclaiming: "The people of France will never make war on the Soviet Union."—*Humanité,* October 1, 1948.

[5] *Cahiers du communisme,* No. 5, May, 1949, 537.

the shores of the North Sea or those of the Atlantic; as long as the Yugoslav defection lasts they can not approach the Mediterranean except through Albania. Nothing can lead one to suppose, therefore, that the USSR wishes to attack western Europe, or what remains of it, militarily.

Even if the arguments from which this conclusion is drawn are to be regarded with caution, we believe that the USSR does not, in fact, intend to regulate its relations with western Europe by means of war. In the first place, the USSR is conducting its policy on a world scale and not just on a European scale. It determines its conduct according to an over-all view, dominated by the need and the desire to avoid the risks of a generalized conflict with the United States. A new outbreak of the Soviet army toward the West would make this conflict almost certain. Besides, if the tanks, following the tracks of Hitler's divisions, reached the English Channel, England would probably react as it did in the summer of 1940.

Within the framework of its general policy, the USSR gains no major advantage by occupying western Europe. Let us say that it does not think it needs to do so, for it is sufficient for it to keep Europe disunited and paralyzed. The USSR has no interest in paying a heavy price, by running a serious risk of war, to control western Europe for its benefit, for it proposes to obtain the same result almost without cost. If France, western Germany, and Italy are "neutralized," if the Ruhr industrial complex ceases to furnish an economic foundation for the defense of the West, if the bonds between France and England and America are greatly loosened, if not broken, the USSR will no longer have anything to fear from that direction. The odd "peace" which it is imposing on the West can advantageously take the place of war in this sector, since it is the equivalent thereof—one might say the cheapest *ersatz*.

The USSR, by conducting a fierce *political* struggle against the West at all times, is fighting on familiar ground, where it has had long experience and has numerous bases. For the Moscow leaders, who have studied Clausewitz, this "odd peace" is also war but waged "by other means."

These means are many and they range from organization to ideology. With respect to organization, Moscow had in the

West two great Communist parties at the beginning of 1953: the French (about 600,000 members) and the Italian (over 2 million). In spite of their size, these parties, if they remained isolated, could not successfully mount guard over Soviet interests. Hence they have tried first of all to eliminate or to infiltrate their nearest competitors among labor: the Socialist parties. Their purpose was to bring about "organic unity" with these parties by incorporating them, by "digesting" them in one way or another, as happened in all the satellite countries, including eastern Germany, where the Socialist-Communist merger was decided in April, 1946.

The fusion of the two parties nearly took place in France also, where, however, it was finally rejected as a result of the return of Leon Blum from his deportation to Germany. The small nucleus of elements closely bound to the Communists left the S. F. I. O.[6] in July, 1948, to form a "Socialist Unity Party," a small group which has been reduced more and more to the role of "maid of all work" of the Communist party.

The fusion between Socialists and Communists did not take place in Italy either. But here the Socialist party, which, in the elections of June, 1946, had obtained more votes than the Communist party (4.67 million to 4.28), linked itself so closely with the Communists by a "unity-of-action" pact that there was finally a split in the party: at the beginning of 1947 a Social Democratic party was formed which had few roots among the working masses, while the majority of the Italian Socialist party, led by Pietro Nenni, ended by constituting politically almost a double of the Communist party, performing with it a sort of division of labor for the support of the Moscow policy and taking as its ideal and model the regimes of the "peoples' democracies" of the satellite countries. In all the other countries of western Europe, the separation, and often the opposition, between Communists (nearly nonexistent) and Socialists remained very marked. In England the Communist party has renewed, since the end of the war, its demand for affiliation with the Labor party, which has rejected it.[7]

[6] Section Française de l'Internationale Ouvrière (French Section of Workers' International).

[7] By 2,678,000 votes against 468,000 at its Congress in June, 1946.

The same "unity" attempts, which were also encouraged by Moscow, were pursued by the Communists on the labor-union level. In only two countries of the West were the Communists successful in obtaining control of the labor-union movement: in France and in Italy. In France a union between the free labor-union organization (C.G.T.)—by far the most important—and the Communist labor unions (C.G.T.U.),[8] took place early in 1936 in consequence of the "Popular Front." It was broken three and a half years later as a result of the German-Soviet pact and the adherence thereto by the Communists. It was reconstituted in the latter period of the German occupation and was again abandoned in December, 1947. The Christian labor unions (C.F.T.C.)[9] in France did not step into the "unity" trap, whereas in Italy, after the Liberation, all labor-union trends were united in the C.G.I.L.,[10] from which the Christian and Socialist labor-union members succeeded in escaping, not without difficulty and losses, toward the middle of 1948.

One cannot lay sufficient stress on the fact that the question of the unity of the political movements and the trade unions, both of them under Communist control and leadership, has not been a formal question of structure, and still less an administrative question—Moscow wanted to make them essential tools of its policy, and especially its foreign policy, in the countries not yet annexed or colonized by it.

The tactics of the Communist parties, like their form of organization, have had but a single purpose in all countries: to defend and reinforce the positions gained by the USSR as a result of the second World War. In the countries of western Europe the strength relationships did not permit of giving the Communist parties the order to seize power, which was done very soon, at a more or less rapid pace, in the countries of eastern Europe which were destined to become "satellites" within a short time.

In the West, tactics were based on the following principle: while renouncing the seizure of power, the Communist parties were to exert pressure in order to control the foreign policy of

[8] Confédération Générale du Travail and C.G.T. unitaire.

[9] Confédération Française des Travailleurs Chrétiens.

[10] Confederazione Generale Italiana del Lavoro.

the governments and orient and aim it in a direction favorable to Soviet interests as conceived in Moscow. That is why (in contrast to what had taken place between the two wars or even at the time of the "Popular Front" in France, when the Communist parties, while supporting the government of 1936—as the rope supports the hanged man—never went so far as to participate in the government) Moscow urged the Communist parties to take part in the government wherever possible. And the Communist parties, from the time of the liberation, did enter the government in France and in Italy and remained in them until May, 1947.[11] It should be noted that in both France and Italy the Communists did not leave the government of their own accord; in France they even clung to it, and it required a decree of the president of the Republic, Mr. Vincent Auriol, to eject the Communist ministers who, although they voted against the government of which they were a part, refused to resign.

Indeed, the Communist parties in the government in France and in Italy obtained great benefits thereby, infiltrating all the machinery of the state and of the administration, and maneuvering in such a way as to multiply the advantages of their power and of the opposition entrusted to the party and the labor unions. But, while the Communist ministers unscrupulously exploited the posts of command which had been entrusted to them, the real reason for their presence in the government, articulated with the activity of their party in the country, was direct support for the consolidation and expansion of the USSR.

Stalin, after having made of France, between 1934 and 1939, the principal pawn in his game in Europe, to the extent to which his effort to arrive at an agreement with Hitler risked failure, took into consideration the role which France might play after the liberation. Hence he encouraged the French Communists, who were not in a position to seize power, to participate in the first De Gaulle government. The first diplomatic act of the new France was the treaty of alliance with the USSR, signed at Moscow on December 10, 1944. The treaty was directed particularly against Germany, but its historic significance, in the mind of General de Gaulle and in Stalin's calculations, was that of

[11] There was also a period of Communist participation in Belgium, which lasted until March, 1947.

the establishment of a policy in which the Franco-Soviet alliance would have allowed France to free herself from all allegiance to England and particularly to the United States, and would have allowed the USSR to cut any too close bonds between France and the Western democracies. Anti-German in its content, the treaty was—by the very play of its mechanism—anti-American. And, while the point aimed at Germany would be blunted by Moscow and the French Communists, the anti-American point would be sharpened and it alone would be grasped and maneuvered by them.

Stalin felt considerable scorn for France because it had been beaten in 1940. But France was still, even in his eyes, the most important power of western Europe—at least as long as Germany remained crushed under the weight of its terrible defeat.

As long as Germany lay prostrate and appeared to be unable to rise, France embodied the course of the West on the European continent. If she were submerged or paralyzed, there would be no more West on the continent; and that prospect could not fail to be enticing to Moscow. During the campaign conducted by the leaders of the French Communist party against Marty and Tillon, they accused the former, in particular, of having been too greatly obsessed by the problems of domestic policy instead of placing those connected with foreign policy in the foreground. Marty is said to have committed the error, in 1943 and especially in 1944 and the following years, of seeing only the Gaullist danger, "relegating to the background," says the resolution of the Political Bureau concerning him, "the effect on our country of American imperialism." He "underestimated the role played by the Socialist leaders as an American tool at a time when the policy of Marshallization of France was being developed with the aid of the parties of the third force whose activity was thereby blunted."[12] In other words, the Gaullists, those "Fascists" or alleged Fascists, were much less dangerous to Moscow than the Socialists and democrats, because the former could rise up against the American measures while the latter supported them.

There is not room here to illustrate in more detail the connection—which, however, is obvious—between the activity of

[12] *Humanité*, October 4, 1952.

the Communist parties of the West and Soviet foreign policy. It is sufficient, in the case of France, to consider the position of the French Communist party with respect to the "colonial" problem to show how close and decisive this connection is.[13] The same conclusions would be reached by examining the attitude of the Italian Communist party toward the Badoglio government and toward the Vatican during the years following the liberation, its attitude with respect to the treaty of peace, the establishment of the Italian frontiers, the entry of Italy into the United Nations, and the question of Trieste. It would be interesting to analyze the reasons and circumstances surrounding the participation of the Communist party in the de Gasperi government in June, 1946, after the proclamation of the Republic, and those surrounding its going over to the opposition. The guiding thread to the actions of this party from 1943 to 1953 is still the same: throwing the greatest possible weight into the balance of international affairs in favor of the Soviet Union over and above any other consideration.

The most conclusive example of the subordination of the Communist parties to Soviet directives and interests is the campaign unleashed by Moscow against the Marshall Plan. When the broad outlines of this plan were known and a conference was called in Paris in June, 1947, to study it and to implement it, Moscow intervened immediately to sabotage it, to prevent its effects from being felt across the iron curtain. The plan was in such close conformity with the interests of the nations of Europe that even the Communist governments of the satellite countries looked upon it with favor. We know what happened, in this respect, at Warsaw and at Prague. It is less well known that in the West, too, the Communist parties in the countries which were in a position to benefit from the plan hesitated in the beginning to take a position. At the Strasbourg congress of the party (June, 1947), Maurice Thorez expressed himself in an equivocal manner in his report:[14] In Italy, where the aid to be furnished

[13] See below p. 251.

[14] An editor of *l'Humanité,* who had in good faith interpreted the words of Thorez in a sense hostile to the Marshall Plan, was disavowed by the party, which treated him almost like an *agent provocateur* and announced measures to be taken against him.

under the plan was almost a question of life or death, the Communist party and its labor unions displayed great caution.[15]

Moscow, through its drastic intervention, resorted to extreme measures. One after another the governments of the satellite countries declared their intention to remain away from the Paris conference. On June 21 the USSR agreed to take part in it, but, in a commentary by the Tass agency, it stated a few days later that it was opposed, in the name of national sovereignty, to the preparation of a European economic program. Thus it gave to the Communist parties of the East as well as of the West the principal slogan under which the struggle against the Marshall Plan was to be conducted. But the alarm caused by the initial hesitation of these parties had been great in Moscow. It was this alarm and the desire to prevent its recurrence which brought about the decision to create the Cominform.

It is not sufficiently kept in mind that the Cominform was essentially created as an element of Soviet strategy intended to coordinate the struggle of the Communist parties against the Marshall Plan. And it was not by chance that the Cominform grouped the Communist parties of all the countries which were " threatened " by the Marshall Plan—those of the countries which were already satellites or were soon to become satellites (Czechoslovakia and Eastern Germany) and those of the two countries of the West which were most likely, on account of their economic conditions, to accept the plan, that is, France and Italy. After the first Cominform conference, which was held in Poland at the end of September, 1947, all the Communist parties took a stand in conformity with the conclusions of this conference (Zhdanov speech and resolution adopted), denouncing the Marshall Plan as "an instrument of preparation for war," as "a plan for the economic and political enslavement of Europe."

In France not only the Communist party but the national committee of the C.G.T., upon orders, pronounced themselves (November 9, 1947) against the Marshall Plan, to combat which the Communist majority did not hesitate to provoke a conflict which aggravated its relations with the minority and was one of

[15] The Communist leader Scoccimarro declared on June 16, 1947, that Italy needed a foreign loan and that the United States was the only country which could supply it.

the chief causes of the labor-union split. In Italy the head of the Communist party, Togliatti, gave the greatest possible impetus to the campaign against the Marshall Plan in the speech which he delivered on November 16 at the congress of Communists of the province of Milan.

In France the struggle against the Marshall Plan engaged all the forces of the party and its labor unions. They strove to sabotage the plan indirectly by sabotaging French production and reconstruction through repeated strikes—notably in the mines, in the nationalized industries and in the public services—such as those which took place in the autumn of 1947 and the latter months of 1948. In this way the contribution of the Marshall Plan to the recovery of the French economy was to be absorbed to a not inconsiderable extent in making up for the losses caused by the economic confusion. At the same time it was explained that if the United States sent help to France it was because it was impelled by the economic crisis raging there, which forced the United States to seek new markets at any cost. The Marshall Plan was denounced as a plan for the "enslavement of the French economy" and they sought to mobilize against it any particular interests which were more or less endangered.

In the course of such mobilization, lies were spread unscrupulously: if the sugar-beet crop was to be curtailed it was not because of the excessive stock of sugar accumulated in the French refineries but because the United States wished an outlet in France for its own sugar; the slump in wine sales was due to the introduction of Coca Cola; the crisis in the French motion-picture industry was nothing but the result of the "invasion of Hollywood films"; it was the "excessive imports" under the Marshall Plan which paralyzed French agriculture, etc., etc. This propaganda and agitation by the party were not without results: by throwing suspicion on the plan and on its intentions, by disseminating lies, they succeeded in taking from the United States part of the political advantages which its aid could and should have assured it and even succeeded in turning this aid against it.

How shall we explain this at least relative political setback? As Mario Einaudi remarked in the preface of a book devoted to communism in western Europe,[16] most of the funds placed by the Economic Cooperation Administration at the disposal of France and Italy were used to surmount critical situations (at times, to meet treasury deficits) and not in basic investments; although very beneficial, these payments were not able to transform the economic structure of these countries permanently by modernizing their industry and their agriculture. Many American citizens have spoken of the " ingratitude " of the peoples who benefitted from this great aid which, being inspired by lofty perspectives, was by that very fact disinterested. In this connection collective psychology has been brought in; it has been said, for example, that the French suffered from the " M. Perrichon complex "—M. Perrichon being the character in a comedy by Labiche who could no longer tolerate a young suitor for the hand of his daughter after the former had saved his life.

The reasons for the limited return from the Marshall Plan appear to us to be deeper but also simpler. At that time the United States perhaps placed too much confidence in economics and the automatism thereof. Actually, struggles fought in the field of economics require, in order to be truly won, a transmutation of their economic results into political results; the contests engaged in may be economic, but the points measuring success or failure are tallied on a political " computing machine." The Communist leaders have waged an essentially political war against the Marshall Plan, and it was during the course of this war that they were able to reduce the benefits which the United States had assured itself by its perspicacious intervention.

In the struggle against the Marshall Plan the USSR was able to turn to its advantage the real difficulties encountered and being encountered by the countries of the West, and particularly Great Britain and France, as a result of the shrinking of the world market which the USSR itself brought about and which dominates its fundamental outlook. Actually, in the minds of the Bolshevik leaders, the fate of the USSR is bound up with the enlargement of the " Socialist world " (USSR, China, " peoples' democracies ") at the expense of the Western " capitalist world " which is condemned to asphyxiation, even if, for tactical reasons or for contingent economic necessities, the USSR sends

[16] *Communism in Western Europe* (Cornell University Press, 1951),

in a few tanks of oxygen from time to time through a certain amount of trade.

The "capitalist" business world is not, moreover, very sensitive to "historical perspectives"; it lives from day to day and, when pressed by its difficulties, it is prone to neglect the political and long-range implications of the solutions to which it is forced to resort in the immediate present. The USSR is never motivated by reasons of "pure" economics, and that is an advantage which is always with it; in its strategy, and in the strategy which it prescribes for the Communist parties and groups of all types which it manipulates, the political side always retains its rightful place. The Marshall Plan had scarcely been presented to the public when the British Communist leader, Harry Pollitt, in the name of his party, wrote [17] a letter to Mr. Attlee advocating sending a British mission to Moscow to negotiate a trade agreement, loosening the bonds "which linked British economy to American imperialism," and recalling to England at least 50 per cent of the troops stationed abroad. Similar leitmotifs in France and in Italy accompanied the Communist campaigns for the resumption of East-West trade, particularly at the time of the economic conference held at Moscow in April, 1952, and at the time of the work of the "experts" on the same problem (Geneva, April, 1953).

Quite recently, upon the occasion of a Franco-Soviet trade agreement signed on July 15, 1953, at the Quai d'Orsay, a certain segment of the press, always the same segment, sought to force this agreement into the perspective of a reversal of French foreign policy, for which it has been working actively for years.

The Soviet Communist campaigns against the Atlantic Pact and against the European Defense Community were carried on in the West with an almost frenzied intensity, especially in France and in Italy. As early as March 7, 1949, the Political Bureau of the French Communist party protested against the decision of the government to sign the Atlantic Pact, stating: "We refuse to consider that this Pact is binding on the word of France"; in Italy the Communist deputies violently obstructed the pact in parliament, and their leader, Togliatti, revealing the

[17] August 31, 1947.

real purpose of their opposition, presented an amendment by which a commitment was undertaken, even though ratifying the pact, "not to permit any foreign power to use the national territory for military bases of any type whatever." It is well known that the Paris and Bonn agreements with respect to the E.D.C. have not yet been ratified by the French parliament[18] and that in all the countries of the West the Communists, their allies and friends are happy over the "crisis of the Atlantic policy" which they seek to aggravate in every way.

Against the military agreements concluded at the instance of the United States, the Western Communist parties have engaged in direct action intended materially to prevent their execution. That is especially true in the case of France. This direct action has taken the following form, referring merely to its principle and public character:

(a) A program in the army and especially among conscripts, whom they try to bring into associations which are intended to maintain contact with them during their military service. This activity is entrusted particularly to Communist youth groups forming part of the *Union des Jeunesses Républicaines de France* (U.J.R.F.) (Union of Republican Youth of France) and it has all the characteristics of "revolutionary defeatism" with a Bolshevik trademark; (b) struggle against the manufacturing, handling, and transportation of any war matériel; (c) struggle against the debarkation, handling and transportation of American war matériel; and (d) campaigns against the "American occupation," directed especially toward preventing the establishment of strategic bases and the enlargement of airports.

Characteristic of all this activity is the essential part taken in it by the labor unions of the C.G.T. in their central, federal, and local organizations and in the plant committees.[19] The

[18] The French Communist party proclaims: "For patriots and for French democrats, two tasks are imperative: to oppose the ratification of the Bonn and Paris agreements and to obtain respect for the treaty of friendship and assistance concluded between France and the USSR in December 1944." *Humanité*, September 29, 1952.

[19] In April, 1950, the national conference of the committees of the metallurgical industry declared that these committees, "with the aid and under the guidance of the labor unions," were "to make an energetic stand against all manufacturing of war matériel, to denounce it, to

secretariat of the C.G.T. instructed one of its members (A. Le Léap—at present under arrest on account of it) to direct the antimilitarist activity of the Communist youth organizations. The struggle was to be carried on through certain special categories of workers: metal-workers, railway workers, dock workers, and sailors, who were in the best position to sabotage the manufacture and transportation of war matériel.

In May, 1950, the C.G.T. organized a conference of the Federation of Government Workers (workers in arsenals and arms manufacturing plants) in order to issue the following instructions: "In manufacturing arms you are working against yourselves. Therefore, do not manufacture any under any circumstances." At the same time the *Fédération Syndicale Mondiale* (World Federation of Labor Unions), meeting at Budapest, expressed in a manifesto its solidarity "with the workers in mechanical engineering in France and Italy who refuse to manufacture arms." The activities under (a) and (d) must be mass actions involving ever broader strata of the population; they must set "practical" objectives, that is to say, whenever possible to smite effectively the military wheels of Western defense.

It is by realizing those aims that the "higher level in the struggle against war" [20] will be reached which the trade unions and the Communist party must strive to attain.

Alongside that direct action, the Communist parties of the West have devoted the greatest efforts to moving and influencing public opinion, which is very strong in this field, by creating a powerful current "for peace and against war." This slogan unquestionably corresponds to the deep sentiment of the masses, especially in countries like France and Italy, where the memory

call on the workers and the people to act against it."—*Humanité*, April 24, 1950.

[20] Document No. 4415, annexed to the minutes of the meeting of October 21, 1952, of the National Assembly, p. 63. This document contains part of the record compiled with a view to the prosecution of five Communist deputies. Jacques Duclos, in his report to the Central Committee of the party, insists that the "political level" of the workers' struggles be raised by articulating them "more and more with the struggle for national independence and the defence of peace" in such a way as to "accentuate the pressure of the working class on the political, economic, and social life of the nation."—*Humanité*, June 17, 1953.

of the suffering endured as a result of the second World War is still very strong. The participation of the Communist parties of France and Italy in the international campaigns connected with the "Partisans of Peace" movement (whose first congress was held in Paris in April, 1949), in the appeals and the collection of signatures against the use of the atomic bomb, in favor of a peace pact between the Five Powers, in the "people's" congresses for peace, etc., has been very intense and has constituted the greater part of their activities. The parallels between these campaigns, even in their nuances, and the great maneuvers of Soviet foreign policy, both the constant factors and the variations, need hardly be pointed out. Nor can we pause here to examine the techniques of their actions and of their propaganda in this field, which attempts, as an appeal of the French Communist party puts it, to reach "*all strata of the population*: workers, peasants, middle classes, men, women, young people; *all democratic and workers' organizations*: labor unions, cooperatives, sports clubs, veterans' associations, family groups, cultural, educational, and religious groups; *all types of individuals*: scholars, writers, journalists, elected officials; everyone who expresses himself in favor of peace." [21]

The essence of this campaign is its unity of purpose: it envelopes everything for the "struggle for peace," including economic claims, by affirming that these claims depend, in the final analysis, on the success of this struggle. A characteristic example of this method is furnished by the report of Pierre Le Brun at the last congress of the French General Confederation of Labor (early in June, 1953) on the organization's economic program, subject to political conditions in which can be found all the slogans of the French Communist party.[22] The campaign "for peace" is like the main sewer to which all the streams are led, pure as well as polluted. It becomes the "fundamental task" of the Communist parties, the basis for their recruitment, and it is under that banner that the French Communist party

[21] *Humanité*, April 7, 1950.

[22] "Cessation of the war in Indo-China; opposition to the rearmament of Western Germany; re-establishment of the full enjoyment of personal liberty; extensive Franco-Soviet trade agreement," *Humanité*, June 9.

conducted its campaign for the parliamentary elections of June, 1951,[23] and for the municipal elections of April-May, 1953, and the Italian Communist party its campaign in June, 1953. Their candidates were the "peace candidates," as their parties are the "peace parties" and as the USSR is "the country of peace."

As soon as there arose, with the Marshall Plan, the possibility that a bridge might be erected between the West and the East, Moscow appealed to the "independence," to the "national sovereignty" of each country. Anything "European" is regarded with suspicion and hostility. Against any attempt at association among themselves by the countries of western Europe and at strengthening their bonds with America, the Communist parties of those countries do not hesitate to appeal to the most rabid nationalism; the presence of United States armed forces is denounced as "occupation." The French Communist party protests against the Military Assistance Program because "a foreign general staff has been installed at Fontainebleau"—after having publicly proclaimed that in case of a Soviet invasion of France, the people, the workers, should array themselves on the side of the invader and support his aims.

For a time, Moscow exploited in France the old fear of the "German peril," which the horrors of Hitler's occupation revived. It was against the German peril that the Franco-Soviet treaty of December, 1944, was drawn up. Moscow did not, despite the treaty, renounce its freedom of action on the chess board of Germany, which was of very great importance for the USSR. Only a few months after the signature of the de Gaulle-Molotov agreements Stalin attempted, in the course of the Yalta conference, to prevent the inclusion of France in the Allied

[23] The electoral manifesto of the French Communist party for the national elections which took place in June initiated a "program of public 'health,'" the first seven points of which concerned foreign policy. They demanded: conclusion of a peace treaty between the Five Powers; denunciation of the Atlantic Pact as well as of the Marshall Plan and the Schuman Plan; reduction of armaments by the great powers; entry into force of the treaty of friendship and alliance between France and the USSR concluded by de Gaulle in December 1944; withdrawal of French troops from Indo-China and Korea, etc."—*Humanité*, April 28, 1951.

Control Commission for Germany; [24] he gave in only because of Anglo-American insistence. Of this complete autonomy of Kremlin policy with respect to Germany—whereby the USSR uses French " chauvinism " whenever convenient and condemns it when it interferes with Soviet plans—two examples should be remembered. They illustrate once more in what direction and with what success Soviet Communist pressures are exerted on the West in general and on France in particular. They concern the Schuman Plan and German rearmament.

Robert Schuman had hardly announced the principles and aims of his plan in a press conference on May 9, 1950, when the French Communist party the very next day began to fight it, charging it with all possible sins: the plan constituted abandonment of national sovereignty; it would liquidate the French steel industry and lower the standard of living of French workers; it would again put into the hands of the Germans an industry which could be used for war and, finally, it constituted a step in the preparation of an anti-Soviet war. The plan was denounced by the Political Bureau of the party as " a plan of treason against French interests " and a " war plan." The French General Confederation of Labor also entered the fight immediately.[25] In mid-June it sent its Secretary-General, Bénoit Frachon, to Berlin to reach agreement with the German trade unions on a fight against the plan.[26] At the beginning of July, Moscow organized a meeting of the Communist parties of France, Germany, Italy, Great Britain, the Netherlands, Belgium, and Luxembourg, at the conclusion of which the Schuman Plan was accused of being " dictated by American imperialists," of being " an important step in the preparation of war against the Soviet Union and the people's democracies," of " consecrating the bringing to heel of the Marshallized countries," of " completing the destruction of the national sovereignty of those countries," and of wanting to create in the Ruhr an " arsenal

[24] The witnesses to that conference (E. Stettinius, J. F. Byrnes, etc.) recalled that Stalin finally agreed that France might also have a zone of occupation in Germany, but only on condition that that zone be carved out of the British and American zones.

[25] *Humanité*, May 10, 11, and 12, 1950.

[26] *Humanité*, June 20, 1950.

of the Atlantic bloc." The plan was said to "facilitate the reconstitution of an army in West Germany under the command of former Hitler generals." [27]

By the same declaration, the Communist parties "commit themselves to redouble their effort to support the Democratic Republic of East Germany."

Soviet policy toward Germany, as imposed on the Communist parties of the West, and especially on the French party, thus finds itself at a crossroad where the appeal to anti-German nationalism and solidarity with East Germany intersect.[28] Immediately after the liberation, the Communist party in France, inspired by Moscow, played its anti-German card; this play permitted it to present itself as a jealously patriotic party and to participate in the government for a little less than three years. It exploited at one and the same time the nationalist vein and the pacifist vein, by demanding the total, permanent disarmament and control of Germany. But, since the creation of the German Democratic Republic, the USSR possesses, or believes it possesses, a more solid basis of action. And it obtains the complete support of the French Communist party. Stalin saluted the establishment of the German Democratic Republic as "a turning point in the history of Europe," which would make "impossible the enslavement of the European countries by the imperialists." [29] The Political Bureau of the French Communist party, in turn, hailed the creation of the new republic in terms which, while somewhat embarrassed, nevertheless point out to "French patriots and democrats" their imperative duty to support the new republic whose aim is to "bring the whole of Germany into the world peace front" which has at its head "the great and powerful Soviet Union." [30]

[27] Text of the declaration in *l'Humanité* of July 4, 1950.

[28] In the struggle against the Schuman Plan we also see another artful use of opposing elements: on the one hand the French Communist party presents it as a fight "against the trusts," one destined to defeat the magnates of capitalism, and on the other hand the same party appeals to French industrialists to oppose ratification of the plan for the sake of the freedom of their enterprises and of their private interests.

[29] Message of October 13, 1949 from Stalin to the President of the new Republic, Pieck, and the Minister President, Otto Grotewohl.

[30] *Humanité*, October 21, 1949.

This position of the party leaders came up against a certain resistance among Communists and fellow-travelers who had taken part in the armed struggle against Hitler Germany, especially on the part of Charles Tillon, former "Black Sea sailor," former Communist Air Minister, and president of the Association des Francs-Tireurs Partisans (F.T.P.). And, since it was a matter of capital interest to Soviet policy, the party leaders publicly took up the struggle against Tillon and his "resisting" friends because they continued to speak of an over-all German peril without differentiating between West Germany and East Germany.[31] The orthodox doctrine was clearly established: there are two Germanys; a democratic, pacifist Germany friendly to the USSR; and a reactionary, warlike Germany subservient to America. East Germany's armament is not dangerous for the peace nor for France; only the armament of West Germany is to be combatted. Putting the campaign against the general rearmament of Germany in the foreground, Tillon and his friends were accused of giving this campaign "a chauvinist character capable of confusing the measures to be taken against the rearmament of West Germany."[32] Some days later, the secretary of the party, Jacques Duclos, addressed to the Socialist Unity Party of East Germany (S.E.D.) a message approving, as Stalin had just done, the "protective measures"—that is, the military measures—which the government of the "German Democratic Republic" had taken.

Another campaign was hatched in the countries of the West: that in favor of their "neutrality" with regard to the USSR-USA conflict. This campaign does not touch the countries of the East and does not interest the Communist parties as such, as they are not and do not wish to be neutral. It has been conducted primarily in France and Italy. In France it found expression in certain organs of the press such as *Le Monde,* which, in 1950, gave space to Professor Gilson of the Collège de France, who has in a way been the evangelist of neutralism. The Communist party adopted with regard to this position an attitude both benevolent and critical—benevolent enough to use to its own advantage the confusion which it caused, and critical

[31] Declaration of the Political Bureau of the French Communist Party in the case of Marty and Tillon, *Humanité,* October 4, 1942.

[32] *Humanité,* October 7, 1952.

enough to eliminate any attenuation of the struggle in favor of the USSR and its policies. On the eve of the French preparatory sessions for the Second World Peace Congress which was to be held in Warsaw, the periodical *Action,* edited by Yves Farges and Pierre Hervé, started a discussion of neutrality[33] clearly oriented in the direction of taking a position in favor of an active struggle in accordance with Soviet slogans. In December a conference of the Progressive Movement was held in Paris, where the initial report was presented by Pierre Cot, who for twenty years has been one of the most intelligent and faithful agents of Soviet policy in France and in the world. M. Cot left no room for misunderstanding of his position when he stated "There is no doubt that if at present peoples all over the world are freeing themselves and progressing, it is through Communism"; this was by way of explanation of the reasons for which he "accepts the policy of neutrality," reasons which were exclusively tactical and provisional. He argued, among other things, that French neutrality would better permit reaching "guaranteed neutralization of Germany."[34]

In Italy it was Pietro Nenni, secretary of the Socialist party of Italy, who made himself the champion of neutrality. The party adopted a cautious attitude with respect to this position, following a wait-and-see tactic. But the neutrality of Mr. Nenni is, like that of the French "neutralists," in one direction only. In the report which he prepared for the thirtieth congress of his party, he speaks of the "conflict started in 1947 by the capitalist world against the Soviet Union and the Socialist states arrayed behind it, which now include China, the advance guard of the liberation of Asia from capitalist domination"; he defines his policy as a policy of "concrete solidarity with the peoples of the East, who are in the vanguard of humanity." He demands "a foreign policy of neutrality of the state, which would return to the Italian Republic its full independence by disengaging it from the Atlantic Pact," etc.[35] Moreover, Nenni advocates an Italo-Soviet nonagression pact.[36] It is also characteristic that in

[33] In the issues from September to November, 1950.

[34] *National Conference of French Progressives,* December 9-10, 1950, edited by "The Progressive Union."

[35] *Avanti,* October 26, 1952.

[36] *Avanti,* November 4, 1952, pp. 5 and 7.

Italy a strong current of former Fascists have similar views. Mr. Nenni did not hesitate to call to arms these circles, as the Communists did for the same purpose among the neo-Fascist students of the MSI (Italian Social Movement). Mr. Nenni published in *Avanti* a letter from a Fascist journalist, Concetto Pettinato, who advocates the armed neutrality of Italy for a policy "of peace and independence," proclaims that the USSR and the Asiatic Orient are "the logical counterbalance to American pressure, which has become intolerable," and that "cultivating the patriotism of Europeans," supported by the national armed forces, could liberate Italy "from the detested yoke of the Atlantic oligarchy." [37]

These positions are employed, especially in France, by those who—while strongly pro-Soviet and often pro-Communist—cultivate the view of France placed equidistant between the "two blocs," even playing the role of arbiter, which recalls the position taken by Pierre Laval under the German occupation, trying to maneuver between the United States and Hitler. We know what the real content of such a policy was, which has now again been taken up by the so-called French neutralists, with the difference that the collaboration would no longer be in favor of Hitler but of Moscow.

One must also call attention to the tendency of the so-called pacifist and neutralist currents to spread from France on an international and especially a Franco-British scale. That is the case with the group formed around the review, *La Tribune des peuples,* "an international review of the left," which began to appear in Paris in March-April, 1953, and was also to be published in London. This review, under the pretext of "Bevanism" and "independence," explicitly or covertly reaches anti-American conclusions. Anti-Americanism is, moreover, the common denominator of all these currents and movements, whether of the "left" or of the "right."

The manifestations of a certain anti-Americanism which prevails in the countries of western Europe would be inexplicable if they were separated from the organization which prepares them, and from the technique perfected to bring them out. To those who ask why such a current arises and develops, there is

[37] *Avanti,* November 2, 1952.

only one answer: whatever the role of certain interests which have been prejudiced, of national sensitivity, of fears and preoccupations aroused by the international situation, nothing serious would result if the anti-Americanism were not methodically cultivated by forces basically dedicated to that aim, led, of course, by the Communist parties. Their tactic is to turn against America all forms of discontent by attributing to her the responsibility therefor.[38] Their aim is not to start a discussion but to create a state of mind. Polemics, accusations, imprecations are heaped one upon the other, and their very absurdity is useful, for it makes them impossible to verify: they are nothing but fuel to kindle and maintain the fire.

The technique of agitation is the one which the Communist parties have always practiced: the sending of letters and delegations to public officials, to the embassies, strikes and demonstrations. Their efforts are concentrated principally in the capitals—Paris and Rome—so as to have the greatest reverberation. The arrival of American public figures is used as a pretext for campaigns and demonstrations, whether it be the "warmonger Acheson" or the "warmonger Dulles," whether it be General Bradley or General Ridgway. The latter has been the target of furious agitation against the Atlantic Pact on the part of the French and Italian Communists, who, virtually mobilizing their forces, denounced him as the "bacteriological-warfare general" and the "microbe killer"; the failure of these demonstrations only caused a redoubling of the anti-American furor on the part of their organizers.[39]

[38] Merely by leafing through a few weeks of *l'Humanité* one finds the following gems: At Brest the police intervene to prevent a demonstration; a scuffle ensues; the police fire and a demonstrator is killed by a pistol shot. Here is the headline "informing" the readers of the event: "The Government fires on Frenchmen with arms furnished by Washington" (April 18, 1950). The Government decides to close several apprenticeship centers: it is because "The American imperialists do not need skilled workers in France; manual laborers . . . are enough for them" (May 3, 1950), etc., etc.

[39] A study of the anti-Ridgway campaign organized in France toward the end of April, 1952, would constitute a very instructive chapter on the methods of propaganda, agitation, and action employed by the French Communist party and its allies.

The problem, for the Communists and their accomplices, is always that of creating a certain climate, which is that of hate. Knowing that the psychology of the masses is often "primitive"—without, alas, excluding the "intellectuals"—they realize that the appeal to hatred is very powerful; they endeavor to create a "basic" hatred against America, a hatred "*per se*," by means of the same procedures through which the Nazis provoked pogroms against the Jews or against the "Marxists."[40] During the French Revolution the "English party" was denounced; now they denounce the "American party," which is, of course, "the war party" and the party of "enslavement of France," so that even sincere pacifist and patriotic sentiments may be transformed as far as possible into hatred of America.

Since the direct seizure of power in the countries of the West is, under present circumstances, impossible, the tactics of the Communist parties, wherever they can be effectively exercised, aim, as we have seen, at controlling the foreign policy of the government. If they cannot orient it in a direction favorable to the Soviet interests, they attempt to prevent any other policy from being practiced. And the best way to paralyze a policy is to paralyze the government itself, to throw pebbles into the gears so that they cease, or almost cease, to function. On the economic level they seek to create difficulties or to profit from existing difficulties, so that the state may never have a balanced budget and drags on from crisis to crisis in such a manner that, weakened thereby, it cannot pursue a policy with any real continuity. In France, for example, the Communists support or create claims and demands of all kinds, applying the principle: "To demand and protest is to weaken the enemy." At the same time, they oppose the reconstruction of the national economy, taking a clear position against increasing the productivity of labor.[41]

[40] We take the liberty of pointing out that we have analyzed the traits common to the technique of hatred among the Fascists and Nazis and among the Soviet Communists in the Preface to the French edition of our *Physiologie du PCF* (*Physiology of the French Communist Party*) (Paris: Self, 1948), xxvii ff.

[41] As done by the last congress of the CGT (see *Humanité* of June 8, 1953, and *Le Peuple* of June 15); and as done in the report of Jacques Duclos to the Central Committee of the Party (*Humanité* of

In Italy, the Communist tactics are more adroit, for they have to take account of the unemployed and of the low standard of living in numerous categories of employed workers; thus the C.G.I.L. takes the initiative in "labor plans," a large part of which are of a demagogic nature, though some appear suitable for application. But whatever the tactics adopted, the goal remains the same: to impose a change of foreign policy and then a change of government.

In France as well as in Italy, the Communists practice a sort of blackmail with the threat of social disorder and civil war; if the government changes its foreign policy, they will make life less hard for it, they will cease their continual harassment, they will allow it to enjoy a sort of truce; otherwise, the most implacable struggle will be conducted against it. The Communists are disposed, in both countries, to go quite far in their alliances with parties or men who adopt their foreign policy; but they are not content with vague promises; they demand firm commitments to be guaranteed even by the composition of the new governments.

In France the Communist party spelled out its attitude during the course of the campaign preceding the national elections of June, 1951. That campaign was opened with a meeting of the Central Committee of the party advocating unity, in a manifesto, in order to bring about "the formation of a government which would be not a foreign government but that of France, not an organizer of war but an artisan of peace." [42] And Jacques Duclos in a speech defined the governmental views of the party: "The Communist party is prepared to work in agreement with Frenchmen of all opinions and all beliefs, with a view to promoting a policy which would permit the creation of the conditions necessary for the formation of a government determined to halt the march toward the abyss. The Communist party is prepared to collaborate with such a government or to support it, the only condition being that it consider it its basic task to make every effort to apply a policy based on the following principles."

June 17). At the same time, the Communists justify the application of the most severe labor norms to the workers of the USSR and of the satellite countries.

[42] *L'Humanité,* April 28, 1951.

There follows a nine-point program, the first eight points of which concern the foreign policy of France, demanding its modification in a pro-Soviet and anti-American direction. This is a position analogous to the one which the party adopted in 1936 at the time of the "Popular Front," but based still more on foreign policy problems and permitting participation in the government itself.

In Italy, party Chief Togliatti proclaimed in a speech to which the party gave wide distribution: "The Communists are prepared to renounce their opposition if the government adopts a policy of peace." Some months before the last Italian elections, the Communist Di Vittorio, the Secretary-General of the C.G.I.L., declared at the national congress of that organization in Naples that it was disposed to "consider favorably participation in a government which was presented as a government of economic progress and social reconstruction, of national unity, and of peace."[43] In April, 1953, in his report on the party's electoral program, Togliatti put in the foreground "the problem of peace and war" and affirmed that a "peace government" would have permitted the "cold war" to be stopped—inside the country, too, and would have prevented domestic schism.[44] After the elections of June, 1953, Togliatti stressed, in statements to *L'Humanité*, the alternatives with which the country is now confronted: change of government and policy, or continuation and aggravation of the Italian political crisis.[45]

[43] Naples Congress of the end of November, 1952.

[44] *Unità*, April 16 and 17, 1953.

[45] *Humanité*, June 12, 1953. Here is the essence of his statements: "The reactionaries of the entire world will be obliged, after the results of the Italian elections, to reflect seriously on the fact that the peoples of capitalist Europe will not let themselves be reduced to slavery in order to serve as cannon fodder in a war against the Socialist countries. We Communists realize that the country must have a stable government with real authority. But, at the same time, where the popular movement has attained the degree of development and strength that it has today in Italy and in France, governmental stability and authority can be based on it alone. If it is attempted to impose the formulas of the anti-Communist governments in the service of foreign imperialism, the crisis in the national political life will be permanent and will only get worse." See also the resolution of the Italian Communist party with respect to the new government.—*Unità*, June 21, 1953.

By the repetition of political crises, by its exploitation of economic difficulties, this Communist policy, which encourages apathy and disunity, engenders a feeling of fatigue and confusion which also spreads to certain official groups. This chaotic pressure in some countries of the West is one of the most redoubtable arms employed by the Communists on behalf of the USSR, for there is the danger of infecting the entire social body in its vital parts, dangerously weakening even the instinct of self-preservation.

The political crises which the Communists nourish in those countries of the West which are of direct interest to the USSR are not the temporary and factitious result of their tactics; they would not be dangerous if they did not, in these countries, and especially in France, parallel a crisis in the ruling classes. We cannot analyze here the complex causes of this crisis. Part of these classes, at the time of liberation, was, so to speak, banished to the fringes of political and social life by a guilt complex resulting from their antinational or opportunist attitude during the German occupation. But even those who participated actively in the fight against Hitlerism often ended by compromising the very cause for which they had fought, by letting themselves be bowled over and evicted in the field of thought, of political and social ideology. It is on the ideological, spiritual level that, in the West, there took place the most dangerous collapses, and mistaken ideas, from which the Soviet Communists profited greatly, were tolerated or even cultivated. There is a proverb to the effect that "it is the head of the fish that rots first," and the ruling classes of the West—after those of East Central Europe—too often allowed the most essential concepts—those of democracy, of progress, and of liberty—to be decomposed by permitting the introduction into the very heart of their civilization of the most glaring falsifications of these concepts and of the concrete values which they imply. The Communists have thus been able to exercise effective pressure to have constitutions enacted, as in France, which permit them to pursue their illegal actions legally.

They have cultivated the presumption (which they do not share) that freedom and progress are menaced only from the "right"; this presumption explains, among other things, why part of the small farmers and artisans of France vote Communist, because they believe that the Communists are a party of the left and that the democratic formula implies that there is " no enemy on the left." " Popular " democracy, when separated from the exigencies of the individual conscience, constitutes an " alienation " of man at least as serious as that which Marx denounced referring to the proletariat torn from his tools; it is to such an alienation, such an uprooting, that the Communist influences lead the few general concepts lingering in the public mind of the Western peoples. That also explains the fierce efforts made by the Communists in intellectual circles, to which they justly attribute great importance. When the principle is valid, as in the case of the emancipation of the " colonial " peoples, the Communists use it to make of these peoples purely material for manipulation in the service of the political and military strategy of the USSR. This case arises notably with respect to the overseas colonies and territories of France and the Netherlands. This does not prove anything against freedom and progress, but it proves even less that the Communists are the guarantors of freedom and progress.

The war which the Soviet Communists are waging against the West comprises various battles: one of the most decisive among them is waged on the ideological level. While the political and economic campaign aims at keeping the Western nations permanently in a state of instability, and at shaking their material foundation, the ideological campaign strikes these nations in the brain, in the spirit, in order to make them incapable of defending themselves, by warping or rocking the spiritual certainties which would assure the strength, the correctness, and the promptness of their reactions.

When one follows the activity of the Communist parties, one is struck by the fact that not only those of the USSR and its satellites but also those of western Europe function with a fundamental uniformity, in spite of the surface eddies, using the same slogans launched at the same time, and everywhere immediately adapting themselves to the exigencies of Soviet foreign policy. Those parties are like armies always on a war footing, always prepared to mobilize at any moment and for any campaign. Today they march in much closer alignment and are much better synchronized than when the Comintern had not yet been officially suppressed. The Cominform, which did not replace it, was, as we have seen, a product of circumstance, and it is not, apparently, destined for a great future, although the two strongest Communist parties of the West are members. The axis of the relations between Moscow and the Communist parties has been displaced more and more toward the Bolshevik party and state; through the increase in its power, the USSR has, since the second World War, acquired a great attractive force which causes the Communist parties to gravitate toward Moscow even more than in the past and to revolve in its orbit.

There is another element which must not be neglected: the greater "political capacity" of the Communist parties. The latter no longer need to be guided step by step like children. We must abandon the concept of these parties as automatons, mechanically put together, moving only so long as the battery lasts, and incapable of action as soon as they are on their own. This does not mean that their subordination to Moscow has become less; these parties can, on the contrary, implement this subordination with greater efficiency. In an address delivered recently on the occasion of the celebration of his sixtieth birthday, Togliatti remarked: "Those who believe that, day after day, hour after hour, we receive directives from the comrades who direct the Communist party of the USSR make me laugh. Do they really believe we have learned nothing in these thirty-four years during which we have fought in the midst of the world Communist movement?" [46]

Unquestionably, orders are still given to the Communist parties, who hasten to carry them out. It was certainly on orders from Moscow that Jacques Duclos signed and published the article transmitted to him regarding the Browder-Forster conflict in the U. S. Communist party; [47] it was on orders and after a trip to Moscow that François Billoux brought back to Paris the directives regarding the stiffening of the anti-American campaign which culminated in the violent demonstrations against

[46] *Unità,* April 10, 1953.

[47] *Cahiers du communisme,* No. 6, April, 1945.

Ridgway.[48] But it suffices for *Pravda* to publish an important political article for it to be reproduced immediately by *L'Humanité* in Paris, by *Unità* in Rome, and by the whole western Communist press; without the need of agents or of special emissaries, these articles are considered as orders; the leaders of the Communist parties have acquired experience which permits them to read between the lines if necessary and base their actions thereon. To these fairly constant directions which come to them from the Muscovite press and are immediately assimilated are added the diplomatic notes from the government of the USSR which, far from being intended for the record, become battle instructions; for all the questions of interest to the Western countries (German question, Atlantic Pact, etc.) the collection of Soviet notes to the governments of these countries has constituted a sort of "red book" furnishing the Communist parties with programs of action.

The unity and the continuity of Soviet policy are the crucible in which are forged the unity and continuity of the policy of all the Communist parties, including those of the West. An essential element in this fusion is furnished by Soviet mysticism, which characterizes the Communist cadres and also spills over into other circles. This could not, however, cause any great ravages if the Communists had not learned to articulate it, in their propaganda, with the problems which arise in each country and with the state of mind which they arouse. The "Soviet paradise" can only be pictured advantageously to miserable peoples and in contrast to the "inferno" to which they are sometimes condemned. The struggle against misery is essentially a struggle against communism, but the two do not entirely coincide.

Other factors intervene to facilitate the Communist game: the "alogical" character of collective passions and the narrow nature of economic interests often permit the Communists to escape from the vise of their contradictions. Passions and interests successively overshadow other passions and interests which, if they continued in the foreground, would turn out to be contradictory. The French Communist party can simultan-

[48] These directives were exposed by the same Billoux in an article in *Cahiers du communisme*, No. 5, May, 1952.

eously utilize the anti-German sentiment, exalt the East German regime, and even take a position on Alsace-Lorraine which recalls the former autonomism and even the former separatism.[49] In the question of Trieste, toward which national Italian sentiment is extremely sensitive, the Italian Communist party has been able to maneuver in such a way as to displace it from the status of an anti-Soviet resentment to that of an anti-Yugoslav resentment, almost obliterating, at the same time, the memory that it was the veto of the USSR which kept Italy out of the UN. Interests are often blind and act only for the immediate future: by tactics of outbidding, the Communists even succeed in attracting groups which are relatively well off, as in the case of the small tenant farmers of central Italy. The latter generally enjoy fair economic conditions and are sometimes well-to-do; but the Communists explain to them that, thanks to the Communists, they will receive all the land and will no longer have to share the produce with the present proprietors. The vision of these new riches and this new status are so seductive that the farmers do not reflect that a victory of the Communist regime will reduce them to the level of simple proletarians and that in the end they will lose everything. In short, the economic problems, in addition to their own weight, which is great, are multiplied and distorted in the societies "without prospects," without a stable government intent on solving them, without a national state which is firmly constructed and linked with the people, their needs, and their future.

RICHARD SCAMMON: *Discussion* *

Chief, Division of Research for Western Europe,
Department of State

I should like to add to Mr. Rossi's most interesting picture of the nature of Communist penetration in western Europe a few comments concerning Germany. First, let us glance

[49] See the articles by F. Billoux devoted to Alsace-Lorraine in the *Cahiers du bolchevisme,* May and June, 1950.

* The interpreter during the discussion period was Miss Alice Libby, Intelligence Research Specialist (Political) of the Department of State.

at democratic Germany—West Germany—the German Federal Republic.

The KPD—the German Communist party—exists today as an outpost of the international movement directed by the Kremlin. But it is interesting to note that this outpost is weaker than it was before the rise of Hitler. I stress this fact because it is only in West Germany among all the powers of western Europe that communism today is weaker than it was before the war. There are many reasons for this—the efficiency of the *Gestapo,* the strong *revanche* feeling among most of West Germany's ten million refugees, the bitter hatred of most Germans for anything Russian. These and many other factors have produced this unique situation in West Germany. But whatever the reason, the fact remains: only in West Germany is communism weaker today than it was before the war.

Moreover, the Communist party in Germany remains apart from the mainstream of current German thought. Aside from a handful of renegade "intellectuals," the party can win support only in isolated working-class sections of the population. Professor Timasheff has referred to the value of election results in the analysis of the growth of communism. These figures are indeed useful in Germany and they stress this isolated character of the appeal of communism in Germany. In Hamburg, in Mannheim and Frankfurt and Ludwigshafen, in Munich and Nürnberg and Stuttgart, in the industrial complex of the Ruhr—in all these centers the Communist party has a measure of support amongst the industrial workers, especially amongst those in the so-called heavy industries. But even this support is waning. In district after district in the Ruhr the Communists polled 20, 25, even 30 per cent of the vote. That vote is now down to 5 and 10 per cent, and I venture to predict it will go even lower.

In East Germany the situation is different. There the melancholy business of bolshevization goes on apace. Supported by the Red army's military machine, the so-called Socialist Unity party of Communist boss Walter Ulbricht disciplines the masses in a new fascism. The HJ has become the FDJ, but it is only the name which has changed. The apparatus of the so-called German Democratic Republic—the East German Soviet satellite—is basically Hitlerite. There may be changes in tactics, zigs and zags as the party pursues its devious ways to the Soviet Valhalla, but that a Bolshevik state is its final aim cannot be doubted.

There are no more "German" Communists than there are "French" or "Italian" or "American." There is but the one breed and that breed is typified by the butcher-man Ulbricht and his concentration camp regime in Soviet Germany.

About East Germany there is too much wishful thinking already. Let us not be led into some false hope that an imagined weakness will force the Soviet tomorrow to give up its satellite peoples in Germany and agree to a new, unified, democratic German state. That they would like us to believe this is possible is, of course, obvious. But the Soviets have learned the lesson of June 17th better perhaps than we. Their state machine is now fully in the hands of the extremist element, fully under the control of Ulbricht. The execution squads and the deportation trains are working overtime. This is no time to expect the USSR to be ready to give up in East Germany, though we may well expect new offers—and even offers that may sound more and more tempting as time develops strength in the West. Such offers will not, however, be translated into actuality because basically the Soviet is not prepared at any price save its own complete control of all of Germany, to unite its terror-ridden eastern zone with the three democratic zones making up the German Federal Republic.

Communist Exploitation of Anti-Colonialism and Nationalism in Africa

D. VERNON McKAY,
Acting Officer in Charge of Trusteeship Affairs, Office of Dependent Area Affairs, Department of State

A continent as vast and varied as Africa is an intriguing subject for a study of the problem of Soviet imperialism. One of the first principles any student of Africa must grasp, however, is the danger of generalizations about an area nearly four times as large as Europe or the United States, which has such a bewildering variety of political subdivisions, cultural groups, economic resources, and geographical features. Having said this, let me acknowledge that I will no doubt violate this *caveat* against generalizations in the following analysis, which will deal first with the character of Communist propaganda concerning Africa, and second with the channels through which Soviet influence reaches that continent.

Russian ideas about Africa have been set forth in many articles in various Soviet journals, including *World Economy and World Politics, The New East, The War and the Working Class, New Times, Soviet Ethnography,* and *Problems of Economics.* Soviet interest, however, is by no means a post-World War II development. Four of the aforementioned periodicals published a total of eighty-eight articles on Africa between 1922 and 1946, a period during most of which the Comintern was actively interested in exploiting nationalism and anticolonialism in Africa. In fact, as students of Tsarist history will recall, Russia has long been interested in the northeastern corner of Africa, particularly Egypt and Ethiopia, and the Russians also participated in the Moroccan settlement in Madrid in 1880 and in the Congo arrangements at Berlin in 1885.

In order to highlight the character of contemporary Soviet propaganda concerning Africa, it may be worth while to call attention to certain key ideas appearing in more recent articles in Soviet periodicals. Foremost among them is the familiar thesis of Lenin and Stalin that the overthrow of capitalism and the destruction of the colonial system are two sides of one and the same task. A second idea is the exaggerated distortion with which Soviet writers picture contemporary Africa as a land of oppressed peoples suffering under colonial slavery. Third is the view that the latest stage in the imperialist struggle for Africa is a great American imperialist drive for the economic, political, and military expansion of United States interests. And finally, mention must be made of the contradictory and ironical picture of the "national bourgeoisie" of Africa which emerges from these writings.

A few examples will illustrate the character of this propaganda. In an article on "The Colonial Policy of the Labor Party and the Position of the Workers in Africa" published in *Problems of Economics* in 1949, I. Lemin writes that the aim of the British Labor Party is "to maintain and strengthen the system of colonial slavery in its most horrible and cruel form." Ignoring statistics of population growth, he says there is danger that the African working population will die out because of monstrous exploitation and low wages. S. R. Smirnov, writing in *Soviet Ethnography* in 1950 on "The British Policy of 'Indirect Rule' in Southeast Nigeria," brands Lugard's well-known technique of administration as Britain's "desperate attempt to hamper the birth of a Nigerian society, an attempt to restrain the headlong development of the national-liberation movement."

As for American imperialism, Lemin contends that "the American military authorities direct all the military measures adopted in Africa," and he similarly exaggerates the efforts of "American monopolists" to grab African trade and investment from the British. The aim of all this, he writes, is to transform Africa "into a base of military operations for the aggressive war which the Anglo-American bloc is preparing."

With regard to the "national bourgeoisie" in Africa, the Communists are, of course, confronted with an ironical dilemma. Committed by doctrine to the principle that revolutionary leadership must be in the hands of the working class, they find in Africa as in other colonial areas that the workers and peasants have not developed to the point of being able to assume such leadership. The Communist appeal must, therefore, be directed at the nationalist-minded bourgeois intelligentsia. This troublesome problem is discussed in a 1950 article in *Soviet Ethnography* by I. I. Potekhin, entitled "The Stalinist Theory of Colonial Revolution and the National-Liberation Movement in Tropical and South Africa," which was first presented as a report to the Scientific Board of the Institute of Ethnography of the USSR Academy of Sciences on the occasion of Stalin's seventieth anniversary. Potekhin warns that the African bourgeoisie "supports the revolutionary movement of the masses of the people only with a view to taking advantage of the fruits of the revolution and seizing political power for the suppression and enslavement of the masses of the people of its own country." At the same time, however, he acknowledges that these reactionary nationalistic elements can be used in "the special strategic stage of the colonial revolution, the stage of the nation-wide anti-imperialist front when the national bourgeoisie still supports the revolutionary movement."

The sardonic implication that African nationalist leaders would be due for liquidation after the Communists are through using them as stepping stones to power ought to be made as clear as we can possibly make it in Africa. Nnamdi Azikiwe, the best known Nigerian nationalist leader, is evidently considered by Potekhin as one of these reactionary nationalistic elements, for he writes that "the ideology and policy of the Azikiwe group is the ideology and policy of petty bourgeois national reformism." Zik's fellow nationalist, Nwafor Orizu, is also branded as one of the national bourgeois leaders who attacks British colonial policy but "at the same time advocates the preservation of the bases of capitalism."

A related aspect of the hypocrisy of the Soviet position, which might profitably be given publicity in Africa, is what Bertram Wolfe has termed "The Agony of Soviet Historians." In its colonial context, this agony is well described by Solomon M. Schwarz in an article on "Rewriting the History of Russian Colonialism" in a recent issue of *Foreign Affairs*. Schwarz points out that in the last fifteen years the Communist party has made a full 180 degree turn in its appraisal of Russian colonial policy. As late as August, 1934, the annexationist-colonialist role of Russian Tsarism was still under official attack, but Soviet historians today must portray Russian colonial expansion even under the Tsars as a " liberation " movement.

The channels through which Communist ideas and influences reach Africa are many and varied. Perhaps the best measure of the weakness of communism, however, is that the most obvious of these channels, local Communist parties, do not even exist in the vast expanse of tropical Africa between the Mediterranean coast and the Union of South Africa. It is only in the advanced and Europeanized areas at the northern and southern ends of the continent that even small party organizations are found.

In fact, the only territory in all of Africa where Communist party strength can still be indicated in general elections is Algeria, in which Communists have polled an average of 20 per cent of the votes for candidates for the French National Assembly. However, the party members, who may number 15,000 or more, are mostly European workers, artisans, and lower civil servants. In neighboring Morocco where there have never been any general elections to reveal electoral strength, the party was outlawed in December, 1952. In Casablanca and other urban areas it may have had a few thousand members at that time. Similarly, in Tunisia, since 1952 government repressive measures against Communists have resulted in the arrest of certain party leaders, the suspension of publications, and the banning of Communist meetings, demonstrations, and foreign newspapers. The size of the small Tunisian party is comparable to that of Morocco.

More than four thousand miles south in the Union of South Africa, where the Malan Government outlawed communism on July 17, 1950, Communist candidates polled 6,806 votes in the national elections of 1943, but only 1,783 votes in the 1948 elections. The party's chief influence was in Capetown and Johannesburg among the working population, especially the Indian and colored communities, but this could hardly be called a good showing for a party founded as long ago as 1921. The South African experience is instructive because of its racial complications. Although South African delegates at the Sixth Comintern Congress in 1928 advocated black and white unity, the Congress went on record in favor of a "Black Republic," a line which was not abandoned until 1935 after it had done considerable damage to the party. Complacency about the future of communism in the Union is unwarranted, however. The fact that the movement has now been driven underground might enhance its appeal to many Africans. One striking indication of African opinion is the fact that after Sam Kahn was recently ousted from Parliament on the charge of Communist party membership, a by-election was held in which Natives of Cape Province overwhelmingly elected Brian Bunting, who was then the editor of the Communist-line weekly *Advance*.

In the absence of party organizations the Communists, of course, turn to other channels for the exploitation of African nationalism, one of which is the labor movement. Here again the maximum effort is concentrated in the industrialized areas of the north and south. Communists dominate the *Confédération Générale du Travail,* which contains nearly half the membership of Algerian unions and belongs to the Communist controlled World Federation of Trade Unions. In Tunisia, one of four labor federations, the *Union Syndicat des Travailleurs de Tunisie* is under Communist control but has lost strength since 1948, when it was reported to have about 25,000 members. A Moroccan affiliate of the CGT, once under Communist leadership, is now largely in nationalist hands. At the other end of the continent, South African Communists have made considerable efforts to penetrate the labor movement, but none of the important unions is wholly controlled by the party.[1]

Labor organization in tropical Africa is too varied for detailed description, but a few facts will highlight the essential point, which is that the small number of European, Asian, and African Communists scattered throughout the area do influence the labor movement. In British West Africa, where the British began a systematic effort to organize African trade unions in the Gold Coast in 1942, and in French West Africa, there are now

[1] Edward Roux, *Time Longer Than Rope* (London, 1949), is a former Communist's informative account of the history of Communist efforts in the Union of South Africa.

several hundred unions. One of the officers of the Nigerian Labor Congress was reported to have returned from Prague early in 1951 with a Communist donation of £2,000. In French West Africa, the African Secretary-General of the Sudan trade unions, Diallo Abdoulaye, is a vice-president of the World Federation of Trade Unions. In fact, a majority of the organized workers in most French territories belong to local affiliates of the Communist controlled CGT.

To meet this threat of Communist infiltration, the International Confederation of Free Trade Unions is making an effort to compete with the WFTU. The ICFTU has now established a West Africa headquarters in the Gold Coast capital, Accra. What its success will be is uncertain, but it should be noted that two newspapers of Prime Minister Nkrumah's Convention People's Party, the *Accra Evening News* and the *Ashanti Sentinel,* printed a series of five articles praising the WFTU and condemning the ICFTU.

In addition to Communist party organizations and Communist infiltration of the labor movement, the three most important African opportunities the Soviet Union has had, particularly since the end of World War II, seem to me to have been (1) the mushroom-like growth of nationalist and other indigenous political parties in certain areas, especially the *Rassemblement Démocratique Africain* in French West and Equatorial Africa, (2) the great increase in the number of African students receiving their higher education in England, France, and other countries, and (3) Soviet exploitation of those United Nations organs which deal with colonial questions. Each of these three subjects is worthy of careful analysis, but I am going to devote particular attention to Soviet conduct in the United Nations because I have had the first-hand opportunity of watching and studying the behavior of Soviet representatives in the Trusteeship Council, the Trusteeship Committee of the General Assembly, and other United Nations bodies for the past five years.

Before analyzing these three major post-war developments, however, I would like to complete this continental round-up of Communist activities by briefly mentioning certain lesser channels for the dissemination of Soviet propaganda. One of these is found in various cultural and other Communist front organizations such as the South African Society for Goodwill and Friendship with the USSR. Attention should also be called to the few Soviet consular and diplomatic posts in Africa. Most publicized among these is the Russian Embassy along with the Soviet Hospital and Permanent Exhibition in Ethiopia, which have been the subject of many exaggerated and fanciful tales, including a rumor that Kikuyu from Kenya are trained in Communist tactics in the Soviet Hospital and are then gradually infiltrated across the Kenya border with wandering herdsmen until they arrive in the White Highlands, where they stir up Mau-Mau violence against the British!

The Russians also have, in addition to their Cairo Embassy, a small Consulate-General in Pretoria and a Consular Agent in Capetown, and Czechoslovakia has a consulate in Leopoldville. On October 15, 1951, however, the Soviet Consulate-General in Algiers ceased to function, and it may also be worth mentioning that the Russians have not taken advantage of their opportunity to participate in the international administration of Tangiers.

A few words are also essential concerning press and radio channels of Soviet propaganda. In Algeria the Communists have one Arabic and three French newspapers, the most important being the *Alger Républicain,* which has a daily circulation of 20,000 and prints the schedule of Soviet and satellite radio broadcasts. Stalin's *Principles of Leninism* are now said to be circulated in Arabic translations in Algeria. Parisian and local Communist publications in Morocco and Tunisia have been suspended or banned since 1952. In the Union of South Africa, the main Communist-line publication is the weekly *Advance* with a circulation of possibly 40,000. A monthly newsletter called *Inkululeko* is also published in several Bantu languages. Moreover, a considerable number of subversive pamphlets, leaflets, and other publications, including those of Paul Robeson's Council on African Affairs in New York, find their way from overseas into tropical Africa, some by ordinary mail and others by clandestine routes. During the past three years, however, several of the colonial governments have taken more vigorous steps to prohibit the importation of certain specified Communist publications.

Outside the Communist press there are numerous African

newspapers in West Africa and certain Indian publications in East Africa which print material unsympathetic to the West in the cold war. The large number of small but uninhibited newspapers, entirely owned, edited and written by Africans, is a distinctive feature of British West African life. Best known among them is *The West African Pilot,* which occasionally contrasts the United States unfavorably with the Soviet Union for its Nigerian readers.

Soviet radio broadcasts also can be heard in tropical Africa, as is indicated by an amusing incident reported not long ago from Nigeria. Radio Moscow, it seems, broadcasts on every frequency used by the British Broadcasting Company and sometimes misleads its listeners by giving the " six pips " of the BBC station break signals. As a result, one of the Monitors of the Nigerian Broadcasting Services thought the Moscow signal was London calling, and therefore inadvertently turned Radio Moscow into the Eastern Nigerian radio re-diffusion system for thirty-five minutes!

Let us now examine the three postwar developments which I have selected for special consideration because of the unusual opportunities they have presented the Communists. First among them is the rapid postwar rise of indigenous political parties. In British West Africa the slogan " Self-Government Now " became the political battle cry of nationalist parties seeking the end of British rule. British Communists had worked hard on the African leaders who had studied in England, but the new political movements in British territories were unquestionably nationalist rather than Communist. It is to the neighboring French territories that one must turn for the most instructive example of Communist penetration in postwar Africa. The great increase in suffrage and political representation granted the peoples of the new French Union inspired the creation of many new parties, the most striking of which is known as the RDA (*Rassemblement Démocratique Africain*).

Partly as a result of the assimilationist trend of French colonial policy in the past, and partly because of the equivocal position of the French Communists, the RDA, in contrast to its counterparts in British West Africa, did not aim at getting rid of its colonial rulers. The RDA had its origins in the Ivory

Coast where in 1945 a wealthy African landowner and physician named Félix Houphouet-Boigny, supported by a Union of African Planters, was elected to the French National Assembly. In Paris he came into contact with Communists who encouraged him to form a large African party, an aim which was evidently facilitated by the fact that certain French officials in the government of the Ivory Coast at that time were Communists or Communist sympathizers. Other African representatives in the French parliament joined him, and a Congress was held at Bamako in the Sudan on October 19–21, 1946, to organize the RDA on the platform of political and social equality, democratic local assemblies, and freely consented union with France. The growth of the party from this date was absolutely phenomenal. By 1949 it claimed a membership of 700,000 of the two and a half million people in the Ivory Coast, and another 300,000 in other French African territories. Even with due allowance for exaggeration of this claim, it is a fact that after the May elections of 1948, the RDA held twenty-five of the twenty-seven seats in the Ivory Coast Representative Assembly.

The RDA was never a Communist party, a fact which was an asset to the Communists because it enabled them to bring strong influence from the outside on a new party of the masses which could be regarded, in the Comintern tradition, as a single national front against imperialism. French Communists, including Raymond Barbe, a member of the Central Committee of the Communist party who attended the 1946 Congress in Bamako, went to the Ivory Coast to help Houphouet-Boigny organize public meetings on the theme "the people of Africa will never fight against the USSR," along with denunciations of the Marshall Plan and American imperialism. Communist study groups were organized in Paris and West Africa to indoctrinate RDA leaders, and in the French National Assembly the RDA and other African deputies formed a voting bloc with the French Communists.

By 1949, however, the peak had passed. RDA membership began to dwindle and, over the next two years, its open alliance with the French Communists came to an end. Although the significance of this fact is not yet entirely clear, the reasons for the split are certainly instructive to a student of communism in

Africa. It was evident from the beginning that a number of important African political leaders outside the Ivory Coast disliked the Communist ties of the RDA, and were possibly annoyed by the idea of an African organization being directed by Frenchmen. As these and other ambitious leaders reshaped and strengthened their own postwar political organizations, they began to make such inroads in RDA voting strength that RDA politicians came to the gradual conclusion that their Communist ties were a political liability. At the same time, as the French government moved to the right in Paris, Communist sympathizers among French officials in Africa were gradually replaced by administrators who suppressed RDA excesses and made efforts to persuade RDA leaders to break with the Communists. Finally, as its decline became apparent in 1949, the RDA antagonized many more Africans by the adoption of extremist tactics in an unsuccessful effort to recoup its strength. Apparently incited by its Communist backers, it deliberately provoked a number of riots in 1949 and 1950 which resulted in many deaths and injuries. As a result of these various developments, the RDA representation in the Ivory Coast Assembly declined, RDA representation in Paris dropped, and RDA deputies stopped voting with the Communists in the French parliament. On October 6, 1951, Houphouet-Boigny announced to a large assemblage of his followers in the Ivory Coast that he had broken with the Communists because, he said, "there should be no class struggle in Africa."

A second postwar African opportunity of the Communists was the great increase of African students in European universities. Today there are about 3,000 African students in England and more than 4,000 in France, as well as over 600 in the United States and even a small number behind the Iron Curtain. British and French Communists have given high priority to ways and means of indoctrinating these Africans before they return home to become leaders of their people. One technique is for young members of "cultural associations" with innocuous names to contact the Africans, arrange sightseeing tours for them, invite them out to meals, and pay their expenses to attend student conferences in other countries. If the prospect seems sufficiently pliable, he may be rewarded with a trip to Prague, Warsaw, or

Moscow. Since the finances of most African students are invariably poor, such opportunities are undeniably attractive.

The number of African students in Soviet and satellite countries is small but could be of some importance in the future. For example, eight Nigerians arrived in the Soviet zone of Berlin during 1951 with scholarships from the Free German Youth organization. The Communists have also sought to aid Africans through the International Union of Students, and the World Fund for Student Aid in Prague, which has raised a sizable scholarship fund. It is too early to judge the impact of these Communist approaches to African students, but its potential significance is clear.

The third major postwar opportunity for Soviet propaganda in Africa is found in the United Nations, a fact which is generally unappreciated except by the colonial powers. Being completely irresponsible, the USSR is able to paint the colonial picture in the same lurid colors used by African nationalists, and Soviet representatives have systematically exploited the official records of the United Nations for this purpose. Since the tears of the Russian bear look very much like those of the crocodile to other UN members, the Soviet point of view carries little weight in the United Nations, even among the anticolonial members who sometimes share the Soviet view on the substance of African problems.

But the point under discussion here is whether Soviet propaganda is having an effect in Africa, not in the United Nations. In answering this question it is important to note an item which is usually billed on the agenda of UN meetings under the innocuous title "the dissemination of information about the United Nations," an admirable cause which is generally supported by all members. In the UN discussion of this item, constant pressure is placed on the British, French, Belgians, and Italians to increase the flow of information about the United Nations, primarily in the form of these official records which are full of Soviet propaganda, to their seven trust territories in tropical Africa. And the Visiting Missions of the Trusteeship Council, four of which have already gone to the African trust territories, check up on the administering authorities by asking in the schools and libraries and other appropriate places to see what United Nations material is available.

The extent to which United Nations documents in libraries and schools may be actually used is of course problematical. There is, however, one important group of Africans to whom many of these documents are sent directly. This is the steadily increasing number of petitioners who send their grievances to the Trusteeship Council. The 1952 Visiting Mission to West Africa, for example, received 4,235 petitions and other communications, many of which were subsequently acted upon by the Council. Since petitioners are at the outset dissatisfied persons, most of whom do not understand the constitutional limitations on what the UN can do for them, they are very likely to be even more dissatisfied when they read the decisions of the Trusteeship Council on their petitions. And when they turn to the summary records of meetings at which their petitions were discussed, which are also sent to them along with other relevant documentation, they may often find that the only country whose representative recommended what they wanted was the USSR.

When the Council began its first examination of African trust territories at its third session in the summer of 1948, the Soviet representative obviously set out to make the most of a valuable propaganda opportunity. His speeches cover approximately 1,000 inches of the 7,700 inches of printed Summary Records of the Third Session, in contrast to 450 inches for the United States representative, who took a very active part in the Council's work. The twofold technique of the Soviet representative is the *exaggerated oversimplification and distortion* of African problems, and the *constant and deliberate repetition* of the same themes. All allegations of misrule in the trust territories are treated as fact by the Soviet delegation, and all answers of the administering authorities to such allegations are discounted as mere whitewash.

To conclude this analysis of Soviet exploitation of the United Nations, brief mention should be made of the main tactics of USSR representatives. First of all, for every trust territory no matter what its stage of development, the Soviet representative introduces the same series of stock recommendations. These are voted down one by one, but the interesting fact about them is that, if taken out of the context of the arguments used in supporting them, they seem relatively harmless. As a result the unwary reader may be inclined to wonder why the other delegations oppose the USSR's apparent effort to help colonial peoples.

A second tactic of the Soviet Delegation is its use and abuse of what the Trusteeship Council terms "individual observations" in the Council's Annual Report to the General Assembly, which is perhaps the most important and most studied Council document. Although the observations and recommendations of each delegation are recorded in the record of the Council's meetings, the Soviet Union, in this case supported by all the other nonadministering members, succeeded in getting these individual observations *also* included in a separate section of the Council's annual report, after a long procedural wrangle which split the administering and nonadministering powers in the Council six to six. Fortunately for the Soviet Union, the other nonadministering members attached great importance to having their individual observations included in the Council's reports to the Assembly.

Finally the Soviet delegation makes a special effort to capitalize on the opportunity for Soviet propaganda presented by the Council's treatment of petitions. The USSR has not been included on the Council's Visiting Missions, and the only one of the Council's committees on which it is now represented is the Standing Committee on Petitions. In order to deal with the mounting accumulation of petitions, this important committee has now been made a permanent body which meets between sessions as well as during Council meetings. The Soviet representative employs the same tactics in the Committee as in the Council, accepting the allegations of petitioners as true, and implying that explanations by the administering authority are false. And, as in the Council, after his proposals are voted down, he manages to get them recorded as individual proposals in the Committee's reports to the Council, which are then sent to the petitioners. He also supports requests for oral hearings before the Trusteeship Council and the General Assembly, whether or not the petitioner has a valid request on a matter of sufficient importance to merit an oral hearing, and he is now participating in a campaign with certain other members to go beyond the Charter of the United Nations by providing for the participation of Africans in the Council's examination of annual reports by the administering authorities.

The evidence presented in this study has demonstrated that the Communists have used many channels for the exploitation of anticolonialism and nationalism in Africa, particularly since the end of World War II. In summary, however, despite an effort of more than thirty years duration, the results thus far achieved seem relatively small. There is not a single Communist party organization in all of tropical Africa between the Mediterranean and the Union of South Africa. The Communists have failed to penetrate or form an alliance with the Arab nationalist parties of French North Africa, and they have lost control of the RDA, their greatest opportunity in tropical Africa, despite the advantages derived from the presence of a strong Communist party in France. It is true that they have succeeded in penetrating the labor movement in a few territories, but only in Algeria does infiltration seem dangerous. Even if it is assumed that Africa is last on the Soviet timetable, and that instead of organizing Communist movements the Russians are now primarily interested in subverting European authority, splitting the Western allies, and neutralizing the Arab-Asian bloc, their record of achievement is still unimpressive.[2]

The reasons for this lack of Communist success, though partly evident from the foregoing analysis, are of course more difficult to explain. Communist mistakes doubtless provide part of the answer. The erratic and opportunistic doctrinal and tactical shifts of a foreign ideology, as well as the ruthless and cynical imperialist expansion of Russia, have certainly tended to undermine the interest of African nationalists in communism. In this context the equivocal position of the French Communists is significant, for many an African must have wondered whether they favor the end of European domination in Africa or whether they simply want European domination under a Communist dictatorship. In any case the French Communists are Europeans, a fact which was probably influential in their failure to penetrate at least the French North African nationalist movements

[2] The Soviet effort to split the West is emphasized by Cyril Brown, "Russian Interest in Africa," *Current History*, July, 1953, 41-46.

which seek the end of European rule. The sophistication of numerous African leaders has also made them aware of the fact that Communist ties would alienate their noncommunist sympathizers, to say nothing of their awareness that "national bourgeoisie" are good prospects for liquidation under Communist rule.

The difficult environment of Africa itself has doubtless been an even greater obstacle to Communist success. The physical difficulty of penetrating a vast continent with very limited facilities for transportation and communications is one barrier. More important are the cultural difficulties involved in working among African peoples with eight-hundred languages, 80 per cent of whom are unable to read and write. Most Africans, moreover, still live in tribal environments with limited horizons, and are resistant to new ideas. In addition it should be recalled that the number of industrial workers is small, that in large parts of Africa there are no great estates available for distribution to peasants, and that the numbers of the reachable African intelligentsia are still quite limited. Finally, there is a strong political obstacle to Communist activity in the power of colonial and other authoritarian governments to suppress agitation whenever it seems worth suppressing.

Many things are changing very rapidly in Africa, however, and the conclusion that Communist influence is now relatively small should not lead to undue optimism about the future. Despite the tortuous course of their history, the Communists do have the asset of a long revolutionary tradition in an era of ferment. Moreover, there are many African leaders who admire what they regard as outstanding Russian achievements in the social and economic field. There seems to be a widespread view among them that the overwhelming economic, social, and educational problems of their countries cannot be solved without a Socialist economic system. Although they do not like Russian methods of achieving a Socialist economy, they consider that Britain and France have demonstrated how socialism can be combined with democracy.

A third Soviet asset is the African view that the Russians believe in the equality of races as opposed to the assumption of racial superiority. This is significant because there is nothing more important to many Africans than race relations, for they live in a continent full of race prejudice and, in many areas, racial discrimination. Current attempts to explode the theory that there is no racial discrimination in Russia have made little or no impression on Africans.

What would happen to Communist chances, it may be asked, if European authority in Africa were to collapse under nationalist pressures? In that event, the chief political obstacle to Communist penetration would disappear, and in the ensuing turmoil, the Communists might be able to overcome many other barriers by capitalizing on the Communist sympathies which still remain in the minds of a number of members of the RDA and other African parties. For the moment, however, European authority is not collapsing. Moreover, any careful student should examine the validity of the oft-heard cliché that Africa will be next to follow in the path of Asia. I do not know whether Africa will or will not follow in the path of Asia, to say nothing of the fact that I don't know what the path of Asia is going to be. Attention should be drawn, however, to a number of differences between the two continents.

First is the presence of five million Europeans in Africa, 80 per cent of whom are concentrated in the strategic northern and southern ends of the continent. Many of these people, especially in the Union of South Africa, have no place else to go, and they are determined to remain at any cost. The second important difference between Africa and Asia lies in the role of force and, in particular, in the fact that Africans are as yet unable to obtain weapons in any way comparable to those acquired by Asians after World War II from Japanese and other sources. Third is the geographical proximity of the USSR to Asia, which greatly facilitates Soviet efforts to feed arms, agitators, and propaganda into that continent. Fourth is the geographical proximity of western Europe to Africa, at least in contrast to its remoteness from Asia, a relationship that facilitates European control over Africa or at least French North Africa. Finally, it should not be ignored that the European powers, in contrast to their prewar policy in Asia, are today spending hundreds of millions of dollars in a two-fold effort to strengthen Europe's economy and to meet African demands for political, economic, social, and educational advancement.

In order to avoid exaggerating the significance of these differences between Africa and Asia, let me say again that I do not know to what extent they will affect the course of African history. With Mau-Mau in Kenya, *Apartheid* in South Africa, and a deep and bitter passion in French North Africa, the future is certainly foreboding. In the words of a recent observer the most important problem in colonial Africa today is not poverty but passion—"passion about the colonial relationship."[3] The West has not yet found the answer to this problem, but the evidence of this study has shown that the Communist answer is also far from effective. It is not my purpose to moralize about what the West should do to take advantage of communism's failure to penetrate Africa, but I will conclude by suggesting that the best means yet devised are the time-tested efforts to accelerate African political advancement, to extend additional technical guidance and economic assistance, and to combat the race prejudice of the white man.

MANFRED HALPERN: *Discussion*

Division of Research for Near East and Africa,
Department of State

In Africa, as in the Middle East, Asia, and Latin America, the traditional system of values and the social system in which it was anchored are crumbling. New elites are emerging. New and radical demands are being made. The importance of this basic social transformation to the problem of Soviet imperialism lies in the fact that Soviet communism has scored its greatest success thus far in the underdeveloped areas of the world—Russia, eastern Europe, and China. Indeed, Soviet communism in practice has turned out to be a formula for ruthlessly and rapidly industrializing, and enhancing the military power of underdeveloped economies.

Its own greatest needs may therefore influence the Soviet Union to believe that the preferable targets for Soviet expansion are highly developed sources of machinery and tools, like Germany and Japan, and not additional areas which, like Africa, are

[3] Walter R. Crocker, *Self-Government in the Colonies* (London, 1950), vi.

in their early state of economic growth. For the present, the Kremlin appears to be content to assign responsibility for counselling and supporting the Communist in the colonies to the parties in Great Britain, France, and Belgium; these, in turn, have left some of their colonial comrades without any but the most ambiguous guidance over a period of years. Soviet effort is limited, on the whole, to the encouragement of native forces which generally need no encouragement to deprive the West of friendship, prestige, military bases, and raw materials. The USSR may be counting on the long-range trend toward instability in Africa and other underdeveloped areas to bring communism inescapably to victory.

Africa may well have a stormy transition from tribal societies and isolated subsistence economies to national status and dynamic, interrelated cash economies. But the rising winds may not blow the fruits into Communist hands. A number of forces are competing for the harvest. European control over all but three [1] of Africa's territories constitutes one of the greatest barriers to Communist activity in Africa at present. For some time to come, European authorities will be able to limit the freedom and scope of the conflict between the Communists and their native competitors. The outcome of this conflict will therefore be determined, to a large degree, by the manner in which European powers exercise their control, the circumstances under which they consent to greater African participation in government, the degree to which they will in fact find it possible to reduce the effects of Africa's social disorganization by developing the continent primarily to satisfy Europe's needs, and the process by which Africa's five million "permanent" European settlers will attempt to achieve permanent status within African society. Because Western powers are so very much more present and in control in Africa than they were in Asia, their possible failure to meet the challenge could be even more serious than it was in parts of Asia.

Among the Communists' native competitors, the Mau-Mau have received particular publicity. The Mau-Mau movement in Kenya cost that colony more than one thousand dead by the summer of 1953, and $600,000.00 a month for the necessary police measures. What gives the Mau-Mau significance in the context of Soviet imperialism is not that it is Communist-in-

[1] By common consent, Egypt is not thought to be in Africa, though Egypt may prove otherwise in the next few years.

spired, Communist-financed, or Communist-led. One may fairly doubt that it is any of these. It merits attention because we shall probably see more such movements arrive in Africa to threaten political stability. In a strategically important colony, the Mau-Mau have already succeeded in compelling a serious diversion of reserve funds intended for social and economic development to police and military activities instead. The excesses of the Mau-Mau have also increased the hostility of Kenya's European settlers to future projects intended to advance the native population. Even though they may be defeated, the Mau-Mau movement will have achieved some lasting victories in setting African against European.

It should be recognized that the Mau-Mau is not a relic, a throw-back to an ancient past. It is a peculiarly modern movement. It was formed within what has always been one of the most advanced tribes of Africa—the Kikuyu—a tribe which more than most has had opportunity to observe Western civilization at close range. Those who organized the Mau-Mau were not the most primitive among the Kikuyu tribe. They include some of the tribe's most advanced elements—men who had seen the world with the British army, or at least observed the ways of city life in Nairobi. They and the West had come close to each other, but closeness merely brought a deeper awareness of deprivation and discrimination, and a deeper conviction that Europeans would only understand the language of force. The Mau-Mau came to pervert and transform tribal traditions—like the oath—in order to find the strength to fight the problem of modernism.

Further inroads of modernism into Africa, unless the benefits of modernism are freely shared, may therefore only further incite the growth of movements like the Mau-Mau. Such movements, because they are often led by detribalized urban elements, may increasingly be capable of uniting tribes under their radical leadership. Communists could infiltrate such urban-led movements. They need not infiltrate in order to allow movements of this type to diminish the strategic value of certain areas of Africa to the West.

Hundreds of thousands of frustrated and discontented Africans who might otherwise join Communist ranks are now also being drawn into the African Separatist Christian Churches. Championing Christianity, not as the missionary teaches it, but with symbols and programs transformed to meet the needs of tribalistic nationalism, these Christian separatist sects have caused many serious political outbreaks, especially in the Union of South Africa, where racial discrimination and native land expropriation have, perhaps, been most extreme.

Organized to protect the interests of a particular tribal group, or transcending such loyalties under the leadership of a healer-prophet, these sects, often secret in character, provide clear-cut issues, clear-cut rituals of behavior, and intense fellowship in a strange and bitter world. The ideology of this protest movement, like that of communism, is ultimately a gift of the West—a Christianity turned into revolutionary and religious utopianism. But unlike communism, it can promise salvation, and possesses sanctions against failure to join that Communists cannot employ—such as social ostracism, ridicule, and the fear of sorcery.

As in Europe at the end of the Middle Ages, when the traditional mold of that continent began to disintegrate, the organization of separatist and chiliastic churches in Africa today is also being accompanied by a renaissance among intellectuals. Increasingly, the latter have been able to lead the religious sects into more radical directions, or draw the masses away entirely into secular nationalist movements.

Yet another religio-political competitor should be taken into account. It is sometimes forgotten that almost the entire northern third of Africa is Islamic by religion. Islam, however, is not only a religion but also a community, and hence, as its history has shown, peculiarly adapted to reacting to what it believes to be exploitation or tyranny with a religio-political crusade. The movement led in the late nineteenth century by the so-called Mad Mahdi of the Sudan is probably the best known such manifestation in Africa. There have been others, before and since.

Islam, whose advance over Africa is far more spectacular than that of Christianity, has given tribes over a large region a common set of symbols and a common faith. A crusade against imperialism and Western modernism and based on Islam could at present draw together intellectuals and masses more effectively than the European doctrine of communism. The bitterness that would follow the inevitable repression of such movements may provide improved opportunities for Communist efforts. Where Islam has been disintegrating under the impact of modernism, Moslems may turn to communism as the most ruthless form of Western modernism which can be employed against internal corruption, and the most useful Western heterodoxy which can be employed against Western domination.

The Mau-Mau, Christian separatist, and Moslem extremist have the advantage over Communists that, while often equally radical, revolutionary, and anti-Western, they possess deep native roots. But they lack any program which might answer Africa's practical needs, and that may prove a fatal weakness in the long run. Still, the violence and terror that compensate for lack of program may have had serious consequences for others before these movements have played themselves out.

Only the secular nationalists of Africa, such as have already come to power in the Gold Coast, or are pressing for power in North Africa, appear to offer a major and modern alternative to communism. But it is too early to tell how that competition may come out.

We can take comfort—for the moment—in the perception that the Communists have devoted still less attention than we to the movement of forces in Africa. The number of articles on Africa in all the major Soviet journals cited by Mr. McKay, for example, average but four a year over a period of twenty-four years. Only one book on Africa was published by the USSR since World War II, and it was condemned by Soviet reviewers as inaccurate and overoptimistic in its predictions.

One may suspect also that Africans who have turned to communism have not thought too seriously about the fact that most regions of Africa lack the head start, the resources, the time, that allowed Russia to make gains over a period of thirty-six years by the use of totalitarian methods. That such men have misjudged communism may also still be a tenuous and temporary advantage to us. Before too long, however, such men may grasp at totalitarianism not out of misguided idealism, but out of resentment and despair.

In the continent of Africa, the loss of social and traditional roots, the fact of racial discrimination, and the burden of great poverty could easily and descisively shape political destiny. The Communists, however, are not fated to take over control. But our discussion suggests that control over African affairs will ultimately go to that among the competing movements—modern nationalist, primitive fascist, or Communist—which turns out to be most radical in character, that is, which insists, in the original and best meaning of the word, on going to the roots of the problem.

Factors Influencing Soviet Imperialism in Latin America

HOBART A. SPALDING,
Intelligence Advisor, Bureau of Inter-American Affairs, Department of State

Let us examine first some of the basic facts concerning the development and significance of the Communist movement in Latin America. A valuable study recently released by the special Subcommittee on Security Affairs of the Senate Committee on Foreign Relations [1] has made these readily available.

As pointed out there, Communist party membership appears to have passed its peak in Latin America, and in none of the American Republics is the Communist party alone, acting as a political party, an important electoral factor. Nor do the Communists as such have any prospect at present of gaining control over the government of any Latin American Republic by electoral means; only in Guatemala is the direct participation of the Communist party in national politics significant.[2]

As emphasized by the Committee, however, numerical strength and participation on an organized basis in national politics are

[1] Senate Committee on Foreign Relations, Special Subcommittee on Foreign Affairs, *Strength of the International Communist Movement*, Government Printing Office, Washington, 1953.

[2] Reference is made here only to the independent Republics of the Americas. Recent events have called attention to Communist potential in certain European possessions in the Caribbean such as British Guiana, where the Peoples Progressive party, reportedly dominated by Communists and fellow-travellers, won eighteen of twenty-four elective seats in the House of Assembly in April, 1953, and to the French Overseas Department of Martinique where two of the Department's three deputies in the French National Assembly are members of the Communist party.

not conclusive assessments of potential strength, for the Communists in Latin America have greatly extended the range of their activities and have captured a substantial following through their use of front groups. It has been estimated that through these methods of attracting support and thus extending both their voice and their audience they may have retained what is described as the " latent sympathy " of perhaps a million or more Latin Americans.

Most important of all, however, is the manner in which communism has penetrated groups which give voice and expression to the new spirit of ultranationalism which is now so widespread in the area and, as the Committee study indicates, as long as Communist parties have cells or strong individual representation in labor, in student and intellectual groups, they can play on their doubts and discontents and utilize emerging nationalist drives to serve the ends of international communism. This they have done under their current " national liberation front " tactics, utilizing slogans and phrases which are frequently barely distinguishable from those of many noncommunist but " progressive " or " nationalist " political parties, turning them in a fashion which makes their attainment appear dependent upon the " elimination of imperialist (i. e. U.S.) exploitation," the " nationalization of raw material resources," and the elimination of " encroachments on national sovereignty " which they allege are involved in all collaboration with the United States.

A broad strategic objective is discernible in this propaganda which is aimed at weakening the potential economic and military contribution of Latin America to the strength of the free world. There are at least two near-term tactical objectives: (1) to hamper our current program of military assistance agreements, and (2) to reduce wherever possible the participation of U. S. capital and technical ability in the development of Latin America's raw material resources.

We should underline, then, the potential danger of communism in Latin America, operating as it does within the framework of nationalist demands which do indeed awaken the sympathy of the peoples of Latin America, and we should stress the possible magnitude of Communist influence if communism is joined to belated nationalistic revolutions and convulsions, emphasizing that an impressive degree of probability does exist that Communist activity will be extended in Latin America in spite of certain tendencies which may work in the opposite direction, to which I wish to turn later.

Meanwhile, two additional factors should be mentioned which may also point to an increase of Communist activity in Latin America in the near future.

The first of these is the apparently increasing degree of priority which the Kremlin places on the area. Thus Secretary of State John Foster Dulles, writing in 1950, could say that "Soviet communism has not made any major effort in Latin America, except in the normal way of spreading propaganda and helping to invigorate local Communist parties" and that, from the point of view of the USSR, "South America has, for the time being, been treated as a secondary theatre." Secretary Dulles goes on to say, however, that "the over-all trend in Latin America has created a situation out of which Soviet communism can manufacture distinctive successes if and when the party judges that the effort is worth while." [3]

It is not suggested that this point has been reached nor that in the Soviet view Latin America is anything but a secondary theatre as yet, but there is some evidence to the effect that Latin America is at least rising on the Kremlin's scale of priority and that aggressive Soviet imperialism may be paying increasing attention to this region. For example, Soviet broadcasts in Spanish and Portuguese to Latin America have greatly increased since 1950, and one estimate has been made to the effect that these may even have doubled since then. It is also said that there has been an attempt to raise the quality of these programs as well as their quantity, and we might in passing contrast this with our own recent action of eliminating all Spanish and Portuguese broadcasts to Latin America. At the same time, the flood of Communist printed propaganda tailored for Latin America has also increased, and such publications as the Spanish edition of the Cominform *Journal* are now put out in a regular air-mail edition and flown into the area.

Similar evidence may be found in the marked increase in the number of individuals who have travelled to Communist-

[3] John Foster Dulles, *War or Peace* (New York, 1950), 150–51.

sponsored and Communist-front meetings of all kinds from Latin America in recent years. Local Communists are reported to have received recently generous financial assistance from international Communist headquarters in support of their program of developing front organizations, and with this financing hundreds of fellow travellers as well as enrolled members and a scattering of noncommunists, evidently identified as likely prospects, have travelled to front conferences within the Soviet orbit both in Europe and in the Far East. There has been a very startling increase in this travel in recent times, and it appears that the Soviet Union too has its "exchange-of-persons" program and its "leader-grants," with Latin America receiving a growing share of these "benefits."

Additional evidence which might be mentioned briefly is the rash of Soviet and satellite trade negotiations which has recently broken out in Latin America. These have been previously dealt with by Mr. Armstrong, from the point of view of trade. Even though, as he suggests, these may not mark a new departure as seen from the Kremlin and, the rigidity of the Soviet apparatus and the meagerness of Soviet production may make Soviet use of trade a relatively secondary weapon, as seen from Latin America, the increasing use of this weapon appears to be a shift of emphasis. It might also be noted that it is surely not coincidental that these Soviet and satellite trade negotiations inevitably turn up in those countries where they appear to think there are grounds for belief that economic relations with the U.S. may, temporarily at least, not be running smoothly.

So far, only one such agreement has been signed, namely, between the USSR and Argentina early in August, 1953, but others are reported to be in the process of negotiation or are threatened. Since these agreements appear to promise the export of capital goods, and since the orbit as a whole is a net importer of capital goods, their political aspect should be obvious.

A second factor which should be mentioned since it may afford a partial explanation of the first, is brought out in a series of studies which have been recently published on the possible future population of Latin America.[4] According to these

[4] Population Bulletin, Vol. IX, No. 6, Population Reference Bureau, Inc., Washington, D. C., 1953.

studies, if present population growth rates continue, it is estimated that by the year 2000, the population of Latin America may well be double that of the United States and Canada combined, having tripled in 47 years, and conceivably reaching the fantastic figure of 550 million. Even if these estimates ultimately prove to be many percentage points off, it is evident that Latin America is in the midst of a " population explosion," and it must be clear that unless industrial development and capital investment keep step with this large and rapid population growth, an increasingly fertile field for the seeds of Soviet communism is surely being created. In other words, both the importance and the vulnerability of Latin America as a target for Soviet imperialism may be increasing significantly and we may expect the Kremlin to react accordingly.

Not all factors which bear on the possible course of Soviet imperialism in Latin America are favorable to its expansion, however, and one of these should be examined in more detail, namely its increasingly apparent interventionist aspect.

The principle of nonintervention is the corner stone both of our own Good Neighbor policy and of the inter-American concept and system as a whole, and it is now embodied in treaty form in the basic document of that system, the Charter of the Organization of American States signed at Bogota in 1948. Nothing will bring a reaction throughout the inter-American system more quickly than violation of this principle, and we can be confident that as the interventionist nature of Communist imperialism becomes more clear, the people and the governments of the American republics will react jointly and severally to combat it. Thus the republics represented at the Ninth International Conference of American States have already declared that " by its anti-democratic nature and its interventionist tendency " the political activity of international communism " is incompatible with the concept of American freedom," and the topic of Communist intervention has been placed on the agenda of the forthcoming Tenth Inter-American Conference to be held at Caracas, Venezuela, in March, 1954.

Communist leaders themselves have left us with no doubts as to their primary allegiance to Moscow since Luis Carlos Prestes' well known declaration to this effect in 1946, echoed shortly thereafter with greater or less vehemence by other Latin American Communist leaders; and one need only read the effulgent declarations of the Latin American representatives to the 19th All-Union Communist Party Congress held in Moscow in October, 1952, to be convinced that their loyalty to and dependence on the leadership of the USSR continues unabated.

It is at this point that the role of those who may be described as the intellectuals becomes of great importance. By intellectuals in this context is meant those scholars, writers, artists, historians, and the like who through travel, reading, and research are perhaps best equipped to understand the basic significance of political forces and to interpret them to their own countrymen and to others. Surely it is one of their tasks to bring about an increasing awareness of the true nature of Soviet imperialism and an awareness of what its expansion to this hemisphere will ultimately mean to the independent republics of the Americas.

There is still widespread sympathy for the Communist " ideal " in many Latin American intellectual circles, but even among those who sympathize there is relatively little knowledge or understanding of the realities of Soviet communism or of the facts of life in Russia today. As stated in the Subcommittee Report referred to above, " it is especially ironic that a movement so completely subservient to dictation from outside the borders of every land (except the Soviet Union) should achieve such incredible success in its false parading under the nationalist banner." The intellectuals of Latin America—those in a position to know and understand Soviet communism—can render great service in relentlessly exposing its fundamental contradictions and making clear the extent to which local or " national " Communist parties are in truth the servants of the Soviet State.

There is, moreover, a second task which falls on the intellectuals of the Americas, and here we must constantly bear in mind the picture of the United States as seen through certain Latin American eyes. It is a simple truth, but one not always realized here, that the United States does in fact enjoy a very bad press in certain circles to the south, a press which is ardently promoted by the Communists and which, as noted above, frequently is made to appear to coincide with emerging nationalist demands.

To what may this be attributed and what if anything may be

done about it? One element has been identified by a great American citizen and public servant, Dr. Alberto Lleras, Secretary General of the Organization of American States, at the Colgate University Conference on American Foreign Policy on July 16, 1953. Speaking on the topic of "Latin America: Are We Losing its Friendship?" Dr. Lleras points out that:

> What I do regard as a menace to the relations between the two great groups of people, the Americans of the North and those of the South, is the dual tendency—which, fortunately, is expanding in neither area—to attribute all the troubles of a confused situation, such as that of the world today, to one's neighbors. In Latin America there are those who blame the United States for everything that happens, whether it be political instability, economic crises, social upheavals, or the general poverty. The great majority of the people do not really believe it, but they keep their peace, because it is only human not to want to break lances in behalf of the strong, particularly if one has cut his teeth on Don Quijote.

Now, it is here again that the role of the intellectual in Latin America becomes important, for much of this tendency corresponds to old habits of thought—formed perhaps in the atmosphere of the nineteen-hundreds—which have never been broken. There are history text books in Latin America which still reflect the "imperialist" view of the United States in its relations with its sister republics as if it were a current approach and which discuss the periods of "dollar diplomacy" and the "big stick" as if these were current policies. It may not be difficult to understand why this is so, and the manner in which this plays into Communist hands is likewise only too clear.

Perhaps it may be said, then, that two important steps must be taken in the Americas against the expansion of Soviet imperialism. The first is to bring about a true understanding of the subservience of local Communist movements to Moscow, no matter how "national" these may proclaim themselves to be; and the second to make sure that the picture we form of each other, North and South, corresponds not to the prejudices of earlier years but to the facts of 1953. In this the intellectuals bear a heavy responsibility and the task is not an easy one.

Soviet Russia is far removed from Latin America while the U.S. is near by—the hand-made whipping boy for Latin America's troubles. Yet we must never allow Soviet propaganda to drive a wedge between us by playing upon animosities which date from the past but bear little relation to the realities of today. If this degree of understanding can be achieved, the Americas can face the problem of Soviet imperialism with confidence.

HOBART A. SPALDING: *Discussion*

Department of State

The discussion which followed first reviewed the importance of the role of the intellectual in Latin America and raised the question of what the United States is doing to attract the Latin American intellectual leader in the fight against communism. It was pointed out that the "bad press" which the U.S. frequently enjoys may very well be the direct result of the attitude of many of Latin America's leading poets and artists who are in many cases strongly anti-U.S. in their attitude. The names of Pablo Neruda and Diego Rivera were cited as examples. It was agreed that the importance of such individuals as these must not be underestimated and that one of the greatest contributions to the problem of "attracting" such individuals must be made by their counterparts in this country. It was felt to be unfortunate that the word "intellectual" has sometimes been regarded as referring to someone withdrawn from the political arena, without political responsibility, peculiarly able to separate the intellectual doctrines to which he subscribes from the political consequences of such doctrines, and attention was called to that curious phenomenon, the "death wish of artists," pointing out that Pablo Neruda's poetry would probably earn for him a bullet in the brain if it were written under a Communist regime. Similarly, surrealism is not permitted in the USSR where only the realism of Socialism is allowed, yet Picasso supports the Communists! Picasso has stated that if imprisoned and forbidden to draw in his Surrealist style, he would slash the veins of his wrists and as his last act paint upon the floor of his cell with his own life's blood. It was agreed that this strange compulsion of certain artists to support the movement which would destroy them and their work is complicated and hard to understand.

Continuing the discussion of promoting better understanding between North and South America, the comment was made that we will always have difficulty in understanding the institutions and slogans of Latin America if words are taken to have the same meaning there as they have in the United States and in Europe. There is a " derivative " character to slogans which Latin America has borrowed from Europe such as Centralist-Federalist, Liberal-Conservative, Socialist-Democratic, Communist-Fascist and so forth. These labels are not accurate and it was contended that the average Latin American Communist and Latin American Fascist may not be the same as thought of in the United States and in Europe. The labels are imitative and unreal. Continuing in the same vein, the comment was made that close students of Latin America have always been aware of an ebb and flow in its political life–thus there may be a rash of *coup d'etats* for a few years followed by a general decline of military dictatorships and the rise of more democratic regimes. Unfortunately, many in the United States only look at Latin American politics when we believe ourselves to be endangered as, for example, by the Communist menace, and we don't take the long look. If we did, it was thought that there might be signs that the tide was again turning and that the certainty would be reached that in any real crisis of mankind, shadowy communism, as well as shadowy fascism, will give way to the fundamental freedoms held dear by all Americans.

The discussion then adverted to the theory that the Latin American intellectual was at present suffering from a " cultural lag " and that while it was true that the United States did go on an " imperialist spree " at the turn of the century when Theodore Roosevelt " took " the Panama Canal zone and gathered control of areas around it, North Americans are basically anti-imperialist and the marines are no longer in the Caribbean. This cultural lag is suffered by intellectuals everywhere, for learning is a painful process and is acquired with difficulty during our years of schooling. Thus, once a few generalizations get established and laboriously memorized, life itself has a way of gradually slipping out from under them. One must continually guard against this and make sure that these painfully acquired preconceptions do not color objective judgment.

The importance of the increasing interchange of intellectual ideas between Latin America and the U.S. was again emphasized and it was noted that during World War II the U.S. government had undertaken a book translation program which has since ceased. It was strongly recommended that this book translation program be resumed by the U.S. on a two-way basis, and the opinion was expressed that the translation of books written in the U.S. on the subject of communism, its history, and its methods would help greatly to clarify the nature of the Communist threat and the American attitude toward it.

Comment was made that the discussion so far had been primarily on the political level and that the economic foundations of inter-American problems had been disregarded, with a warning of the importance of appreciating the vulnerability of the Latin American economy rather than discussing inter-American difficulties in the rarified atmosphere of the attitudes of intellectuals. It was recognized that the economic problem was, of course, a fundamental consideration and attention was called again to the speaker's remarks on Latin America's current "population explosion," indicating that this made a solution of underlying economic difficulties both imperative and at the same time less subject to easy and ready panaceas.

The present program of the U.S. was then referred to of bringing Latin American leaders of free trade unions to the United States to observe our methods of labor organization and activity, and the question raised of the impact of this program on the Latin American labor movement and the position of these leaders on returning home. Do they win or lose support among their local unions on return? The opinion was expressed that no long-range assessment of this program was yet possible and hence no categorical reply could be made as to the effect it might have on Latin American labor movements, but that to date the program appeared to be successful, one interesting feature being the opportunity extended to such groups of labor leaders to attend classes at the leadership training school of the American Regional Organization of the anti-Communist International Confederation of Free Trade Unions in Puerto Rico for several months, before continuing their studies with travel and observation in continental United States.

The discussion was closed with a reference to the influences of religion on the development of communism in the Latin American countries. The clear position of the Roman Catholic Church in relation to communism was noted and the opinion expressed that the Roman Catholic Church had undoubtedly provided, and could be counted on to provide, a real bulwark against the spread of communism in the area and an important channel through which to expose communism's unmitigated atheism.

PART V

The Soviet Challenge in the Near and Far East

The Eastern Mediterranean in the East-West Conflict

T. CUYLER YOUNG,
Princeton University

The eastern Mediterranean has been important in the development of Western civilization ever since the Bronze Age. Together with the land bridge that separates this sea from the Arabian-Syrian desert, it has served as a means of communication and acculturation between Europe, Africa, and Asia and has bound the parts of these continents bordering the sea into a single cultural unit. War and trade, ethnic migrations and cultural differentiations have been patterned by the *obiter dictum* of this geographical fact of land and sea, with its triangulated tension points of entrance and exit—the narrows off Sicily, the Dardanelles, and the Suez isthmus. Whether it be Phoenicians, Greeks, or Romans, Turks, British, or Americans, those who have controlled this basin have dominated history in this cultural center.

So when considering the world's bipolarization of power and the problem of Soviet imperialism, it is only logical that the Russian imperialist threat to the eastern Mediterranean come under scrutiny. It is only natural that first the mind turns to the strategic significance of this area, then to the political, economic, social, and cultural challenge of Russia to the area and its peoples.

Ever since Russia established herself on the shores of the Black Sea in the latter half of the eighteenth century, she has been concerned with gaining control of access to the Mediterranean through the Straits connecting these seas. For over two centuries Turkish-Russian relations have turned upon this pivot, with the Russians always aiming at opening the Straits for Black Sea powers and closing them for non-Black Sea powers. Up to 1914 this aim was continuously and successfully opposed by Great Britain, sometimes in concert with the other European powers, sometimes not. Just as Russia seemed within grasp of her goal on the basis of the secret Allied agreements of 1915, came the Bolshevist revolution and postponement—until 1945 when the Kremlin tried to intimidate Turkey into bi-power negotiation of the question. With United States and British support Turkey declined to budge, except to agree to a reconsideration of the Montreux Convention of 1936 if the signatories to that agreement currently regulating the Straits under Turkish sovereignty, together with the United States, were also to be consulted. Soviet pressure has been renewed in recent weeks, but for all its milder form it has met with the same Turkish resistance: all of which probably points to Soviet denunciation of the Montreux Convention in 1955, as will be her legal right, thus forcing some reconsideration of the question.

Turkey's resistance has been possible because Western diplomatic backing has been expressed in military and economic aid to Greece and Turkey involved in the Truman Doctrine, with these countries sharing in the Marshall Plan, finally becoming an integral part of the North Atlantic Treaty Organization.

In this strategy of meeting the Soviet challenge at the Straits, Greece is equally as important as Turkey, for the Dardenelles can actually be controlled from the Greek islands in the Aegean Sea. Indeed, in reality, all this history and traditional challenge of Russia is modified, if not largely negated, by long-distance air power in the Atomic Age; but just how much is not yet altogether clear.

In the years immediately after World War II, the challenge of the USSR in this region was also felt in the drive through Yugoslavia to Italy and Sicily, which, coupled with the demand for a trusteeship in Libya, could have put the Soviets astride the Mediterranean. Such a position would have outflanked the Straits and neutralized the third triangular tension point of the Suez. The recent resurgence of both the right and the left in Italy and subsequent overthrow of the De Gasperi government are at once a sad commentary on the ironical effect of NATO and the Marshall Plan in a return to politics-as-usual, and a disturbing hint that the threat of Soviet pressure through Italy on the center of the Mediterranean is not permanently eliminated. But for intervening Titoism this shift in the Italian scene could be even more disturbing. The threat is always potential and demanding of Western attention.

Not unrelated to all this was the Soviet attempt to outflank Turkey on the east by the Iranian Azerbaijan separatist movement of 1945–46 and the nondiplomatic war of nerves in claiming the eastern Turkish provinces of Kars and Ardahan, originally wrested from the Ottomans by Russia in 1878 and then returned to Turkey after the revolution. Although the more direct challenge of the Soviets in Iran was countered by the Western powers there and in the United Nations during 1946–47, it is still in 1953 indirectly potent and unmet there, howbeit in a different situation and set of circumstances. The threat aimed at the eastern provinces, as a part of the total challenge to Turkey, has been countered by the general strengthening of Turkey and specifically by the United States aid to Turkey which has mechanized and motorized the Turkish army on new strategic roads, supported by new ports in the northeastern corner of the Mediterranean, and by airfields under the shadow of the Taurus and Amanus Mountains, with all these in turn covered by the fixed aircraft carrier of British-held Cyprus. Behind all these developments, of course, are the British-American fleets in the Mediterranean and the airbases of northern Africa, stretching from Tripoli to Morocco.

Thus upon Turkey and Greece on the northeastern Mediterranean have centered efforts to counter the Soviet challenge to the eastern Mediterranean, which in turn controls direct communications by land, sea, and air between the members of the British Commonwealth, between Europe and the Near and Middle East. These efforts so far have been successful. Yet they have been seriously compromised by inability to secure the Iranian flank of Turkey and the Arab environment of the Suez, for this hinterland of the eastern Mediterranean not only shares the strategic aspects of the region but embraces its economic assets. Except for the petroleum resources of the Persian Gulf, this general region constitutes an economic liability and problem rather than an asset. But oil sufficient to supply the needs of the Middle East and Europe, with some to spare for importation on our own Atlantic seaboard, constituting approximately two-thirds of the potential production of the world, is important and can scarcely be ignored: important for what it means in positive power to the Western world, as well as for what it means in the denial of such power to the communist area.

Yet seething Iran and Egypt, with restive Iraq between, point up the current failure of the West to secure this strategic and oil-rich hinterland in friendly cooperation and alliance against the present potential threat of the USSR. To anyone skeptical of this, it need only be pointed out that it is now almost two years since the Middle East Defense Organization under American, British, French, and Turkish sponsorship was proposed, and to date there has been no favorable response, not even from Egypt which was invited to be a founding sponsor. The reason for this failure would appear to be the West's inability to appraise correctly the political climate of the eastern Mediterranean, as well as the nature of the political threat of the Soviets in the area.

In this region the aim of the USSR has been the elimination of British influence and the prevention of its replacement by the United States, with the Soviets prepared to fill the power vacuum thus created. The degree of their success has become disturbing, and to counter it the West will have to do better than it has to date.

In Iran the British have been eliminated, with negligible hope of return. Eventual United States solidarity with Britain on the oil question has compromised the previously favorable position. Iranian political acumen and realism have been badly damaged and an almost pathological and unnatural xenophobia developed. All three governments are responsible for the result, with the United States unappreciated by either of the other two. Only the USSR stands to gain, with the harvest delayed by Iran's long-standing and ingrained fear of Russian aggression and by apparent Soviet reluctance to force the issue until it can fit cheaply and quietly into a larger and carefully prepared strategy. At present Russia would seem to be right in believing that time is on her side.

Almost equally disturbing is the Egyptian political scene and its anti-Western potential, despite all the encouraging signs of the Nagib regime's determination to tackle pressing internal problems and inadequacies, and to resist the temptation to indulge in a compensatory emotional crusade of anti-British nationalism. Tension has been relieved some by the British-Egyptian accord on the Sudan, but the craft of this settlement is far from smooth sailing considering the storms that have already broken in efforts to implement a plebiscite.

But the problem of the Suez still threatens. The unbelievable happened in Iran; and it can happen in Egypt if "too little" constructive attention is brought to bear upon the problem "too late." The legal position of both parties has been sullied if not compromised: by the British maintenance of such large numbers of troops, although explained as technically within the treaty provisions; and by the Egyptian unilateral denunciation of the treaty before its 1956 terminus. Settlement must be upon a broader basis. With good will and mutual confidence, it should not be impossible. Unfortunately it is just these assets which are lacking, especially the confidence. In such circumstances it devolves upon the stronger, the more and longer privileged to exercise both restraint and magnanimity, consonant with responsibility. Whether the British can demonstrate more resiliency and realism than in the Iranian dispute remains to be seen; equally uncertain is whether the United States can do a smoother job of honest brokerage.

Not a little depends upon the result. The Soviets have had almost nothing to do directly with the creation of the situation and tension, but they are certainly interested in, and bound to gain by, its continuance or further deterioration.

Closely related is the whole major problem of Arab-Israel relations, the unresolved state of which contributes much to the overcast, humidity, and electric potential of the eastern Mediterranean political weather. It is now over four years since the Arab-Israel armistice, and the parties appear no nearer to peace. The merits of the question aside and all contrary assurances notwithstanding, there is no doubt the Arab peoples regard the establishment of Israel as a threat of Western aggression pointed at the heartland of their domain and culture. The economic support of the new state in dollars equal to, if not more, than the total given to all the Arab states can scarcely remove their skepticism and fear. The reasons and responsibility for it aside, the continuance of at least three-fourths of a million Arab refugees in unproductive and unsettled conditions constitutes a serious threat to the political and social stability of the region. The economic prosperity that accrues from oil to nearby Arab countries, together with all the aid given by the United States, does not make up for the political debits incurred by the current policy of the West, which, in this case, means primarily that of the United States; and all the positive credit secured in a Western-aligned Israel would scarcely seem to change materially or decidedly the totals of the political balance sheet, as it is concerned strictly with the East-West conflict in the eastern Mediterranean. Indeed, the end result to date would seem amply to justify the Soviet departure from ideological doctrine and indulgence in tongue-in-cheek practical tactics when in 1947 the USSR joined the Western powers—on one of those so rare occasions—and voted in the United Nations for Palestinian partition, following it the next year with *de jure* recognition of the new state of Israel.

This estimate or political balance sheet is scarcely modified by the special treaty position still enjoyed by Great Britain in Jordan and recently attained in the newly independent state of Libya. The former is resented in neighboring Arab states and is not as secure a relationship as it was before the assassination of King Abdullah in 1951. The new alliance with Libya is bound to be received coolly among the Arab states, which have been glad enough to back Libyan independence, but not slow to point out the anomaly of such a country attaining independence while Tunis and Morocco remain under French control. Such treaty arrangements are useful, but provide neither the best nor permanent security since they are dictated by poverty and bought with subsidies. In the long run alliances must be established on more community of interest than this, and such bargains can only contribute to lasting peace and security if both parties make a sincere effort to see that the economic and political needs which initiated them are eliminated as rapidly as possible.

This leads to the heart of the more basic psychological problem that lies behind all such political maneuvers and alliances with newly independent and sovereign states. This is the obvious and elementary, yet often neglected, principle of true equality in all dealings. In considering this area, the temptation of the strong Westerner is to think in terms of strategy and power only, with their cheapest price possible named and maintained. However important these may be, in the long run it is the people who inhabit the region who give substance to the strategy and finally determine the tactical utilization of power, be it that of geography or geology. And any Western security in meeting the threat of Soviet imperialism must be based upon the good will, confidence, and cooperation of the people. That is, unless the West is prepared to reestablish with force the old nineteenth century imperialism, and indulge in the ruthless totalitarianism of the Kremlin's twentieth century refinement of imperialism to maintain it. Since Western democracy can scarcely do this, then it is submitted that its only recourse is to go the reasonable and responsible limit of its convictions and treat with all peoples in the true spirit of the free world.

In few areas is this more important than among peoples who are just emergent from colonial or semicolonial status into independence, still backward when measured against modern technical and scientific standards. To them *amour-propre* is priceless and dear. They are often prepared to admit realistically the discrepancy between their achievements and those of Western peoples, but only when spiritually secure and confident that their own inherent worth as persons and peoples is being recognized and respected. Partnership can be endured, even by the poorer of the partners; but patronage cannot, is bound to be resented, and eventually rejected. It is not the colonial burden that Easterners so much object to as it is the smugness with which Westerners carry it. The Anglo-Saxon has not been famed for his humility or ability to put others at ease on a comradely basis. Yet in the eastern Mediterranean where civilization is old and quite self-conscious this spiritual problem is basic, and an integral part of the challenge offered by the proletarian comrades from Moscow.

The fundamental problem in the area is that of imperialism: the peaceful liquidation of that which has dominated, and the effective prevention of that which seeks to replace it. Soviet propaganda is right enough about the first, but either self-deceived or hypocritical about the second.[1]

In any political controversy between the "ins" and the "outs," present and practical advantages of maneuver and pressure are generally with the incumbents who are in possession; while future and ideological advantages of criticism and promise are with the challengers of such incumbent power. Those in control have to stand on their record of achievement, those bidding for power largely on their promises. As between Western democratic imperialism—admitting its reality, at least for the moment—and the Soviet totalitarian version, obviously the advantage is with the Soviets who have no qualms about ruthless self-entrenchment, once power has been seized.

The issue depends upon whether the present Western incumbents of power in this area can demonstrate in deeds—and soon—their determination to turn from all forms of the old imperialism, the elimination of which has become a highly charged battle slogan in the Near East. Sober history will eventually place much to the credit of the British government and people in preparing this area for its rightful place in the free world. But along with such benefits have gone such sins of commission and omission, such exploitative practices and inadequate visions, that awakened and aware peoples have become too impatient to accept the old-fashioned pace of tutelage. There are many Britishers, in and out of government, particularly of the younger generation, who realize this and give themselves unstintingly to new ideas, new ways, and new relationships. But they are severely handicapped by the entail of the still living colonial personnel and mind, much of it shifted from India to the Near East; and—what is more important—by the entail of evil bequeathed them by dead imperialists, long-repressed resentment of whom now bursts ugly and unruly from the limbo of the Near Eastern subconscious. Although inexcusable, some of the irrational outbursts of feeling and passion on the part of Near Eastern peoples are still quite explicable in these terms, goaded

[1] Perhaps the academician may at this point be indulged in a bit of philological irony and a crocodile tear over the fall of Beria, whose Transcaucasian name is of Persian origin and in that language is pronounced "biriya," which, being interpreted, is "without hypocrisy."

as they are by their own so often unadmitted weaknesses and inadequacies when faced with the stern demands of this age of crisis. The tragedy of the situation is marked by Near Eastern misinterpretation and misrepresentation of sincere British efforts to make amends for the past in better programs for the present.

Let no one interpret these strictures as arising from any insensitivity to the same strains in the American character and governmental conduct. For confirmation of this one need only seek the point of view of a Latin American who can document "dollar diplomacy." Yet the Good Neighbor Policy and the New Deal internal revolution have substantially affected, if not completely eliminated, this pattern. Besides, attention is here centered on the eastern Mediterranean where it is Britain who carries on as the major responsible power and heir to the past. Moreover, let it be candidly noted that in this area today there are too many Americans who are as imperialist as any Briton in this so-called "American Century." As between these two major allies, it is mainly a question of degree of involvement.

In any case, unquestionably one of the most important and difficult aspects of this situation is the problem of British-American relations. The very exigencies of the situation have demanded more and more participation of the United States, as British resources have proved inadequate to meet the staggering demands. Yet, except for certain spots, such as Turkey, Greece, and Saudi Arabia, this American participation has never been detached from British leadership and responsibility. The result has often made for friction and working at cross purposes. If Britain has seemed lethargic and unresponsive to the new demands of the people, the United States has appeared brash and irresponsible in abetting those demands. If Britain has been embarrassed and misunderstood because of her Cromers and Curzons, the United States has been equally on a spot when expected to apply instantly on demand the Wilsonian Fourteen Points or Rooseveltian Atlantic Charter. If British liberals are the heirs of the ubiquitous merchants and exploiters, American officials are legatees of the legends of humanitarian educators and missionaries. Be it said that American officials, faced with general global and specific area responsibilities, have come to have more sympathy and respect for British planning and performance.

Yet the old-timer and the newcomer differ in their area diagnosis, hence their prescriptions, however often united they may be in the dogmatics with which these are set forth. Inevitably, problems in such a partnership loom large and threaten to neutralize its efforts, if not undermine its very existence. More resolute facing of this basic problem, with less internecine quarrelling and maneuvering on the part of the partners, must be forthcoming before there is a more effective meeting of the challenge posed by the march of events and by the Soviets just beyond these events ready to mould them to their purposes and ends.

In this context, although already covered in principle, it may be fruitful to spell this out in terms of Western policy toward Near Eastern nationalism. We may well begin by getting in the proper spiritual mood by recognizing and reflecting upon our own groups of superpatriots—their irrational emotionalism, raucous flag-waving, immature irresponsibility, and timid opportunism. If we have our troubles in this regard—in one of the richest and most powerful nations in the world—after a century and three quarters of relatively secure independence, what sympathy should we have for these newly emergent nation-states which have so lately gained a precarious independence, and which have so recently been caught in the maelstrom of imperialist rivalries, as to have difficulty in discerning whether what they have acquired is the genuine thing or but a nominal or phantom facsimile.

From which you will rightly conclude that I believe, in spite of all its real and many shortcomings, that the West must cooperate with nationalism in this area. After all, it is the one major Western ideological importation that has taken deep root, and we had best not be caught branding our own progeny as illegitimate just because of his adolescent extravagances and immaturities, embarrassing though they may be in front of company whom we may wish to impress. Near Eastern nationalism merits our sympathy and patience, for only by its proper growth can the vitality of the strong patriarchalism of this society be newly institutionalized on a scale and in a pattern that will enable these really highly individualistic peoples to fulfill themselves in the kind of a large social entity and pattern so essential for existence and growth in this technological age.

Let it be admitted that this heightens the difficulties in Anglo-American relations in the area. To epitomize this one could, on the one hand, quote from any one of our Founding Fathers and, on the other, recall those words of Lord Curzon to the American delegation at the first session of the Lausanne Conference in 1923, when he stormed about the room following Ismet Inönü's walking out of the Conference: ". . . for four mortal hours [we have listened to] the same old banalities—independence and sovereignty."[2] Yet in all fairness to our British friends, let it be noted that we and many of these obstreperous Near Easterners acquired much of this thirst for liberty and independence at the springs of English literature and constitutionalism.

Deeper than all political maneuvers and diplomatic problems is the social challenge presented by the eastern Mediterranean peoples. Moreover, the emphasis is upon the people. The main difference between this and the preworld-war era is that now appeal must be to an ever increasing and more articulate substantial portion of the people, rather than to a selected few of the ruling elite. It is difficult for some of the old-timers to realize that the center of gravity of social and political power has shifted from the few at the right, toward the center. Mass communications, especially the radio—to be found in almost every village—have effected a new pattern of political awareness and power. The old methods of manipulating the elite, well mastered by the British, were comparatively easy and cheap; but they do not produce results in most places today and must be replaced by more widely based appeals. Moreover, in the midst of current rapid social change the Western powers necessarily often find themselves, sometimes against their better judgment, dealing with the now-outdated elite, which still clings desperately to its privilege but is rapidly being repudiated, often to the embarrassment of the supporting big power.

There is no doubt about the tactics and strategy, the methods and aims of the USSR: its appeal is to the masses, the long submerged and now restless majority, all the way from the frustrated intellectuals to the oppressed peasant. Diplomatic protocol will be observed, but brazen appeals will be made simultaneously

[2] Joseph C. Grew, *The Turbulent Years* (Boston, 1952), Vol. 1, 551.

over the heads of governments directly to the people. This may be regarded as interference, but it can be effective if the governments are not making headway in meeting the basic economic and social demands of their peoples.

No such comparable techniques have been discovered by the West in its efforts to appeal to the people and the groups genuinely interested in progress and reform. Americans especially are rigidly bound by the absolutist dogma of noninterference, not realizing that any great power is going to be held responsible for both its action and inaction, blamed if the result is ill and little thanked if it turns out well. Somewhere between the correct principle of respect and noninterference and the evil program of subversion and consequent tyranny must be devised a democratic moral pressure, translated into tangible deeds, that will give the people as a whole full confidence that Western friendship and cooperation will get them farther and faster toward their goal of the more abundant life.

For just this possibility, envisioned by the masses of these peoples, is a major significant fact in the area. For centuries, if not millenia, convinced that their general pattern of life is fixed and decreed in an economy of scarcity, they have now awakened to the realization that this is no longer necessary in a technological economy of plenty. Both the US and the USSR din their ears full of the wonders of modern science and technology at the service of the common man, till they have dared to believe that the age-old enemies of poverty, disease, and ignorance may be routed. This is truly revolutionary in the history of the Near East.

But by whom is the battle to be led? The Western democracies, whose average GI many have seen able to command what to them seem luxuries even in the midst of war? Or the Eastern Communist who boasts of his industrial transformation and attainment of power within almost a single generation, and by methods allegedly workable in neighboring eastern countries similiarly backward? First chance of proving their respective claims lies with the presently incumbent West, but soon and surely must appear some tangible results in better bread and cheese or the Near Easterner will turn in desperation to the other claimant for his confidence.

To this end Point IV and United Nations technical assistance are a beginning, but no more. If solidly based and locally adapted, not allowed to be prostituted to more immediate and ephemeral political goals and gains, they can help to set pointers along profitable roads for local development. But even this program, granting the boldness which it has never been allowed by congress to develop, is not enough. Granting that most of the economic development of the area must be accomplished by the peoples themselves, some boost and fillip must be found to get this underway and kept dynamically expansive. Large loans from the international banks may help; but only if the risk capital of the West is brought to the task can hope of large-scale advancement be entertained. Given the trade traditions and psychology of the Near East itself, the volatile uncertainty of the present political atmosphere, and a number of other complicating factors, this development is not likely to occur naturally. But some such new formula must be found by dynamic and enlightened Western business if the economic challenge of the USSR is to be met in the Near East.

All Iron Curtain peoples, most Europeans, and too many Britishers are unaware of the recent American business revolution and modifications of North American capitalism that not only outdate all Communist and European Socialist critiques, but give promise of furnishing the dynamism necessary to spark economic development around the world if properly harnessed and then given enough rein. At the base of it is the American drive for an ever-expanding production, with higher wages, small margin of profit, widespread ownership, and relatively free competition for efficiency. This clashes with the old-style theory of limited production, low wages, widest possible margin of profit, restricted ownership, and cartelization wherever possible. Some of the Anglo-American problems in the Near East arise from these different business philosophies. But the main point being made here is the necessity for American concentration on the problem of how to team business dynamism with governmental responsibility abroad in a formula that will avoid the evils of imperialism, yet bring to bear its goods upon underdeveloped regions. Admittedly a difficult task, not even accomplished within the United States, it is nonetheless a goal at which we should aim.

Beyond all this, there is an even deeper level at which decision must be made by Near Eastern peoples in the East-West conflict: that which concerns their way of life and pattern of culture. The struggles for political independence and demand for economic betterment are not primarily ends in themselves, but rather means to insure uninhibited control of the forces that determine mores and social institutions, basic beliefs, and cultural patterns. There is no question of the terrific force of the impact of Western civilization upon the eastern Mediterranean, which will never be the same again because of it. Yet just as Hellenism once reached its crest and receded before a powerful reaction, so today Semitic Islam is stiffening and raising its questioning guard. It is far too early to descry the outcome; suffice it to observe that never before has Western civilization moving east been accompanied by such a total technological revolution as in modern times.

It is no mere piece of political and economic legerdemain that has anchored the eastern arm of NATO on Turkey. This laic Republic has been founded upon a frank and full acceptance of the West. However resolute and strong this Westernized Turkey may seem, it is just this which causes the Arabs and Iranians to balk at her leadership and medial tie to the West. These peoples of the eastern Mediterranean and beyond wish above all else to choose what of the West they will adopt and adapt, without foreign duress and determination. The West has a golden opportunity to demonstrate economic and social solidarity and fraternity in programs of aid and mutually beneficial cooperation, with a sincere respect for Near Eastern corporate and cultural personalities and a scrupulous avoidance of even the semblance of spiritual imperialism.

This will take a bit of doing, particularly on the part of Americans who are tempted to an overdose of messianic smugness and belief that all would be well if only other peoples could be moulded in their image or be persuaded to adopt their political, economic, and social institutions. I am not decrying American evangelism, per se, for I believe there is much we have learned and tested of the Great American Dream that can help our fellowmen around the world; I am only deprecating the provincial assumption that we alone have been entrusted with the true Gospel for humanity. The ancient peoples of the eastern Mediterranean are not likely to take kindly to the preachments of such Far Western grandchildren, howsoever they may welcome their material aid and spiritual comradeship if proffered in humility and respect.

But what of the Soviet bid for this area at this deeper cultural level? It can scarcely be successful if the truth and consequences of that bid are clearly known and understood. Only if by some default, such as Near Eastern political frustration and economic desperation, it gains an entrance by falsehood and blandishment. Communism may garb itself as a fellow-Eastern Asiatic movement, but most Near Easterners should know it as a Western ideology that has been transplanted to Russian soil, now serving basic Russian imperialism. Even though it may demonstrate vitality and viability in China and the Far East, this does not mean its totalitarianism, rigid centralization, or dialectical materialism would be acceptable to the eastern Mediterranean peoples, among whom a remarkable degree of individualism has flourished even in despotically ruled societies, by whom centralization in government has often been successfully resisted, and from whom has come that spiritual and ethical monotheism which is the ground and guarantee of freedom and liberty.

This basically Western cultural plant may often have gone to seed and even degenerated here, but it is native to the soil, and is not likely to succumb, especially if strengthened by ingrafting from younger and hardier forms of the species developed elsewhere.

Viewed relatively in total time and space, eastern Mediterranean culture, for all its differences, is much a part of the West, to which at times in history it has contributed so much. Not only for its own sake and for what it may again contribute to our common culture, but also because of its bridging role between the West and the Farther East, it would be tragedy of the first order if Russian imperialism should enslave the area and deflect it from the fulfillment of its birthright, in which we all share far more than we shall ever know.

EDWIN M. WRIGHT: *Discussion*

Officer in Charge of Turkish Affairs,
Department of State

I am not going to attempt a recapitulation or expansion of Mr. Young's paper, for I find myself in general agreement with its analysis. But I would like to comment on three points which are implied in his argument but not explicitly stated.

One. Although the largest contribution to our Western culture comes from the lands of the eastern Mediterranean, it seems to be the area least understood or studied by the Western world—particularly in the United States. Without the contributions of the Middle East in mathematics, our banks could not operate; without its contribution in religion and ethics, we would be barbarians; without its creation of symbols of speech and ideas, we could not communicate with one another as we do today.

Yet in 1879, a candidate for a Ph. D. at Harvard used some Arabic source material in his thesis, and no professor in Harvard—or in fact in the whole of the United States—was able to judge as to the proper translation of the Arabic quotations. The first course in Modern Middle Eastern History and Languages was offered at Princeton in 1936. There are now four universities giving well-rounded postgraduate courses in Middle Eastern studies and a few others which give partial courses.

This lateness in indicating an interest in the area is also shown by the fact that President Eisenhower is the first United States president to have even visited a part of the Middle East before his term as president—he visited Greece and Turkey as a North Atlantic Treaty Organization Chief of Staff in 1951—and this spring Mr. Dulles was the first secretary of state to visit the Middle East while in office.

Two. The Middle East is undergoing fundamental and rapid change so that anyone who has not recently visited it finds himself out of date within a short span of time. I have heard of an Irish Municipal Council which voted three resolutions at one meeting. They were: (1) Because the old jail is inadequate and collapsing, the jail should be torn down and rebuilt. (2) For the purpose of economy, the old materials in the jail should be used in the rebuilding. (3) The prisoners should be housed in the old jail till the new one is constructed.

This is an exact description of what is happening in the Middle East today. The peoples of the area have decided their traditional patterns are inadequate and must be reformed. They wish to salvage as much from the past as is possible while they rebuild on new and revolutionary patterns. Meanwhile, they must occupy the area while the process of renovation is being pushed.

Three brief illustrations can drive this point home. Until recently, Iran had never heard of a "referendum." There seems to be no word for this idea in the languages of Iran, so the English—or Latin—word was borrowed and given an Iranian accent. Suddenly the Iranian people were notified they were to have a "referendum" on the dissolution of parliament. It is hard to know what meaning this strange word has to the Iranian masses. They were told, by the government, that it was a patriotic duty to sign their names to a vote and cast it into a box marked "Pro-dissolution" for the parliament and that only British agents were opposed to this act. However, they could vote against dissolution if they wished to sign their names and insert the votes in a box which they were told marked opposition to the government. The radio, the government press, and government releases identified all opposition as treason. But the referendum is now one of the political realities in Iran—where it was unknown before 1953—although what it means to the man in the street in Iran is a far cry from what it means in the United States.

Recently the Egyptian Broadcasting System issued a statement from the office of the president—itself a new fact in Egyptian life. The broadcast appealed to the Egyptian people to discard outworn monarchial and aristocratic symbols of speech such as "noble" or "blessed" when referring to the president. The revolution has made all Egyptians equal and they should so act. Kissing of the hand of the leader is a relic of servility and should be stopped. Applauding or rising to greet the president when he enters houses of worship—synagogues, churches, or mosques—disturbs the attitude and violates the new spirit in Egypt. While this type of instruction is being issued in Egypt, the United States press keeps echoing phrases about pharaohs and pashas. Just what these new ideas mean demand careful and sympathetic study by people living in the area.

A still more dramatic symbol of change is to be found in the Sudan. In the summer of 1952 an international commission was assigned with an Indian as chairman to supervise the preparation for the election of a constituent assembly of Sudan. In their visits, they stopped to visit the Diuka tribesmen of Southern Sudan. The Diuka tribesmen are among the worlds' most primitive people, and are among the largest professional and permanent nudist colonies to be found. They have ritualistic associations connected with their main source of wealth—cattle. The nude Diuka male takes the name of his bull and every morning rolls in white wood ashes in a ritual which neither he nor the white man can rationalize. In 1953, to these simplest children of nature, there swoops down out of the skies an international commission which asks them whether they prefer direct or indirect representation in a Constituent Assembly which will decide whether Sudan will choose independence within Egyptian Unity, total independence or independence within the British Commonwealth. To the average Diuka and the other three million people of southern Sudan, all peoples living north of the Sudan are Turks—harking back to memories of the days when Mohammed Ali and the Khedive Ismail annexed the Sudan as part of the Turkish Empire.

The old pattern of living is rapidly being changed, so that it not only confuses the people living in this "house of the Middle East" but also confuses the outside observer.

My third point follows the latter part of Mr. Young's paper on the threat of Soviet imperialism and the problems of Anglo-United States cooperation. Up to the end of 1952, one might say the Soviet Union was our best ally in driving the peoples of the Middle East into our arms. The Soviet Union used every means of terror at its command. It demanded territorial acquisitions, military bases, it organized subversive movements, it blustered, threatened, and interfered with the internal affairs of Middle Eastern states. When the Western powers made mistakes, it did not seem to matter so much because the brutal nature and tone of Soviet imperialism could be held up as the greater danger.

But since the rule of Saint Malenkov this is no longer true. The Soviet line has changed. The USSR no longer has territorial claims, it is anxious to settle amicably all frontier, financial and other problems. The new Malenkov "imperialism" has put on a garb of friendliness, and helpfulness—especially in helping the Middle Eastern peoples to rid themselves of the vestiges of traditional colonial rule. This new approach is not going to make two mistakes to our one. Under these circumstances, unless we wish to lose by default, we can no longer afford the luxury of making mistakes. For I believe that as in the past, so in the future, the integration of the Middle East with the Western world will play a far greater part in both our fates than most of us would ever dream.

India and the East-West Struggle

MERRILL R. GOODALL,
Visiting Professor in Political Science,
University of Delhi

The political process is one of decision-making. By decisions policies are made and executed. The problem of making decisions is not one exclusively possessed by statesmen, politicians, and administrators. All of us make choices, and the choices we make, even though they may be defined and dated, reflect our fundamental processes, our early experience, and perhaps the results of previous decisions we have made. While the decisions made by public officials in this no war–no peace era represent similar processes, they may be of tremendous moment to the survival and welfare of a country.

This report on " India and the East-West Struggle " searches for those decisions of the government of India which enable us to identify that government's response to Communist imperialism. In discussing such policy choices, we want to identify the objectives of Indian government and the tactics selected by the government in an effort to achieve its goals. We will expect, then, to find whatever there may be in the way of recurrent elements in the government of India's approach to the problem of Communist expansion.

It will be noticed at once that the decisions discussed here are not " comprehensive," all the decisions of Indian government are not tabulated and classified. Our discussion is necessarily selective, and it may seem to consist of a proportionately small sample. Yet these are not isolated decisions. They are those acts in situations over which India exercises control, areas in which her decisions are meaningful and not merely interesting declarations of point of view. There are, of course, other methods of considering the role of India with respect to Communist organization, methods not specifically centered on the decisions of government but which illumine the course of decision-making. The latter include descriptions of electoral behavior, party campaign methods, the structure of public opinion, press editorials, and attitudes found in such institutions as the college and university and professional society. But political decisions, the Indian government choices on the issue of Communist expansion, are basic acts in the exercise of political power. They provide the organizing theme of the following pages.

On the issue of Communist party organization and tactics inside India, the government's position is unambiguous. While the party is legal, the Preventive Detention Act (1950) is a frequently used weapon against Communist subversive activities. Prime Minister Nehru has often ridiculed the "extra-territoriality" of the Communists and has attacked the Communist party as "counter-revolutionary and completely out of date."[1] And again quoting Nehru, "The Communists, whatever their ideology, have followed a path of violence and open warfare against the State. No State can tolerate that. Their object appears to have been to create chaos and disruption out of which perhaps something might come. To some extent they have varied their policies and tactics recently, but basically their approach continues to be the same as before."[2]

But less well known are the protective measures taken by the government of India, especially since late 1949 when Tibet's relationship to China became a subject of concern to India. These security decisions of the government, particularly with respect to such Himalayan areas as Bhutan, Sikkim, and Nepal, deserve notice. As Dr. K. Shridharani said, for India to have to alert her border allies against China marked "one of the greatest somersaults in history."[3]

Defensive Outposts: Three Illustrations

Bhutan, in the eastern Himalaya, is bordered on the north and east by Tibet, on the west by the Tibetan district of Chumbi

[1] *Hindustan Times* (New Delhi), May 23, 1952.

[2] Jawaharlal Nehru, *Report to the All India Congress Committee* (New Delhi, 1951), 18.

[3] *Amrita Bazar Patrika* (Calcutta), May 5, 1952.

and by Sikkim, and on the south by the Indian states of West Bengal and Assam. The people are nominal Buddhists and maintain trade and cultural associations with Tibet; indeed, two centuries ago the country was subjugated by Tibetan military adventurers. On August 8, 1949, following India's intitiative, Bhutan and India signed a treaty replacing earlier ones effected by the British in 1865 and 1910. The government of Bhutan "agrees to be guided by the advice of the government of India in regard to external relations" (Article 2). The government of India, in addition, is given supervisory privileges over the importation of "warlike material or stores [which] may be required or desired for the strength and welfare of Bhutan" (Article 6). Bhutan, as well, is to receive an annual subsidy of 500,000 rupees (approximately $100,000.00). Since October, 1951, when the Dalai Lama and the Panchen Lama were appointed members of the Consultative Conference of the Chinese People's Republic, suggesting that Tibet had become an integral part of China, Indian-sponsored defense activities in Bhutan such as the construction of road links and defensive frontier posts have increased both in number and tempo.[4]

Sikkim, which faces Tibet on the north, Tibet and Nepal on the east, Tibet and Bhutan on the west, and West Bengal on the South, is a Buddhist country. The main trade route between India and Tibet lies from Bengal through Sikkim.

On the basis of treaties between Great Britain and China, effected in 1890 and 1893, Sikkim became a protectorate of Britain. In 1949 the Maharaja's administration was threatened by a "no tax" campaign, and tenants' strikes broke out in scattered sections of the country. The government of India, on June 7, 1949, intervened "in the interest of law and order" through a force of soldiers under the general direction of its ICS-trained political officer who resides at Gangtok and represents India in Bhutan as well.[5] The government of India then nominated an officer to serve as Dewan of Sikkim, a position which somewhat resembles that of chief commissioner of a class C Indian state. On December 5, 1950, a treaty between India and Sikkim regularized relations. Sikkim was formally desig-

[4] For one account see *Hindustan Times* (New Delhi), June 5, 1952.
[5] New York *Times*, June 8, 1949.

nated a " Protectorate of India " (Article 2). Subsequent articles made India " responsible for the defense and territorial integrity of Sikkim " and gave India the right to construct and maintain communications for " strategic purposes," and " to take such measures as it considers necessary for the defense of Sikkim or the security of India, whether preparatory or otherwise, and whether within or outside Sikkim. In particular the government of India shall have the right to station troops anywhere within Sikkim." These arrangements were generally approved by parliament, except for Communist opposition, and since the Communist occupation of Tibet the Indian military establishment has been strengthened substantially.

Nepal confronts Tibet across a common frontier of approximately five-hundred miles. On the east the country borders Sikkim and West Bengal; on the south and west, the Indian states of Bihar and Uttar Pradesh. Nepal is an independent state and, compared with Bhutan and Sikkim, its relations with India are far more complicated, tenuous, and significant strategically.

From 1846 to 1951 Nepal was ruled by a military oligarchy with power concentrated in the office of Prime Minister, an office which was inherited by the brothers and cousins of the Rana family. This political order stems from a document, the Panjpatra, negotiated between 1846 and 1848 with the king. The Panjpatra gave the Ranas the premiership, the title of Maharaja, and autocratic powers; the king was accorded merely ceremonial activities.

By the nineteen twenties, Nepalese students in Indian universities, notably Benares Hindu University, had been exposed to democratic themes and the tactics of the Indian National Congress. But not until 1946, in Calcutta, were the various anti-Rana leaders able to consolidate their forces in a new organization, the Nepali National Congress, Bisheswar Pradad Koirala being elected president. On April 10, 1950, a section of the Nepali National Congress and a newer organization, the Nepali Democratic Congress, merged into the Nepali Congress under the leadership of Matrika Prasad Koirala, B. P. Koirala's elder half-brother. The Nepali Congress, built on the model of the Indian congress, stood as the country's major political grouping until the organization in June, 1953, of the National Democratic party, headed by M. P. Koirala who in 1952 left the congress.

The efforts of the Nepali Congress to modify Rana rule, or end it, received the wholehearted support of Pandit Nehru. On numerous occasions he has said that peace in Nepal is essential to Indian independence and possible only through orderly democratic reform. On December 7, 1950, Nehru declared: "The principal barrier to India lies on the other side of Nepal. We are not going to tolerate any person coming over that barrier. Therefore, much as we appreciate the independence of Nepal, we cannot risk our own security by anything not done in Nepal which permits either that barrier to be crossed or otherwise leads to the weakening of our frontiers." And on January 10, 1952, he said: "Where the question of India's security is concerned, we consider the Himalaya mountains as our border. They lie on the other side of Nepal" (i. e., not on the India-Nepal border). These general declarations of policy of the Indian Prime Minister have been applied on innumerable occasions.

The record of Indian interest and decision in Nepalese politics and administration includes the following:

(1) In response to the Nepali Congress civil disobedience movement, the Rana Prime Minister, on February 11, 1947, announced that he wanted to "associate the people even more closely than at present with the government." The Report of the Reform committee which was appointed in April was the product by and large of Sri Prakasa, an India member who served the committee with Nehru's backing. Much of the Report's terminology was borrowed directly from Indian experience.

(2) This dosage of reform was too much for the Ranas as a group and the sponsoring Prime Minister was forced out in 1948 by a considerably less liberal cousin, Mohan Shamsher Jung Bahadur Rana. The tempo of political agitation, however, quickened, and on September 24, 1950, the Prime Minister purged his ranks in Katmandu; those fortunate enough to escape joined the opposition movement in India. On November 6, 1950, King Tribhuvan, who had been restricted to his palace by the Ranas since September, took refuge in the Indian embassy and five days later was flown, with all members of his family excepting

only his three year old grandson, Gyanendra, to New Delhi in Indian Air Force planes.

(3) The Ranas then declared Gyanendra king, a step New Delhi did not recognize.

(4) On November 11, 1950, armed Nepali Congress forces, recruited in India, attacked Nepal at Biranj and other border points. The government of India made no move to deter this uprising which the Rana regime was able to suppress.

(5) The government of India intervened on November 27 and invited several top Nepali officials to New Delhi for discussion. After several rounds of negotiation, India announced on January 8, 1951, that King Tribhuvan would return to Katmandu and a Constituent assembly would be called not later than 1952.

In the summer of 1951, the Communist-organized United Democratic Front sponsored a number of public demonstrations which led in November to general *satyagraha* (nonviolent disobedience) against the government. In the same month, the Rana Prime Minister, the tenth and last Rana to hold the post, resigned in response to "recent developments." Matrika Prasad Koirala was summoned to head the first all-commoner cabinet. Under Indian tutelage, Nepal, according to Nehru's review of these events in Parliament (on March 4, 1952), had "seen a change from the very rigid authoritarian regime" of the Ranas. He again declared that where the question of India's security was concerned "the Himalaya mountains are our border." And, "Apart from that, we do not wish to interfere. We wish to help."

Since November, 1951, however, India has had to "help" on more than one occasion. Disharmony and rivalry inside the Nepali Congress and increasing Communist interest in Nepal provide background for such help. Factionalism inside the congress led to the expulsion from the party of Prime Minister M. P. Koirala by the organizational leader, B. P. Koirala, and the eventual resignation (on August 10, 1952) of the M. P. Koirala ministry. The king, with an advisory board, governed uneasily until June 15, 1953, when M. P. Koirala, in the name of the National Democratic party, a new organization which he formed and heads, reassumed the prime ministership.

As important as the inability of the Koirala brothers to patch up their differences as a factor in evoking Indian concern is the increasing Communist action in Nepal. In November, 1951, Yang Shang-kin, chief of the Central office of the Chinese Communist party, said in a message to Nepal that "after the liberation of Tibet, the Chinese people and the Nepalese people will unite in closer solidarity in the common struggle for the sake of defending Asia and preserving world peace." Further spur to Indian interest came on the night of January 22, 1952, when a segment of the Raksha Dal [6] revolted and freed their former leader, Dr. K. I. Singh. By the twenty-third the rebels had occupied all the key areas and installations of Katmandu, including the airfield, arsenal, and broadcasting station. Singh declared that he would "fight to the finish" for (1) "all party Government" including the Communists but excluding the revivalist Gurkha Dal; and (2) "foreign relations on the basis of equality" [7] rather than "of special friendship with any country." [8] He added: "We do not mind this country becoming another Korea if our demand is not met." Although the revolt was quelled, Singh escaped into Lhasa, Tibet, where he remains today with a number of his followers, despite the recurrent Nepali request that he be returned to Katmandu.

On January 25, reportedly on the advice of the Indian ambassador, Nepal banned the Communist party and in the following weeks India acted to step up its support of the Nepali administration. A loan of 150,000,000 rupees (approximately $30,000,000.00) was negotiated, the bulk of the sum to develop communications, especially an India-Nepal road link and an all-year air field at Katmandu. A 126-man Indian military

[6] The Raksha Dal was a "Home Guard" made up of men who took part in the Nepali Congress uprising of 1950. They had been given sole responsibility for guarding strategic points because the Nepali Congress government feared that the army's loyalty was to the Ranas.

[7] *Statesman* (New Delhi), January 25, 1952.

[8] Ambassadors representing India, Great Britain, and the United States, among others, are accredited to Katmandu, although only the representatives of India and Britain reside there. China has no diplomatic link whatever with Nepal and the United States' suggestion of a permanent diplomatic mission was put off by Katmandu on the grounds that if this were accomplished then China would require similar privileges.

mission entered the country to reorganize the Nepali army. Indian civilian advisers, including teams from the Planning Commission, became active inside Nepali administration. Govind Narain, ICS, continued as Tribhuvan's personal adviser. The India-Nepal relationship thus encompasses Nepalese administration, army, and the economy.

Despite the widening scope of Indo-Nepali collaboration, it is nevertheless true that Indian leadership operates in a most hazardous environment. As matters stand, only M. P. Koirala's National Democratic party defends Indian assistance. Men of that party benefited most from India's decisive role in displacing the Rana regime. Rival parties, including the Nepali Congress, the rightist Gurkha Dal, the leftist Praja Parishad, and the outlawed Communists demand withdrawal of the Indian missions.[9] The Congress and Gurkha Dal do so because of nationalistic resentment of the strong neighbor. Their vociferous, often violent, anti-Indian demonstrations are designed to embarrass the government, and are presumably staged to build up internal political capital. The Praja Parishad and the Communists, through the United Democratic Front, argue that India not China is the threat and charge that India's declared aim to strengthen the frontier against Chinese expansionism is a mask for Indian imperialism.

Indian influence, of course, has not always been exercised circumspectly. This is a new role for Indian government and some of her representatives have been tactless, unsympathetic to Nepali culture, and in a few cases more interested in comparative economic advantage than in a stable Nepal. Many of the administrative procedures written by Indian specialists do not appear to be related to the needs of the relatively undeveloped Nepali institutions. Administration digs deep into culture and cannot be transmitted easily. On the other hand, New Delhi has been willing to recall those of its officials most liable before Nepali opinion of commercial imperialism charges.

In other respects, quite aside from the party battle, India hardly controls the situation. Together with the agricultural missions of U.S.–Technical Cooperation Administration and

[9] See the *Statesman* (New Dehli), March 16, 1953, for one account of these demands.

U.N.–Food and Agricultural Organization, India has experienced difficulty in effecting a constructive administrative relationship with a country just beginning to lay its administrative foundations. The free advice given Nepal by these various technical assistants varies greatly in substance and, indeed, one of the missions has had great difficulty in determining internally what it wants to do in Nepal. A young government, short of managerial personnel, and with limited knowledge of its own country outside the Katmandu valley, is not always in a position to sift the conflicting and sometimes changing views of foreigners. The Indian effort has given priority to strategic needs, not economic development. Yet her military projects have had to be pushed in an administrative situation in which responsibilities inside the Nepal bureaucracy are only vaguely allocated; in which administrative personnel, largely inherited from the Ranas, are untrained in the requirements of democratic administration, that is, the necessities of consultation with the public and themselves; and in which the basic minimum of factual data regarding resources and their use, data so necessary to economic or military planning, are largely absent. Above all, important areas of social policy are so far untouched. Two-thirds of the arable land remain the exclusive property of about forty Ranas; there is no adequate tax structure, and the bulk of the population live and die impoverished. In this country, important segments of which have appeared on Chinese maps since late 1951 as Tibetan, India is trying to mount a defense.

These and similar security decisions represent direct Indian reflex to a changing political geography. Except for the Nepali involvement, this protective program has not been costly of men or money and has meant little in the way of administrative readjustment. Even so, the fact that independent India was required to erect such defenses at all has served to modify the view that the Chinese Communists' exclusive concern is the elimination of Western control. Hostility to Western imperialism remains a persisting theme in Indian public opinion. In the last half-dozen years, however, that theme has been severely undercut, first by the Independence Act of 1947, more recently by events following what the government of India[10] declared

[10] In a note to the Chinese Communist government on October 26, 1950.

as the "deplorable" use of force by the Chinese in its invasion of Tibet.

More than defensive frontier outposts, however, are needed if the Communist danger to India is to be dispelled. India is in competition with the Chinese Communist régime, a competition in which the comparative efficiencies of democratic and Communist economic development operations are to be tested. And for India this major internal effort is to be undertaken in areas which include the three southern states of Hyderabad, Madras, and Travencore-Cochin and the border northern state of Tripura, areas with a recent history of Communist terrorism and of substantial Communist electoral success.

In this competition the central Indian defense is the Five Year Plan. The Plan is the result of democratic processes. A Draft Outline was addressed to the country for discussion in July, 1951. For more than eighteen months the Draft was scrutinized by unofficial and official groups, the press and educational institutions. While a comparison of the Draft with the finalized version, approved by parliament on December 20, 1952, indicates that the principal revisions are traceable to groups inside the Secretariat, the Planning Commission sought earnestly to give every citizen an opportunity to participate.

Nevertheless, the Plan in either its 1951 or 1952 version cannot be called a plan of development. Its aim is the increased production of food; no structural change in Indian economy is sought. Scant attention is accorded India's approximately forty-five million unemployed, or underemployed, landless agricultural laborers and the tough administrative issues which their utilization in more productive, specialized urban-industrial environments would pose. Yet the Plan, if its targets are reached, paves the way for economic development in subsequent five year periods. India, unlike most Asian countries, is required to import heavy food supplies. Though the adjustment is by no means automatic, decreases in the amount of foreign exchange spent on food imports can be applied to the import of those capital goods necessary to non-agricultural production. As matters stand, however, it is a plan of expenditure, or rather an estimate of public expenditure in a five year period. The industrial side of the Plan is primarily a record of discussions conducted by the

Planning Commission with representatives of the business community.

Even so, the Plan and its administration are linked directly to the cold war. The Plan budgets about 1,500 crores rupees (three billion dollars) for expenditure in the public sector over the five year period. This is a modest investment and with luck, it should return the country to 1938–39 living standards; more likely, the investment targets are such that the growing population can count only on being supplied with the tools and other capital equipment it needs to maintain economic activity at present consumption levels. Of the funds budgeted, there is a balance of 387 crores rupees (775 million dollars) in deficit. That sum, the Commission judges, cannot be extracted from the community; the low level of per capita incomes leaves little for savings. Domestic resources are inadequate and the government is unlikely to enforce further privation upon its citizens, a goal that could be attained only through oppressive means. In this situation an undeveloped country is likely to look to its wealthier, democratic partners for the needed resources. Here is an edge democratic-oriented India holds over China.

The decision to operate the Plan raises other issues of moment to both East and West. One of these relates to the export of the Plan from its place of inception, New Dehli, and into its operational areas, the states. Few of the Indian central ministries possess regional offices (i. e., administrative offices in the field staffed and financed by the parent Centre ministry) and are thus dependent on state governments for programming and operations. A *Times of India* editorial (October 29, 1952) phrased the issue better than most foreign academic observers:

> The real snag would appear to be that the Centre is completely at the mercy of the State Governments, when it comes to the execution of all the well-laid plans of the Centre. Incompetent or indifferent State Governments could often prove a drag on the Centre and on the other States. And knowing as we do the calibre of the Governments in many of the States, it would be optimistic to expect better results. In this, as in many other matters, the Centre is helpless and can do no more than take the horse to the river. . . . It is not enough for a planning

commission to prepare blueprints for an integrated progress of the country; we must also have a central machinery to chase up and execute the national plans.

One illustration may serve to specify the nature of this dependent administrative relationship. In the approved Plan, the Planning Commission warned that "for the period of the Five Year Plan, rationing and procurement, together with certain minimum imports must be regarded as a key to the maintenance of a stable system of food controls." As recently as April, 1953, the parliament by special resolution confirmed this policy; controls, it asserted, are needed if food grains are to be available everywhere in India at reasonable prices and for sustained periods. Yet, administration of this major policy decision rests with the states who are inclined to take a provincial view of the situation. By May, 1953, controls over food grains had been relaxed in the Punjab, Uttar Pradesh, Mysore, and Ajmer. The availability of food grains, moreover, varies from state to state. In 1950–51 the figures for Madhya Pradesh was twenty ounces; for the Punjab, seventeen ounces; and for Bombay State, twelve ounces. Despite Centre policy, states with surplus food supplies have been unwilling to lift their bans against the export of food into deficit states.[11]

The organization of linguistic states underscores the significance of the Centre's dependence on the states for administration. On March 25, 1953, the Congress government was forced to concede to the agitation for an independent Andhra State, to be constituted on October 1, 1953, from Telegu-speaking areas in southern India. The linguistic fragmentation of India has been sponsored by the Communists, among others. It so happens that the new Andhra State will include areas in which the Communists were successful in the 1952 elections. A Karnatic-speaking state, also in south India, is the next target. The Communist party may, therefore, govern on a state-wide scale in the near future, an event of significance both for the party and for administration of the Five Year Plan.

In other respects, the operation of this Plan in as highly

[11] *Bulletin,* Reserve Bank of India, May, 1953; and N. V. Sovani, "The Food Situation in India," *Far Eastern Survey* (July, 1953).

stratified a rural society as India is hazardous. Economic development as a function of government is novel to Indian local administration. The single most important unit of administration of the Plan is the district. The district, in fact, is the basic setting for administrative operations in India. Revenue administration, civil and criminal justice, education, public health, police, jail, and irrigation are all concentrated at district headquarters. The district officer, usually known as deputy commissioner, is responsible for district administration. Whether his administration can be equipped to discharge its new tasks is in question; certainly what is now expected from it is far removed from its traditional emphasis on law and order. Administrative traditions change slowly, especially so at local levels in rural societies. As a further complication, the principal link between the district officer and state government is about to be severed. The divisional commissioner is responsible for a division consisting of five to seven districts. This office does not now exist in Madras and Orissa, and moves to abolish the post elsewhere, in the interest of economy, are underway.

The problem of how to elicit a wide degree of public cooperation in economic development operations is partly dependent on the strength and responsiveness of communication from New Delhi and the provincial centers to the operating field administrators. District administration is subject to various social pressures in this agrarian economy characterized as it is by exploitative patterns of credit and tenure. Existing social and economic organization, symbolized by such personalities as the district congress president, a landlord, or sugar cane mill owner, may thus represent an obstacle to the assimilation of new capital equipment and technical assistance. In fact, if economic development operations in India are identified with established community leadership, then elements outside that leadership—the lower social echelons—will remain outside and beyond the reach of the program. "Grass-roots" administration, where the organized "grass-roots" are unrepresentative of the community as a whole, will endow the articulate and voluble with additional channels of influence and result in the granting of significant concessions to the organized segments. In time, survival of the program itself may depend upon the support which the interest groups the administrator had initially contacted are willing to give it. Such groups then assume a commanding role in the operations, and at the expense of other, more newly organized groups. Great ingenuity is needed if the program is to be brought to each of the many publics. And in the absence of far-reaching changes in landlord-tenant relations or in the provision of alternative economic opportunities, any rural development plan will be modified extensively by unsympathetic "grass-roots."[12]

Such at least is the experience of the well-known Etawah pilot project, an agricultural improvement scheme inaugurated some eight years ago by Uttar Pradesh government with the assistance of American farm technicians employed by Uttar Pradesh. Village opinion studies made in 1952 indicate that less than 5 per cent of the district's population cooperated with the program, a typical observation being:

> The development is meant for the rich and for those who are cultivators, for us there is nothing—as a matter of fact we are getting no work.

Economic studies suggest that one consequence of increased agricultural efficiency is the production of more landless agricultural laborers. Such enhancement of existing economic advantage has affected seriously the attitudes of the less fortunate, and Communist organization has responded sensitively to this fact.

Economic development, of course, need not be channeled everywhere through existing local institutions. New, centrally directed public agencies, which fuse energetic leadership from the Centre and local powers, might be given formal jurisdiction over development operations. Or, voluntary and cooperative associations might be encouraged and used in an effort to bypass unsuitable established institutions and create a new avenue of appeal to the citizen. The administration of the Plan would thus tend to move outside the influence of formal organization and find itself bolstered locally despite the presence of traditional

[12] These paragraphs borrow on Chapter 2 of my *Administration for Economic Development* (Delhi School of Economics, 1952).

and customary resistances. Along these lines the Plan announces "cooperative village management" as the "ultimate objective" and proposes village production councils and cooperative farm societies, though the operational steps to be taken in this general direction are not specified.

Distrust of Western colonial control is an important, long-term influence in Indian political thinking. In 1949 it was possible for sizable sections of the Indian press, part of the leadership in the great urban universities, and even for certain public officials to regard the Chinese Communists as nothing more than patriotic, sincere opponents of Western imperialism. Such a view is not now so widely held. India, like Pakistan, retains a Commonwealth link and has seen independence come to her sister nations of Burma and Ceylon. The Communists, increasingly active along the northern borderlands, have contributed to the growth of a new Indian outlook, as evidenced by government of India decision-making in Bhutan, Sikkim, and Nepal. American Point 4 and the Commonwealth Colombo Plan, though modestly endowed, offer notice, on the other hand, of the West's interest in the growth of Indian democracy and the country's independent existence.

Inside India, the near-complete dominance of the Congress party and nation-wide popularity of its leader have tended to hide certain of the inherent weaknesses in the country's administrative structure. Andhra and other state governments moving in different directions may undermine the effectiveness of Centre policies. Administration of the economic program is undertaken in a fluid political situation, full of democratic potential but as yet lacking in governmental decision and leadership and thus open to Communist aggrandizement.

On balance, however, India's impressive postindependence achievements suggest that the country will be able to strengthen its democratic structure. The country's accomplishments are substantial. British India and 552 princely states have been consolidated, a constitution adopted, free elections held, and an economic plan written. The West would be wise to ask only that India remain independent. The country's defensive arrangements seek the same goal. We are in a position to help internally by investing our surplus capital as India perfects its economic goals and administrative techniques. In both respects, in defense against Communist expansion and Communist subversion, our destiny is linked with India's.

WILLIAM C. JOHNSTONE, JR.: *Discussion*

Former Deputy Administrator of Field Programs, International Information Administration, Department of State.

It has been stated that there is a lack of expert knowledge of the Near East and the Eastern Mediterranean on the part of Americans and a lack of understanding of America by the peoples of this area. If this is true for the eastern Mediterranean, where there have been considerable American cultural and commercial interests for a century or more, it is glaringly true for the Indian subcontinent.

In the past, the American concept of India has been that of a land of maharajah's palaces, tiger shooting, strange customs, sacred cows, and impoverished people. The Indian picture of America has been that of a land of mechanical marvels, shocking morals, mass luxury, and unlimited wealth. Since 1947, however, a better understanding has begun to develop. Americans have discovered India's diversity, likewise a characteristic of their own country. They have found that India is less than the sole source of spiritualism and Asian humanitarianism her protagonists have proclaimed, while the Indians, on their side, have discovered that Americans can be spiritual, that moral values are rated above the materialistic things high-lighted in the Indian picture of America.

This process of mutual discovery between Indians and Americans needs to be accelerated so that these two great peoples can act toward each other in a spirit of mutual faith and trust based on an appreciation of their particular culture and character of their people. Americans need to understand Indian problems in all their complexities, for American policy toward events in south Asia cannot be based on emotional reaction. Whether the United States decides it can or cannot act in a situation such as the Communist take-over of Tibet, our decision must be based on better understanding of this part of the world than we have had in the past.

Unfortunately, in the postwar years, American Far Eastern

policy seems not to have been formulated with a clear analysis of issues, but has been beclouded by the process of postmortem, in which skilled surgeons—including elected representatives of the people and their student interns—have thoroughly dissected past American Far Eastern policy and exposed the infection in the form of civil servants and foreign service officers who should have known better. It may be imagined that such postmortems may some day be held on American policy in south Asia and such presently unknown areas as Tibet, Nepal, Sikkim, and Bhutan will make the headlines.

In fact, however, no foreign policy can be made by a postmortem process—although it can be made without proper and adequate understanding of problems and even without full information. Professor Goodall, therefore, rightly devoted almost the first half of his paper to the Indian reaction to Chinese Communist control of Tibet. The people of a country react to their history, and in Indian history it has been the northwest frontier, not the northeast frontier which was a vital area. Past invasions of India have come through the passes to the northwest. Danger in that area now would evoke an immediate reaction. It is all the more significant, as Professor Goodall points out, that Indian reaction to the situation on her northeast frontier was immediate and positive.

The Chinese Communist expansion into Tibet seemed a remote and minor affair to most Americans, whose knowledge of Tibet, if they knew anything, was limited to remembrance of *National Geographic* pictures. Between 1946 and 1949, it is possible that action by the United States, neither costly nor extensive, could have basically changed the character of the situation in Tibet, had there been recognition of the significance of Chinese Communist control of that seemingly remote country. But support of such action came only from a few Americans and Indians who had the advantage of location in New Delhi only three hundred miles from potential, now probably actual, Tibetan airfields.

Nepal is given detailed treatment in Professor Goodall's paper and quite correctly. The history and politics of this little country are so little known in America and so briefly reported that the succinct and clear record of postwar Nepalese political troubles deserves thoughtful attention. Indian relationships with Nepal also need careful study as they demonstrate many of the basic elements of international politics which produce much the same results in different areas and at different times.

Professor Goodall's discussion of Indian economic development focussed attention on certain aspects of these problems which are often overlooked. In particular, it is important to note his reference to the current demands being made for creation of "linguistic states" in central and in south India. Americans are apt to forget that India is a federal republic of twenty-eight or more states in a constitutional framework bearing many resemblances to our own federal union. In central and south India the creation of the new "linguistic" states has been supported by the Communists and the possibility of future Communist-controlled governments in these states is very real. Thus the possibility exists that Communist control of the Indian government might be achieved through the states to the center, rather than the reverse. It is equally possible, however, that the federal system in India may provide greater protection against Communist domination than that of a centralized state.

In assessing the strength of the Communist movement in India and other Asian nations, it is important to determine where and to whom the Communist appeal is made. The cliche that the Communists are successful in Asian countries because they offer to fill the empty stomachs of the masses is unsupported in fact. It is true that Communist propaganda in some areas is designed with an appeal to the mass population, but the bulk of Communist effort is directed at carefully selected groups. In India, a substantial Communist effort goes into the intellectual groups and the university students. These latter form the corps of future leaders in India from which will come the government officials at all levels. The 250,000 Indian university students represent a group of great potential importance which can be swung to a revolutionary Communist movement or to the support of a democratic India.

The advantage of the Communist appeal to youth in India lies in the fact that the Communists offer them an "action" program. Prior to 1947, the Congress party exerted a tremendous influence on Indian youth because it was a revolutionary party aimed at the independence of the country from British rule. Its activities offered every opportunity to young people for militant and almost constant action. Distribution of literature, mass meetings, work in the villages, and many other forms of action caught the imagination and held the loyalty and absorbed the energies of college-age young people.

Now, however, the Congress party is in a position of responsible leadership within the government. Freedom from Britain has been won. The often dreary business of running a government, the slow process of translating paper plans into action is quite a different environment for youth than the pre-independence days. Youth's impatience with economic and social progress under the new Indian government makes the university student particularly susceptible to Communist appeals. Communist success with youth would deprive the Indian government of trained people badly needed to carry out their ambitious economic development programs. On the other hand, it is possible that the current five-year program, particularly its large-scale village improvement scheme, will provide an opportunity and an appeal to the youth and offer to them action more rewarding than agitation and subversion.

American irritation at India's seeming " neutrality " and the apparent sympathy evinced by Indians for the Communist regime in China should not blind us to the importance of this vast country in Asian politics and on the world stage. Much patience will be needed along with a better understanding of India's problems by Americans. If American policy is wise, if Americans who administer it are sensitive and humble in their task, the bonds between India and America can be strengthened and the understanding between their peoples can grow to their mutual benefit. The Indian federal republic could be the means of demonstrating to all the peoples of Asia the values and ideals which Americans cherish and which they find it most difficult to demonstrate to other peoples directly.

Former Ambassador Bowles has stated this possibility succinctly in a recent article in *Foreign Affairs,* where he states that " the future of Asia, and eventually the world balance of power, may rest on the competition between democratic India on the one hand and Communist China on the other. If democracy succeeds in India, regardless of what happens in China, millions of Asian doubters will develop new faith in themselves, in their ancient cultures and in the ideals of the free world."

In the discussion which followed, one of the first questions concerned the present political role of M. N. Roy in fighting communism in India and his relationship to Prime Minister Nehru and the present Indian government. It was pointed out that Roy had been in China in 1937 but was no longer a Communist. He now publishes a newspaper called the *Radical Humanist* which has a circulation of about eight to nine thousand readers.

The possibility of retarding population growth in India as

a method of improving living standards was raised, and it was stated that the Indian government's Five Year Plan includes an appropriation of $150,000.00 for pilot projects in birth-control studies. Also, the All-India Family Conference has explored the techniques of birth-control methods and their applicability to India.

Comment was requested on official Indian attitudes toward the possibility of a revived Japan, economically expansive and militarily strong. It was stated that the Indian government appears to place less reliance upon Japan than upon the United States. In 1950-51, K. P. S. Menon commented that Japan is "essentially unreliable." There is little Japanese capital investment in India apart from the fruit-canning industry. India rebuffed the steel commission sent from Japan and Japanese attempts to organize a coal combine were rejected by the West Bengal and Bihar governments.

In reference to statements made concerning Communist penetration in the areas of Madras, Travancore, and Hyderabad, the question was raised as to whether the Indian government, in executing the five year plan, was emphasizing economic development in these areas over and above economic development within India as a whole. It was stated that the best answer to this question would be to superimpose a map showing electoral strength of the Congress party in 1951 and 1952 over a map of development schemes being put forth under the five year plan. If one were to do this, one would note that the areas of concentration of Congress party strength and the areas in which there were community development programs almost perfectly coincided. It was further stated that American *TCA* grants envisage the expenditure of about $150 million over a period of from five to fifteen years. It was left to the imagination to determine what will be accomplished by such grants, spread over such a vast area as India with its huge population.

Two questions reflected almost opposite points of view in respect to Indian foreign policy. It was first suggested that if we were to show more sympathy for India's desire to remain neutral in the East-West conflict, India might become more sympathetic to the Western point of view. On the other hand, the question was raised that it is not enough to say that all we want of India is to remain independent. It was stated that we want India to cherish freedom everywhere, including China where the Indian tendency is to gloss over Soviet imperialism by treating its puppet government as the representative of Chinese national interests while treating the Chinese Nationalist government as an outlaw or pariah. It was suggested that we ought to help India keep its independence, but that the world is not so parochial that anyone's independence can be secure unless he cherishes the independence of others.

In response to the expression of these two points of view it was stated that, in the controversial situation of "two Chinas," India reflects the point of view of the British Commonwealth. It is not feasible, in terms of the Indian environment of today, to expect an Indian-United States "marriage." The difficulty lies with Indian popular opinion. One can't expect that, with their background of "anti-imperialist" dogma, Indians will immediately accept the American point of view. India is not going to go along with the United States policy toward the Chinese Nationalist government. The outstanding questions heard in India over a one month period after President Eisenhower "demilitarized" the Formosa zone were, "What is going to happen there? Don't you people have any sense?."

This reply evoked discussion in which it was stated that British foreign policy appears sometimes to be a combination of Marx and Freud. It is Marxian in the sense that it wished to turn over the last profitable dollar, and Freudian in the sense that it appeared to have a "death wish." More was to be expected of India, it was stated, than of Britain since Nehru is now supporting a puppet government in China which is analogous to the puppet government in India which the Congress party overthrew. Another questioner immediately asked whether it was realized that both China and Soviet Russia are closer to the borders of India. In response, it was pointed out that voices from Washington suggesting a Middle East defense organization encountered sharp resistance in India.

Another point of view was stated concerning British foreign policy which, it was suggested, was not so much a combination of Marx and Freud as a combination of Richard Cobden, who stood for peace through trade, and of William James, who stood for dealing with problems pragmatically.

A final question related to the Indian reaction to the number of Americans and the variety of their activities in the country and whether this represented a net asset or a net liability to the United States in the East-West struggle. In response it was stated that Indian reaction varied with the type of activity. The successes of Ambassador Chester Bowles were cited and an example was given of his talk at the School of Economics of Delhi University.

There Ambassador Bowles spoke extemporaneously for one and a half hours in a spirit of scientific analysis and with warmth and sympathy for Indian problems. At the end of his address over sixty students studying for the doctorate gave him a rising ovation that lasted for over six minutes, a sharp contrast to the initially cold reception of his audience. This approach of Americans to Indian attitudes is always well received and generally results in good feeling for the United States but without long-lasting effects.

As an example of the importance of Indian attitudes, it was stated that the *American Reporter,* a United States Information Service publication, has a larger circulation than any Indian publication. In 1951-52, this publication devoted 66 per cent of its coverage to Indian internal development. It included, without overemphasis, the part played by American assistance and enjoyed a very high circulation. Although this was due in part to lack of information of these internal developments from the Indian government, there was genuine interest expressed in Indian-American cooperative activities by the readers. During the last three months, however, this publication has been devoting nearly 70 per cent of its space to articles on the cold war and the Communist threat, particularly from China. The result was that the publication has become far less popular, less influential and persuasive in putting across the story of economic development through democratic methods. It was felt that in the present climate of Indian opinion, the story of a direct Communist threat from the Chinese mainland and the importance of the continued existence of the Chinese Nationalist government just will not get across.

Current Techniques of Communist Penetration in Southeast Asia

GERALD F. WINFIELD,
Technical Cooperation Administration,
Rangoon, Burma

The contention that Asia holds top priority in the timetable of world Soviet imperialism is supported by much evidence. The speeches of Communist leaders, the manifestoes and theses of party congresses, the outlines of tactics published by the Communists over the past thirty years are punctuated with the theme that the way to Paris and London lies through Saigon, Singapore, Rangoon, and New Delhi. The leaders of Soviet imperialism have long recognized colonial Southeast Asia as the " soft underbelly " of the noncommunist world.

It is significant that, after the fall of China, five of the six countries where the Communists have used overt military action are in Asia; and four—Indo-China, Burma, Malaya and the Philippines—in Southeast Asia.

There are many reasons why Southeast Asia should have a high priority. Look at what Burma, Thailand, Indo-China, Malaya, Indonesia, and the Philippines have that the Communist world covets. *Raw materials*: Rubber, oil, tin, tungsten and a number of the rare metals now in great demand, teak and other forest products. *Land and food*: Huge areas yet to be plowed, three countries with large rice surpluses capable of further increase. *Manpower*: Almost 170,000,000 people to swell the ranks of controlled labor.

The loss of Southeast Asia would inflict grave damage on the free world. The dislocations of war, the freeing of colonies, and the loss of Asian markets behind the iron curtain have already demonstrated the importance of Asian trade to Europe. European trade with Southeast Asia comprises a respectable portion of Europe's overseas commerce. Its loss to the Soviets would be a heavy blow to Europe's economic position.

Should Southeast Asia join China under Soviet control, the economic pull on Japan with her expanding population forced back into her tiny islands would be irresistible. A mutually profitable trade between Japan and Southeast Asia must be an important element in Japan's survival.

India too would be exposed to increased economic pressure from a Soviet dominated Southeast Asia, while its physical fall would open another even more vulnerable Indian military flank.

The over-all situation in Southeast Asia is highly favorable to Communist penetration.

Colonial control has left a heritage that " sets up " the region for the Communists. The dominant fact that should be kept in mind in discussions and planning about Southeast Asia is that the large majority of all its people are strongly anticolonial.

Anticolonialism has several aspects. At its deepest level, it is a profound hatred for colonial rule. This emotion spills over into anti-Western and anti-whiteman feelings that range from deep suspicion to visceral, murderous hatred. It is this emotion that is the most important single reason why, after seven years, it is still possible for the Vietminh to obtain plenty of volunteers to fight the French in Indo-China. It underlies the suspicion and fear of the West that tinges the attitude of even the wisest and most friendly leaders of the Southeast Asian peoples.

Indigenous nationalism is the political expression of anticolonialism. It unhesitatingly chooses independence under national leadership regardless of risks or difficulties. It prefers national rule, no matter how weak and inefficient, to the best colonial administration. It stands ready to risk Communist enslavement rather than accept the possibility of return to even the appearance of colonial status.

Because of colonialism almost all productive enterprise and trade is owned by non-nationals. There is almost no owning class except landowners. There is no middle class. There is a strong feeling against economic imperialism. There is no adequate group of experienced administrators for either government or business. The dominant national groups are determined to use their political power to get trade and business into their own hands. All this creates a predilection for state economic enterprises and provides fertile ground for collectivist economic revolution.

A further consequence of colonialism is the lack of fear of losing personal freedom under communism. Having not had individual economic and political freedom, the peoples of Southeast Asia are unmoved by anticommunist arguments based on the risk of enslavement and the loss of individual freedom.

Communist penetration in Southeast Asia is easier because of economic and social backwardness. Age-old socio-economic patterns and more recent colonialism have left the countries of Southeast Asia seriously underdeveloped. Communism attributes this underdevelopment to "capitalist exploitation," and many facts well-known to the peoples of the region strongly support this contention. It is easy for Communists to gain acceptance of their contention that a totally new socio-economic system is the only means of overcoming this backwardness. The emotional appeal to youth to build new nations on a new pattern is vivid and effective. Overpopulation coupled with much tenantry and hard living conditions create Communist exploitable peasant unrest in a number of areas.

Distance from the major centers of the noncommunist world makes penetration of Southeast Asia attractive to communism. This distance means that activities designed to check communism must be long-term and planned months to years in advance. The noncommunist world does not always think that far ahead. Now, with the signing of a Korean armistice, it is highly probable that communism will increase its pressure on Southeast Asia.

The long, almost impossible to guard, frontier between Red China, Burma, and Indo-China is an important Communist advantage. Across it seep personnel and materiel for subversion and armed insurrection.

Communist objectives in Southeast Asia are easily stated. They seek to seize power through subversion and armed insurrection by indigenous Communist parties with Russian and Chinese assistance. They use every means to disrupt economic and social life and to discredit existing governments. They seek to win the support of the majority of the population, resting their power seizure on as broad a base as possible. They try to appear as the champions of popular nationalist aspirations.

Techniques of Communist Penetration

In their drive to attain these objectives, the Communists are using techniques that range from armed rebellion to covert penetration. A few principles are almost universally followed:

All techniques are applied with pinpoint precision.

Carefully planned and constantly improved organization by disciplined and dedicated cadres is used in every sphere of activity.

Coercion through the application of every type of suasion and force is ruthlessly used to compel the desired actions or attitude.

Basic appeals are highly emotional, supported by an over-all seemingly logical philosophy.

Activities are carried on by Asians, mostly indigenous individuals and groups in each country.

Great efforts are made to have people achieve a sense of participation.

The Use of Armed Force

In Indo-China, Burma, the Philippines, and Malaya, the Communists are using armed force. Let us briefly look at each of these Communist led wars.

The largest, oldest, and most successful is the six and one-half year old war in Indo-China. During World War II, Moscow-trained Ho Chi Minh developed, with allied assistance, an underground nationalist organization, the Vietminh, which seized power at the end of the war. Ho took a leading part in re-establishing civil order in a nationalist government willing to work with the French to establish an independent Indo-China. In 1946, after much negotiation, the French refused to meet the demands of the Indo-Chinese, and Ho led his largely nationalist following in revolt. Following Ho's revolt and recognition by Moscow, the French implemented a plan of limited independence by organizing the Associated States of Vietnam, Cambodia and Laos. In Vietnam, they got the former Annamese Emperor

Bao Dai to organize a Vietnamese government with himself as head of state. However, the majority of Vietnamese and most Southeast Asians still think of the Vietminh as nationalist patriots.

This war is extremely bitter, marked by much brutality on both sides. It has slowly grown until now more than 400,000 Franco-Vietnam troops are fighting the Vietminh. Of these, about 200,000 are in the Vietnam army raised and trained in the past two years, using American supplied equipment. During the early stages the Vietminh fought entirely with guerrilla and terroristic tactics. As their strength grew, they began using regular army tactics. During the past year and a half, they have repeatedly used as many as 30,000 to 40,000 troops in a single engagement or campaign. They are now reported to have almost 300,000 fighting men.

The Vietminh are receiving important help from Communist China such as material and training given Vietminh fighters at bases safe in China. Chinese technicians have participated in planning campaigns and some have helped fight; but there has been no large-scale participation of Chinese "volunteers" in the war. Now with a Korean armistice it seems probable that Chinese assistance will increase.

The Vietminh have taken full advantage of the anticolonial, anti-French feelings of the majority of Indo-Chinese. They continue to attract both supporters and fighters by promising four things: political control by nationalists, completely free of colonial interference from France; active participation in a new socio-economic order designed primarily to benefit the people of the country; land for the landless peasant; and the chance to kill Frenchmen.

The physical battlefield in Indo-China is fluid and ill-defined. The country is dotted with Franco-Vietnam islands consisting of the principal cities and many smaller places. Surrounding these islands are shifting no-man's lands that the French control during the daytime and the Vietminh prowl at night. The principal French lines of communication reach out tenuously to connect secure centers. These daytime controlled areas include hundreds of villages and much of the best rice land. At night the French forces pull back into the secure areas or into heavily fortified watchtowers and forts along the roads and in the larger villages. These village forts surround rice storage warehouses where families in outlying villages can store their grain to prevent Vietminh looting. The Vietminh control extensive areas usually in the hills surrounding densely populated rice growing plains.

An important phase of the war is the struggle to control these no-man's land villages. Persuasion, propaganda, and force are used by both sides. The Vietminh propaganda has been successful because of its appeal to anticolonialism. But the Vietminh success has also resulted from pinpoint coercion. Force is applied to the individual where it will get the maximum result. The French apply their force almost indiscriminately to the whole community. The Vietminh know accurately who in each village has what influence—who is for them, who is against them. The French and their Vietnamese partners have much less precise information and are never sure how far they dare trust anyone. It is as though two men were trying to force a third to do contrary things. One stands at the victim's back with a pistol pressed against his spine, the other stands a half block away with a shot gun. There is no question which one the man will obey. So it is in the villages of Indo-China. Even when the pistol is withdrawn, because of the temporary arrival of the French, the villager knows that it will return with precision. While it is away, the feel of that pistol remains at his spine.

The French frequently burn, fine, or otherwise punish a whole village because individuals cooperate with the Vietminh. Such shotgun tactics have made tens of thousands of ardent Communist followers out of people formerly either indifferent or hostile to them.

Ultimately, the battleground in Indo-China is in the hearts and minds of the people. Neither side can long command the people by force alone. Thus far the Vietminh are winning the war because the French have not been willing to meet the people's demand for independence.

Vietminh controlled areas are thoroughly organized in typical Communist patterns. Under the direction of a politburo and war council, there is a Peasant's Union that exercises effective control at the community level. Carefully selected, thoroughly schooled Communists or procommunists hold key positions in these village associations. A Woman's Association and organized Youth and Labor groups also play their part both in indoctrination and in guiding the activity of every individual.

Each community has a series of committees responsible for specialized activities: local security and home defense; production, for greater agricultural and small industry production; aid-the-war, to provide volunteer and impressed labor for the armed forces; medical and health, to improve general health and care for wounded and sick soldiers; literacy, for mass literacy education; and, of course, propaganda, to spread official news and propaganda about the program, activities, and successes of the Vietminh.

These committees and the women's and youth organizations all work under "democratic centralism." The centralized will of the party is carried out by the mass of the population through group discussion of a problem until the conclusion the party has decided to be "correct" is reached.

In community organization as in the use of force, the principle of precise pinpoint activity is applied.

There have been hundreds of assassinations and attempted assassinations of specific persons in the cities of Vietnam. During the busy hours, hand grenades are thrown on Saigon streets. They are rolled down theater aisles and tossed among the tables of restaurants. This generalized terror is to remind those who remain in the cities that the Vietminh are serious in their pursuit of war. It also forms the basis for the extortion of considerable protection money. Such terror attacks have reduced the effectiveness of American economic aid in many ways.

Communist armed force in Indo-China has been highly successful. In spite of the French effort and much United States military aid, there is no reason to believe that the ability of the Vietminh to continue fighting has been diminished.

The noncommunist world is caught in a serious dilemma in Indo-China. If French forces are withdrawn, the Vietminh will take the country despite growing Vietnamese strength. But the presence of the French is a constant demonstration that the Vietminh will fight for independence.

Recent French political concessions may help create the favorable political atmosphere required for a successful drive to defeat the Vietminh, but they will have to be dramatically implemented if they are to convince the weary and skeptical people of Indo-China. To win Indo-China, the free world must sustain and improve its military action, arrange for the withdrawal of French forces as rapidly as they can be replaced by Vietnamese, provide the Vietnamese an adequate political motive for which to fight by giving real independence at an accelerated rate, institute effective social reforms in urban and rural areas, and continue practical technical assistance and economic aid to the people of Indo-China.

In contrast with Indo-China, Communist armed rebellion in Burma has been much less successful. This is because colonialism is not an issue in the Burma struggle. The Burmese government is headed by honest men who hold their positions both because they led Burma to independence and have been confirmed in office by popular democratic elections.

The history of armed insurrection in Burma is complicated. Late in World War II, the Burmese nationalists who had welcomed the Japanese invasion as liberation, rose against the invaders and helped the allies retake Rangoon and clear the country. The political instrument used was a coalition called the Anti-Fascist Peoples Freedom League (AFPFL) that included the Socialist party, the Burma Communist party, the Peoples Volunteer Organization, and several other groups. Soon after British government was re-established, the demand for independence arose. The AFPFL under General Aung San, while accepting responsibility for forming a provisional administration, opened negotiations with the Atlee government for independence from Crown and Commonwealth. The Burmese leaders' willingness to negotiate caused rising tension within the AFPFL, because the Communists insisted that independence must be won by bloody struggle.

As Burma worked on a constitution, tension also developed between the Burman majority and several minorities. All but one minority was satisfied by the establishment of states in the Union. The Karens, however, were not given a separate state because they did not reside in a compact geographic area. Special minority rights were created by the constitution for the

Karens and other minorities not given states. But the Karens, who feared they would fare badly after independence, were not satisfied.

At this point, tragedy struck. U Saw, a pro-British politician hoping to stop Burma from leaving the Commonwealth and gain power for himself, engineered the assassination of General Aung San and eight of his provisional government cabinet. The expected reassertion of British power did not come. U Saw was caught, tried, and executed. U Nu, the present Prime Minister, took AFPFL leadership, obtained the election of a constituent assembly, proceeded to adopt a constitution and negotiate the Nu-Atlee agreement that gave Burma independence on January 4, 1948.

Within a few weeks, four groups revolted against U Nu's infant state. The most serious insurrection had nothing to do with political ideology. It was the Karen-Burmese minority issue. Almost two thirds of the Burma army was Karen. Most of them followed the Karen National Defense Organization in its fight against the government. They took large sections of the country and fought to within a few miles of Rangoon. The situation became so bad that U Nu and his lieutenants made plans to go underground if they lost their last centers. At that point the Karens were stopped.

In the meantime, three ideological revolts, two Communist and one strongly procommunist, took place. The Stalinist White Flag Communists received orders to seize the revolutionary opportunity presented by the weak new state beset by the powerful Karen revolt. The Red Flag Communist (Trotskyites) and the Peoples Volunteer Organization also took up arms.

Over the past five years the Union of Burma has slowly fought and worked out of the desperate position in which it lived the first two years of its life. It has gradually overcome much of the Karen revolt and has contained and begun to beat down the Communist led insurrections. As the Karen insurrection has faded, the ideological revolts have come to have greater importance.

Because the Communists are fighting a National government, they are finding the going tough. Lacking the appeal of anti-colonialism that is the sparkplug of the Indo-China war, Burmese Communists do not have the popular support that the Vietminh have. They have to insist that the Union of Burma is not what it obviously is, a genuinely independent country. Government propaganda that vigorously attacks those " who long for the aunt instead of the mother " is effective in branding the Burmese Communists as the agents of a foreign power.

The armed action used in Burma includes disruption of lines of communication by attacks on the railway and damage to highway bridges. Now and then the Communists attack government police or military outposts. In recent months the Burma army has applied more and more pressure throughout the country, forcing the Communist guerrillas out of many areas. Last spring the three Communist groups signed a tripartite agreement that divided the country into spheres of activity and provided for coordination of military effort.

The amount of assistance Burmese Communists receive from China is unknown. The government officially denies any knowledge of such assistance. However, there are frequent local press reports that the Communists are training a considerable number of Burmese in China to strengthen the waning Communist forces.

Some months ago, an official Moscow newspaper story, praising the Communist insurgents for their struggle to " liberate " Burma, caused much indignation in the Burmese press. That frank Soviet statement connected the Communist revolts in all Southeast Asian countries with international communism, praising their efforts as part of the world Communist revolution.

The Burmese Communists use methods of organization in rural areas similar to those described for Indo-China. Because they are in the early stages of gaining power, their dealings with the peasants are still lenient and idealistic. They use land reform as a propaganda weapon. It is not too effective because of the government of Burma's land-reform program and because the land ownership problem in Burma has not been acute since the Indian landlords were driven out by the Japanese.

The Communist insurrection in Burma is not yet defeated, but the trend is favorable to the Burma government.

At the end of World War II, the Communists in the Philippines stirred peasant dissatisfaction with poverty and landlordism to armed revolt. For the past two years, the Peoples Liberation Army (Huks) has fought under the official banner of the Philippine Communist party. The party has a complete organization from politburo to local cell, active connections with Red China, and support from some wealthy Chinese.

A little over two years ago when the Philippine government launched its successful campaign against the Huks, the Communist movement in the Philippines was growing rapidly. It controlled considerable areas in central Luzon and the Visyans. Its armed forces numbered six thousand, supported by nine thousand part-time fighters, more than three thousand active political workers, and tens of thousands of sympathizers. The government's campaign combined vigorous armed action including much attack by night, effective propaganda exposing methods and goals, and a program of economic aid and resettlement for those peasants who surrendered and promised to maintain the peace. Much of the supporting apparatus was smashed by capturing Filipino leaders and deporting Communist Chinese.

These methods have crippled the Communist movement and reduced its military action to scattered guerrilla attacks. However, the hard core of the party and its army has not been destroyed. Many observers believe that it cannot be finally eradicated until overcrowding and high tenantry cease to generate peasant poverty and dissatisfaction in central Luzon and elsewhere. The strong opposition of many top Philippine politicians to land reform, modeled after successful programs in Japan and Formosa and recommended by American aid experts, underlines the difficulties in solving this problem. It seems clear that the final elimination of communism will come only when the basic social and economic conditions that breed it are dealt with.

In Malaya, Communist armed action has seriously delayed the development of the country, but it has not broken the economy. Most armed Communists have been overseas Chinese. These fighters have used guerrilla and terrorist tactics. They have had much support from Chinese and Malayan groups because they fought the British.

For the last year and a half, British action in Malaya has been increasingly successful. This success stems from improved methods of jungle fighting, the use of effective propaganda and physical pressure on civilian groups who support the guerrillas, and from British policies designed to create a Malayan state in which all racial groups, including the Chinese, can find security and opportunity to move toward complete self rule.

The absence of a frontier with Red China is of immense importance in easing the task both of the independent Philippine government and the colonial Malayan government in dealing with armed Communists.

Communist rebellion is increasingly successful in Indo-China, while its effectiveness is being sharply reduced in Burma and the Philippines. In Malaya armed Communists are being dealt with successfully, but with relatively more difficulty than in Burma or the Philippines. The dominant factors that produce these results are:

Colonialism: The more colonial the situation, the more successful the Communist armed force. Rebellion is being dealt with more successfully by independent nationalist governments even though weaker and less well organized than by colonial governments and their subservient national factions.

Contiguity to Red China: The closer the contact with Red China, the greater the effectiveness of Communist armed action.

Social and economic program: The more concerned with human welfare the social and economic program of a government, the stronger its position in combatting communism.

Above Ground Political Action

Only in Indonesia is the Communist party legal with members in parliament. In Burma, the Burma Workers and Peasants Party (BWPP) and several Marxist splinter groups are legal parties that follow closely the official Communist line and are strongly antigovernment in policy and action.

The power of the Communist party in Indonesia was seriously damaged by action taken against it by the Indonesian government in mid-August, 1951. On allegations that, aided by an unnamed foreign government, the Communists were attempting to overthrow the government, one-hundred and fifty people including sixteen Communist members of parliament, the editor of the leading Chinese Communist paper, journalists working for a number of Indonesian language papers and several officials of the Ministry of Labor, were arrested on August 16. Guards were posted at the headquarters of the Communist Central Committee and at the Central Labor Congress (Sobsi). In the next two months, fifteen-thousand more were rounded up. Anti-government activity of all kinds dropped sharply. The principal leaders of the Communist party, however, escaped capture.

Since the majority of Indonesians are Muslims with strong religious loyalties opposed to communism, the crack-down was widely welcomed. A number of labor groups turned from Communist dominated unions to noncommunist ones.

These actions, however, did not eliminate the Communist party. In October, 1951, the Prime Minister told a New York *Times* correspondent that while the "Communists are not numerous, they are tough and well organized, and still a danger." He went on to say they had infiltrated many groups and organizations and that Communist ideas are prevalent among certain elements of the people including part of the youth.

In the ensuing months, many of those arrested were released when it was shown they had no direct connection with the plot. By early 1953, however, the Communists decided to follow a nationalist, united-front line, to lessen the growing anticommunist sentiments rising from their pro-China line. They reduced Chinese activity in their program and associated themselves with noncommunist Indonesians. They succeeded in getting several new well-known people to serve on their National Peace Committee.

This shift to a nationalistic line shows that the Communists recognize the failure of their pro-Chinese line and that their tactics remain flexible.

The Burma Workers and Peasants party denies it is Communist, but follows the line closely and is regarded as the above-ground representative of communism. The party has a few seats in parliament, a considerable organization in several parts of the country, and is actively working to increase its vote-getting power. It carries on a full propaganda program using congresses and mass meetings. It accuses the government of leaning to the West and not following its "neutral" foreign policy. The

BWPP made a play for peasant support, recently, by demanding a sharp rise in the internal price of rice to give the cultivator a bigger share of the wide profits now being earned by the government sale of export rice. It has consistently opposed the American Economic aid program, and constantly supports the World Peace Congress and lauds Russia and Red China.

In recent months the BWPP has taken a more nationalist and less procommunist line. This is evidence that the anticommunist position of the AFPFL is effective and that close association of a Burmese party with China and Russia is becoming a political liability.

The BWPP and the Burma Communist party repeatedly make attempts to pursuade or force the AFPFL to accept one or both of them in a coalition government.

In late February and early March of 1953, a series of incendiary fires set by the Karens burned the bamboo and thatch huts of some 25,000 refugee squatters in Rangoon. At the same time, the Burma government launched a military campaign to drive the Nationalist Chinese remnants that have roamed the mountains of northeastern Burma since 1949, back east of the Salween and force their surrender or withdrawal from the country. Thinking that the government thus beset would welcome a coalition, the Communists promised wholeheartedly to join the fight against the Chinese nationalists. The government of Burma flatly refused the coalition. It took the Chinese Nationalist problem to the UN and flung its old challenge to the Communists to come out into the political arena and seek power by democratic processes.

Penetration of Groups and Organizations

The Communists in Southeast Asia work to penetrate every type of group or organization. The largest, most widespread group that they constantly use and carefully work to control is the overseas Chinese.

Most Chinese in Southeast Asia have been there for generations. They are a minority group that is much distrusted. They are considered by Peiping to still be Chinese citizens. Recently they have been asked to elect representatives to the new Red Chinese parliament. Prior to China's fall, the Kuomintang had strong organizations in all overseas Chinese communities. Now a bitter struggle is on between the Reds and the Kuomintang for control of the overseas Chinese.

There are almost half a million Chinese in Burma. When the Communists seized power in Peiping, there was a nonideological mass movement by Burma Chinese to tie up with them because of disillusionment at the failure of the Kuomintang, and national pride that China at last was under a Chinese regime without overt ties to any foreign country. By 1950, the Communists controlled 80 per cent of the Chinese schools, many clan organizations, and the Chinese Chamber of Commerce. The controlling organization is the little-publicized China Democratic League. Their well-known organizations are Teachers, Shop Employees, and Clerks Unions that form a Federation of Labor; a Students Association and a Women's Association. The connection between these organizations and the Chinese embassy in Rangoon is not clear. Through the Teachers Union the Communists use textbooks from Red China. In the struggles to control the schools, there have been acts of violence including the killing of at least one school principal.

By 1950 Communist organizations among the Chinese were well extended. The anticommunist Double Tenth celebration in October, 1950, marked the beginning of resistance and was more successful than its organizers had hoped. The powerful secret societies are still all noncommunist. The crack-down on all private business by the Communists in China has frightened many Burma Chinese.

As the struggle has intensified, the Chinese Communists have used economic pressure as a weapon. They have subsidized new competing stores near the shops of many anticommunists and noncommunists. Party discipline is used to shunt trade from the old into these new shops. When a shop owner agrees to cooperate the competitive heat is turned off.

The Communists pay particular attention to youth. The Students Association now dominates the activity of most Chinese schools. On many occasions they are turned out to take part in propaganda and political activities. A common sight in Rangoon is half a dozen chartered busses hauling the entire membership of the Students Association of some school to the airfield to meet or send off a Communist or procommunist individual or delegation on its way to or from China or eastern Europe.

A further activity to control overseas Chinese youth is a program to send them to China for education. Thousands of students are being smuggled out of Southeast Asian countries. Many from wealthy families run away from home to go. So determined are they to capture all the youth that they have pressed the services of a mandarin-speaking teacher for her three-year-old son on the widow of a Chinese professional man who migrated to Burma to escape the Reds.

The labor movement, next to the overseas Chinese, is the most important target for the Communists. In Burma the Communists and procommunists split the labor movement about three years ago and took almost half of the workers out of the Trades Union Congress (Burma) into their new Burma Trades Union Congress. Since that time, however, the struggle has gone in favor of the noncommunist unions, principally because the AFPFL has thrown its weight behind them and now the Communists control only a fraction of those who went with them at the time of the split.

Students comprise another group among whom the Communists are hard at work in Southeast Asia. At the University of Rangoon there has been a long fight for control of the Students Union. The well organized Communists have tended to dominate student politics. Recently a trend has developed toward the noncommunist majority assuming responsibility and pushing the Communists out. In the other countries there are active Communist cells in most institutions. Marxist study and discussion groups are numerous. Communism's bold assertion that all the ills of the world are due to the institution of private property, its claim that it will destroy that institution and create a new world free of injustice, its demand of sacrifice, and its promise of personal and group power for its followers provides an attraction that is almost irresistible to youth.

Propaganda

Southeast Asia is flooded with Communist propaganda. The media and method of dissemination vary from country to country as formal relations with Russia and China and the legal position of the Communist party vary. In Burma and Indonesia, there is a steady flow of propaganda from Soviet and Chinese embassies. Many news and feature stories about Russia and China appear in most of the newspapers. In Burma one paper, " The People," is Communist and several others are procommunist. Burma has many Communist book shops and newsstands that sell books and magazines in English, Burmese, and Chinese. Much of this literature is printed in China, some in Burma.

The contrast between a Communist newsstand and one that sells American publications is startling. The Communist stand is stocked with serious items that deal with political, economic, and social problems inside dignified covers featuring portraits of leaders or the accomplishments of Russia and China. American publications on sale are almost entirely frivolous. Most of them have covers showing crime or scantily clad girls. The best of them deal with photography, but most are concerned with crime, detective stories, confessions and " love." The better and more serious American magazines are conspicuously absent. They are too expensive and tuned to American reading interests to command a paying market. The Communist publications are designed with Eastern taste and interests in mind and subsidized for cheap sale. Ours are those which will sell at a profit. The two bookstalls do not present us in a very favorable light.

The official United States Information Service program with its excellent libraries and its good but limited publication work never can offset the effect of these trashy commercial publications because the ordinary Asian feels that the latter show the real America. The Communists take full advantage of this situation.

The Communists see that their books and magazines are available in every school, openly if possible, clandestinely if necessary.

Where they have recognition, Russian and Red Chinese commercial movies are distributed. In Burma, a subsidized movie distributing company headed by Burmese has been organized to distribute these films. One rented theater in Rangoon shows Communist country films exclusively. Only a small number of Russian and Chinese entertainment films are popular because they carry too much propaganda. The Communist embassies carry on active noncommercial film programs.

All of Southeast Asia is blanketed with Communist radio. News, features, music, and propaganda are available in all the languages of the region for long periods each day. While the number of receivers in the area is limited, they are widely distributed and much that is heard is passed on by word of mouth.

The themes used in Communist propaganda are well tailored to the interests and psychology of the various people whom they seek to reach. Highly emotional appeals are the rule. The Communists seek to move people to some sort of specific action. Anticolonialism, anti-imperialism, anti-exploitation, warmongering, Western disregard for Asian opinion, and dictatorial handling of international relations are among the negative themes that are iterated and reiterated. The building of a better world for the proletariat, the seizure of power in behalf of the masses and the achievements of socialism in Russia and China are positive themes.

Cultural Relations

In the neutralist countries, the Communists have active cultural relations programs. In Burma, there are Burma-China and Burma-USSR friendship organizations with programs for cultural exchange. They have sponsored or assisted with the exchange of official Cultural Missions between Burma and China. Such missions have been effective partly because of the deep desire of all Asians to reaffirm the cultural heritage of the whole Asian area, and partly because the Chinese Communists get credit for much in China that was precommunist in origin.

Procommunist groups in Burma organized a delegation to the Moscow International Trade Conference two years ago. The mission and Russia got much favorable publicity out of it, but one prominent noncommunist Burmese writer who was taken along to give prestige to the delegation wrote a book, *Through the Iron Curtain by the Back Door,* which was devastating in its debunking of Russia.

The Communists recognize the importance of Southeast Asia and are using every means at their command short of international military conquest to gain control. Propaganda and ideology are still important weapons that support armed insurrection and legal political activity by Communists and procommunists. The idealistic claim of communism to leadership in building a better society still has much potency, though in recent months Communist action in eastern Europe and in Russia itself has begun to cause many Burmese to question this claim.

In spite of the varied methods and great extent of the Communist efforts, Southeast Asia is not yet lost. Within the nationalist groups in many of the countries are elements of strength that are strongly resisting Communist efforts to seize power. The immediate and acute task is to find and pursue policies that will support and strengthen these groups.

EDMUND GULLION: *Discussion*

Policy Planning Staff,
Department of State

We might usefully focus here on the differences in Communist and free world tactics in Southeast Asia and seek to discern any pattern that may exist in the fluctuations of these respective approaches over the past few years. Certainly the importance of Southeast Asia to the international Communist movement can hardly be overestimated, and it has been fully recognized in the Kremlin from the earliest days.

The patristic writers of the revolution and its first apostles stressed the great asset which revolution in China would bring to communism; they were especially awake to the effects it could have in the area to the south and in the South Pacific. They seemed to have expected that it would signal disintegration in the colonial areas which would be at once a symptom of, and contribute to, the " crisis of capitalism."

Thus Manuilsky wrote in 1926: ". . . liberated China will become the magnet for all the peoples of the yellow race, who inhabit the Philippines, Indonesia, and the numerous islands of the Pacific."

At the foundation of the Cominform in 1947, Zhdanov asserted that " the crisis in the colonial system has placed the rear of the Capitalist system in jeopardy."

It is interesting that the Soviet Union spokesmen dwell in this way on the two faces of the Southeast Asia problem; they see not only the prospect of adding enormous numbers of people —poverty-stricken and colored peoples—to the Communist world, but also this sapping of the metropolitan West. I do not know to what extent the attitude of the Chinese Communists and the Kremlin would vary on this point. It is interesting to speculate, however, on whether the Chinese Communists are as much preoccupied with the drain on the West as their Kremlin partners, or whether they are primarily interested in seeing the countries on their southern borders, particularly the vassal states of past dynasties, brought once more under friendly control.

Certainly we in this country are keenly aware that the problem has both an Asian and a European face. For example, we are increasingly convinced that a satisfactory solution of the Indo-China war would greatly ease the burden of metropolitan France, and strengthen the whole NATO concept. A growing preoccupation with the problem of strengthening of the Western alliance has balanced an earlier American tendency to consider the Asian revolution rather exclusively in an Asian context and in terms of self-determination for formerly dependent peoples. At the same time, this sympathy for the aspirations of colonial peoples is deeply rooted in our psychology and history and antedates our assumption of major responsibilities in a European coalition.

We can trace the cycles in American reactions by reference back to the close of the war. This was the period when sympathy for nationalist aspirations in India, Burma, Indonesia, and Indo-China was least tempered by the realization of what the Communists could do in some of these countries to subvert the new nationalism. It is significant, however, that communism made least progress in those countries where the grant of independence was quickest, widest, and most audacious.

Then as the cold war intensified, there was increasing understanding and sympathy for the problems of the ex-colonial countries—our NATO allies—who were trying to stand against Communist pressure on two fronts. This was especially true after China fell to the Communists and the Korean War began. In some quarters this seemed to be accompanied by a tendency to oversimplify Asian problems and assess Asian attitudes on world issues in terms of black and white, ignoring the all-important intermediate greys.

At the present time, there is a wide awareness of the vital importance of our alliance with our European friends and an understanding of both their problems and their good intentions with respect to former colonies. At the same time our people feel that the Southeast Asian peoples must have confidence in their progress toward independence if they are to resist the Communists who have tried to usurp the nationalist movement.

Thus, while American opinion is preoccupied simultaneously with increasing independence for colonial peoples and with our alliance with the colonial powers, I think most Americans are confident that there is no inconsistency and that we can support genuine nationalism and NATO at one and the same time.

The principal ideological challenge from the Communists in Southeast Asia is their pretension to represent true nationalism; they also pose as defenders of the yellow race, and givers of land to the landless.

These are consistent themes, accompanied or not, as the case may be, by a resort to armed force.

There seem to be definite turning points in the history of their use of force. First, just after the war, the Communists fostered armed uprisings in various countries, but also tried, as in Indo-China, to create " coalition " regimes and to achieve their objectives through Trojan Horse tactics. By 1948, however, (following the organization of the Cominform) the emphasis increasingly shifted to " armed struggle."

The idea of winning power through armed struggle seems to have a particular *mystique* for the Chinese Communists. The hard-bitten Asian Communist idealogues would probably not consider their control of a country as complete or valid unless and until it had been consolidated and ratified, as it were, by armed struggle during which Communist leadership would be exalted.

This " armed struggle " phase may be associated with the Indian Party Congress of February, 1948, and the Calcutta Youth Conference of that time. Decisions or resolutions in support of the idea of " armed struggle " were taken at those meetings. Besides the Indo-China war, which was already a flourishing affair from their point of view, the Communists were actively pushing armed rebellions in Malaya, Burma, Indonesia, and the Philippines.

The triumph of the Chinese Communists in 1949 must have augured well in the Communist view for the victory of the armed struggle in Southeast Asia.

Yet the results for the Communists in the next few years were mediocre; the United States' and United Nations' stand in Korea and the stiffening of Southeast Asia with our aid certainly had a damaging effect on the time table.

Consequently, without abandoning any ultimate objectives

or renouncing reliance on force, the Communist leadership seems to have tried out another approach in at least four of the Southeast Asia countries. A kind of modified " united front " or " unified action " manoeuvre was and still is being tested. The Communists are not neglecting opportunities to work through the vulnerable and nascent party and parliamentary systems in the new countries. In Burma they are active in the Burma Workers and Peasant party which demands formation of a coalition government. In Indonesia they have succeeded in getting a number of sympathetic members into the new government, and are cleverly playing a number of popular nationalist themes. In the Philippines, while the Huks seem to be losing out, the Communists are making a determined effort to penetrate elements of what might be called the " national bourgeoisie," as well as the workers, peasants, and landless groups.

The basic appeals of the Communists seem unvarying: land, nationalism, a chance to shoot white men; these may seem inconsistent with Kremlin communism as we know it, or as it has evolved from its earlier days; but Asiatic communism may conceive of itself as in an earlier intermediate stage of tactics.

One thing is certain: the Communists make their strongest appeal at the village level, with simple themes, with the minimum of ostensible foreign overhead, and a pretense to offer the greatest good to the greatest number. And it is in the village that we must meet them and contest the issue. We must not only show up the Communist fraud but we must show that the democratic revolution is more positive and humanist than theirs. We have been fighting the good fight in these rice paddy villages for some time now, and we have learned something about what to do and what not to do. The contest for the minds of Asia could perhaps be described in the history of that effort.

China's Role in the Communist Movement in Asia

U. ALEXIS JOHNSON,
Deputy Assistant Secretary for Far Eastern Affairs, Department of State

The rapid conquest of China in 1949 by Mao's Communist armies radically altered the balance of power in Asia and gave a new impetus to the Asian Communist movement. Mao's triumph refocused the Kremlin's attention sharply on the revolution in Asia and emboldened the Communist leadership to embark on a new and aggressive program there. Thus, in a speech on the thirty-second anniversary of the October Revolution (November, 1949) Malenkov hailed Mao's victory as the precursor of the rapid extension of Communist power in Asia. As he put it:

> The national struggle of liberation of the peoples of Asia, the Pacific Ocean basin, and of the whole colonial world has risen to a new and considerably higher stage.

Through his conquest of China, Mao strengthened the Communist movement in Asia psychologically, militarily, and politically. Both the decisiveness of the Chinese Communist military triumph and the character of their revolution proved to be psychologically advantageous to the Asian movement. The apparent ease with which the Chinese Red army rolled down over China from the northeast in 1948–49 inspired confidence in the Communist world and spread defeatism in the free world. It created an atmosphere conducive to acceptance of the line assiduously promoted by Communist propagandists that the events taking place in China represented the " wave of the future " in

Asia. Mao's "Sinification" of Marxism-Leninism and his utilization of nationalism as the means of achieving success in his revolution contributed a further psychological advantage to the Communist movement in Asia by confusing many noncommunists as to the real significance of the events of 1949, thus allowing the Communists to exploit their victory in China as a triumph of Asian nationalism.

Of greater long-range significance than the psychological impact of the Communist victory in China was the increased military potential it gave to the Communist movement in Asia. With the example of Korea before us, it is necessary to dwell on this aspect. It is important to note, however, that the Kremlin had long been aware of the potentialities of China as a Soviet ally. A typical appraisal of China's strategic importance as an ally of the Soviet Union was expressed by Kitaigorodsky in January, 1927, as follows:

> A future war in the Pacific will have a rear of 400 million Chinese. This fact and China's position in this war represent a tremendous factor which the imperialist states will have to take into consideration and examine in calculating all the chances of an armed conflict.

Thus Mao's victory in China added to the Communist bloc's potential military power not only a great reservoir of manpower but also a vast geographical base which provided security in the rear to the arsenals of Communist imperialism in the Soviet Union. It also exposed important noncommunist Asiatic countries to Communist military power for the first time. This extension of Communist military power to the borders of Asian countries was in itself an important psychological advantage to the Communist bloc in that the bloc could now exercise the threat of direct military pressure to intimidate noncommunist states. It would be difficult to overestimate the importance of these military factors in facilitating the advancement of Communist objectives in Asia, not merely through the direct application of force, as in Korea, but also through the political utilization of the threat of force. As a result of Mao's conquest of China, therefore, the balance of power in Asia, which had already been altered significantly by the elimination of Japanese military strength and the extension of Soviet power into Manchuria, shifted still further to the benefit of the Communist movement in Asia.

Another important aspect of Mao's victory in China for the Communist movement was the method by which it was accomplished. The Chinese Communists under Mao Tse-tung had developed a technique for the organization of violence peculiarly adapted to the environment of China. In the jargon of the Communists, China was a "semicolonial country." Since most Asian countries are described by the Communists as "colonial and semicolonial areas," Mao's techniques of revolution were immediately hailed throughout the Communist world as the model on which the Communist movement in the other Asian countries should be based. For the Communists it was a case of "nothing succeeds like success"—Mao's methods were successful in China; they must hold the key to success in comparable areas. More recently, however, the Communists, at least in the Soviet Union, seem to have had second thoughts on this score. Thus, at a conference of Soviet oriental experts, held in November, 1951, one conclusion was that "Chinese revolutionary experience should not be applied mechanically to the rest of Asia."

The "China way" for conducting revolution was distinguished by several special characteristics. Most significant was the basing of the revolutionary movement on the peasantry rather than on the urban proletariat, as called for by classic Marxist-Leninist theory. This does not mean that the Chinese Communist party was "of the peasantry." The party had no roots in any one segment of Chinese society; it was based on no particular class. It took individuals from all walks of life and integrated them into a disciplined instrument for the acquisition of power. Since the days of the Chinese Soviets, it has been more of a militaristic bureaucracy than a political party. But though the party was not based on the peasantry, the revolution was. Wherever the party went it stirred up class warfare between peasant and landlord, utilizing this struggle to promote itself to power.

Another important feature of the Chinese Communist rise to power was the development by the party of its own army, composed largely of peasants. The concept of "armed struggle" was basic to the Chinese Communist movement. This had been recognized as early as 1926 by Stalin, who declared that victory by Communist forces within China could be achieved only by a revolutionary army. Stalin expressed himself as follows:

> In China, it is not the unarmed people against the troops of their own government, but the armed people in the form of its revolutionary army. In China, armed revolution is fighting against armed counterrevolution.
>
> The Chinese revolutionaries, including the communists, must make a special study of things military, they must not regard military questions as something of secondary importance, for military questions in China are at present the most important factor in the Chinese revolution.

The Chinese Communists took this dictum of Stalin's to heart and gave their military arm the central role in their drive for power. Though not surprising, it is nevertheless ominous that nearly four years after their acquisition of power the Chinese Communists continue to give it special attention.

Another Chinese Communist innovation was the establishment of secure geographical " war bases " from which the party-controlled army could operate. An important development in the " war base" concept took place in 1934 when the Chinese Communists, whose war bases in south China were in danger of strangulation by Chiang Kai-shek's encircling armies, undertook their " long march " to northwest China, where their flank could be safely protected by the USSR. This security in the rear was an important asset to the Communists in their subsequent struggle with Chinese government forces, and was further enhanced in 1945 by the Soviet occupation of Manchuria. The importance of a secure rear to the prosecution of Communist revolution was recently emphasized by the Indian Communist leader Ghosh in an article in *Bharat Jyoti*, published in Bombay. Ghosh wrote:

> The Chinese Communists had the initial advantage of a revolutionary army to start with. In India there is no such army. Above all, after Manchuria was liberated, the Chinese comrades had a firm rear in the Soviet Union. There is no such advantage in India today.

Under Mao Tse-tung, too, the concept of the " united front " was exploited to the full. According to this concept, the indigenous Communist party allies itself with other national groups against a real or imagined foreign enemy and its alleged domestic accomplices. Mao Tse-tung had early recognized the utility of harnessing nationalism to the Communist cause by his declaration of war against Japan in the name of the Chinese Soviets in 1932. On this basis he called for a united front of all patriotic Chinese groups, including the Chinese government, to fight Japan. He succeeded, after Moscow promulgated a united front policy in 1935, in achieving this end with the signing of the Communist-Kuomintang agreement of 1937.

Whether or not the Mao strategy of revolution in China, which by reason of its success became the classic strategy of revolution in the so-called colonial and semicolonial areas, represented a doctrinal heresy is a moot question, but in any event it seems to be largely an academic one. Mao's innovations were certainly radical enough to lead a great many observers to conclude that the Chinese Communist movement was something quite distinct from the communism of Russia. Yet, it is quite clear that Mao Tse-tung and his party colleagues have always regarded themselves as orthodox Marxist-Leninists, and loyal to the international leadership of Stalin. The writings of Mao and other leading Chinese Communists abound in passages attesting to this. Typical is the following excerpt from a speech by Liu Shao-ch'i to the Central China Party School on July 2, 1941, entitled "On the Intra-Party Struggle":

> The Chinese Communist party was established after the October Revolution and after the Russian Bolshevik Party had already achieved victory in living form. Therefore from the beginning it was under the guidance of the Communist International and was established according to the principles of Lenin.

As a convinced Communist, Mao's primary concern was to make the Communist movement in China succeed. His was a practical problem, not a doctrinal one. Mao felt that the answer to his problem lay in analyzing existing conditions in China and capitalizing on them to promote Communist objectives. In the opening day ceremonies at the party school at Yenan on February 1, 1942, which launched the party reform movement of 1942–44, Mao stressed this theme, as he did again and again through the reform period. The following passage from his speech on this occasion is illustrative:

> Theory and practice can be combined only if men of the Chinese Communist Party take the standpoints, concepts, and methods of Marxism-Leninism, apply them to China, and create a theory from conscientious research on the realities of the Chinese Revolution and Chinese history.

The distinctive features of the Chinese Communist movement, of which the most distinctive was the basing of the revolution on the peasant masses rather than on the urban proletariat, can all be related directly to special conditions existing in China upon which Mao capitalized for the benefit of the Communist movement. Thus China had no urban proletariat to speak of, and the attempts during the late twenties, under the leadership of Li Li-san, to organize violence based on the urban proletariat had failed dismally. A shift to a peasant base was requisite to the survival of the revolution. Likewise, the development of geographic war bases, the organization of a party-controlled peasant army within the bases, and the promotion of a united front were all moves designed to capitalize on conditions peculiar to China in the thirties and forties.

Thus it seems clear that the innovations which distinguished the Chinese Communist movement from previous Communist revolutionary theory and practice were a direct outgrowth of Mao's preoccupation with adaptation of Marxist-Leninist theory to the China scene, rather than of any wavering in his belief in Marxism-Leninism or of a desire to pursue other than accepted Communist goals. In fact, Mao's insistence on "the adaptation of theory to national conditions" was in itself an orthodox concept. Thus Stalin writing in *Pravda* on February 3, 1925, made the following statements, which were to be echoed by Mao in later years:

> When formulating any slogan or directive, the Party should not rely on memorized formulas or historical comparisons but on the concrete conditions of the revolutionary movement—on results of a close analysis of concrete national and international conditions; at the same time, it must take into consideration the experience of the various national revolutions.

This same concept was subsequently stressed by Dimitrov at the Seventh Congress of the Comintern in 1935.

We have seen that Mao's victory made important psychological, political, and military contributions to the Communist movement in Asia. With their control firmly established over China, the Chinese Communists have continued to contribute heavily to the advancement of Communist objectives in Asia since 1949. Peiping's military contributions to the Communist cause have been as conspicuous as they have been tragic. Its political contributions have also been significant, however, and since they have been less obvious I shall devote primary attention to them.

Communist China's ability to make decisive military contributions to the Asian Communist movement is all too familiar and needs no elaboration. The Peiping regime's intervention in Korea and its crucial assistance to Ho Chi Minh's forces in Indo-China are obvious examples of Communist China's important military role. The extension of Peiping's military power to the borders of Burma in 1950, and to those of India, Bhutan, and Nepal in late 1951, through the subjugation of Tibet, have also contributed to the advancement of Communist objectives. Not only have these moves enhanced the Communist military potential in Asia, but they have created psychological pressures on the neighboring noncommunist countries favorable to the advancement of Communist political objectives with respect to those countries. These moves have been important too, because they have made the border areas of these countries potential sites for native Communist "war bases" on the Chinese model, secured in the rear by foreign Communist armies, and providing an avenue of infiltration and clandestine supply from outside.

Peiping's political contributions to the Communist movement in Asia have been both diversified and intensive. Even prior to its final acquisition of power, the Chinese Communist party had established itself through organizational ties and by the political exploitation of its successes in China in a leadership position within the Asian Communist movement. Since 1949, the Chinese Communists have expanded this political role still further.

A brief summary of the Chinese Communist party's organizational ties with Communist parties elsewhere in Asia will serve to point up the extent to which the Chinese party is able to wield a significant influence in the Asian Communist movement.

1. The Chinese Communist party controls the small Communist organization in Thailand, whose personnel are almost entirely Chinese.

2. Chinese branches are strong in the parties of Malaya and the Philippines but have been rebuffed by native elements in a bid for dominance.

3. The Burmese Communist party, after internal disagreement, decided to seek Chinese Communist aid but has not demonstrated the independent capabilities apparently required of a recipient of Peiping's assistance. However, Chinese money and guidance have poured into the Burma Workers and Peasants party, a Communist-front organ.

4. The Indian Communist party apparently retains its organizational freedom, but may receive aid from China. However, the movement in Nepal is torn between gravitation to the influence of the Chinese Communist party and loyalty to the Indian Communist party.

5. The Japanese Communist party evidences increasingly close organizational ties with Communist China. Some of the purged leaders of the Japanese Communist party appear to be in Peiping. The main foreign organ of Communist propaganda to Japan is Radio Free Japan, located in Communist China. The Japanese Communist party may be receiving substantial financial help from China and contacts across the China Sea are increasing.

6. Since the entry of China into the Korean War, Yenan elements in the North Korean party have regained a strong position.

7. Indigenous Soviet-oriented elements continue to control the Indonesian Communist party, but financial help from China and active propaganda under the guidance of the Chinese Embassy in Djakarta appear to be on the increase.

8. A recent instance of the clearance of a Ho Chi Minh speech by Peiping suggests the close organizational ties between

the two parties. Despite Chinese Communist military aid and the presence of Chinese Communist advisers, Ho's movement continues to display a strong orientation to the USSR, as well as to China.

Quite apart from these organizational ties, the Chinese Communist regime and its leaders have been a major ideological force in the Asian Communist movement. Peiping's ideological leadership since 1949 has taken diverse forms. It was exercised at international conferences of Communists and fellow travelers in Peiping, in editorial comments in official Chinese Communist party organs (like the *Jen Min Jih Pao*), through radio contacts with Asian countries (Radio Free Japan beamed at Japan, special broadcasts in most Asian languages, etc.), through personal contacts between Asian and Chinese "cultural" and other delegations, and through the precedents Peiping established in its domestic and foreign policies. Peiping often acts as a spokesman for international communism. Even in these cases, however, Peiping appears to exercise considerable discretion in details and a voice in basic policy.

On the occasion of the 1949 Peiping conferences of "Asian and Australasian Trade Unions," Peiping, acting primarily as a spokesman for a world Communist policy, formulated the doctrines of "armed struggle" and of "legal and illegal struggle" as they applied to Asia at that time. The conference served to bring under a common denominator the various policies Asian Communist movements were following and was one of the first steps in an effort to define the meaning of China's revolutionary experience for other Asian parties.

The analogous Peiping "Asian and Pacific Peace Conference" of 1952, though not designed to formulate Communist strategy, served to set the tone for subsequent Communist "peace" efforts in Asia, designed to undermine the bases of Western support in Asia. Most of the propaganda themes of the conference have since been widely disseminated through the great variety of Communist and front organizations and individuals represented at Peiping.

Although Peiping was acting as an Asian spokesman in the world Communist "peace" campaign, its treatment of the "peace" line has occasionally varied in details from that of the Kremlin. For example, Peiping's propaganda treatment of the newly-independent Asian governments has often been milder than Moscow's, as was Peiping's propaganda treatment of the Socialists who met in Rangoon last year. On the latter occasion, Peiping joined with Moscow in castigating Socialist leaders accused of " collaborating " with Tito, Attlee, or the U. S., but it withheld its venom from the rank-and-file participants, thus no doubt facilitating the efforts of those parties, like the Japanese Communist party, that were attempting to create a basis for Communist-sponsored " unified action " against pro-Western alignments in Asia.

The Communist regime of Ho Chi Minh in Indo-China can be cited as an example of the influence of Chinese Communist precedents, most of them differing significantly from corresponding Soviet precedents. During recent months the Ho regime has instituted an agrarian program modeled closely upon that of Communist China during the wartime period, with variations culled from more recent practices. The regime followed Chinese Communist practice in detail in such fields as judicial reform, anticorruption campaigns, and the rewriting of history. Ho Chi Minh has, in recent months, been described by the propaganda organs of his regime in terms paralleling exactly the terms used by the Chinese Communists in reference to Mao. Thus Ho's " contribution " in combining " theory with practice " is hailed, as is his " discovery " of the importance of peasants in the revolution led by the " proletariat " (i. e. by the Communist party). Similar parallels can be cited between Ho's and Mao's military tactics, the most recent of which is the resort by Ho Chi Minh to the device of " volunteers " in his invasion of Laos.

The position of leadership which the Chinese Communist party and later Communist China has developed in the Communist movement in Asia rests in part on certain advantages which Communist China enjoys over the Soviet Union as a purveyor of communism in Asia. The first advantage lies in the fact that Communist China is distinctly an Asian power while the Soviet Union is at best half European. In any case, it does not appear that the leaders in the Kremlin are regarded by Asian public opinion as Asians. The fact that the Chinese Communist leader, Mao Tse-tung, is an Asian gives him a special kind of prestige in Asia, and inclines many Asians to believe that because he is an Asian leader he could not be so firmly wedded to the ideology and objectives of the Kremlin as he appears to us to be. Consequently, I believe it is correct to estimate that the activities of Mao Tse-tung and of his Chinese Communist followers are looked upon with less suspicion than similar activities conducted in Asia by the Russians.

Another advantage of Communist China in the promotion of international Communist objectives in Asia lies in its geographical proximity to other Asian nations. This fact provides the Chinese Communists with opportunities for the exertion of direct pressure and for maintaining contact with subversive forces over the border and other opportunities which are not available to the Soviet Union thousands of miles distant from most Asian countries. A third obvious advantage which Communist China has over the Soviet Union in many of the Asian countries is the existence of large communities of overseas Chinese. These communities have never been well integrated into the indigenous societies where they dwell and have traditionally looked towards China as their homeland and primary loyalty. The Chinese Communist regime is thus provided with many opportunities for utilizing overseas Chinese, not only for subversive activities but as instruments of collective pressure against the local government. With such advantages as the foregoing, Communist China, although using the same techniques and following the same policies as the Soviet Union, is able to play a unique part in the furtherance of international communism's objectives in Asia.

While the role of Communist China in the Communist movement is unique, because Peiping is in a position to make a unique contribution, it is at the same time firmly integrated with that of the Soviet Union. Thus Peiping's role cannot be fully understood without examining the nature of Sino-Soviet relations. The Peiping-Moscow alliance (which was formalized by the Treaty of February, 1950) appears to be a very solid one. It is based on a mutually advantageous power relationship as well as on a commonly held political creed. Either factor alone would be sufficient for an alliance; together they ensure its strength.

Mao's dedication to the Soviet political creed and his loyalty to Soviet leadership made it inevitable that this power alliance should take place after his victory in China. Since 1949 the Chinese Communists have put even greater stress upon the ideological leadership role of the Kremlin and upon Communist China's indebtedness to the Soviet Union. This has been a principal theme of the Sino-Soviet Friendship Associations which have been so vigorously sponsored by the Peiping regime throughout China. Moreover, the Chinese Communist leadership has deliberately sought to increase the direct ideological influence of Moscow in the Chinese party and to remodel its administration more closely on the Soviet pattern. Significant also has been Peiping's shift of emphasis from organization of the peasants to that of the urban workmen, in a reversion to traditional Marxist-Leninist concepts.

While the ideological basis of the Peiping-Moscow relationship is obviously of fundamental, and perhaps of overriding importance, this relationship, and consequently Peiping's role in the Communist bloc, cannot be understood without an appreciation of the power factors involved. It is the existence of these factors that makes it highly questionable, at least within the immediate future, that Communist China will go the way of Yugoslavia. The similarities between Tito's rise to power and that of Mao are frequently considered as evidence that Mao is likely to break with Moscow if given an opportunity, notwithstanding his record of devotion to the principles of Marxism-Leninism and of loyalty to the Kremlin's leadership. However, there are important differences between Yugoslavia and Communist China that must not be overlooked.

These differences lie primarily in the realm of power factors. Perhaps the most significant difference is that Yugoslavia is a country of 99,044 square miles, having a population of 16,545,000 and an army of approximately 500,000; while Communist China is 3,845,000 square miles in area, contains approximately 450,000,000 people, and boasts an army well over 2,000,000 strong. Another important difference lies in the Peiping regime's decisive importance to the Communist movement in Asia. Mao's victory in China greatly increased the momentum of the Asian movement, placing it in a position of top priority in the

Kremlin's plans. Mao thus became more vital to the Kremlin than Tito ever was.

Tito had little power either to resist or to assist the Kremlin, but Mao's strength is sufficient to allow him to work closely with Moscow without serious risk of obliteration, while the military, political, and psychological assets at his disposal are of transcending importance to the promotion of the Kremlin's objectives in Asia. In Moscow's special treatment of Peiping as compared with other Communist countries, there is strong evidence that the Kremlin is being careful not to take the risk of losing these assets. In brief, the difference in the power position of Tito and Mao is so considerable as probably to overshadow other parallels between them.

While the advantages of preserving the intimate Sino-Soviet relationship to the Kremlin are apparent, what are the advantages in terms of power politics to the Peiping regime? The tie with Moscow spells power to the Chinese Communist leaders. It brings them guns, jet aircraft, aid to their industry—the means of strengthening the territory under their control and particularly their army. It helps them to establish China as the most powerful country in Asia, a position it occupied for centuries in the past. It helps to protect them from the only rival they fear in Asia—Japan, and from Japan's powerful ally—the United States. These are the advantages in Chinese Communist eyes of their alliance with the Soviet Union. If they pay a steep price for the Kremlin's aid and protection, they do not blink at exacting it from those they have brought under their heel. And, for the reasons I have stated, we can by no means assume that the Kremlin will push the price higher than the Chinese Communists are able to pay.

It is apparent that the Peiping regime exercises a significant degree of influence in the determination of Communist strategy in Asia and of discretion in its execution. While Moscow probably still exercises the major voice in shaping broad aspects of the Communist movement in Asia, by reason both of its acknowledged ideological leadership and of its greater economic and military strength, Peiping also has a real voice and plays a role in its own right. Because the Peiping regime possesses military and political assets which enable it to play an important role of its own, it is a far more formidable adversary of freedom in Asia than if it were merely an automaton directed from a control room in the Kremlin. It is potentially a major threat in its own right, and it would be folly to assume that its aggressive policies and hostility to the West stem entirely from its relationship with the Soviet Union.

If correct estimates of Communist moves in Asia are to be made, therefore, it is necessary to take into account Chinese Communist as well as Soviet factors. Thus such factors as internal developments in Communist China, Peiping's aspirations for industrialization and a powerful modernized military establishment, its fear of Japan, its sensitivity to the security of its borders, the history of the Chinese Communist party's rise to power, and the personalities of its leaders, all must be continually analyzed and evaluated if we are to be able to devise sound policies to overcome the threat of Communist imperialism in Asia.

K. A. WITTFOGEL: *Discussion*

University of Washington

Mr. Johnson has warned against accepting Mao's China, as the Communists want us to do, as the Wave of the Future in Asia. The Communists present the Asian "revolution" as a historical process which advanced irrestibly and unilineally. This concept has become a powerful weapon in the Communist ideological arsenal; and Mr. Johnson's warning is therefore eminently timely.

To acknowledge the existence of serious economic and national conflicts does not mean to accept the Communist claim that these conflicts can be solved only by violent revolution and only in one way—the Communist way. To cite an example from the sphere of economic conflict: The excellent land policy, which, under our guidance, was initiated and implemented in Japan, made the bulk of the Japanese peasants the owners of their land; and it did so through an honest reform and not through a dishonest revolution Communist style—that is, an agrarian revolution that uses temporary land distribution to buy temporary peasant support and that reverses this distribution, as soon as the new Communist masters are strong enough to plow the peasants under. Or to cite an example from the sphere of national conflict: India and other former colonies have recently become independent by means of an intelligently promoted peaceful change, and not by means of a violent revolution.

Thus, whatever political and institutional developments present-day Asia may require need not be revolutionary in the Communist sense of the term; and they certainly need not follow the Chinese Communist pattern. The underlying concept of the necessary—and necessarily progressive—Asian Communist revolution overlooks elementary institutional facts and basic human values. Measured by a multiplicity of criteria, which in addition to technical advances also include the freedom to check the "big" forces of society, the freedom of creative activity and the freedom of silence, it is manifest that historical developments may be retrogressive as well as progressive. Lenin himself recognized this in 1906 when he admitted that a new Russian revolution might lead not to socialism, but to what he, following Plekhanov, called an Asiatic Restoration—a return to an Orientally despotic regime. Lenin underrated the institutional novelty and unique oppressiveness of the regime he helped to create. But we will do well to remember his concept of a possible Asiatic Restoration, when the Communists try to impose upon us their myth of the inevitable (and inevitably progressive) Communist "wave of the future."

It depends on a number of factors, our own policy being one, whether or not the rest of Asia goes the Chinese way. And this Chinese way, although it is definitely more than the restoration of an outmoded type of Oriental despotism, is certainly closer to an Asiatic restoration than to the "association of free producers" that the Marxist Socialists, perhaps utopianly, set out to establish.

Other points of Mr. Johnson's analysis also have significance for Asia as a whole, but specifically they focus on the Chinese Communists and on Mao Tse-tung's leadership. The myth of a special Maoist version of communism, which Mr. Johnson clearly and, in my opinion, correctly rejects, involves among other things an emphasis on the strategic role of the peasants in the first phase of the Chinese Communist revolution.

There is nothing originally "Maoist" in this emphasis. As early as 1905, Lenin assigned a decisive role in the next Russian revolution to the revolutionary peasants; and in 1920, at the Second World Congress of the Communist International, he recognized the applicability of this strategy to the so-called "colonial and semi-colonial countries," particularly in Asia. Simultaneously he asserted the possibility of peasant Soviets in such countries. Lenin formulated this idea tentatively and with the expectation that its details would be worked out when the opportunity presented itself.

The decisive role of the agrarian revolution for China was postulated by Stalin prior to the Sixth World Congress of the Comintern, which took place in the summer of 1928. And it was at this Congress that the concept of peasant Soviets was elaborated with express reference to Lenin's original theses. As Lenin assumed there were many adjustments and developments of detail. But any attempt to base the assumption of a covertly anti-Leninist "Maoism" on the Chinese Communists' temporary policy of "limited" Soviets in essentially agrarian areas disregards fundamental and easily verifiable facts of Comintern doctrine.

Mr. Johnson also rejects another part of the Maoist myth, when he stresses the Soviet background of the United Front, which the Chinese Communists concluded with the Nationalist government in 1937. After the Japanese invasion of Manchuria in 1931, the Chinese Communists cried out against Japanese aggression; but for several years, and in accordance with the Comintern line, they were careful not to single out Japan, but to denounce all "imperialist powers" for encroaching upon China. During this period Moscow was trying to ally itself in the West with Hitler, and in the Far East with Japan. It was only when these attempts failed that the great swing toward the United Front began, in the West in 1934, and in the Far East, after the conspicuous rapprochement between Hitler and Japan, in 1935. Far from spontaneously responding to national embitterment, the Chinese Communists followed what they later called their "sectarian" anti-Kuomintang policy—until the summer of 1935. Six weeks prior to the Seventh World Congress of the Comintern, on June 15, Mao's government still advocated a United Front "against Japanese imperialism and Chiang Kai-shek," and it solemnly declared "that it had sentenced Chiang Kai-shek to death." The Comintern Congress began on July 25, and the first major speech by Piek clearly laid down the new United Front line. Only on August 1—that is, a week after the opening of the Congress—did the Chinese Communists proclaim their version of the United Front policy by offering an alliance to the Nationalist Government.

Obviously Soviet strategy of expansion relies on more than internal fifth columnists (native Communists and their friends) and external military aggression. As Lenin said pointedly, and as Stalin repeated in his last public utterances, there is still a third weapon: the careful use of all tensions and "contradictions" in the free world for weakening the noncommunist camp through the promotion of open conflicts, whose final fruits the Kremlin expects to reap.

Stalin's German policy, which by paralyzing the antifascist forces fatally contributed to bringing Hitler to power and which, through the pact, paved the way for Hitler's attack on western Europe, involved enormous risks; and temporarily it endangered the very existence of the USSR. But the state of Europe after World War II demonstrates the formidable possibilities of this third weapon of Soviet imperialism in the West.

The Soviet support of Chiang Kai-shek from the middle thirties on, which crucially influenced Chiang's decision to go to war against Japan, was much less risky than Stalin's Hitler policy (the former immediately lessened the danger of a Japanese attack against the USSR); and it enabled the Chinese Communists to expand so vigorously that, at the close of the war, Mao could claim control over more than a hundred million people. Thus in the Far East too, the third weapon destroyed the previous balance of power, and this again to the great advantage of the USSR.

Mr. Rossi has painted a grim picture of how today in France and Italy this third weapon is being used successfully to keep Western Europe fragmented and separated from America. A great deal of cool thinking is required to counter this gigantic campaign and to make all countries concerned realize the overriding importance of the interests which they have in common and the overriding need for coordinated action. Cool thinking also is required in evaluating the possibility that the masters of such powerful Communist countries as China may desert the USSR and turn "Tito."

Mr. Johnson has offered impressive reasons of sentiment, ideology, and power politics to show why a Titoist development of Communist China is highly improbable. Supplementing his arguments, I would point to the fact that a China that wishes to see its modest industry grow can least of all afford to break with the USSR, since China's industrially most important area, Manchuria, is open to, and half encircled by, the Far Eastern provinces of the Soviet Union.

But this geo-military consideration, however valid it may be, still does not touch upon the core of the matter. The chances of a Titoist development in Communist China can be properly weighed only if we put ourselves in the position of the Chinese Communist leaders. These leaders adhere—and adhere fanatically—to a Marxist-Leninist doctrine that appraises power in terms of economy. They are fully aware that, within the Communist orbit, the great centers of industry, and particularly heavy industry, today lie in the Eurasian Communist heartland, the USSR. At the Sixth World Congress of the Comintern, Bukharin stated that even in a global Communist order there would be a "world town" as well as a "world village"; and that naturally the world town would remain in a position of leadership.

From the Marxist standpoint, this argument is indeed entirely convincing. And while we may expect Mao and his lieutenants to struggle for as much power as they can obtain within the economically determined international hierarchy of Communist "production-relations," there is no reason to believe that, in their own hearts, they doubt the legitimacy of the hierarchy itself—at least for the foreseeable future, which involves not only the growth of industry in China, but also a further and substantial growth of industry in the already massive industrial centers of the USSR.

In this foreseeable future, to carry the Communist perspective still further, Mao might become the super-Gauleiter of all the peasants of East and South Asia. And yet Moscow would know, and Mao would know too, that he would still remain a giant junior partner.

But as such a junior partner, Mao would exert power beyond anything he could hope for, if he broke with the USSR. And in a war between the Communist and capitalists world (a war which the Chinese Communists, like all other Communists, consider unavoidable) a Mao Tse-tung, who has broken with the USSR, will be a loser, whichever side wins, since a victorious West (this *must* be his Marxist-Leninist conviction) will not tolerate his kind of communism, if it is strong enough to crush the " number one " Communist power, the Soviet Union. Mao can hope to survive this war successfully only if he remains what he has been up to now and most rewardingly: a member of the Communist camp.

To survive and to grow as a giant junior partner in a Eurasian or global Communist system of total power is an ideologically consistent and a practically immensely attractive goal. Abysmal stupidities in Soviet policy excluded—which are of course possible, but not too probable—we may conclude that, in view of Mao's Marxist-Leninist interpretation of the world situation, we have no right to base our Far Eastern policy on the likelihood of a Titoist development of Communist China.

The United States in the Face of the Communist Challenge

PAUL H. NITZE,
Former Director of the Policy Planning Staff, Department of State

There is a wide area of agreement on most of the important questions of fact as to Soviet capabilities, Soviet techniques, and the bases of Soviet policy. On one salient question, however, two somewhat different points of view have been brought out. It is the question whether the course of events following on Stalin's death indicates a profound or a merely superficial modification in the nature of the Soviet threat.

It, perhaps, is too early to find a wholly conclusive answer to this question when it is put in this way. The discussion tends toward a semantic difficulty over the meaning of "superficial" and "profound."

A more useful approach may be to sort out those aspects presenting reasonably firm grounds for judgment and to proceed on the remainder by the method of testing out alternative assumptions.

First let us list the elements falling into the category of questions as to which the grounds for a judgment are reasonably firm.

It seems virtually certain that the small band of Kremlin conspirators will not soon break up to such an extent as to deprive the Soviet rulers of the power of decision.

It appears certain that the control of the survivors over the Russian and satellite peoples will be maintained, if necessary by increased severity and discipline.

It further seems clear that Soviet economic and military capabilities, including atomic, will continue to grow.

Finally, it seems certain enough that the unappeasable hostility of the ruling group in the Kremlin toward power centers not under their control, particularly the United States, will continue.

Now let us turn to the questions in the second category—those as to which we can best proceed by the method of testing alternate assumptions. These relate to the more subtle factors bearing on the probable intentions of the surviving Soviet leadership.

Let us assume for the moment that not only the Russian people but also leading cadres of the Communist party had become disillusioned with certain of the more Byzantine elements which Stalin had superimposed on the Bolshevik point of view.

Let us assume that the transition from one line of control and of policy to another line of control and of policy can be accomplished only after further internal struggles such as that which presumably led to the Beria purge.

Let us assume further that the easing of internal economic pressures and the expansion of the intellectually aware segment of the Russian population present the rulership with new and different internal problems.

Then let us assume that in international affairs the surviving group in control finds it to its interest to make certain real or apparent concessions in order to relax international tensions and thus reduce the danger of a major external crisis at a time when the rulership is new and perhaps divided.

Let us now examine the bearing of these assumptions on the main elements of our policy as it relates to the Soviet threat.

At this point it may be helpful to restate the broad outlines of our policy. It has three major elements. The first is strength and unity, based upon an informed public, here in the United States. The second is leadership among, and assistance to, the other nations of the free world menaced in varying degrees by the Communist threat. The third element has been determined opposition with superior power to aggression or encroachment by Soviet power.

For the past six or seven years these three elements of our policy have been relatively clear and obvious to all who have had to deal responsibly with the question of our proper reaction to the Soviet threat. Within the framework of this broad agreement, differences developed over such questions as the degree of urgency of execution and on the way to resolve the dilemmas involved in translating policy into action. For instance, the necessity of developing, in support of our world position, a stronger and more flexible military posture than was being provided became clear as early as 1946 or 1947. The dilemma involved in choosing between an unbalanced budget, higher taxes, and more stringent economic controls on the one hand, and an adequate military posture on the other hand was not resolved at the policy decision level until some three months prior to the outbreak of the North Korean aggression. Those decisions were translated into specific action only after the aggression into South Korea had given concrete and bloody confirmation to the conclusions already produced by analysis.

For the last six or seven years, the main elements of what we ought to do have been clear enough. To a considerable, if uneven extent, we have done it.

Assuming as actual a purported shift of Soviet intentions toward relaxation of international tensions, we must ask whether it is reasonable to suppose that such a modification would have occurred if we had been less unified and strong at the center, if we had not provided leadership and assistance to the other nations of the world menaced by the Soviet threat, and if determined and effective resistance to aggression had not been manifested in Berlin, in Greece, in Iran, and in Korea.

The internal factors and developments producing such modifications as those assumed to have taken place in the Soviet regime are inseparable from the external situation of the Soviet Union. Clearly the strength, unity, and power of resistance developed by the non-Soviet world in the past six or seven years were essential preconditions. The primary purpose of these policies and of the sacrifices in casualties and in wealth, and of the steadfastness of effort involved, has been to create such conditions outside the Soviet Union as would lead to just such a modification within the Soviet Union.

Let us ask whether these sacrifices continue to be necessary if there has in fact been a shift in Soviet intentions. Taxes are high. People are apathetic. Unpleasant dilemmas are arising. Our allies are irritated by certain aspects of our leadership.

In my view, to relax at the first glimmering of hope of success is the sure road to failure in any serious enterprise. Developments confirming the rightness of a policy should rather lead to still more unity and resolve in carrying it forward to a positive result.

Let us not deceive ourselves into believing we are doing more to daunt the Soviet Union than we are; or that we are strong where we are not. Rather, consciousness of building true strength should enable us to quiet our tone and to negotiate with greater authority. It should permit us to foster situations enabling the Kremlin rulers to undertake still further modifications without that loss of face which would in itself make modification impossible.

Now let us test the alternative assumptions with respect to a shift in Kremlin intentions. Let us assume that Malenkov's lack of that unique prestige which was associated with Stalin's name makes it even more necessary than before for the ruling group to play up hatred and contempt of the foreign devil as a means of generating domestic support and unity. Let us assume that to maintain themselves in power will require them to give to the military a larger role than Stalin ever did. Let us anticipate also a possible Communist resort to a Hitlerian policy of external adventure and boldness after a reasonable period for consolidation. If these assumptions were to be closer to the fact than our previous assumptions, then every instinct of sheer survival would support the urgent implementation of the three broad elements of our national policy developed over the last six or seven years.

Either assumption—a shift in Soviet intentions in the direction of relaxation of international tensions, or of a shift toward a more adventuresome policy—supports the main lines of our own policy: growing unity and strength at home, appropriate leadership and assistance to the other nations of the free world, and firm and determined resistance wherever the Soviets encroach.

This is in the realm of the reasonably clear and obvious. It is supported by almost all responsible students of the problem whether in the last administration, in this present administration, or in neither.

The controversial issues arise in the attempt to resolve the dilemmas inhering in the application of these policies. Differing points of view stem in part from varied interpretations of the facts, in part from variations in the sense of urgency.

At this point, I wish to throw out certain ideas without undertaking fully to support them.

The opportunity for developing domestic unity and strength respecting our external problems seems to me to have improved—provided the problem is tackled in any serious way. The attitude prevailing in some quarters of ascribing our dangers to internal causes—such as incompetence, ill will, or even disloyalty on the part of those in power—rather than to the factors of the international scene, has been a basic divisive factor in the past. This illusion was deeply held by many. In some of its forms it lingers on and may unhappily endure for a long period. The fact of a change of administration, however, has taken the heart out of any basis for that illusion. Different men are now in power. Some of them shared in that illusion before coming into responsibility for decisions affecting the national interest and into intimate acquaintance with the obdurate, irreducible facts of the external scene. A widening awareness of the persistence of the problems on the international scene, notwithstanding a change of faces in Washington, is a main factor which should make possible the closing of the former divisions and provide a base for greater support of a proper response to the Soviet threat.

More general agreement on the location and nature of the danger should enable us to act with greater sureness in resolving certain of the subsidiary dilemmas. One such set of dilemmas lies in those interrelated decisions necessary to a determination of the over-all size of our military establishment, the balance between its components, and the level of taxation and the other economic measures necessary to meet the costs. The attainment of greater unity in our appreciation of the external threat should make possible a clearer view of the problems of financing an adequate military posture. It should result in a clearer comprehension that the expansion of our economic base increases our capability to carry the load. One can hope that it will make clear that a willingness to shoulder the financial burden of defense in whatever measure necessary involves less risk to the nation than an inadequate unbalanced military posture.

The establishment of firm and general recognition of these simple propositions should make it possible to bring into the open and to act upon the major elements necessary to provide an integrated and effective defense against the possibility of overwhelming atomic attack. This is an essential element in an adequate military posture for the United States. One may concede the impracticability of absolute defense and the impossibility of foreseeing now the course of technological developments of the next ten or twenty years. Nevertheless, one is warranted in saying that the use of technical developments already practical and the expenditure over a period of years of two or at most three billion dollars a year above the level of this year's expenditures budgeted for this purpose would transform our presently vulnerable position into one of far greater security. That new action in this field is urgently necessary has for months and even years been clear to all who have seriously analyzed the problem. It would be tragic indeed if even Malenkov's statement were not enough to convert analysis into action.

Provision of effective leadership and assistance to the loose coalition of the nations of the non-Soviet world seems to me to be more difficult but for that very reason deserving of even greater care than our more directly domestic problems. We talk too much about leadership in the abstract. The essence of leadership is the successful resolution of problems and the successful attainment of objectives which impress themselves as being important to those whom one is called upon to lead.

In this we have not been without success. Soviet forces withdrew from Iran. The Berlin blockade was lifted. The economy of Europe has risen to levels substantially above prewar. The aggression into South Korea was thrown back. A third world war has for the time at least been averted.

But much remains to be done, and failure to succeed—and to succeed in time—can have the most frightful consequences.

The situation in Iran continues to fester. We have yet to adopt and carry through on an approach to that problem offering a reasonable prospect of success.

The repulsion of Communist forces in Indo-China remains an item of unfinished and dangerous business after almost eight years of effort.

Germany continues to present unresolved questions as to its future relations to its European neighbors and as to its role as a factor in the equations of power in the world.

Many knotty problems of economic relationships still remain, notwithstanding the improvements made in the free world economies.

Clearly no coalition strong enough to stand up to the Kremlin and its satellites is possible without the continuing participation of a strong United States. No one else is in a position to provide effective coordination to the free world coalitions. Let us devote to that responsibility all the care, patience, and objectivity indicated by the examples of history as necessary for success in such a role. History is replete with instances of the difficulty and annoyance inherent in the development of unity and power of decision in coalitions. History is also replete, however, with coalitions which were successful in developing superior over-all strength and staying power, even while less efficient than the centrally controlled opponent in the coordination of effort and in concentration on the immediately important tactical objective.

Adaptability to the rapid historical and technological changes of this century is certainly a factor of great and continuing importance in the confrontation between the Soviet-ruled domain and the nations disposed to stand free and independent. As the newest and most radical regime thrown up by the upheavals of World War I, the Soviet regime seemed to many to be likely to have the advantage in this respect. The course of Soviet development convinces me otherwise.

The peculiar requirements of a small conspiratorial group in maintaining themselves in power forced a hard crystallization of their basic position and have made them basically less adaptable than others. In tactical aspects, the Soviet rulers have shown great flexibility, but in a strategic sense the accidents of their own development appear to have robbed them of an essential power of adaptation. Having built a regime upon the primacy of force, they find it almost impossible to move to a basis of consent or a frame of legitimacy. Their recent experience in East Germany must reconfirm them in this and heighten their anxiety lest any relaxation of control by coercion will be interpreted as weakness and will be utilized to give expression to the pent-up hatreds engendered by their own oppressions.

In the view prevailing in our institutions, consent is the primary component of leadership. Consent may have to be foregone in favor of coercion in the exigencies of particular situations, but the return to consent comes naturally with the passing of the circumstances requiring the use of force. In a certain basic sense then, on our side flexibility and strategic opportunity for adaptation to the changing requirements of the modern world are greater than on the Soviet side.

Far from being on the Soviet side, time and history are on our side if we but live up to the potentialities and opportunities of our position and keep alive our sense of urgency.

We can then eschew policies born of frustration. We can play for the long pull. Though unable now to foresee how the rigidities of the Soviet regime will encompass its eventual profound modification or downfall, we should go forward concentrating primarily on our own proper adaptation to the changing world scene and building our own strength and unity and that of the non-Soviet world while playing for the breaks of history.

Index